Sources of the American Mind

A COLLECTION OF DOCUMENTS AND TEXTS IN AMERICAN
INTELLECTUAL HISTORY

Sources of the American Mind

A COLLECTION OF DOCUMENTS AND TEXTS
IN AMERICAN INTELLECTUAL HISTORY

Volume II

LOREN BARITZ

PROFESSOR OF HISTORY
UNIVERSITY OF ROCHESTER

JOHN WILEY & SONS, INC.   New York   London   Sydney

To Joe

Contents

1. Industrialism   1
   A. The Problem of Reform   1
       I. Henry George, Progress and Poverty, 1879   3
       II. William Graham Sumner, The Absurd Effort to Make the
       World Over, 1894   12
   B. The Impact of Darwin   22
       III. Thorstein Veblen, Why Is Economics Not an Evolu-
       tionary Science? 1898   24
   C. The Religious Response   39
       IV. Russell H. Conwell, Acres of Diamonds, 1915   40
       V. Walter Rauschenbusch, A Theology for the Social
       Gospel, 1917   48
   D. The Progressive Response   69
       VI. Henry Demarest Lloyd, Wealth against Commonwealth,
       1894   70
       VII. Louis D. Brandeis, Competition, 1913   88

2. The Attack on Idealism   101
       VIII. Oliver Wendell Holmes, The Path of the Law, 1897   102
       IX. William James, The Varieties of Religious Experience,
       1902   110
       X. William James, What Pragmatism Means, 1907   126
       XI. Herbert Croly, The Promise of American Life, 1909   143
       XII. John Dewey, The Scientific Factor in Reconstruction
       of Philosophy, 1920   155

3. The Republic of Letters   167
   A. Cynicism   167
       XIII. Ambrose Bierce, Ashes of the Beacon, 1909   168
   B. The Woman and Democracy   179
       XIV. Henry Adams, The Dynamo and the Virgin, 1900   180
       XV. Henry James, Washington, 1907   190

C. The Challenge   208
    XVI. Randolph S. Bourne, This Older Generation, 1915   209
D. The Twenties   218
    XVII. Sinclair Lewis, Main Street, 1920   219
    XVIII. Edmund Wilson, Night Thoughts in Paris, 1922   225
    XIX. Ernest Hemingway, The Sun Also Rises, 1926   230
    XX. Joseph Wood Krutch, The Modern Temper, 1929   236

4. Depression Realism   247
A. The Meaning of the Economy   247
    XXI. Adolf A. Berle, Jr. and Gardiner C. Means, The
        Modern Corporation and Private Property, 1932   248
    XXII. Rexford G. Tugwell, The Economics of the Recovery
        Program, 1933   264
    XXIII. Thurman W. Arnold, The Folklore of Capitalism,
        1937   277
B. The Tenant   291
    XXIV. James Agee, Let Us Now Praise Famous Men, 1936   292
    XXV. John Steinbeck, The Grapes of Wrath, 1939   300
C. Neo-orthodoxy   316
    XXVI. Reinhold Niebuhr, Ten Years That Shook My
        World, 1939   317

5. Social Responsibilities   327
A. War   327
    XXVII. Archibald Macleish, The Irresponsibles, 1940   328
B. Cold War   340
    XXVIII. George F. Kennan, America and the Russian Future,
        1951   341
C. Resource Allocation   357
    XXIX. John Kenneth Galbraith, The Affluent Society, 1958 357
D. The American Negro   369
    XXX. Ralph Ellison, Invisible Man, 1947   370

6. Apocalypse   379
    XXXI. Norman O. Brown, Apocalypse: The Place of Mystery
        in the Life of the Mind, 1961   380

Sources of the American Mind

A COLLECTION OF DOCUMENTS AND TEXTS IN AMERICAN
INTELLECTUAL HISTORY

CHAPTER 1
Industrialism

A. The Problem of Reform *to where?*

I. INTRODUCTION

Henry George (1839–1897) was born and raised in Philadelphia in an
intensely religious home. He left school at the age of fourteen and
sailed as a foremast boy in a ship bound for Australia and India. Upon
his return to the United States when he was seventeen, he took a job
with a printing office in order to learn typesetting. In 1857 he sailed
for San Francisco where he eventually found employment as a composi-
tor. He married, and his economic plight steadily worsened. At one
point a doctor informed George that his wife and second child were
starving.

In 1868 he visited New York City, where he discovered what he
thought to be the necessary association between wealth and poverty.
His eldest son later explained how George's masterpiece, *Progress and
Poverty*, came to be written:

"Out of the open West came a young man of less than thirty to this
great city of New York. He was small of stature and slight of build.
His alma mater had been the forecastle and the printing office. He was
poor, unheralded, unknown. He came from a small city rising at the
western portals of the country to set up here for a struggling little
newspaper there, a telegraphic news bureau, despite the opposition of
the combined powerful press and telegraph monopolies. The struggle
was too unequal. The young man was overborne by the monopolies and
his little paper crushed. This man was Henry George and the time was
1869. But though defeated Henry George was not vanquished. Out of
the struggle had come a thing that was to grow and grow until it
should fill the minds and hearts of multitudes. For in the intervals of
rest from his newspaper struggle in this city the young correspondent
had musingly walked the streets. As he walked he was filled with
wonder at the manifestations of vast wealth. Here as nowhere he had
dreamed of were private fortunes that rivaled the riches of the fabled

Monte Cristo but here also side by side with the palaces of the princely rich was to be seen a poverty and degradation, a want and shame, such as made the young man from the open West sick at heart. Why in a land so bountifully blessed with enough and more than enough for all should there be such inequality of conditions, such heaped wealth interlocked with such deep and debasing want. Why amid such super-abundance should strong men vainly look for work. Why should women faint with hunger and little children spend the morning of life in the treadmill of toil. Was this intended in the order of things. No, he could not believe it. And suddenly there came to him there in the daylight in this city street a burning thought, a call, a vision. Every nerve quivered and he made it a vow that he would never rest until he had found the cause of and if he could the remedy for this deepening poverty amid advancing wealth. Returning to San Francisco soon after his telegraphic news failure and keeping his vow nurtured in his heart, Henry George perceived that land speculation locked up vast territories against labor. Everywhere he perceived an effort to corner land, an effort to get it and hold it. Not for use but for a rise. . . . Those who had a monopoly of the land would practically own those who had to use the land."

Progress and Poverty was written in 1879, ten years after Henry George had visited New York City. The book exerted a steady and growing influence virtually throughout the world. It was estimated that two million copies of *Progress and Poverty*, in several languages, had been published in the first twenty-five years of the book's existence.

The economic argument of *Progress and Poverty* is based on two essential assumptions: Produce minus rent equals wages plus interest; industrialism stimulates monopoly of ownership of land. From his first assumption it naturally followed that an increase in rent would cause a decrease in wages. From his second assumption it followed that economic crisis and human hardship were built into the very texture of an industrialized economy. The unearned increment in rent literally determined the fact of slums and deprivation, the kind of hardship Henry George had himself experienced in the early years of his marriage. Reduced to its simplest terms, his solution was the confiscation of the unearned increment in rent by the government, a single tax on land values.

In the following selection, both the moral intensity and some of the substance of George's influential book may readily be seen.

Produce — rent = wages + interest.

I.

Henry George

PROGRESS AND POVERTY

1879

If chattel slavery be unjust, then is private property in land unjust.

For let the circumstances be what they may—the ownership of land will always give the ownership of men, to a degree measured by the necessity (real or artificial) for the use of land. This is but a statement in different form of the law of rent.

And when that necessity is absolute—when starvation is the alternative to the use of land, then does the ownership of men involved in the ownership of land become absolute.

Place one hundred men on an island from which there is no escape, and whether you make one of these men the absolute owner of the other ninety-nine, or the absolute owner of the soil of the island, will make no difference either to him or to them.

In the one case, as the other, the one will be the absolute master of the ninety-nine—his power extending even to life and death, for simply to refuse them permission to live upon the island would be to force them into the sea.

Upon a larger scale, and through more complex relations, the same cause must operate in the same way and to the same end—the ultimate result, the enslavement of laborers, becoming apparent just as the pressure increases which compels them to live on and from land which is treated as the exclusive property of others. Take a country in which the soil is divided among a number of proprietors, instead of being in the hands of one, and in which, as in modern production, the capitalist has been specialized from the laborer, and manufactures and exchange, in all their many branches, have been separated from agriculture. Though less direct and obvious, the relations between the owners of the soil and the laborers will, with increase of population and the improvement of the arts, tend to the same absolute mastery on the one hand and the same abject helplessness on the other, as in the case of the island we

SOURCE. Henry George, *Progress and Poverty,* Garden City, N.Y.: Doubleday, Page and Co., 1911, pp. 345–355.

have supposed. Rent will advance, while wages will fall. Of the aggregate produce, the land owner will get a constantly increasing, the laborer a constantly diminishing share. Just as removal to cheaper land becomes difficult or impossible, laborers, no matter what they produce, will be reduced to a bare living, and the free competition among them, where land is monopolized, will force them to a condition which, though they may be mocked with the titles and insignia of freedom, will be virtually that of slavery.

There is nothing strange in the fact that, in spite of the enormous increase in productive power which this century has witnessed, and which is still going on, the wages of labor in the lower and wider strata of industry should everywhere tend to the wages of slavery—just enough to keep the laborer in working condition. For the ownership of the land on which and from which a man must live is virtually the ownership of the man himself, and in acknowledging the right of some individuals to the exclusive use and enjoyment of the earth, we condemn other individuals to slavery as fully and as completely as though we had formally made them chattels.

In a simpler form of society, where production chiefly consists in the direct application of labor to the soil, the slavery that is the necessary result of according to some the exclusive right to the soil from which all must live, is plainly seen in helotism, in villeinage, in serfdom.

Chattel slavery originated in the capture of prisoners in war, and, though it has existed to some extent in every part of the globe, its area has been small, its effects trivial, as compared with the forms of slavery which have originated in the appropriation of land. No people as a mass have ever been reduced to chattel slavery to men of their own race, nor yet on any large scale has any people ever been reduced to slavery by this kind of conquest. The general subjection of the many to the few, which we meet with wherever society has reached a certain development, has resulted from the appropriation of land as individual property. It is the ownership of the soil that everywhere gives the ownership of men that live upon it. It is slavery of this kind to which the enduring pyramids and the colossal monuments of Egypt yet bear witness, and of the institution of which we have, perhaps, a vague tradition in the biblical story of the famine during which the Pharoah purchased up the lands of the people. It was slavery of this kind to which, in the twilight of history, the conquerors of Greece reduced the original inhabitants of that peninsula, transforming them into helots by making them pay rent for their lands. It was the growth of the *latifundia,* or great landed estates, which transmuted the population of ancient Italy, from a race of hardy husbandmen, whose robust virtues conquered the world, into a race of cringing bondsmen; it was the appropriation of the land as the absolute property of their chieftains which gradually turned the descendants of free and equal Gallic, Teutonic and Hunnish warriors into colonii and villains, and which changed the independent burghers of Sclavonic village communities into the boors of Russia and the serfs of Poland; which instituted the feudalism of China and Japan, as well as that of Europe, and which made the High Chiefs of Polynesia the all but absolute masters of their fellows. . . . And could we find the key to the records of the long-buried civilizations that lie entombed in the gigantic ruins of Yucatan and Guatemala, telling at once of the pride of a ruling class and the unrequited toil to which the masses were condemned, we should read, in all human probability, of a slavery imposed upon the great body of the people through the appropriation of the land as the property of a few—of another illustration of the universal truth that they who possess the land are masters of the men who dwell upon it.

The necessary relation between labor and land, the absolute power which the ownership of land gives over men who cannot live but by using it, explains what is otherwise inexplicable—the growth and persistence of institutions, manners, and ideas so utterly repugnant to the natural sense of liberty and equality.

When the idea of individual ownership, which so justly and naturally attaches to things of human production, is extended to land, all the rest is a mere matter of development. The strongest and most cunning easily acquire a superior share in this species of property, which is to be had, not by production, but by appropriation, and in becoming lords of the land they become necessarily lords of their fellow-men. The ownership of land is the basis of aristocracy. It was not nobility that gave land, but the possession of land that gave nobility. All the enormous privileges of the nobility of medieval Europe flowed from their position as the owners of the soil. The simple principle of the ownership of the soil produced on the one side, the lord, on the other, the vassal—the one having all rights, the other none. The right of the lord to the soil acknowledged and maintained, those who lived upon it could do so only upon his terms. The manners and conditions of the times made those terms include services and servitudes, as well as rents in produce or money, but the essential thing that compelled them was the ownership of land. This power exists wherever the ownership of land exists, and can be brought out wherever the competition for the use of land is great enough to enable the landlord to make his own terms. The English land owner of to-day has, in the law which recognizes his exclusive right to the land, essentially all the power which his predecessor the feudal baron had. He might command rent in services or servitudes. He might compel his tenants to dress themselves in a particular way, to profess a particular religion, to send their children to a particular school, to submit their differences to his decision, to fall upon their knees when he spoke to them, to follow him around dressed in his livery, or to sacrifice to him female honor, if they would prefer these things to being driven off his land. He could demand, in short, any terms on which men would still consent to live on his land, and the law could not prevent him so long as it did not qualify his ownership, for compliance with them would assume the form of a free contract or voluntary act. And English landlords do exercise such of these powers as in the manners of the times they care to. Having shaken off the obligation of providing for the defense of the country, they no longer need the military service of their tenants, and the possession of wealth and power being now shown in other ways than by long trains of attendants, they no longer care for personal service. But they habitually control the votes of their tenants and dictate to them in many little ways. . . . The principle that permits this is the same principle that in ruder times and a simpler social state enthralled the great masses of the common people and placed such a wide gulf between noble and peasant. Where the peasant was made a serf, it was simply by forbidding him to leave the estate on which he was born, thus artificially producing the condition we supposed on the island. In sparsely settled countries this is necessary to produce absolute slavery, but where land is fully occupied, competition may produce substantially the same conditions. Between the condition of the rack-rented Irish peasant and the Russian serf, the advantage was in many things on the side of the serf. The serf did not starve.

Now, as I think I have conclusively proved, it is the same cause which has in every age degraded and enslaved the laboring masses that is working in the civilized world to-day. Personal liberty—that is to say, the liberty to move about—is everywhere conceded, while of political and legal inequality there are in the United States no vestiges, and in the most backward civilized countries but few. But the great cause of inequality remains, and is manifesting itself in the unequal distribution of wealth. The essence of slavery is that it takes from the laborer all he produces save enough to support an animal existence, and to this minimum the wages of free labor, under existing conditions, unmistakably tend. Whatever be the increase of productive power, rent steadily tends to swallow up the gain, and more than the gain.

Thus the condition of the masses in every civilized country is, or is tending to become, that of virtual slavery under the forms of freedom. And it is probable that of all kinds of slavery this is the most cruel and relentless. For the laborer is robbed of the produce of his labor and compelled to toil for a mere subsistence; but his taskmasters, instead of human beings, assume the form of imperious necessities. Those to whom his labor is rendered and from whom his wages are received are often driven in their turn—contact between the laborers and the ultimate beneficiaries of their labor is sundered, and individuality is lost. The direct responsibility of master to slave, a responsibility which exercises a softening influence upon the great majority of men, does not arise; it is not one human being who seems to drive another to unremitting and ill-requited toil, but "the inevitable laws of supply and demand," for which no one in particular is responsible. The maxims of Cato the Censor—maxims which were regarded with abhorrence even in an age of cruelty and universal slaveholding—that after as much work as possible is obtained from a slave he should be turned out to die, become the common rule; and even the selfish interest which prompts the master to look after the comfort and well-being of the slave is lost. Labor has become a commodity, and the laborer a machine. There are no masters and slaves, no owners and owned, but only buyers and sellers. The higgling of the market takes the place of every other sentiment.

When the slaveholders of the South looked upon the condition of the free laboring poor in the most advanced civilized countries, it is no wonder that they easily persuaded themselves of the divine institution of slavery. That the field hands of the South were as a class better fed, better lodged, better clothed; that they had less anxiety and more of the amusements and enjoyments of life than the agricultural laborers of England there can be no doubt; and even in the Northern cities, visiting slaveholders might see and hear of things impossible under what they called their organization of labor. In the Southern States, during the days of slavery, the master who would have compelled his negroes to work and live as large classes of free white men and women are compelled in free countries to work and live, would have been deemed infamous, and if public opinion had not restrained him, his own selfish interest in the maintenance of the health and strength of his chattels would. But in London, New York, and Boston, among people who have given, and would give again, money and blood to free the slave, where no one could abuse a beast in public without arrest and punishment, barefooted and ragged children may be seen running around the streets even in the winter time, and in squalid garrets and noisome cellars women work away their lives for wages that fail to keep them in proper warmth and nourishment. Is it any wonder that to the slaveholders of the South the demand for the abolition of slavery seemed like the cant of hypocrisy?

And now that slavery has been abolished, the planters of the South find they have sustained no loss. Their ownership of the land upon which the freedmen must live gives them practically as much command of labor as before, while they are relieved of responsibility, sometimes very expensive. The negroes as yet have the alternative of emigrating, and a great movement of that kind seems now about commencing, but as population increases and land becomes dear, the planters will get a greater proportionate share of the earnings of their laborers than they did under the system of chattel slavery, and the laborers a less share— for under the system of chattel slavery the slaves always got at least enough to keep them in good physical health, but in such countries as England there are large classes of laborers who do not get that.

The influences which, wherever there is personal relation between master and slave, slip in to modify chattel slavery, and to prevent the master from exerting to its fullest extent his power over the slave, also showed themselves in the ruder forms of serfdom that characterized the earlier periods of European development, and aided by religion, and, perhaps, as in chattel slavery, by the more enlightened but still selfish interests of the lord, and hardening into custom, universally fixed a limit to what the owner of the land could extort from the serf or peasant, so that the competition of men without means of existence bidding against each other for access to the means of existence, was nowhere suffered to go to its full length and exert its full power of deprivation and degradation. The helots of Greece, the metayers of Italy, the serfs of Russia and Poland, the peasants of feudal Europe, rendered to their landlords a fixed proportion either of their produce or their labor, and were not generally squeezed past that point. But the influences which thus stepped in to modify the extortive power of land ownership, and which may still be seen on English estates where the landlord and his family deem it their duty to send medicines and comforts to the sick and infirm, and to look after the well-being of their cottagers, just as the Southern planter was accustomed to look after his negroes, are lost in the more refined and less obvious form which serfdom assumes in the more complicated processes of modern production, which separates so widely and by so many intermediate gradations the individual whose labor is appropriated from him who appropriates it, and makes the relations between the members of the two classes not direct and particular, but indirect and general. In modern society, competition has free play to force from the laborer the very utmost he can give, and with what terrific force it is acting may be seen in the condition of the lowest class in the centers of wealth and industry. That the condition of this lowest class is not yet more general, is to be attributed to the great extent of fertile land which has hitherto been open on this continent, and which has not merely afforded an escape for the increasing population of the older sections of the Union, but has greatly relieved the pressure in Europe—in one country, Ireland, the emigration having been so great as actually to reduce the population. This avenue of relief cannot last forever. It is already fast closing up, and as it closes, the pressure must become harder and harder.

It is not without reason that the wise crow in the Ramayana, the crow Bushanda, "who has lived in every part of the universe and knows all events from the beginning of time," declares that, though contempt of worldly advantages is necessary to supreme felicity, yet the keenest pain possible is inflicted by extreme poverty. The poverty to which in advancing civilization great masses of men are condemned, is not the freedom of distraction and temptation which sages have sought and philosophers have praised; it is a degrading and embruting slavery, that cramps the higher nature, dulls the finer feelings, and drives men by its pain to acts which the brutes would refuse. It is into this helpless, hopeless poverty, that crushes manhood and destroys womanhood, that robs even childhood of its innocence and joy, that the working classes are being driven by a force which acts upon them like a resistless and unpitying machine. The Boston collar manufacturer who pays his girls two cents an hour may commiserate their condition, but he, as they, is governed by the law of competition, and cannot pay more and carry on his business, for exchange is not governed by sentiment. And so, through all intermediate gradations, up to those who receive the earnings of labor without return, in the rent of land, it is the inexorable laws of supply and demand, a power with which the individual can no more quarrel or dispute than with the winds and the tides, that seem to press down the lower classes into the slavery of want.

But in reality, the cause is that which always has and always must result in slavery—the monopilization by some of what nature has designed for all.

Our boasted freedom necessarily involves slavery, so long as we recognize private property in land. Until that is abolished, Declarations of Independence and Acts of Emancipation are in vain. So long as one man can claim the exclusive ownership of the land from which other men must live, slavery will exist, and as material progress goes on, must grow and deepen!

This . . . is what is going on in the civilized world to-day. Private ownership of land is the nether millstone. Material progress is the upper millstone. Between them, with an increasing pressure, the working classes are being ground.

II. INTRODUCTION

Darwin's conception of evolution provided the intellectual background for a very different response to industrialism than the position taken by Henry George. Applying Darwin's mechanism of biological change to the social organism, a number of men argued that the struggle for survival, resulting in the success of the most fit, was the tool of analysis which could pry loose the secrets of social development. William Graham Sumner (1840–1910) was among the most articulate and influential of the social Darwinists. An ordained priest in the Episcopal Church, Sumner followed the bent of his mind toward questions of political economy and accepted a chair of political and social science at Yale University in 1872. With the new freedom of his academic post, Sumner spent the rest of his life in search of the laws of political economy whose universal applicability would allow men to cooperate with necessity. He opposed protectionism, inflation, the opposition to big business, socialism, and imperialism.

Among his most important books are the following: *A History of American Currency*, 1874; *American Finance*, 1875; *The Financier and Finances of the American Revolution* (two volumes), 1891; *What Social Classes Owe to Each Other*, 1883; *Folkways*, 1907; and *Science of Society*, 1927, brought out by Albert G. Keller after Sumner's death.

Sumner's essential position can be quickly seen in his own language: "Perhaps the most fundamental fact which makes this a world of toil and self-denial is that two men cannot eat the same loaf of bread. This pitiless and hopeless monopoly is . . . the reason for capital and rent, for property and rights, for law and estate, for poverty and inequality." Man's relationship to a grudging and unsentimental nature meant that all human beings must struggle against the probability of their own death by starvation.

The social system, as Sumner understood it, is a life process, a result and not a plan, an integral part of the natural world, and not the design of ingenious political economists. Man had, in Sumner's words, ". . . no more right to life than a rattlesnake; he has no more right to liberty than any wild beast; his right to the pursuit of happiness is nothing but a license to maintain the struggle for existence if he can find within himself the power with which to do it." The power of capital was the most powerful weapon men could use in their struggle to survive. He put his general view this way:

"Such is the system of nature. If we do not like it, and if we try to amend it, there is only one way in which we can do it. We can take from the better and give to the worse. We can deflect the penalties of those who have done ill and throw them on those who have done better. . . . We shall thus lessen the inequalities. We shall favor the survival of the unfittest, and we shall accomplish this by destroying liberty. Let it be understood that we cannot get outside this alternative: liberty, inequality, survival of the fittest; liberty, equality, survival of the unfittest. The former carries and favors all its worst members."

This inevitable antagonism between man and nature necessarily resulted in the sorting out of individuals into those groups that succeeded and those that failed, between, that is, the rich and the poor. The attempts of reformers to redress the balance would be unnatural and therefore foredoomed enterprise. "The truth is," Sumner said, ". . . that the social order is fixed by laws of nature precisely analogous to those of the physical order. The most that man can do is by ignorance and self-conceit to mar the operation of social laws. The evils of society are to a great extent the result of the dogmatism and self-interest of statesmen, philosophers and ecclesiastics who in past time had done just what the socialists now want to do. Instead of studying the natural laws of the social order, they assumed that they could organize the society as they chose. They made up their minds what kind of society they wanted to make and they planned their little measures for the ends they had resolved upon. It will take centuries of scientific study of the facts of nature to eliminate from human society the mischievous institutions and traditions which said statesmen, philosophers and ecclesiastics have introduced into it."

Sumner's war on sentimentality in the name of natural economic force and law is strikingly clear in the following selection.

II.

William Graham Sumner
THE ABSURD EFFORT
TO MAKE THE WORLD OVER
1894

It will not probably be denied that the burden of proof is on those who affirm that our social condition is utterly diseased and in need of radical regeneration. My task at present, therefore, is entirely negative and critical: to examine the allegations of fact and the doctrines which are put forward to prove the correctness of the diagnosis and to warrant the use of the remedies proposed.

The propositions put forward by social reformers nowadays are chiefly of two kinds. There are assertions in historical form, chiefly in regard to the comparison of existing with earlier social states, which are plainly based on defective historical knowledge, or at most on current stock historical dicta which are uncritical and incorrect. Writers very often assert that something never existed before because they do not know that it ever existed before, or that something is worse than ever before because they are not possessed of detailed information about what has existed before. The other class of propositions consists of dogmatic statements which, whether true or not, are unverifiable. This class of propositions is the pest and bane of current economic and social discussion. Upon a more or less superficial view of some phenomenon a suggestion arises which is embodied in a philosophical proposition and promulgated as a truth. From the form and nature of such propositions they can always be brought under the head of "ethics." This word at least gives them an air of elevated sentiment and purpose, which is the only warrant they possess. It is impossible to test or verify them by any investigation or logical process whatsoever. It is therefore very

SOURCE. William Graham Sumner, *Essays,* Volume I, eds. A. G. Keller and M. R. Davies, New Haven: Yale University Press, 1934, pp. 91–106. Reprinted with the permission of Yale University Press.

difficult for anyone who feels a high responsibility for historical statements, and who absolutely rejects any statement which is unverifiable, to find a common platform for discussion or to join issue satisfactorily in taking the negative.

When anyone asserts that the class of skilled and unskilled manual laborers of the United States is worse off now in respect to diet, clothing, lodgings, furniture, fuel, and lights; in respect to the age at which they can marry; the number of children they can provide for; the start in life they can give to their children, and their chances of accumulating capital, than they ever have been at any former time, he makes a reckless assertion for which no facts have been offered in proof. Upon an appeal to facts, the contrary of this assertion would be clearly established. It suffices, therefore, to challenge those who are responsible for the assertion to make it good.

If it is said that the employed class are under much more stringent discipline than they were thirty years ago or earlier, it is true. It is not true that there has been any qualitative change in this respect within thirty years, but it is true that a movement which began at the first settlement of the country has been advancing with constant acceleration and has become a noticeable feature within our time. This movement is the advance in the industrial organization. The first settlement was made by agriculturists, and for a long time there was scarcely any organization. There were scattered farmers, each working for himself, and some small towns with only rudimentary commerce and handicrafts. As the country has filled up, the arts and professions have been differentiated and the industrial organization has been advancing. This fact and its significance has hardly been noticed at all; but the stage of the industrial organization existing at any time, and the rate of advance in its development, are the absolutely controlling social facts. Nine-tenths of the socialistic and semi-socialistic, and sentimental or ethical, suggestions by which we are overwhelmed come from failure to understand the phenomena of the industrial organization and its expansion. It controls us all because we are all in it. It creates the conditions of our existence, sets the limits of our social activity, regulates the bonds of our social relations, determines our conceptions of good and evil, suggests our life-philosophy, molds our inherited political institutions, and reforms the oldest and toughest customs, like marriage and property. I repeat that the turmoil of heterogeneous and antagonistic social whims and speculations in which we live is due to the failure to understand what the industrial organization is and its all-pervading control over human life, while the traditions of our school of philosophy lead us always to approach the industrial organization, not from the side of objective study, but from that of philosophical doctrine. Hence it is that we find that the method of measuring what we see happening by what are called ethical standards, and of proposing to attack the phenomena by methods thence deduced, is so popular.

The advance of a new country from the very simplest social coordination up to the highest organization is a most interesting and instructive chance to study the development of the organization. It has of course been attended all the way along by stricter subordination and higher discipline. All organization implies restriction of liberty. The gain of power is won by narrowing individual range. The methods of business in colonial days were loose and slack to an inconceivable degree. The movement of industry has been all the time toward promptitude, punctuality, and reliability. It has been attended all the way by lamentations about the good old times; about the decline of small industries; about the lost spirit of comradeship between employer and employee; about the narrowing of the interests of the workman; about his conversion into a machine or into a "ware," and about industrial war. These lamentations have all had reference to unquestionable phenomena attendant on advancing organization. In all occupations the same movement is discernible—in the learned professions, in schools, in trade, commerce, and transportation. It is to go on faster than ever, now that the continent is filled up by the first superficial layer of population over its whole extent and the intensification of industry has begun. The great inventions both make the intension of the organization possible and make it inevitable, with all its consequences, whatever they may be. I must expect to be told here, according to the current fashions of thinking, that we ought to control the development of the organization. The first instinct of the modern man is to get a law passed to forbid or prevent what, in his wisdom, he disapproves. A thing which is inevitable, however, is one which we cannot control. We have to make up our minds to it, adjust ourselves to it, and sit down to live with it. Its inevitableness may be disputed, in which case we must re-examine it; but if our analysis is correct, when we reach what is inevitable we reach the end, and our regulations must apply to ourselves, not to the social facts.

Now the intensification of the social organization is what gives us greater social power. It is to it that we owe our increased comfort and abundance. We are none of us ready to sacrifice this. On the contrary, we want more of it. We would not return to the colonial simplicity and the colonial exiguity if we could. If not, then we must pay the price. Our life is bounded on every side by conditions. We can have this if we will agree to submit to that. In the case of industrial power and product the great condition is combination of force under discipline and strict coordination. Hence the wild language about wage-slavery and capitalistic tyranny.

In any state of society no great achievements can be produced without great force. Formerly great force was attainable only by slavery aggregating the power of great numbers of men. Roman civilization was built on this. Ours has been built on steam. It is to be built on electricity. Then we are all forced into an organization around these natural forces and adapted to the methods or their application; and although we indulge in rhetoric about political liberty, nevertheless we find ourselves bound tight in a new set of conditions, which control the modes of our existence and determine the directions in which alone economic and social liberty can go.

If it is said that there are some persons in our time who have become rapidly and in a great degree rich, it is true; if it is said that large aggregations of wealth in the control of individuals is a social danger, it is not true.

The movement of the industrial organization which has just been described has brought out a great demand for men capable of managing great enterprises. Such have been called "captains of industry." The analogy with military leaders suggested by this name is not misleading. The great leaders in the development of the industrial organization need those talents of executive and administrative skill, power to command, courage, and fortitude, which were formerly called for in military affairs and scarcely anywhere else. The industrial army is also as dependent on its captains as a military body is on its generals. One of the worst features of the existing system is that the employees have a constant risk in their employer. If he is not competent to manage the business with success, they suffer with him. Capital also is dependent on the skill of the captain of industry for the certainty and magnitude of its profits. Under these circumstances there has been a great demand for men having the requisite ability for this function. As the organization has advanced, with more impersonal bonds of coherence and wider scope of operations, the value of this functionary has rapidly increased. The possession of the requisite ability is a natural monopoly. Consequently, all the conditions have concurred to give to those who possessed this monopoly excessive and constantly advancing rates of remuneration.

Another social function of the first importance in an intense organization is the solution of those crises in the operation of it which are called the conjuncture of the market. It is through the market that the lines of relation run which preserve the system in harmonious and rhythmical operation. The conjuncture is the momentary sharper misadjustment of supply and demand which indicates that a redistribution of productive effort is called for. The industrial organization needs to be insured against these conjunctures, which, if neglected, produce a crisis and catastrophe; and it needs that they shall be anticipated and guarded against as far as skill and foresight can do it. The rewards of this function for the bankers and capitalists who perform it are very great. The captains of industry and the capitalists who operate on the conjuncture, therefore, if they are successful, win, in these days, great fortunes in a short time. There are no earnings which are more legitimate or for which greater services are rendered to the whole industrial body. The popular notions about this matter really assume that all the wealth accumulated by these classes of persons would be here just the same if they had not existed. They are supposed to have appropriated it out of the common stock. This is so far from being true that, on the contrary, their own wealth would not be but for themselves; and besides that, millions more of wealth, many-fold greater than their own, scattered in the hands of thousands, would not exist but for them.

Within the last two years I have traveled from end to end of the German Empire several times on all kinds of trains. I reached the conviction, looking at the matter from the passenger's standpoint, that, if the Germans could find a Vanderbilt and put their railroads in his hands for twenty-five years, letting him reorganize the system and make twenty-five million dollars out if it for himself in that period, they would make an excellent bargain.

But it is repeated until it has become a commonplace which people are afraid to question, that there is some social danger in the possession of large amounts of wealth by individuals. I ask, Why? I heard a lecture two years ago by a man who holds perhaps the first chair of political economy in the world. He said, among other things, that there was great danger in our day from great accumulations; that this danger ought to be met by taxation, and he referred to the fortune of the Rothschilds and to the great fortunes made in America to prove his point. He omitted, however, to state in what the danger consisted or to specify what harm has ever been done by the Rothschild fortunes or by the great fortunes accumulated in America. It seemed to me that the assertions he was making, and the measures he was recommending, ex-cathedra, were very serious to be thrown out so recklessly. It is hardly to be expected that novelists, popular magazinists, amateur economists, and politicians will be more responsible. It would be easy, however, to show what good is done by accumulations of capital in a few hands— that is, under close and direct management, permitting prompt and accurate application; also to tell what harm is done by loose and unfounded denunciations of any social component or any social group. In the recent debates on the income tax the assumption that great accumulations of wealth are socially harmful and ought to be broken down by taxation was treated as an axiom, and we had direct proof how dangerous it is to fit out the average politician with such unverified and unverifiable dogmas as his warrant for his modes of handling the direful tool of taxation.

Great figures are set out as to the magnitude of certain fortunes and the proportionate amount of the national wealth held by a fraction of the population, and eloquent exclamation-points are set against them. If the figures were beyond criticism, what would they prove? Where is the rich man who is oppressing anybody? If there was one, the newspapers would ring with it. The facts about the accumulation of wealth do not constitute a plutocracy, as I will show below. Wealth, in itself considered, is only power, like steam, or electricity, or knowledge. The question of its good or ill turns on the question how it will be used. To prove any harm in aggregations of wealth it must be shown that great wealth is, as a rule, in the ordinary course of social affairs, put to a mischievous use. This cannot be shown beyond the very slightest degree, if at all.

Therefore, all the allegations of general mischief, social corruption, wrong, and evil in our society must be referred back to those who make them for particulars and specifications. As they are offered to us we cannot allow them to stand, because we discern in them faulty observation of facts, or incorrect interpretation of facts, or a construction of facts according to some philosophy, or misunderstanding of phenomena and their relations, or incorrect inferences, or crooked deductions.

Assuming, however, that the charges against the existing "capitalistic" —that is, industrial—order of things are established, it is proposed to remedy the ill by reconstructing the industrial system on the principles of democracy. Once more we must untangle the snarl of half ideas and muddled facts.

Democracy is, of course, a word to conjure with. We have a democratic-republican political system, and we like it so well that we are prone to take any new step which can be recommended as "democratic" or which will round out some "principle" of democracy to a fuller fulfillment. Everything connected with this domain of political thought is crusted over with false historical traditions, cheap philosophy, and undefined terms, but it is useless to try to criticize it. The whole drift of the world for five hundred years has been toward democracy. That drift, produced by great discoveries and inventions, and by the discovery of a new continent, has raised the middle class out of the servile class. In alliance with the crown they crushed the feudal classes. They made the crown absolute in order to do it. Then they turned against the crown and, with the aid of the handicraftsmen and peasants, conquered it. Now the next conflict which must inevitably come is that between the middle capitalist class and the proletariat, as the word has come to be used. If a certain construction is put on this conflict, it may be called that between democracy and plutocracy, for it seems that industrialism must be developed into plutocracy by the conflict itself. That is the conflict which stands before civilized society to-day. All the signs of the times indicate its commencement, and it is big with fate to mankind and to civilization.

Although we cannot criticize democracy profitably, it may be said of it, with reference to our present subject, that up to this time democracy never has done anything, either in politics, social affairs, or industry, to prove its power to bless mankind. If we confine our attention to the United States, there are three difficulties with regard to its alleged achievements, and they all have the most serious bearing on the proposed democratization of industry.

1. The time during which democracy has been tried in the United States is too short to warrant any inferences. A century or two is a very short time in the life of political institutions, and if the circumstances change rapidly during the period the experiment is vitiated.

2. The greatest question of all about American democracy is whether it is a cause or a consequence. It is popularly assumed to be a

cause, and we ascribe to its beneficent action all the political vitality, all the easiness of social relations, all the industrial activity and enterprise which we experience and which we value and enjoy. I submit, however, that, on a more thorough examination of the matter, we shall find that democracy is a consequence. There are economic and sociological causes for our political vitality and vigor, for the ease and elasticity of our social relations, and for our industrial power and success. Those causes have also produced democracy, given it success, and have made its faults and errors innocuous. Indeed, in any true philosophy, it must be held that in the economic forces which control the material prosperity of a population lie the real causes of its political institutions, its social class-adjustments, its industrial prosperity, its moral code, and its world-philosophy. If democracy and the industrial system are both products of the economic conditions which exist, it is plainly absurd to set democracy to defeat those conditions in the control of industry. If, however, it is not true that democracy is a consequence, and I am well aware that very few people believe it, then we must go back to the view that democracy is a cause. That being so, it is difficult to see how democracy, which has had a clear field here in America, is not responsible for the ills which Mr. [Edward] Bellamy [author of *Looking Backward,* 1888] and his comrades in opinion see in our present social state, and it is difficult to see the grounds of asking us to intrust it also with industry. The first and chief proof of success of political measures and systems is that, under them, society advances in health and vigor and that industry develops without causing social disease. If this has not been the case in America, American democracy has not succeeded. Neither is it easy to see how the masses, if they have undertaken to rule, can escape the responsibilities of ruling, especially so far as the consequences affect themselves. If, then, they have brought all this distress upon themselves under the present system, what becomes of the argument for extending the system to a direct and complete control of industry?

3. It is by no means certain that democracy in the United States has not, up to this time, been living on a capital inherited from aristocracy and industrialism. We have no pure democracy. Our democracy is limited at every turn by institutions which were developed in England in connection with industrialism and aristocracy, and these institutions are of the essence of our system. While our people are passionately democratic in temper and will not tolerate a doctrine that one man is not as good

as another, they have common sense enough to know that he is not; and it seems that they love and cling to the conservative institutions quite as strongly as they do the democratic philosophy. They are, therefore, ruled by men who talk philosophy and govern by the institutions. Now it is open to Mr. Bellamy to say that the reason why democracy in America seems to be open to the charge made in the last paragraph, of responsibility for all the ill which he now finds in our society, is because it has been infected with industrialism (capitalism); but in that case he must widen the scope of his proposition and undertake to purify democracy before turning industry over to it. The socialists generally seem to think that they make their undertakings easier when they widen their scope, and make them easiest when they propose to remake everything; but in truth social tasks increase in difficulty in an enormous ratio as they are widened in scope.

The question, therefore, arises, if it is proposed to reorganize the social system on the principles of American democracy, whether the institutions of industrialism are to be retained. If so, all the virus of capitalism will be retained. It is forgotten, in many schemes of social reformation in which it is proposed to mix what we like with what we do not like, in order to extirpate the latter, that each must undergo a reaction from the other, and that what we like may be extirpated by what we do not like. We may find that instead of democratizing capitalism we capitalized democracy—that is, have brought in plutocracy. Plutocracy is a political system in which the ruling force is wealth. The denunciation of capital which we hear from all the reformers is the most eloquent proof that the greatest power in the world to-day is capital. They know that it is, and confess it most when they deny it most strenuously. At present the power of capital is social and industrial, and only in a small degree political. So far as capital is political, it is on account of political abuses, such as tariffs and special legislation on the one hand and legislative strikes on the other. These conditions exist in the democracy to which it is proposed to transfer the industries. What does that mean except bringing all the power of capital once for all into the political arena and precipitating the conflict of democracy and plutocracy at once? Can anyone imagine that the masterfulness, the overbearing disposition, the greed of gain, and the ruthlessness in methods, which are the faults of the master of industry at his worst, would cease when he was a functionary of the State, which had relieved him of risk and endowed him with authority? Can anyone imagine that politicians would no longer be corruptly fond of money, intriguing, and crafty when they were charged, not only with patronage and government contracts, but also with factories, stores, ships and railroads? Could we expect anything except that, when the politician and the master of industry were joined in one, we should have the vices of both unchecked by the restraints of either? In any socialistic state there will be one set of positions which will offer chances of wealth beyond the wildest dreams of avarice; *viz.,* on the governing committees. Then there will be rich men whose wealth will indeed be a menace to social interests, and instead of industrial peace there will be such war as no one has dreamed of yet: the war between the political ins and outs—that is, between those who are on the committee and those who want to get on it.

We must not drop the subject of democracy without one word more. The Greeks already had occasion to notice a most serious distinction between two principles of democracy which lie at its roots. Plutarch says that Solon got the archonship in part by promising equality, which some understood of esteem and dignity, others of measure and number. There is one democratic principle which means that each man should be esteemed for just what he is, without regard to birth, wealth, rank, or other adventitious circumstances. The other principle is that each one of us ought to be equal to all the others in what he gets and enjoys. The first principle is only partially realizable, but, so far as it goes, it is elevating and socially progressive and profitable. The second is not capable of an intelligible statement. The first is a principle of industrialism. It proceeds from and is intelligible only in a society built on the industrial virtues, free endeavor, security of property, and repression of the baser vices; that is, in a society whose industrial system is built on labor and exchange. The other is only a rule of division for robbers who have to divide plunder or monks who have to divide gifts. If, therefore, we want to democratize industry in the sense of the first principle, we need only perfect what we have now, especially on its political side. If we try to democratize it in the sense of the other principle, we corrupt politics at one stroke; we enter upon an industrial enterprise which will waste capital and bring us all to poverty, and we set loose greed and envy as ruling social passions.

If this poor old world is as bad as they say, one more reflection may check the zeal of the headlong reformer. It is at any rate a tough old world. It has taken its trend and curvature and all its twists and tangles from a long course of formation. All its wry and crooked gnarls and knobs are therefore stiff and stubborn. If we puny men by our arts can do anything at all to straighten them, it will only be by modifying the tendencies of some of the forces at work, so that, after a sufficient time, their action may be changed a little and slowly the lines of movement may be modified. This effort, however, can at most be only slight, and it will take a long time. In the meantime, spontaneous forces will be at work, compared with which our efforts are like those of a man trying to deflect a river, and these forces will have changed the whole problem before our interferences have time to make themselves felt. The great stream of time and earthly things will sweep on just the same in spite of us. It bears with it now all the errors and follies of the past, the wreckage of all the philosophies, the fragments of all the civilizations, the wisdom of all the abandoned ethical systems, the debris of all the institutions, and the penalties of all the mistakes. It is only in imagination that we stand by and look at and criticize it and plan to change it. Everyone of us is a child of his age and cannot get out of it. He is in the stream and is swept along with it. All his sciences and philosophy come to him out of it. Therefore the tide will not be changed by us. It will swallow up both us and our experiments. It will absorb the efforts at change and take them into itself as new but trivial components, and the great movement of tradition and work will go on unchanged by our fads and schemes. The things which will change it are the great discoveries and inventions, the new reactions inside the social organism, and the changes in the earth itself on account of changes in the cosmical forces. These causes will make of it just what, in fidelity to them, it ought to be. The men will be carried along with it and be made by it. The utmost they can do by their cleverness will be to note and record their course as they are carried along, which is what we do now, and is that which leads us to the vain fancy that we can make or guide the movement. That is why it is the greatest folly of which a man can be capable, to sit down with a slate and pencil to plan out a new social world.

B. The Impact of Darwin

III. INTRODUCTION

In every sense of the word Thorstein Veblen (1857–1929) was a maverick. Raised on a Wisconsin farm, he eventually made his way to Yale University where he earned a Ph.D. in philosophy in 1884, and where he worked with William Graham Sumner. First unable to get any kind of academic position and later unable to hold those he did get, Veblen wandered through American academe smashing the idols of the American capitalistic establishment wherever he went. At the universities of Chicago, Stanford, and Missouri, he lectured on questions of political economy in his rambling, erudite, and inaudible fashion.

His mature intellectual position was a combination of American populism, Marxism, and the application of evolution to the discipline of economics.

The Theory of the Leisure Class, 1899, Veblen's first book, was greeted with almost universal rejection by his academic critics, and he suffered and enjoyed widespread notoriety. A biting and productive scholar, Veblen published a number of other iconoclastic works on the nature of the political economy: *The Theory of Business Enterprise,* 1904; *The Instinct of Workmanship,* 1914; *Imperial Germany and the Industrial Revolution,* 1915; *An Inquiry into the Nature of Peace,* 1917; *The Higher Learning in America,* 1918; *The Vested Interests and the State of the Industrial Arts,* 1919; *The Engineers and the Price System,* 1921; and *Absentee Ownership and Business Enterprise in Recent Times,* 1923.

In the selection reprinted here, Veblen argued essentially that economics must be freed from idealisms of all kinds. As a leading exponent of the attack on classical economics, Veblen in the following article—as well as in a series of other essays and books—was beginning to formulate the intellectual basis of institutional economics. The need for, but the absence of, a theoretical basis for all of the social sciences, including economics, meant to Veblen that none of those disciplines met the standards of modern science, especially those of evolutionary biology. It was his lifelong quest to substitute a theory of causal analysis for the merely mechanical sequence of earlier scholars in economics. To abandon rationalistic ideas like natural law became essential to his search for economic realism. To destroy concepts like "normality" and purposefulness in nature or in the social structure was equally essential to him. An almost existential stress on action, in place of the older ideals of human nature that stressed essences, increasingly began to characterize his mature work.

In this selection, he asserts that an evolutionary economics must be an explanation and conceptualization of cultural development as that is conditioned or determined by the material context of human life.

III.

Thorstein Veblen

WHY IS ECONOMICS NOT AN EVOLUTIONARY SCIENCE?

1898

M. G. de LaPouge recently said, "Anthropology is destined to revolution-ise the political and the social sciences as radically as bacteriology has revolutionised the science of medicine." In so far as he speaks of economics, the eminent anthropologist is not alone in his conviction that the science stands in need of rehabilitation. His words convey a rebuke and an admonition, and in both respects he speaks the sense of many scientists in his own and related lines of inquiry. It may be taken as the consensus of those men who are doing the serious work of modern anthropology, ethnology, and psychology, as well as of those in the biological sciences proper, that economics is helplessly behind the times, and unable to handle its subject-matter in a way to entitle it to standing as a modern science. The other political and social sciences come in for their share of this obloquy, and perhaps on equally cogent grounds. Nor are the economists themselves buoyantly indifferent to the rebuke. Probably no economist to-day has either the hardihood or the inclination to say that the science has now reached a definitive formulation, either in the detail of results or as regards the fundamental features of theory. . . . With the economists who are most attentively looked to for guidance, uncertainty as to the definitive value of what has been and is being done, and as to what we may, with effect, take to next, is so common as to suggest that indecision is a meritorious work. Even the Historical School, who made their innovation with so much home-grown applause some time back, have been unable to settle down contentedly to the pace which they set themselves.

The men of the sciences that are proud to own themselves "modern" find fault with the economists for being still content to occupy themselves

SOURCE. Thorstein Veblen, *The Place of Science in Modern Civilization,* New York: Viking Press, 1930, pp. 36–81. Copyright 1919 by B. W. Huebsch, 1947 by Ann B. Sims and Becky Meyers. Reprinted with the permission of The Viking Press, Inc.

with repairing a structure and doctrines and maxims resting on natural rights, utilitarianism, and administrative expediency. This aspersion is not altogether merited, but is near enough to the mark to carry a sting. These modern sciences are evolutionary sciences, and their adepts contemplate that characteristic of their work with some complacency. Economics is not an evolutionary science—by the confession of its spokesmen; and the economists turn their eyes with something of envy and some sense of baffled emulation to these rivals that make broad their phylacteries with the legend, "Up to date."

Precisely wherein the social and political sciences, including economics, fall short of being evolutionary sciences, is not so plain. At least, it has not been satisfactorily pointed out by their critics. Their successful rivals in this matter—the sciences that deal with human nature among the rest—claim as their substantial distinction that they are realistic: they deal with facts. But economics, too, is realistic in this sense: it deals with facts, often in the most painstaking way, and latterly with an increasingly strenuous insistence on the sole efficacy of data. But this "realism" does not make economics an evolutionary science. The insistence on data could scarcely be carried to a higher pitch than it was carried by the first generation of the Historical School; and yet no economics is farther from being an evolutionary science than the re-ceived economics of the Historical School. The whole broad range of erudition and research that engaged the energies of that school com-monly falls short of being science, in that, when consistent, they have contented themselves with an enumeration of data and a narrative ac-count of industrial development, and have not presumed to offer a theory of anything or to elaborate their results into a consistent body of knowledge. . . .

Of the achievements of the classical economists, recent and living, the science may justly be proud; but they fall short of the evolutionist's standard of adequacy, not in failing to offer a theory of a process or of a developmental relation, but through conceiving their theory in terms alien to the evolutionist's habits of thought. The difference between the evolutionary and the pre-evolutionary sciences lies not in the insistence on facts. There was a great and fruitful activity in the natural sciences in collecting and collating facts before these sciences took on the character which marks them as evolutionary. Nor does the difference lie in the ab-sence of efforts to formulate and explain schemes of process, sequence, growth, and development in the pre-evolutionary days. Efforts of this

kind abounded, in number and diversity; and many schemes of development, of great sublety and beauty, gained a vogue both as theories of
organic and inorganic development and as schemes of the life history
of nations and societies. It will not even hold true that our elders overlooked the presence of cause and effect in formulating their theories and
reducing their data to a body of knowledge. But the terms which were
accepted as the definitive terms of knowledge were in some degree different in the early days from what they are now. The terms of thought
in which the investigators of some two or three generations back definitively formulated their knowledge of facts, in their last analyses, were
different in kind from the terms in which the modern evolutionist is
content to formulate his results. The analysis does not run back to the
same ground, or appeal to the same standard of finality or adequacy, in
the one case as in the other.

The difference is a difference of spiritual attitude or point of view
in the two contrasted generations of scientists. To put the matter in other
words, it is a difference in the basis of valuation of the facts for the scientific purpose, or in the interest from which the facts are appreciated.
With the earlier as with the later generation the basis of valuation of
the facts handled is, in matters of detail, the causal relation which is
apprehended to subsist between them. This is true to the greatest extent
for the natural sciences. But in their handling of the more comprehensive
schemes of sequence and relation—in their definitive formulation of
the results—the two generations differ. The modern scientist is unwilling
to depart from the test of causal relation or quantitative sequence. When
he asks the question, Why? he insists on an answer in terms of cause
and effect. He wants to reduce his solution of all problems to terms of
the conservation of energy or the persistence of quantity. This is his last
recourse. And this last recourse has in our time been made available for
the handling of schemes of development and theories of a comprehensive process by the notion of a cumulative causation. The great deserts
of the evolutionist leaders—if they have great deserts as leaders—lie, on
the one hand, in their refusal to go back of the colorless sequence of
phenomena and seek higher ground for their ultimate syntheses, and, on
the other hand, in their having shown how this colorless impersonal
sequence of cause and effect can be made use of for theory proper, by
virtue of its cumulative character.

For the earlier natural scientists, as for the classical economists, this
ground of cause and effect is not definitive. Their sense of truth and

substantiality is not satisfied with a formulation of mechanical sequence. The ultimate term in their systematisation of knowledge is a "natural law." This natural law is felt to exercise some sort of a coercive surveillance over the sequence of events, and to give a spiritual stability and consistence to the causal relation at any given juncture. To meet the high classical requirement, a sequence—and a developmental process especially—must be apprehended in terms of a consistent propensity tending to some spiritually legitimate end. When facts and events have been reduced to these terms of fundamental truth and have been made to square with the requirements of definitive normality, the investigator rests his case. Any causal sequence which is apprehended to traverse the imputed propensity in events is a "disturbing factor." Logical congruity with the apprehended propensity is, in this view, adequate ground of procedure in building up a scheme of knowledge or of development. The objective point of the efforts of the scientists working under the guidance of this classical tradition, is to formulate knowledge in terms of absolute truth; and this absolute truth is a spiritual fact. It means a coincidence of facts with the deliverances of an enlightened and deliberate common sense.

The development and the attenuation of this preconception of normality or of a propensity in events might be traced in detail from primitive animism down through the elaborate discipline of faith and metaphysics, overruling Providence, order of nature, natural rights, natural law, underlying principles. But all that may be necessary here is to point out that, by descent and by psychological content, this constraining normality is of a spiritual kind. It is for the scientific purpose an imputation of spiritual coherence to the facts dealt with. The question of interest is how this preconception of normality has fared at the hands of modern science, and how it has come to be superseded in the intellectual primacy by the latter-day preconception of a non-spiritual sequence. This question is of interest because its answer may throw light on the question as to what chance there is for the indefinite persistence of this archaic habit of thought in the methods of economic science.

Under primitive conditions, men stand in immediate personal contact with the material facts of the environment; and the force and discretion of the individual in shaping the facts of the environment count obviously, and to all appearance solely, in working out the conditions of life. There is little of impersonal or mechanical sequence visible to primitive men in their every-day life; and what there is of this kind in the processes of brute nature about them is in large part inexplicable and passes for inscrutable. It is accepted as malignant or beneficent, and is construed in the terms of personality that are familiar to all men at first hand,—the terms known to all men by first-hand knowledge of their own acts. The inscrutable movements of the seasons and of the natural forces are apprehended as actions guided by discretion, will power, or propensity looking to an end, much as human actions are. The processes of inanimate nature are agencies whose habits of life are to be learned, and who are to be coerced, outwitted, circumvented, and turned to account, much as the beasts are. At the same time the community is small, and the human contact of the individual is not wide. Neither the industrial life nor the non-industrial social life forces upon men's attention the ruthless impersonal sweep of events that no man can withstand or deflect, such as becomes visible in the more complex and comprehensive life process of the larger community of a later day. There is nothing decisive to hinder men's knowledge of facts and events being formulated in terms of personality—in terms of habit and propensity and will power.

As time goes on and as the situation departs from this archaic character,—where it does depart from it,—the circumstances which condition men's systematisation of facts change in such a way as to throw the impersonal character of the sequence of events more and more into the foreground. The penalties for failure to apprehend facts in dispassionate terms fall surer and swifter. The sweep of events is forced home more consistently on men's minds. The guiding hand of a spiritual agency or a propensity in events becomes less readily traceable as men's knowledge of things grows ampler and more searching. In modern times, and particularly in the industrial countries, this coercive guidance of men's habits of thought in the realistic direction has been especially pronounced; and the effect shows itself in a somewhat reluctant but cumulative departure from the archaic point of view. The departure is most visible and has gone farthest in those homely branches of knowledge that have to do immediately with modern mechanical processes, such as engineering designs and technological contrivances generally. Of the sciences, those have wandered farthest on this way (of integration or disintegration, according as one may choose to view it) that have to do with mechanical sequence and process; and those have best and longest retained the archaic point of view intact which—like the moral, social, or spiritual sciences—have to do with process and sequence that is less tangible, less traceable by the use of the senses, and that therefore less immediately forces upon the attention the phenomenon of sequence as contrasted with that of propensity.

There is no abrupt transition from the pre-evolutionary to the post-evolutionary standpoint. Even in those natural sciences which deal with the processes of life and the evolutionary sequence of events the concept of dispassionate cumulative causation has often and effectively been helped out by the notion that there is in all this some sort of a meliorative trend that exercises a constraining guidance over the course of causes and effects. The faith in this meliorative trend as a concept useful to the science has gradually weakened, and it has repeatedly been disavowed; but it can scarcely be said to have yet disappeared from the field.

The process of change in the point of view, or in the terms of definitive formulation of knowledge, is a gradual one; and all the sciences have shared, though in an unequal degree, in the change that is going forward. Economics is not an exception to the rule, but it still shows too many reminiscences of the "natural" and the "normal," of "verities" and "tendencies," of "controlling principles" and "disturbing causes" to be classed as an evolutionary science. This history of the science shows a long and devious course of disintegrating animism,—from the days of the scholastic writers, who discussed usury from the point of view of its relation to the divine suzerainty, to the Physiocrats, who rested their case on an *"ordre naturel"* and a *"loi naturelle"* that decides what is substantially true and, in a general way, guides the course of events by the constraint of logical congruence. There has been something of a change from Adam Smith, whose recourse in perplexity was to the guidance of "an unseen hand," to Mill and Cairnes, who formulated the laws of "natural" wages and "normal" value. . . .

The standpoint of the classical economists, in their higher or definitive syntheses and generalisations, may not inaptly be called the standpoint of ceremonial adequacy. The ultimate laws and principles which they formulated were laws of the normal or the natural, according to a preconception regarding the ends to which, in the nature of things, all things tend. In effect, this preconception imputes to things a tendency to work out what the instructed common sense of the time accepts as the adequate or worthy end of human effort. It is a projection of the accepted ideal of conduct. This ideal of conduct is made to serve as a canon of truth, to the extent that the investigator contents himself with an appeal to its legitimation for premises that run back of the facts with which he is immediately dealing, for the "controlling principles" that are conceived intangibly to underlie the process discussed, and for the "tendencies" that run beyond the situation as it lies before him. As instances of the use of this ceremonial canon of knowledge may be cited the "conjectural history" that plays so large a part in the classical treatment of economic institutions, such as the normalized accounts of the beginnings of barter in the transactions of the putative hunter, fisherman, and boat-builder. . . . Of a similar import is the characterisation of money as "the great wheel of circulation" or as "the medium of exchange." Money is here discussed in terms of the end which, "in the normal case," it should work out according to the given writer's ideal of economic life, rather than in terms of causal relation.

With later writers especially, this terminology is no doubt to be commonly taken as a convenient use of metaphor, in which the concept of normality and propensity to an end has reached an extreme attenuation. But it is precisely in this use of figurative terms for the formulation of theory that the classical normality still lives its attenuated life in modern economics; and it is this facile recourse to inscrutable figures of speech as the ultimate terms of theory that has saved the economists from being dragooned into the ranks of modern science. The metaphors are effective, both in their homiletical use and as a labor-saving device,—more effective than their user designs them to be. By their use the theorist is enabled serenely to enjoin himself from following out an elusive train of causal sequence. He is also enabled, without misgivings, to construct a theory of such an institution as money or wages or land-ownership without descending to a consideration of the living items concerned, except for convenient corroboration of his normalised scheme of symptoms. By this method the theory of an institution or a phase of life may be stated in conventionalised terms of the apparatus whereby life is carried on, the apparatus being invested with a tendency to an equilibrium at the normal, and the theory being a formulation of the conditions under which this putative equilibrium supervenes. In this way we have come into the usufruct of a cost-of-production theory of value which is pungently reminiscent of the time when Nature abhorred a vacuum. The ways and means and the mechanical structure of industry are formulated in a conventionalised nomenclature, and the observed motions of this mechanical apparatus are then reduced to a normalised scheme of relations. The scheme so arrived at is spiritually binding on the behavior of the phenomena contemplated. With this normalised scheme as a guide, the permutations of a given segment of the apparatus are worked out according to the values assigned the several items and features comprised in the calculation; and a ceremonially consistent formula is constructed to cover that much of the industrial field. This is the deductive method. The formula is then tested by comparison with observed permutations, by the polariscopic use of the "normal case"; and the results arrived at are thus authenticated by induction. Features of the process that do not lend themselves to interpretation in the terms of the formula are abnormal cases and are due to disturbing causes. In all this the agencies or forces causally at work in the economic life process are neatly avoided. The outcome of the method, at its best, is a body of logically consistent propositions concerning the normal relations of things—a system of economic taxonomy. At its worst, it is a body of maxims for the conduct of business and a polemical discussion of disputed points of policy.

In all this, economic science is living over again in its turn the experiences which the natural sciences passed through some time back. In the natural sciences the work of the taxonomist was and continues to be of great value, but the scientists grew restless under the régime of symmetry and system-making. They took to asking why, and so shifted their inquiries from the structure of the coral reefs to the structure and habits of life of the polyp that lives in and by them. In the science of plants, systematic botany has not ceased to be of service; but the stress of investigation and discussion among the botanists to-day falls on the biological value of any given feature of structure, function, or tissue rather than on its taxonomic bearing. All the talk about cytoplasm, centrosomes, and karyokinetic process, means that the inquiry now looks consistently to the life process, and aims to explain it in terms of cumulative causation. . . .

In the days of the early classical writers economics had a vital interest for the laymen of the time, because it formulated the common sense metaphysics of the time in its application to a department of human life. But in the hands of the later classical writers the science lost much of its charm in this regard. It was no longer a definition and authentication of the deliverances of current common sense as to what ought to come to pass; and it, therefore, in large measure lost the support of the people out of doors, who were unable to take an interest in what did not concern them; and it was also out of touch with that realistic or evolutionary habit of mind which got under way about the middle of the century in the natural sciences. It was neither vitally metaphysical nor matter-of-fact, and it found comfort with very few outside of its own ranks. Only for those who by the fortunate accident of birth or education have been able to conserve the taxonomic animus has the science during the last third of a century continued to be of absorbing interest. The result has been that from the time when the taxonomic structure stood forth as a completed whole in its symmetry and stability the economists themselves, beginning with Cairnes, have been growing restive under its discipline of stability, and have made many efforts, more or less sustained, to galvanise it into movement. At the hands of the writers of the classical line these excursions have chiefly aimed at a more complete and comprehensive taxonomic scheme of permutations; while the historical departure threw away the taxonomic ideal without getting rid of the preconceptions on which it is based; and the later Austrian group struck out on a theory of process, but presently came to a full stop because the process about which they busied themselves was not, in their apprehension of it, a cumulative or unfolding sequence.

But what does all this signify? . . . What are we going to do about it? The question is rather, What are we doing about it? There is the economic life process still in great measure awaiting theoretical formulation. The active material in which the economic process goes on is the human material of the industrial community. For the purpose of economic science the process of cumulative change that is to be accounted for is the sequence of change in the methods of doing things,—the methods of dealing with the material means of life.

What has been done in the way of inquiry into this economic life process? The ways and means of turning material objects and circumstances to account lie before the investigator at any given point of time in the form of mechanical contrivances and arrangements for compassing certain mechanical ends. It has therefore been easy to accept these ways and means as items of inert matter having a given mechanical structure and thereby serving the material ends of man. As such, they have been scheduled and graded by the economists under the head of capital, this capital being conceived as a mass of material objects serviceable for human use. This is well enough for the purposes of taxonomy; but it is not an effective method of conceiving the matter for the purpose of a theory of the developmental process. For the latter purpose, when taken as items in a process of cumulative change or as items in the scheme of life, these productive goods are facts of human knowledge, skill, and predilection; that is to say, they are, substantially, prevalent habits of thought, and it is as such that they enter into the process of industrial development. The physical properties of the materials accessible to man are constants: it is the human agent that changes,—his insight and his appreciation of what these things can be used for is what develops. The accumulation of goods already on hand conditions his handling and utilisation of the materials offered, but even on this side—the "limitation of industry by capital"—the limitation imposed is on what men can do and on the methods of doing it. The changes that take place in the mechanical contrivances are an expression of changes in the human factor. Changes in the material facts breed further change only through the human factor. It is in the human material that the continuity of development is to be looked for; and it is here, therefore, that the motor forces of the process of economic development must be studied if they are to be studied in action at all. Economic action must be the subject-matter of the science if the science is to fall into line as an evolutionary science.

Nothing new has been said in all this. But the fact is all the more significant for being a familiar fact. It is a fact recognised by common consent throughout much of the later economic discussion, and this current recognition of the fact is a long step towards centering discussion and inquiry upon it. If economics is to follow the lead or the analogy of the other sciences that have to do with a life process, the way is plain so far as regards the general direction in which the move will be made.

The economists of the classical trend have made no serious attempt to depart from the standpoint of taxonomy and make their science a genetic account of the economic life process. As has just been said, much the same is true for the Historical School. The latter have attempted an account of developmental sequence, but they have followed the lines of pre-Darwinian speculations on development rather than lines which modern science would recognise as evolutionary. They have given a narrative survey of phenomena, not a genetic account of an unfolding process. In this work they have, no doubt, achieved results of permanent value; but the results achieved are scarcely to be classed as economic theory. . . .

In all the received formulations of economic theory, whether at the hands of English economists or those of the Continent, the human material with which the inquiry is concerned is conceived in hedonistic terms; that is to say, in terms of a passive and substantially inert and immutably given human nature. The psychological and anthropological preconceptions of the economists have been those which were accepted by the psychological and social sciences some generations ago. The hedonistic conception of man is that of a lightning calculator of pleasures and pains, who oscillates like a homogeneous globule of desire of happiness under the impulse of stimuli that shift him about the area, but leave him intact. He is an isolated, definitive human datum, in stable equilibrium except for the buffets of the impinging forces that displace him in one direction or another. Self-imposed in elemental space, he spins symmetrically about his own spiritual axis until the parallelogram of forces bears down upon him, whereupon he follows the line of the resultant. When the force of the impact is spent, he comes to rest, a self-contained globule of desire as before. Spiritually, the hedonistic man is not a prime mover. He is not the seat of a process of living, except in the sense that he is subject to a series of permutations enforced upon him by circumstances external and alien to him.

The later psychology, reënforced by modern anthropological research, gives a different conception of human nature. According to this conception, it is the characteristic of man to do something, not simply to suffer pleasures and pains through the impact of suitable forces. He is not simply a bundle of desires that are to be saturated by being placed in the path of the forces of the environment, but rather a coherent structure of propensities and habits which seeks realisation and expression in an unfolding activity. According to this view, human activity, and economic activity among the rest, is not apprehended as something incidental to the process of saturating given desires. The activity is itself the substantial fact of the process, and the desires under whose guidance the action takes place are circumstances of temperament which determine the specific direction in which the activity will unfold itself in the given case. These circumstances of temperament are ultimate and definitive for the individual who acts under them, so far as regards his attitude as agent in the particular action in which he is engaged. But, in the view of the science, they are elements of the existing frame of mind of the agent, and are the outcome of his life up to the point at which he stands. They are the products of his hereditary traits and his past experience, cumulatively wrought out under a given body of traditions, conventionalities, and material circumstances; and they afford the point of departure for the next step in the process. The economic life history of the individual is a cumulative process of adaptation of means to ends that cumulatively change as the process goes on, both the agent and his environment being at any point the outcome of the last process. His methods of life to-day are enforced upon him by his habits of life carried over from yesterday and by the circumstances left as the mechanical residue of the life of yesterday.

What is true of the individual in this respect is true of the group in which he lives. All economic change is a change in the economic community,—a change in the community's methods of turning material things to account. The change is always in the last resort a change in habits of thought. This is true even of changes in the mechanical processes of industry. A given contrivance for effecting certain material ends becomes a circumstance which affects the further growth of habits of thought— habitual methods of procedure—and so becomes a point of departure for further development of the methods of compassing the ends sought and for the further variation of ends that are sought to be compassed. In all this flux there is no definitively adequate method of life and no definitive or absolutely worthy end of action, so far as concerns the science which sets out to formulate a theory of the process of economic life. What remains as a hard and fast residue is the fact of activity directed to an objective end. Economic action is teleological, in the sense that men always and everywhere seek to do something. What, in specific detail, they seek, is not to be answered except by a scrutiny of the details of their activity; but, so long as we have to do with their life as members of the economic community, there remains the generic fact that their life is an unfolding activity of a teleological kind.

It may or may not be a teleological process in the sense that it tends or should tend to any end that is conceived to be worthy or adequate by the inquirer or by the consensus of inquirers. Whether it is or is not, is a question with which the present inquiry is not concerned; and it is also a question of which an evolutionary economics need take no account. The question of a tendency in events can evidently not come up except on the ground of some preconception or prepossession on the part of the person looking for the tendency. In order to search for a tendency, we must be possessed of some notion of a definitive end to be sought, or some notion as to what is the legitimate trend of events. The notion of a legitimate trend in a course of events is an extra-evolutionary preconception, and lies outside the scope of an inquiry into the causal sequence in any process. The evolutionary point of view, therefore, leaves no place for a formulation of natural laws in terms of definitive normality, whether in economics or in any other branch of inquiry. Neither does it leave room for that other question of normality, What should be the end of the developmental process under discussion?

The economic life history of any community is its life history in so far as it is shaped by men's interest in the material means of life. This economic interest has counted for much in shaping the cultural growth of all communities. Primarily and most obviously, it has guided the formation, the cumulative growth, of that range of conventionalities and methods of life that are currently recognized as economic institutions, but the same interest has also pervaded the community's life and its cultural growth at points where the resulting structural features are not chiefly and most immediately of an economic bearing. The economic interest goes with men through life, and it goes with the race throughout its process of cultural development. It affects the cultural structure at all points, so that all institutions may be said to be in some measure economic institutions. This is necessarily the case, since the base action—the point of departure—at any step in the process is the entire organic complex of habits of thought that have been shaped by the past process. The economic interest does not act in isolation, for it is but one of several vaguely isolable interests on which the complex of teleological activity carried out by the individual proceeds. The individual is but a single agent in each case; and he enters into each successive action as a whole, although the specific end sought in a given action may be sought avowedly on the basis of a particular interest; as e.g., the economic, æsthetic, sexual, humanitarian, devotional interests. Since each of these passably isolable interests is a propensity of the organic agent man, with his complex of habits of thought, the expression of each is affected by habits of life formed under the guidance of all the rest. There is, therefore, no neatly isolable range of cultural phenomena that can be rigorously set apart under the head of economic institutions, although a category of "economic institutions" may be of service as a convenient caption, comprising those institutions in which the economic interest most immediately and consistently finds expression, and which most immediately and with the least limitation are of an economic bearing.

From what has been said it appears that an evolutionary economics must be the theory of a process of cultural growth as determined by the economic interest, a theory of a cumulative sequence of economic institutions stated in terms of the process itself. . . .

We are now ready to return to the question why economics is not an evolutionary science. It is necessarily the aim of such an economics to trace the cumulative working-out of the economic interest in the cultural sequence. It must be a theory of the economic life process of the race or the community. The economists have accepted the hedonistic preconceptions concerning human nature and human action, and the conception of the economic interest which a hedonistic psychology gives does not afford material for a theory of the development of human nature. Under hedonism the economic interest is not conceived in terms of action. It is therefore not readily apprehended or appreciated in terms of a cumulative growth of habits of thought, and does not provoke, even if it did lend itself to, treatment by the evolutionary method. At the same time the anthropological preconceptions current in that common-sense apprehension of human nature to which economists have habitually turned has not enforced the formulation of human nature in terms of a cumulative growth of habits of life. These received anthropological preconceptions are such as have made possible the normalized conjectural accounts of primitive barter with which all economic readers are familiar, and the no less normalized conventional derivation of landed property and its rent, or the sociologico-philosophical discussions of the "function" of this or that class in the life of society or of the nation.

The premises and the point of view required for an evolutionary economics have been wanting. The economists have not had the materials for such a science ready to their hand, and the provocation to strike out in such a direction has been absent. Even if it has been possible at any time to turn to the evolutionary line of speculation in economics, the possibility of a departure is not enough to bring it about. So long as the habitual view taken of a given range of facts is of the taxonomic kind and the material lends itself to treatment by that method, the taxonomic method is the easiest, gives the most gratifying immediate results, and best fits into the accepted body of knowledge of the range of facts in question. This has been the situation in economics. The other sciences of its group have likewise been a body of taxonomic discipline, and departures from the accredited method have lain under the odium of being meretricious innovations. The well-worn paths are easy to follow and lead into good company. Advance along them visibly furthers the accredited work which the science has in hand. Divergence from the paths means tentative work, which is necessarily slow and fragmentary and of uncertain value.

It is only when the methods of the science and the syntheses resulting from their use come to be out of line with habits of thought that prevail in other matters that the scientist grows restive under the guidance of the received methods and standpoints, and seeks a way out. Like other men, the economist is an individual with but one intelligence. He is a creature of habits and propensities given through antecedents, hereditary and cultural, of which he is an outcome; and the habits of thought formed in any one line of experience affect his thinking in any other. Methods of observation and of handling facts that are familiar through habitual use in the general range of knowledge, gradually assert themselves in any given special range of knowledge. They may be accepted slowly and with reluctance where their acceptance involves innovation; but, if they have the continued backing of the general body of experience, it is only a question of time when they shall come into dominance in the special field. The intellectual attitude and the method of correlation enforced upon us in the apprehension and assimilation of facts in the more elementary ranges of knowledge that have to do with brute facts assert themselves also when the attention is directed to those phenomena of the life process with which economics has to do; and the range of facts which are habitually handled by other methods than that in traditional vogue in economics has now become so large and so insistently present at every turn that we are left restless, if the new body of facts cannot be handled according to the method of mental procedure which is in this way becoming habitual.

In the general body of knowledge in modern times the facts are apprehended in terms of causal sequence. This is especially true of that knowledge of brute facts which is shaped by the exigencies of the modern mechanical industry. To men thoroughly imbued with this matter-of-fact habit of mind the laws and theorems of economics, and of the other sciences that treat of the normal course of things, have a character of "unreality" and futility that bars out any serious interest in their discussion. The laws and theorems are "unreal" to them because they are not to be apprehended in the terms which these men make use of in handling the facts with which they are perforce habitually occupied. The same matter-of-fact spiritual attitude and mode of procedure have now made their way well up into the higher levels of scientific knowledge, even in the sciences which deal in a more elementary way with the same human material that makes the subject-matter of economics, and the economists themselves are beginning to feel the unreality of their theorems about "normal" cases. Provided the practical exigencies of modern industrial life continue of the same character as they now are, and so continue to enforce the impersonal method of knowledge, it is only a question of time when that (substantially animistic) habit of mind which proceeds on the notion of a definitive normality shall be displaced in the field of economic inquiry by that (substantially materialistic) habit of mind which seeks a comprehension of facts in terms of a cumulative sequence.

The later method of apprehending and assimilating facts and handling them for the purposes of knowledge may be better or worse, more or less worthy or adequate, than the earlier; it may be of greater or less ceremonial or æsthetic effect; we may be moved to regret the incursion of underbred habits of thought into the scholar's domain. But all that is beside the present point. Under the stress of modern technological exigencies, men's every-day habits of thought are falling into the lines that in the sciences constitute the evolutionary method; and knowledge which proceeds on a higher, more archaic plane is becoming alien and meaningless to them. The social and political sciences must follow the drift, for they are already caught in it.

C. The Religious Response

IV. INTRODUCTION

The impact of industrial change in America was felt virtually throughout society. Religious thought, along with other areas, had somehow to make its peace with the facts of industrialism. A theology that was relevant to industrial capitalism seemed, to some, a desperate need of the post-Civil War period.

One of the phenomena of the religious response to industrialism was Russell H. Conwell (1843–1925). A Baptist minister, philanthropist, and founder of Temple University, Conwell was a self-made man who began his adult career as a lawyer. None of his achievements, however, equal in importance a lecture he called "Acres of Diamonds," which he delivered approximately 6,000 times to approximately thirteen million people. The reasons for the popularity of Conwell's lecture are immediately obvious. He told American audiences that it was their Christian duty to get rich. He explained that getting money honestly was, in fact, like preaching the gospel. No greater defense of the capitalistic American establishment could be offered than his assertion that 98 per cent of the rich men in America were honest, along with his affirmation that their honesty had been the cause of their wealth. The poor, he explained, were poor because of their own personal deficiencies.

The individualism of Conwell's approach was obviously found congenial by his vast audiences. His celebration of wealth, and his sup-

posed reconciliation of enormous power with Christianity also contributed to the applause of that same audience which relished Horatio
Alger. Absolutely denying any superiority of the social organization,
Conwell held out the hope to each individual in his audience that each
one could look forward to the day when he would be surrounded with
gold, if only each one would exert himself, believe in Conwell's Lord,
and seek his fortune in his own backyard. The fact of the social pre-
eminence of the captains of industry in America meant that those
millions who thrilled to Conwell's assurances were themselves nour-
ished by the hope that someday they too would be able to buy their way
into the controlling segment of American life, and be able to pay the
expensive toll presumably demanded by St. Peter before he would
allow an individual to pass through his bejewelled gate.

IV.

Russell H. Conwell
ACRES OF DIAMONDS
1915

The opportunity to get rich, to attain unto great wealth, is . . . within the
reach of almost every man and woman who hears me speak to-night, and
I mean just what I say. I have not come to this platform even under these
circumstances to recite something to you. I have come to tell you what
in God's sight I believe to be the truth, and if the years of life have been
of any value to me in the attainment of common sense, I know I am right;
that the men and women sitting here, who found it difficult perhaps to
buy a ticket to this lecture or gathering to-night, have within their reach
"acres of diamonds," opportunities to get largely wealthy. . . . I say it is
the truth, and I want you to accept it as such; for if you think I have come
to simply recite something, then I would better not be here. I have no
time to waste in any such talk, but to say the things I believe, and unless
some of you get richer for what I am saying to-night my time is wasted.

I say that you ought to get rich, and it is your duty to get rich. How
many of my pious brethren say to me, "Do you, a Christian minister,

SOURCE. Russell H. Conwell, *Acres of Diamonds,* New York: Harper and
Brothers, 1915, pp. 17–24, 27–28, 30–32, 34–35, and 50–51. Copyright 1915,
1943 by Harper and Brothers. Reprinted with the permission of Harper and Row,
Publishers.

spend your time going up and down the country advising young people to get rich, to get money?" "Yes, of course I do." They say, "Isn't that awful! Why don't you preach the gospel instead of preaching about man's making money?" "Because to make money honestly is to preach the gospel." That is the reason. The men who get rich may be the most honest men you find in the community.

"Oh," but says some young man here to-night, "I have been told all my life that if a person has money he is very dishonest and dishonorable and mean and contemptible." My friend, that is the reason why you have none, because you have that idea of people. The foundation of your faith is altogether false. Let me say here clearly, and say it briefly, though subject to discussion which I have not time for here, ninety-eight out of one hundred of the rich men of America are honest. That is why they are rich. That is why they are trusted with money. That is why they carry on great enterprises and find plenty of people to work with them. It is because they are honest men.

Says another young man, "I hear sometimes of men that get millions of dollars dishonestly." Yes, of course you do, and so do I. But they are so rare a thing in fact that the newspapers talk about them all the time as a matter of news until you get the idea that all the other rich men got rich dishonestly.

My friend, you take and drive me—if you furnish the auto—out into the suburbs . . . and introduce me to the people who own their homes around this great city, those beautiful homes with gardens and flowers, those magnificent homes so lovely in their art, and I will introduce you to the very best people in character as well as in enterprise in our city, and you know I will. A man is not really a true man until he owns his own home, and they that own their homes are made more honorable and honest and pure, and true and economical and careful, by owning the home.

For a man to have money, even in large sums, is not an inconsistent thing. We preach against covetousness, and you know we do, in the pulpit, and oftentimes preach against it so long and use the terms about "filthy lucre" so extremely that Christians get the idea that when we stand in the pulpit we believe it is wicked for any man to have money—until the collection-basket goes around, and then we almost swear at the people because they don't give more money. Oh, the inconsistency of such doctrines as that!

Money is power, and you ought to be reasonably ambitious to have it. You ought because you can do more good with it than you could without it. Money printed your Bible, money builds your churches, money sends your missionaries, and money pays your preachers, and you would not have many of them, either, if you did not pay them. I am always willing that my church should raise my salary, because the church that pays the largest salary always raises it the easiest. You never knew an exception to it in your life. The man who gets the largest salary can do the most good with the power that is furnished to him. Of course he can if his spirit be right to use it for what it is given to him.

I say, then, you ought to have money. If you can honestly attain unto riches . . . it is your Christian and godly duty to do so. It is an awful mistake of these pious people to think you must be awfully poor in order to be pious.

Some men say, "Don't you sympathize with the poor people?" Of course I do, or else I would not have been lecturing these years. I won't give in but what I sympathize with the poor, but the number of poor who are to be sympathized with is very small. To sympathize with a man whom God has punished for his sins, thus to help him when God would still continue a just punishment, is to do wrong, no doubt about it, and we do that more than we help those who are deserving. While we should sympathize with God's poor—that is, those who cannot help themselves—let us remember there is not a poor person in the United States who was not made poor by his own shortcomings, or by the shortcomings of some one else. It is all wrong to be poor, anyhow. Let us give in to that argument and pass that to one side.

A gentleman gets up back there, and says, "Don't you think there are some things in this world that are better than money?" Of course I do, but I am talking about money now. Of course there are some things higher than money. Oh yes, I know by the grave that has left me standing alone that there are some things in this world that are higher and sweeter and purer than money. Well do I know there are some things higher and grander than gold. Love is the grandest thing on God's good earth, but fortunate the lover who has plenty of money. Money is power, money is force, money will do good as well as harm. In the hands of good men and women it could accomplish, and it has accomplished, good.

I hate to leave that behind me. I heard a man get up in a prayer-meeting in our city and thank the Lord he was "one of God's poor." Well, I wonder what his wife thinks about that? She earns all the money that comes into that house, and he smokes a part of that on the veranda. I don't want to see any more of the Lord's poor of that kind, and I don't believe the Lord does. And yet there are some people who think in order to be pious you must be awfully poor and awfully dirty. That does not follow at all. While we sympathize with the poor, let us not teach a doctrine like that.

Yet the age is prejudiced against advising a Christian man (or, as a Jew would say, a godly man) from attaining unto wealth. The prejudice is so universal and the years are far enough back, I think, for me to safely mention that years ago up at Temple University there was a young man in our theological school who thought he was the only pious student in that department. He came into my office one evening and sat down by my desk, and said to me: "Mr. President, I think it is my duty sir, to come in and labor with you." "What has happened now?" Said he, "I heard you say at the Academy, at the Peirce School commencement, that you thought it was an honorable ambition for a young man to desire to have wealth, and that you thought it made him temperate, made him anxious to have a good name, and made him industrious. You spoke about man's ambition to have money helping to make him a good man. Sir, I have come to tell you the Holy Bible says that 'money is the root of all evil.' "

I told him I had never seen it in the Bible, and advised him to go out into the chapel and get the Bible, and show me the place. So out he went for the Bible, and soon he stalked into my office with the Bible open, with all the bigoted pride of the narrow sectarian, or of one who founds his Christianity on some misinterpretation of Scripture. He flung the Bible down on my desk, and fairly squealed into my ear: "There it is, Mr. President; you can read it for yourself." I said to him: "Well, young man, you will learn when you get a little older that you cannot trust another denomination to read the Bible for you. You belong to another denomination. You are taught in the theological school, however, that emphasis is exegesis. Now, will you take that Bible and read it yourself and give the proper emphasis to it?"

He took the Bible, and proudly read, "The love of money is the root of all evil."

Then he had it right, and when one does quote aright from that same old Book he quotes the absolute truth. I have lived through fifty years of the mightiest battle that old Book has ever fought, and I have lived to see its banners flying free; for never in the history of this world did the great minds of earth so universally agree that the Bible is true—all true— as they do at this very hour.

So I say that when he quoted right, of course he quoted the absolute truth. "The love of money is the root of all evil." He who tries to attain unto it too quickly, or dishonestly, will fall into many snares, no doubt about that. The love of money. What is that? It is making an idol of money, and idolatry pure and simple everywhere is condemned by the Holy Scriptures and by man's common sense. The man that worships the dollar instead of thinking of the purposes for which it ought to be used, the man who idolizes simply money, the miser that hordes his money in the cellar, or hides it in his stocking, or refuses to invest it where it will do the world good, that man who hugs the dollar until the eagle squeals has in him the root of all evil. . . .

There are some over-pious Christian people who think if you take any profit on anything you sell that you are an unrighteous man. On the contrary, you would be a criminal to sell goods for less than they cost. You have no right to do that. You cannot trust a man with your money who cannot take care of his own. You cannot trust a man in your family that is not true to his own wife. You cannot trust a man in the world that does not begin with his own heart, his own character, and his own life. . . . I have no more right to sell goods without making a profit on them than I have to overcharge him dishonestly beyond what they are worth. But I should so sell each bill of goods that the person to whom I sell shall make as much as I make.

To live and let live is the principle of the gospel, and the principle of every-day common sense. Oh, young man, hear me; live as you go along. Do not wait until you have reached my years before you begin to enjoy anything of this life. If I had the millions back, or fifty cents of it, which I have tried to earn in these years, it would not do me anything like the good that it does me now in this almost sacred presence to-night. Oh, yes, I am paid over and over a hundredfold to-night for dividing as I have tried to do in some measure as I went along through the years. I ought not speak that way, it sounds egotistic, but I am old enough now to be excused for that. I should have helped my fellow-men, which I have tried to do, and every one should try to do, and get the happiness of it. The man who goes home with the sense that he has stolen a dollar that day, that he has robbed a man of what was his honest due, is not going to sweet rest. He arises tired in the morning, and goes with an unclean conscience to his work the next day. He is not a successful man at all, although he may have laid up millions. But the man who has gone through life dividing always with his fellow-men, making and demanding his own rights and his own profits, and giving to every other man his rights and profits, lives every day, and not only that, but it is the royal road to great wealth. The history of the thousands of millionaires shows that to be the case. . . .

The moment a young man or woman gets more money than he or she has grown to by practical experience, that moment he has gotten a curse. It is no help to a young man or woman to inherit money. It is no help to your children to leave them money, but if you leave them education, if you leave them Christian and noble character, if you leave them a wide circle of friends, if you leave them an honorable name, it is far better than that they should have money. It would be worse for them, worse for the nation, that they should have any money at all. Oh, young man, if you have in-herited money, don't regard it as a help. It will curse you through your years, and deprive you of the very best things of human life. There is no class of people to be pitied so much as the inexperienced sons and daugh-ters of the rich of our generation. I pity the rich man's son. He can never know the best things in life.

One of the best things in our life is when a young man has earned his own living, and when he becomes engaged to some lovely young woman, and makes up his mind to have a home of his own. Then with that same love comes also that divine inspiration toward better things, and he begins to save his money. He begins to leave off his bad habits and put money in the bank. When he has a few hundred dollars he goes out in the suburbs to look for a home. He goes to the savings-bank, perhaps, for half of the value, and then goes for his wife, and when he takes his bride over the threshold of that door for the first time he says in words of eloquence my voice can never touch: "I have earned this home myself. It is all mine, and I divide with thee." That is the grandest moment a human heart may ever know.

But a rich man's son can never know that. He takes his bride into a finer mansion, it may be, but he is obliged to go all the way through it and say to his wife, "My mother gave me that, my mother gave me that, and my mother gave me this," until his wife wishes she had married his mother. I pity the rich man's son.

The statistics of Massachusetts showed that not one rich man's son out of seventeen ever dies rich. I pity the rich man's sons unless they have the good sense of the elder Vanderbilt, which sometimes happens. He went to his father and said, "Did you earn all your money?" "I did, my son. I began to work on a ferry-boat for twenty-five cents a day." "Then," said his son, "I will have none of your money," and he, too, tried to get em-ployment on a ferry-boat that Saturday night. He could not get one there, but he did get a place for three dollars a week. Of course, if a rich man's son will do that, he will get the discipline of a poor boy that is worth more than a university education to any man. He would then be able to take care of the millions of his father. But as a rule the rich men will not let their sons do the very thing that made them great. As a rule, the rich man will not allow his son to work—and his mother! Why, she would think it was a social disgrace if her poor, weak, little lily-fingered, sissy sort of a boy had to earn his living with honest toil. I have no pity for such rich men's sons. . . .

The best thing I can do is to illustrate by actual facts well-known to you all. A. T. Stewart, a poor boy in New York, had $1.50 to begin life on. He lost 87½ cents of that on the very first venture. How fortunate that young man who loses the first time he gambles. That boy said, "I will never gamble again in business," and he never did. How came he to lose 87½ cents? You probably all know the story how he lost it—because he bought some needles, threads, and buttons to sell which people did not want, and had them left in his hands, a dead loss. Said the boy, "I will not lose any more money in that way." Then he went around first to the doors and asked the people what they did want. Then when he had found out what they wanted he invested his 62½ cents to supply a known demand. Study it wherever you choose—in business, in your profession, in your housekeeping, whatever your life, that one thing is the secret of success. You must first know the demand. You must first know what people need, and then invest yourself where you are most needed. A. T. Stewart went on that principle until he was worth what amounted afterward to forty millions of dollars, owning the very store in which Mr. Wanamaker carries on his great work in New York. His fortune was made by his losing something, which taught him the great lesson that he must only invest himself or his money in something that people need. When will you salesmen learn it? When will you manufacturers learn that you must know the changing needs of humanity if you would succeed in life? Apply yourselves, all you Christian people, as manufacturers or merchants or workmen to supply that human need. It is a great principle as broad as humanity and as deep as the Scripture itself. . . .

But there are two other young men here to-night, and that is all I will venture to say, because it is too late. One over there gets up and says, "There is going to be a great man in Philadelphia, but never was one." "Oh, is that so? When are you going to be great?" "When I am elected to some political office." Young man, won't you learn a lesson in the primer of politics that it is a *prima facie* evidence of littleness to hold office under our form of government? Great men get into office sometimes, but what this country needs is men that will do what we tell them to do. This nation—where the people rule—is governed by the people, for the people, and so long as it is, then the office-holder is but the servant of the people, and the Bible says the servant cannot be greater than the master. The Bible says, "He that is sent cannot be greater than Him who sent Him." The people rule, or should rule, and if they do, we do not need the greater men in office. If the great men in America took our offices, we would change to an empire in the next ten years.

I know of a great many young women, now that woman's suffrage is coming, who say, "I am going to be President of the United States some day." I believe in woman's suffrage, and there is no doubt but what it is coming, and I am getting out of the way, anyhow. I may want an office by and by myself; but if the ambition for an office influences the women in their desire to vote, I want to say right here what I say to the young men, that if you only get the privilege of casting one vote, you don't get anything that is worth while. Unless you can control more than one vote, you will be unknown, and your influence so dissipated as practically not to be felt. This country is not run by votes. Do you think it is? It is governed by influence. It is governed by the ambitions and the enterprises which control votes. . . .

V. INTRODUCTION

The social gospel movement was a result of the combination of several impulses: the impact of Darwin on religion, along with its secularization; the growing recognition that the social question demanded the attention of the clergy; and the mounting wave of general criticism of the industrial capitalism that was continuing to develop in the United States. Of the several men who represented the social gospel movement, Walter Rauschenbusch (1861–1918) developed the most serious body of thought. In *A Theology for the Social Gospel*, 1917, Rauschenbusch articulated the intellectual basis of the social gospel. It was his major contention that the incorporation into Christian theology of questions concerning the political economy would result in a newly relevant and scientifically accurate Christianity. What he called traditional Christianity, that is, the Christianity of the individual, had been superannuated by social developments.

Rauschenbusch's position depended upon the assertion of the primacy of the community over the putative rights of the individual. The contrast between his position and that of Russell H. Conwell (Reading IV) is obvious.

The concept of sin, as it was worked out by Rauschenbusch, held that when the individual self came into conflict with the good of the community, when the self conflicted with God, sin was the necessary and inevitable result. In such a view, sin became the exploitation of labor even more than it was taking the Lord's name in vain. The system of business and politics, rather than the devil, constituted man's temptation. The social conception of God, rather than individual belief or faith, was a determining idea in the philosophy of the social gospel. Rauschenbusch's flat assertion that "God is against capitalism," placed the force of the social gospel in the camp of those who were growing disaffected with the nature of the American political economy.

The seriousness, pungency, and learning of Rauschenbusch's argument can be seen in the following selections from his major work.

V.

Walter Rauschenbusch

A THEOLOGY FOR THE SOCIAL GOSPEL

1917

The social movement is the most important ethical and spiritual movement in the modern world, and the social gospel is the response of the Christian consciousness to it. Therefore it had to be. The social gospel registers the fact that for the first time in history the spirit of Christianity has had a chance to form a working partnership with real social and psychological science. It is the religious reaction on the historic advent of democracy. It seeks to put the democratic spirit, which the Church inherited from Jesus and the prophets, once more in control of the institutions and teachings of the Church.

The social gospel is the old message of salvation, but enlarged and

SOURCE. Walter Rauschenbusch, *A Theology for the Social Gospel,* New York: The Macmillan Co., 1917, pp. 4–8, 10–21, 45–56, 167–168, 170, 172–175 and 177–187. Reprinted with the permission of The Macmillan Co. Copyright 1917, The Macmillan Co., copyright renewed 1945 by Pauline E. Rauschenbusch.

intensified. The individualistic gospel has taught us to see the sinfulness of every human heart and has inspired us with faith in the willingness and power of God to save every soul that comes to him. But it has not given us an adequate understanding of the sinfulness of the social order and its share in the sins of all individuals within it. It has not evoked faith in the will and power of God to redeem the permanent institutions of human society from their inherited guilt of oppression and extortion. Both our sense of sin and our faith in salvation have fallen short of the realities under its teaching. The social gospel seeks to bring men under repentance for their collective sins and to create a more sensitive and more modern conscience. It calls on us for the faith of the old prophets who believed in the salvation of nations. . . .

The adjustment of the Christian message to the regeneration of the social order is plainly one of the most difficult tasks ever laid on the intellect of religious leaders. The pioneers of the social gospel have had a hard time trying to consolidate their old faith and their new aim. Some have lost their faith; others have come out of the struggle with crippled formulations of truth. Does not our traditional theology deserve some of the blame for this spiritual wastage because it left these men without spiritual support and allowed them to become the vicarious victims of our theological inefficiency? If our theology is silent on social salvation, we compel college men and women, workingmen, and theological students, to choose between an unsocial system of theology and an irreligious system of social salvation. It is not hard to predict the outcome. If we seek to keep Christian doctrine unchanged, we shall ensure its abandonment.

Instead of being an aid in the development of the social gospel, systematic theology has often been a real clog. When a minister speaks to his people about child labour or the exploitation of the lowly by the strong; when he insists on adequate food, education, recreation, and a really human opportunity for all, there is response. People are moved by plain human feeling and by the instinctive convictions which they have learned from Jesus Christ. But at once there are doubting and dissenting voices. We are told that environment has no saving power; regeneration is what men need; we can not have a regenerate society without regenerate individuals; we do not live for this world but for the life to come; it is not the function of the church to deal with economic questions; any effort to change the social order before the coming of the Lord is foredoomed to failure. These objections all issue from the theological consciousness created by traditional church teaching. These half-truths are the proper product of a half-way system of theology in which there is no room for social redemption. Thus the Church is halting between two voices that call it. On the one side is the voice of the living Christ amid living men to-day; on the other side is the voice of past ages embodied in theology. Who will say that the authority of this voice has never confused our Christian judgment and paralysed our determination to establish God's kingdom on earth? . . .

I have entire sympathy with the conservative instinct which shrinks from giving up any of the dear possessions which have made life holy for us. We have none too much of them left. It is a comfort to me to know that the changes required to make room for the social gospel are not destructive but constructive. They involve addition and not subtraction. The social gospel calls for an expansion in the scope of salvation and for more religious dynamic to do the work of God. It requires more faith and not less. It offers a more thorough and durable salvation. It is able to create a more searching sense of sin and to preach repentance to the respectable and mighty who have ridden humanity to the mouth of hell.

The attacks on our inherited theology have usually come from the intellectuals who are galled by the yoke of uncritical and unhistorical beliefs brought down from pre-scientific centuries. They are entirely within their right in insisting that what is scientifically impossible shall not be laid as an obligatory belief on the neck of modern men in the name of religion. But the rational subtractions of liberalism do not necessarily make religion more religious. We have to snuff the candle to remove the burnt-out wick, but we may snuff out the flame, and all the matches may prove to be damp. Critical clarifying is decidedly necessary, but power in religion comes only through the consciousness of a great elementary need which compels men to lay hold of God anew. The social gospel speaks to such a need, and where a real harmony has been established it has put new fire and power into the old faith.

The power of conservatism is not all due to religious tenderness and loyalty. Some of it results from less worthy causes. Doctrinal theology is in less direct contact with facts than other theological studies. Exegesis and church history deal with historical material and their business is to discover the facts. New facts and the pressure of secular scientific work compel them to revise their results and keep close to realities. Doctrinal theology deals with less substantial and ascertainable things. It perpetuates an esoteric stream of tradition. What every church demands of its systematic theologians is to formulate clearly and persuasively what that church has always held and taught. If they go beyond that they are performing a work of supererogation for which they do not always receive thanks.

Theoretically the Church is the great organization of unselfish service. Actually the Church has always been profoundly concerned for its own power and authority. But its authority rests in large part on the stability of its doctrine. The Roman Catholic Church has always been in the nature of a defensive organization to maintain uniformity of teaching. The physical suppression of heresy was merely the last and crudest means employed by it to resist change. The more subtle and spiritual forms of pressure have doubtless been felt by every person who ever differed with his own church, whatever it was. This selfish ecclesiastical conservatism is not for the Kingdom of God but against it.

Theology needs periodical rejuvenation. Its greatest danger is not mutilation but senility. It is strong and vital when it expresses in large reasonings what youthful religion feels and thinks. When people have to be indoctrinated laboriously in order to understand theology at all, it becomes a dead burden. The dogmas and theological ideas of the early Church were those ideas which at that time were needed to hold the Church together, to rally its forces, and to give it victorious energy against antagonistic powers. To-day many of those ideas are without present significance. Our reverence for them is a kind of ancestor worship. To hold laboriously to a religious belief which does not hold us, is an attenuated form of asceticism; we chastise and starve our intellect to sanctify it by holy beliefs. The social gospel does not need the aid of church authority to get hold of our hearts. It gets hold in spite of such authority when necessary. . . .

Every forward step in the historical evolution of religion has been marked by a closer union of religion and ethics and by the elimination of non-ethical religious performances. This union of religion and ethics reached its highest perfection in the life and mind of Jesus. After him Christianity quickly dropped back to the pre-Christian stage. Ceremonial actions and orthodox beliefs became indispensable to salvation; they had a value of their own, quite apart from their bearing on conduct. Theology had the task of defending and inculcating these non-ethical ingredients of religion, and that pulled theology down. It is clear that our Christianity is most Christian when religion and ethics are viewed as inseparable elements of the same single-minded and wholehearted life, in which the consciousness of God and the consciousness of humanity blend completely. Any new movement in theology which emphatically asserts the union of

religion and ethics is likely to be a wholesome and christianizing force in
Christian thought.

The social gospel is of that nature. It plainly concentrates religious
interest on the great ethical problems of social life. It scorns the tithing
of mint, anise and cummin, at which the Pharisees are still busy, and insists
on getting down to the weightier matters of God's law, to justice and
mercy. It ties up religion not only with duty, but with big duty that stirs
the soul with religious feeling and throws it back on God for help. The
non-ethical practices and beliefs in historical Christianity nearly all centre
on the winning of heaven and immortality. On the other hand, the Kingdom of God can be established by nothing except righteous life and action.
There is nothing in social Christianity which is likely to breed or reinforce
superstition. The more the social gospel engages and inspires theological
thought, the more will religion be concentrated on ethical righteousness.
The social gospel is bound to be a reformatory and christianizing force
inside of theology.

Theology is the esoteric thought of the Church. Some of its problems
are unknown and unintelligible except where the Church keeps an interest
in them alive. Even the terminology of theology is difficult for anyone to
understand unless he has lived under church influence for years. Jesus and
his followers were laymen. The people felt that his teaching was different
from the arguments of their theologians, less ponderous and more moving. When Christianity worked its way from the lower to the higher
classes, its social sympathies became less democratic and fraternal, its language less simple, and its ideas more speculative, elaborate and remote.
Origen felt he had to apologize for the homely Greek and the simple
arguments of Jesus. Theology became an affair of experts. The first duty
of the laymen was to believe with all their hearts what they could not
possibly understand with all their heads. . . .

Now, many of the fears and burdens which drove men to the altars of
their gods in the past are being eased in modern life. People are learning
to trace diseases to natural causes instead of the evil eye, or the devil, or
the anger of God. Even the streptococcus has a friendlier look than the
omnipresent devils that haunt a Burmese hill tribe. Men used to feel acute
guilt if they had committed some ritual oversight, such as touching a
taboo thing, eating meat on Friday, or working on the Sabbath. The better teachings of modern Christianity and general religious indifference
have combined to reduce that sort of fear and guilt.

On the other hand we are becoming much more sensitive about collective sins in which we are involved. I have a neighbour who owns stock in a New England cotton mill. Recently the company opened a factory in North Carolina and began to employ child labour. This man's young daughter faded away when she was emerging from childhood, and so he thinks of the other girls, who are breathing cotton fluff for him. A correspondent wrote me whose husband, a man of national reputation, had bought stock in a great steel company. She is a Jewess and a pacifist. When the plant began to devote itself to the manufacture of shrapnel and bombs in 1915, she felt involved. But what was her husband to do with the stock? Would it make things better if he passed the war-stained property to another man? I know a woman whose father, back in the nineties, took a fortune out of a certain dirty mill town. She is now living on his fortune; but the children of the mill-hands are living on their misfortune. No effort of hers can undo more than a fraction of the evil which was set in motion while that fortune was being accumulated.

If these burdens of conscience were foolish or morbid, increased insight and a purer Christian teaching would lift them. But it is increased insight and Christian feeling which created them. An unawakened person does not inquire on whose life juices his big dividends are fattening. Upper-class minds have been able to live parasitic lives without any fellow-feeling for the peasants or tenants whom they were draining to pay for their leisure. Modern democracy brings these lower fellow-men up to our field of vision. Then if a man has drawn any real religious feeling from Christ, his participation in the systematized oppression of civilization will, at least at times, seem an intolerable burden and guilt. Is this morbid? Or is it morbid to live on without such realization? Those who to-day are still without a consciousness of collective wrong must be classified as men of darkened mind.

These are distinctly modern burdens. They will continue to multiply and increase. Does the old theology meet them? Was it competent to meet the religious problems raised by the war? Can personal forgiveness settle such accounts as some men run up with their fellow-men? Does Calvinism deal adequately with a man who appears before the judgment seat of Christ with $50,000,000 and its human corollaries to his credit, and then pleads a free pardon through faith in the atoning sacrifice?

Religious experience, as William James has shown us, has many varieties, and some are distinctly higher than others. The form most common among us has come through an intense concentration on a man's own sins, his needs, his destiny. In the Old Testament we have a number of accounts describing how men of the highest type of God-consciousness made their fundamental experience of God and received their prophetic mission. In none of these cases did the prophet struggle for his personal salvation as later Christian saints have done. His woe did not come through fear of personal damnation, but through his sense of solidarity with his people and through social feeling; his hope and comfort was not for himself alone but for his nation. This form of religious experience is more distinctively Christian than any form which is caused by fear and which thinks only of self. It contains larger possibilities of personal growth and religious power. . . .

Connect these two propositions: that an experience of religion through the medium of solidaristic social feeling is an experience of unusually high ethical quality, akin to that of the prophets of the Bible; and second, that a fresh and clearly marked religious experience reacts on theology. Can we not justly expect that the increasing influence of the social gospel and all that it stands for, will have a salutary influence on theology? The social gospel has already restored the doctrine of the Kingdom of God, which held first place with Jesus but which individualistic theology carefully wrapped in several napkins and forgot. Theology always needs rejuvenation. . . .

THE NATURE OF SIN

It is not easy to define sin, for sin is as elastic and complicated as life itself. Its quality, degree, and culpability vary according to the moral intelligence and maturity of the individual, according to his social freedom, and his power over others. Theologians have erred, it seems to me, by fitting their definitions to the most highly developed forms of sin and then spreading them over germinal and semi-sinful actions and conditions.

We are equipped with powerful appetites. We are often placed in difficult situations, which constitute overwhelming temptations. We are relatively ignorant, and while we experiment with life, we go astray. Some of our instincts may become rampant and overgrown, and then trample on our inward freedom. We are gifted with high ideals, with a wonderful range of possibilities, with aspiration and longing, and also weighted with inertia and moral incapacity to achieve. We are keenly alive to the call of the senses and the pleasures of the moment, and only dimly and occasionally conscious of our own higher destiny, of the mystic value of personality in others, and of God.

This sensual equipment, this ignorance and inertia, out of which our moral delinquencies sprout, are part of our human nature. We did not order it so. Instead of increasing our guilt, our make-up seems to entitle us to the forbearing judgment of every onlooker, especially God. Yet no doubt we are involved in objective wrong and evil; we frustrate our possibilities; we injure others; we disturb the divine harmonies. We are unfree, unhappy, conscious of a burden which we are unable to lift or escape.

Sin becomes guilt in the full sense in the degree in which intelligence and will enter. We have the impulse to live our life, to exercise our freedom, to express and satisfy the limitless cravings in us, and we are impatient of restraint. We know that our idleness or sensuality will cripple our higher self, yet we want what we want. We set our desires against the rights of others, and disregard the claims of mercy, of gratitude, or of parental love. Our self-love is wrought up to hot ill-will, hate, lying, slander, and malevolence. Men press their covetousness to the injury of society. They are willing to frustrate the cause of liberty and social justice in whole nations in order to hold their selfish social and economic privileges. Men who were powerful enough to do so, have left broad trails of destruction and enslavement through history in order to satisfy their selfish caprice, avarice, and thirst for glory.

Two things strike us as we thus consider the development of sin from its cotyledon leaves to its blossom and fruit. First, that the element of selfishness emerges as the character of sin matures. Second, that in the higher forms of sin it assumes the aspect of a conflict between the selfish Ego and the common good of humanity; or, expressing it in religious terms, it becomes a conflict between self and God.

The three forms of sin,—sensuousness, selfishness, and godlessness,— are ascending and expanding stages, in which we sin against our higher self, against the good of men, and against the universal good.

Theology with remarkable unanimity has discerned that sin is essentially selfishness. This is an ethical and social definition, and is proof of the unquenchable social spirit of Christianity. It is more essentially Christian than the dualistic conception of the Greek Fathers, who thought of sin as fundamentally sensuousness and materiality, and saw the chief consequence of the fall in the present reign of death rather than in the reign of selfishness.

The definition of sin as selfishness furnishes an excellent theological basis for a social conception of sin and salvation. But the social gospel can contribute a good deal to socialize and vitalize it.

Theology pictures the self-affirmation of the sinner as a sort of solitary duel of the will between him and God. We get a mental image of God sitting on his throne in glory, holy and benevolent, and the sinner down below, sullenly shaking his fist at God while he repudiates the divine will and chooses his own. Now, in actual life such titanic rebellion against the Almighty is rare. Perhaps our Puritan forefathers knew more cases than we because their theological God was accustomed to issue arbitrary decrees which invited rebellion. We do not rebel; we dodge and evade. We kneel in lowly submission and kick our duty under the bed while God is not looking.

The theological definitions of sin have too much the flavour of the monarchical institutions under the spiritual influence of which they were first formed. In an absolute monarchy the first duty is to bow to the royal will. A man may spear peasants or outrage their wives, but crossing the king is another matter. When theological definitions speak of rebellion against God as the common characteristic of all sin, it reminds one of the readiness of despotic governments to treat every offence as treason.

Sin is not a private transaction between the sinner and God. Humanity always crowds the audience-room when God holds court. We must democratize the conception of God; then the definition of sin will become more realistic.

We love and serve God when we love and serve our fellows, whom he loves and in whom he lives. We rebel against God and repudiate his will when we set our profit and ambition above the welfare of our fellows and above the Kingdom of God which binds them together.

We rarely sin against God alone. The decalogue gives a simple illustration of this. Theology used to distinguish between the first and second table of the decalogue; the first enumerated the sins against God and the second the sins against men. Jesus took the Sabbath commandment off the first table and added it to the second; he said the Sabbath is not a taboo day of God, but an institution for the good of man. The command to honour our parents is also ethical. There remain the first three commandments, against polytheism, image worship, and the misuse of the holy name. The worship of various gods and the use of idols is no longer one of our dangers. The misuse of the holy name has lost much of its religious significance since sorcery and magic have moved to the back-streets. On the other hand, the commandments of the second table grow more important all the time. Science supplies the means of killing, finance the methods of stealing, the newspapers have learned how to bear false witness artistically to a globeful of people daily, and covetousness is the moral basis of our civilization.

God is not only the spiritual representative of humanity; he is identified with it. In him we live and move and have our being. In us he lives and moves, though his being transcends ours. He is the life and light in every man and the mystic bond that unites us all. He is the spiritual power behind and beneath all our aspirations and achievements. He works through humanity to realize his purposes, and our sins block and destroy the Reign of God in which he might fully reveal and realize himself. Therefore our sins against the least of our fellow-men in the last resort concern God. Therefore when we retard the progress of mankind, we retard the revelation of the glory of God. Our universe is not a despotic monarchy, with God above the starry canopy and ourselves down here; it is a spiritual commonwealth with God in the midst of us.

We are on Christian ground when we insist on putting humanity into the picture. Jesus always deliberately and energetically bound man and God together. He would not let us deal with man apart from God, nor with God apart from man. We can not have forgiveness from God while we refuse forgiveness to any man. "What ye have done to these, ye have done to me; what ye have not done to these, ye have not done to me." This identification of the interests of God and man is characteristic of the religion of Jesus. Wherever God is isolated, we drop back to a pre-Christian stage of religion.

Sin is essentially selfishness. That definition is more in harmony with the social gospel than with any individualistic type of religion. The sinful mind, then, is the unsocial and anti-social mind. To find the climax of sin we must not linger over a man who swears, or sneers at religion, or denies the mystery of the trinity, but put our hands on social groups who have turned the patrimony of a nation into the private property of a small class, or have left the peasant labourers cowed, degraded, demoralized, and without rights in the land. When we find such in history, or in present-day life, we shall know we have struck real rebellion against God on the higher levels of sin.

We have defined sin. But we need more than definition. We need realization of its nature in order to secure the right religious attitude toward it.

Sin is always revealed by contrast to righteousness. We get an adequate measure of it and feel the proper hate and repugnance for it only when we see it as the terrible defeat and frustration of a great good which we love and desire.

Theology has tried to give us such a realization of sin by elaborating the contrast between the sinless condition of Adam before the fall and his sinful condition after it. But there are objections to this. In the first place of course we do not know whether Adam was as perfect as he is portrayed. Theology has ante-dated conceptions of human perfection which we have derived from Jesus Christ and has converted Adam into a perfect Christian. Paul does nothing of the kind. In the second place, any interpretation of the nature of sin taken from Adam will be imperfect, because Adam's situation gave very limited opportunities for selfishness, which is the essence of sin. He had no scope to exhibit either the virtues or the sinful vices which come out in the pursuits of commerce or politics. The only persons with whom he could associate were God, Eve, and Satan. Consequently, theology lacked all social details in describing his condition before and after the fall. It could only ascribe to him the virtues of knowing and loving God and of having no carnal concupiscence, and, by contrast, after the fall he lost the love and knowledge of God and acquired carnal desires. Thus a fatal turn toward an individualistic conception of sin was given to theology through the solitariness of Adam.

A better and more Christian method of getting a religious realization of sin is to bring before our minds the positive ideals of social righteousness contained in the person of Christ and in the Kingdom of God, and see sin as the treasonable force which frustrates and wrecks these ideals and despoils the earth of their enjoyment. It is Christ who convicts the world of sin and not Adam. . . .

It follows that a clear realization of the nature of sin depends on a clear vision of the Kingdom of God. We can not properly feel and know the reign of organized wrong now prevailing unless we constantly see it over against the reign of organized righteousness. Where the religious conception of the Kingdom of God is wanting, men will be untrained and unfit to see or to estimate the social manifestations of sin. . . .

It would be unfair to blame theology for the fact that our race is still submerged under despotic government, under war and militarism, under landlordism, and under predatory industry and finance. But we can justly blame it for the fact that the Christian Church even now has hardly any realization that these things are large-scale sins. We can blame it in part for the fact that when a Christian minister in our country speaks of these sins he is charged with forgetting the simple gospel of sin and salvation, and is in danger of losing his position. This comes of shelving the doctrine of the Kingdom of God, or juggling feeble substitutes into its place. Theology has not been a faithful steward of the truth entrusted to it. The social gospel is its accusing conscience.

This is the chief significance of the social gospel for the doctrine of sin: it revives the vision of the Kingdom of God. When men see the actual world over against the religious ideal, they become conscious of its constitutional defects and wrongs. Those who do their thinking in the light of the Kingdom of God make less of heresy and private sins. They reserve their shudders for men who keep the liquor and vice trade alive against public intelligence and law; for interests that organize powerful lobbies to defeat tenement or factory legislation, or turn factory inspection into sham; for nations that are willing to set the world at war in order to win or protect colonial areas of trade or usurious profit from loans to weaker peoples; and for private interests which are willing to push a peaceful nation into war because the stock exchange has a panic at the rumour of peace. These seem the unforgivable sins, the great demonstrations of rebellious selfishness, wherever the social gospel has revived the faith of the Kingdom of God.

Two aspects of the Kingdom of God demand special consideration in this connection: the Kingdom is the realm of love, and it is the commonwealth of labour.

Jesus Christ superimposed his own personality on the previous conception of God and made love the distinctive characteristic of God and the supreme law of human conduct. Consequently, the reign of God would be the reign of love. It is not enough to think of the Kingdom as a prevalence of good will. The insitutions of life must be fundamentally fraternal and co-operative if they are to train men to love their fellow-men as co-workers. Sin, being selfish, is covetous and grasping. It favours institutions and laws which permit unrestricted exploitation and accumulation. This in turn sets up antagonistic interests, increases law suits, class hostility, and wars, and so mis-educates mankind that love and co-operation seem unworkable, and men are taught to put their trust in coercive control by the strong and in the sting of hunger and compulsion for the poor.

Being the realm of love, the Kingdom of God must also be the commonwealth of co-operative labour, for how can we actively love others without serving their needs by our abilities? If the Kingdom of God is a community of highly developed personalities, it must also be an organization for labour, for none can realize himself fully without labour. A divinely ordered community, therefore, would offer to all the opportunities of education and enjoyment, and expect from all their contribution of labour.

Here again we realize the nature of sin over against the religious ideal of society. Sin selfishly takes from others their opportunities for self-realization in order to increase its own opportunities abnormally; and it shirks its own labour and thereby abnormally increases the labour of others. Idleness is active selfishness; it is not only unethical, but a sin against the Kingdom of God. To lay a heavy burden of support on our fellows, usually on the weakest classes, and to do no productive labour in return, is so crude a manifestation of sinful selfishness that one would suppose only an occasional instance of such delinquency could be found, and only under medical treatment. But in fact throughout history the policy of most States has been shaped in order to make such a sinful condition easy and perpetual. Men who have been under the teachings of Christianity all their lives do not even see that parasitism is a sin. So deeply has our insight into sin been darkened by the lack of a religious ideal of social life. . . . We shall not be doing our thinking in a Christian way until we agree that productive labour according to the ability of each is one of "the conditions of salvation." . . .

THE SOCIAL GOSPEL AND THE CONCEPTION OF GOD

The conception of God held by a social group is a social product. Even if it originated in the mind of a solitary thinker or prophet, as soon as it becomes the property of a social group, it takes on the qualities of that group. . . . If every individual had to work out his idea of God on the basis of his own experiences and intuitions only, it would be a groping quest, and most of us would see only the occasional flitting of a distant light. By the end of our life we might have arrived at the stage of voodooism or necromancy. Entering into a high conception of God, such as the Christian faith offers us, is like entering a public park or a public gallery of art and sharing the common wealth. When we learn from the gospels, for instance, that God is on the side of the poor, and that he proposes to view anything done or not done to them as having been done or not done to him, such a revelation of solidarity and humanity comes with a regenerating shock to our selfish minds. Any one studying life as it is on the basis of of real estate and bank clearings, would come to the conclusion that God is on the side of the rich. It takes a revelation to see it the other way. . . .

Our imagination has only a short reach. In conceiving a higher world we have to take the familiar properties and figures of our material world, and enlarge and refine them as best we can. As long as kings and governors were the greatest human beings in the public eye, it was inevitable that their image should be superimposed on the idea of God. Court language and obeisances were used in worship and when men reasoned about God, they took their illustrations and analogies from those who were a close second to God. . . .

Scholastic arguments reach few people; imaginative pictures of spiritual ideas are subtle and pervasive. God was imagined far above, in an upper part of the universe, remote from humanity, but looking down on us, fully aware of all we do, interfering when necessary, but very distinct. In Greek theology this distinctness was due to philosophical influences. In popular theology the remoteness of great men perhaps had more to do with shaping this idea than philosophy.

The sense of fear which has pervaded religion has doubtless been, at least in part, a psychological result of the despotic attitude of parents, of school-masters, of priests, and of officials all the way from the town beadle to the king. To uncounted people God has not been the great Comforter but the great Terror. The main concern in religion was to escape from his hands. Luther longed that he "might at last have a gracious God"—*einen gnädigen Gott;* the word is the same which was applied to princes and nobles when they were good-natured. Luther sweated with fear when he walked alongside the body of the Lord in a Corpus Christi procession. To what extent was this due to the fact that he was constantly beaten by his parents and by his school-masters, and taught to be afraid of everything? Men enriched the Church enormously with gifts of land as insurance premiums that God would not do anything horrible to them. When farmers are afraid enough to part with land, it must be a deep fear.

The medieval methods of earning religious merit and of securing intercession were the product of fear and a close duplicate of the conditions existing under economic and political despotism. God was a feudal lord, holding his tenants in a grip from which there was no escape, exacting what was due to him, and putting the delinquent in a hot prison which was even worse than the terrible holes underneath the duke's castle. By special self-denial the religious peon could win "merit" to offset his delinquencies. The saints and the blessed Virgin had much merit. The Church had power to assign some of this to those who stood in with the Church. The intercession of the saints counted; every one knew that it was a great thing for a poor man if a nobleman spoke for him to the judge; it would be so in heaven too. Things go by favour; the more aristocracy, the more pull.

Thus the social relations in which men lived, affected their conceptions about God and his relations to men. Under tyrannous conditions the idea of God was necessarily tainted with the cruel hardness of society. This spiritual influence of despotism made even the face of Christ seem hard and stern. The outlook into the future life was like a glimpse into a chamber of torture.

The conflict of the religion of Jesus with autocratic conceptions of God is therefore part of the struggle of humanity with autocratic economic and political conditions. This carries the social movement into theology. Theologians therewith have their share in redeeming humanity from the reign of tyranny and fear, and if we do not do our share emphatically and with a will, where do we belong, to the Kingdom of God or the Kingdom of Evil? The worst form of leaving the naked unclothed, the hungry unfed, and the prisoners uncomforted, is to leave men under a despotic conception of God and the universe; and what will the Son of Man do to us theologians when we gather at the Day of Doom?

Here we see one of the highest redemptive services of Jesus to the human race. When he took God by the hand and called him "our Father," he democratized the conception of God. He disconnected the idea from the coercive and predatory State, and transferred it to the realm of family life, the chief social embodiment of solidarity and love. He not only saved humanity; he saved God. He gave God his first chance of being loved and of escaping from the worst misunderstandings conceivable. The value of Christ's idea of the Fatherhood of God is realized only by contrast to the despotic ideas which it opposed and was meant to displace. We have classified theology as Greek and Latin, as Catholic and Protestant. It is time to classify it as despotic and democratic. From a Christian point of view that is a more decisive distinction. . . .

The social gospel is God's predestined agent to continue what the Reformation began. It arouses intelligent hatred of oppression and the reign of fear, and teaches us to prize liberty and to love love. Therefore those whose religious life has been influenced by the social gospel are instinctively out of sympathy with autocratic conceptions of God. They sense the spiritual taint which goes out from such ideas. They know that these religious conceptions look tolerable, necessary, and desirable. Like Paul, the social gospel has not "received the spirit of bondage again unto fear." It is wholly in sympathy with the conception of the Father which Jesus revealed to us by his words, by his personality, and by his own relations to the Father.

This reformatory and democratizing influence of the social gospel is not against religion but for it. The worst thing that could happen to God would be to remain an autocrat while the world is moving toward democracy. He would be dethroned with the rest. For one man who has forsaken religion through scientific doubt, ten have forsaken it in our time because it seemed the spiritual opponent of liberty and the working people. This feeling will deepen as democracy takes hold and becomes more than a theory of government. We have heard only the political overture of democracy, played by fifes; the economic numbers of the program are yet to come, and they will be performed with trumpets and trombones.

The Kingdom of God is the necessary background for the Christian idea of God. The social movement is one of the chief ways in which God is revealing that he lives and rules as a God that loves righteousness and hates iniquity. A theological God who has no interest in the conquest of justice and fraternity is not a Christian. It is not enough for theology to eliminate this or that autocratic trait. Its God must join the social movement. The real God has been in it long ago. The development of a Christian social order would be the highest proof of God's saving power. The failure of the social movement would impugn his existence.

The old conception that God dwells on high and is distinct from our human life was the natural basis for autocratic and arbitrary ideas about him. On the other hand the religious belief that he is immanent in humanity is the natural basis for democratic ideas about him. When he was far above, he needed vice-gerents to rule for him, popes by divine institution and kings by divine right. If he lives and moves in the life of mankind, he can act directly on the masses of men. A God who strives within our striving, who kindles his flame in our intellect, sends the impact of his energy to make our will restless for righteousness, floods our subconscious mind with dreams and longings, and always urges the race on toward a higher combination of freedom and solidarity, —that would be a God with whom democratic and religious men could hold converse as their chief fellow-worker, the source of their energies, the ground of their hopes.

Platonic philosophy in the first century made God so transcendent that it had to devise the Logos-idea to bridge the abyss between the silent depths of God and this world, and to enable God to create and reveal himself. Theology shrank from imputing suffering to God. Patripassianism seemed a self-evident heresy. To-day men want to think of God as close to them, and spiritually kin to them, the Father of all spirits. Eminent theologians insist that God has always suffered with and for mankind and that the cross is a permanent law of God's nature: "The lamb has been slain from the beginning of the world." Through the conception of evolution and through the social movement we have come to see human life in its totality, and our consciousness of God is the spiritual counterpart of our social consciousness. Some, apparently, would be willing to think of God as less than omnipotent and omniscient if only he were working hard with us for that Kingdom which is the only true Democracy.

Two points still demand discussion. The first is the problem of suffering.

The existence of innocent suffering impugns the justice and benevolence of God, both of which are essential in a Christian conception of God.

The simplest solution is to deny the existence of unjust suffering; to trust that good and ill are allotted according to desert; and if the righteous Job suffers great disaster, to search for his secret sin. This explanation broke down before the facts. How about the man born blind? What personal sin had merited his calamity?

Dualism took the other extreme. It acknowledged that the good suffer, and stressed the fact. But it exculpated the good God by making the evil God the author of this world, or at least its present lord.

Christianity has combined several explanations of suffering. It grounds it in general on the prevalence of sin since the fall. It has ascribed a malignant power of afflicting the righteous to Satan and his servants. It has taken satisfaction when justice was vindicated in some striking case of goodness or wickedness. It has held out a hope of a public vindication of the righteous in the great judgment, and of an equalization of their lot by their bliss in heaven and the suffering of the wicked. . . . Finally, Christianity has taught that God allots suffering with wise and loving intent, tempering it according to our strength, relieving it in response to our prayer, and using it to chasten our pride, to win us from earthliness to himself, and to prepare us for heaven. This interpretation does not assert the justice of every suffering, taken by itself, but does maintain its loving intention.

All these are powerful and comforting considerations. But they are shaken by the bulk of the unjust suffering in sight of the modern mind. These Christian ideas are largely true as long as we look at a normal village community and its individuals and families. But they are jarred by mass disasters. The optimism of the age of rationalism was shaken by the Lisbon earthquake in 1755, when 30,000 people were killed together, just and unjust. The War has deeply affected the religious assurance of our own time, and will lessen it still more when the excitement is over and the aftermath of innocent suffering becomes clear. But that impression of undeserved mass misery which the war has brought home to the thoughtless, has long been weighing on all who understood the social conditions of our civilization. The sufferings of a single righteous man could deeply move the psalmists or the poet of Job. To-day entire social classes sit in the ashes and challenge the justice of God who has afflicted them by fathering the present social system. The moral and religious problem of suffering has entered on a new stage with the awakening of the social consciousness and the spread of social knowledge.

If God stands for the present social order, how can we defend him? We can stand the pain of travail, of physical dissolution, of earthquakes and accidents. These are the price we pay for the use of a fine planet with lovely appurtenances and for a wonderful body. We can also accept with reasonable resignation the mental anguish of unrequited love, of foiled ambition, or of the emptiness of life. These are the risks we run as possessors of a highly organized personality amid a world of men. But we can not stand for poor and laborious people being deprived of physical stature, youth, education, human equality, and justice, in order to enable others to live luxurious lives. It revolts us to see these conditions perpetuated by law and organized force, and palliated or justified by the makers of public opinion. None of the keys offered by individualistic Christianity fit this padlock.

The social gospel supplies an explanation of this class of human suffering. Society is so integral that when one man sins, other men suffer, and when one social class sins, the other classes are involved in the suffering which follows on that sin. The more powerful an individual is, the more will he involve others; the more powerful a class is, the more will it be able to unload its own just suffering on the weaker classes. These sufferings are not "vicarious"; they are solidaristic.

Our solidarity is a beneficent part of human life. It is the basis for our greatest good. If our community life is righteous and fraternal, we are enriched and enlarged by being bound up with it. But, by the same law, if our community is organized in a way that permits, encourages, or defends predatory practices, then the larger part of its members are through solidarity caged to be eaten by the rest, and to suffer what is both unjust and useless.

It follows that ethically it is of the highest importance to prevent our beneficent solidarity from being twisted into a means of torture.

Physical pain serves a beneficent purpose by warning us of the existence of abnormal conditions. It fulfils its purpose when it compels the individual to search out the cause of pain and to keep his body in health. If he takes "dope" to quiet the consciousness of pain without healing the causes, the beneficent purpose of pain is frustrated.

Social suffering serves social healing. If the sense of common humanity is strong enough to set the entire social body in motion on behalf of those who suffer without just cause, then their troubles are eased and the whole body is preserved just and fraternal. If the predatory forces are strong enough to suppress the reactions against injustice and inhumanity, the suffering goes on and the whole community is kept in suicidal evil. To interpret the sufferings imposed by social injustice in individualistic terms as the divine chastening and sanctification of all the individuals concerned, is not only false but profoundly mischievous. It is the equivalent of "dope," for it silences the warning which the suffering of an innocent group ought to convey to all society without abolishing the causes. It frustrates the only chance of redemptive usefulness which the sufferers had.

All this applies to our conception of God. The idea of solidarity, when once understood, acts as a theodicy. None of us would want a world without organic community of life, any more than we would want a world without gravitation. The fact that a careless boy falls down stairs does not condemn gravitation, nor does the existence of evil community life condemn God who constituted us social beings. The innocent suffering of great groups through social solidarity simply brings home to us that the tolerance of social injustice is an intolerable evil. The great sin of men is to resist the reformation of predatory society. We do not want God to be charged with that attitude. A conception of God which describes him as sanctioning the present social order and utilizing it in order to sanctify its victims through their suffering, without striving for its overthrow, is repugnant to our moral sense. Both the Old Testament and the New Testament characterizations of God's righteousness assure us that he hates with steadfast hatred just such practices as modern communities tolerate and promote. If we can trust the Bible, God is against capitalism, its methods, spirit, and results. The bourgeois theologians have misrepresented our revolutionary God. God is for the Kingdom of God, and his Kingdom does not mean injustice and the perpetuation of innocent suffering. The best theodicy for modern needs is to make this very clear.

Finally, the social gospel emphasizes the fact the God is the bond of racial unity.

Speaking historically, it is one of the most universal and important characteristics of religion that it constitutes the spiritual bond of social groups. A national god was always the exponent of national solidarity. A common religion created common sympathies. Full moral obligation stopped at the religious boundary line. The unusual thing about the Good Samaritan was that he disregarded the religious cleavage and followed the call of humanity pure and simple.

The mingling of populations and religions in modern life makes the influence of religion less noticeable, but it still works as a bond of sympathy. It is easiest to trace it where the religious cleavage coincides with the racial or political cleavages. The French Catholics in Quebec and the English Protestants in Ontario; the Irish and the Ulstermen; the Catholic Belgians and the Protestant Dutch; the Latin nations of America and the United States;—the mention of the names brings up the problem. The Balkans are a nest of antagonisms partly because of religious differences. It has been fortunate for the American negro that the antagonism of race and social standing has not been intensified in his case by any difference of religion.

The spread of a monotheistic faith and the recognition of a single God of all mankind is a condition of an ethical union of mankind in the future. This is one of the long-range effects of Christian missions. The effects of Christianity will go far beyond its immediate converts. Every competing religion will be compelled to emphasize its monotheistic elements and to allow its polytheistic ingredients to drop to a secondary stage.

But it is essential to our spiritual honesty that no imperialism shall masquerade under the cover of our religion. Those who adopt the white man's religion come under the white man's influence. Christianity is the religion of the dominant race. The native religions are a spiritual bulwark of defence, independence, and loyalty. If we invite men to come under the same spiritual roof of monotheism with us and to abandon their ancient shelters, let us make sure that this will not be exploited as a trick of subjugation by the Empires. As long as there are great colonizing imperialisms in the world, the propaganda of Christianity has a political significance.

God is the common basis of all our life. Our human personalities may seem distinct, but their roots run down into the eternal life of God. In a large way both philosophy and science are tending toward a recognition of the truth which religion has felt and practised. The all-pervading life of God is the ground of the spiritual oneness of the race and of our hope for its closer fellowship in the future.

The consciousness of solidarity, therefore, is of the essence of religion. But the circumference and spaciousness of the fellowship within it differ widely. Every discovery of a larger fellowship by the individual brings a glow of religious satisfaction. The origin of the Christian religion was bound up with a great transition from a nationalistic to an international religious consciousness. Paul was the hero of that conquest. The Christian God has been a breaker of barriers from the first. All who have a distinctively Christian experience of God are committed to the expansion of human fellowship and to the overthrow of barriers. To emphasize this and bring it home to the Christian consciousness is part of the mission of the social gospel, and it looks to theology for the intellectual formulation of what it needs. . . .

D. The Progressive Response

VI. INTRODUCTION

Of the Muckrakers who were probing beneath the skin of American life during the Progressive period, the first and one of the most articulate was Henry Demarest Lloyd (1847–1903). Among those who followed Lloyd's lead were Lincoln Steffens, Gustavus Myers, Ida Tarbell, and David G. Phillips. The general position taken by many of the Muckrakers was that American life had become corrupt because of a conspiracy between government and business. The supposedly frantic search for profit had contributed to the "treason of the senate," "the shame of the cities," and "frenzied finance." The American industrial system, according to Lincoln Steffens, had converted American political democracy into a plutocracy. Virtually in chorus, the Muckrakers said that no American institution was safe from the corruption of money.

In *Wealth Against Commonwealth,* Lloyd's major work from which selections are reprinted here, those major themes are made explicit. With a high moral temperature and a certain intensity of expression, Lloyd said that wealth was now the master of men, that the corporation had grown stronger than the state. It was the stress on individualism, for Lloyd as well as for Rauschenbusch and Henry George, that presumably constituted the intellectual source of contemporary decadence. The dominant feature of the American landscape, according to Lloyd, was its poverty. Captains of industry were guilty of making war on all of civilization, and Lloyd, obviously touched by the social gospel movement himself, asserted that every true Christian principle was social and tended toward the establishment of an authentic community. The greed of the majority was no substitute for community, and that greed could result only in a new aggregate of individual monsters who would become more dangerous through the principle of majority rule. Only the greatest good of all members of society was a sufficiently inclusive goal to restrict the insatiable greed of men, including that of the industrial giants. It is clear that William Graham Sumner and Henry Demarest Lloyd occupied polar positions, both of which represented sections of the American public of the time.

VI.

Henry Demarest Lloyd
WEALTH AGAINST COMMONWEALTH
1894

The corn of the coming harvest is growing so fast that, like the farmer standing at night in his fields, we can hear it snap and crackle. We have been fighting fire on the well-worn lines of old-fashioned politics and political economy, regulating corporations, and leaving competition to regulate itself. But the flames of a new economic evolution run around us, and we turn to find that competition has killed competition, that corporations are grown greater than the State and have bred individuals greater than themselves, and that the naked issue of our time is with property becoming master instead of servant, property in many necessaries of life becoming monopoly of the necessaries of life.

We are still, in part, as Emerson says, in the quadruped state. Our industry is a fight of every man for himself. The prize we give the fittest is monopoly of the necessaries of life, and we leave these winners of the powers of life and death to wield them over us by the same "self-interest" with which they took them from us. In all this we see at work a "principle" which will go into the records as one of the historic mistakes of humanity. Institutions stand or fall by their philosophy, and the main doctrine of industry since Adam Smith has been the fallacy that the self-interest of the individual was a sufficient guide to the welfare of the individual and society. Heralded as a final truth of "science" this proves to have been nothing higher than a temporary formula for a passing problem. It was a reflection in words of the policy of the day.

When the Middle Ages landed on the shores of the sixteenth century they broke ranks, and for three hundred years every one has been scurrying about to get what he could. Society was not highly developed enough to organize the exploration and subjugation of worlds of new things and ideas on any broader basis than private enterprise, personal

SOURCE. Henry Demarest Lloyd, *Wealth against Commonwealth*, New York: Harper and Brothers, 1894, pp. 494–515. Reprinted with the permission of Harper and Row, Publishers.

adventure. People had to run away from each other and from the old ideas, nativities, guilds, to seize the prizes of the new sciences, the new land, the new liberties which make modern times. They did not go because the philosophers told them to. The philosophers saw them going and wrote it down in a book, and have believed themselves ever since to be the inventors of the division of labor and the discoverers of a new world of social science. But now we are touching elbows again, and the dream of these picnic centuries that the social can be made secondary to the individual is being chased out of our minds by the hard light of the crisis into which we are waking.

"It is a law of business for each proprietor to pursue his own interest," said the committee of Congress which in 1893 investigated the coal combinations. "There is no hope for any of us, but the weakest must go first," is the golden rule of business. There is no other field of human associations in which any such rule of action is allowed. The man who should apply in his family or his citizenship this "survival of the fittest" theory as it is practically professed and operated in business would be a monster, and would be speedily made extinct, as we do with monsters. To divide the supply of food between himself and his children according to their relative powers of calculation, to follow his conception of his own self-interest in any matter which the self-interest of all has taken charge of, to deal as he thinks best for himself with foreigners with whom his country is at war, would be a short road to the penitentiary or the gallows. In trade men have not yet risen to the level of the family life of animals. The true law of business is that all must pursue the interest of all. In the law, the highest product of civilization, this has long been a commonplace. The safety of the people is the supreme law. We are in travail to bring industry up to this. Our century of the caprice of the individual as the law-giver of the common toil, to employ or disemploy, to start or stop, to open or close, to compete or combine, has been the disorder of the school while the master slept. The happiness, self-interest, or individuality of the whole is not more sacred than that of each, but it is greater. They are equal in quality, but in quantity they are greater. In the ultimate which the mathematician, the poet, the reformer projects the two will coincide.

Our world, operated by individual motive, is the country of the Chinese fable, in which the inhabitants went on one leg. Yes, but an "enlightened self-interest"? The perfect self-interest of the perfect individual is an admirable conception, but it is still individual, and the world is social. The music of the spheres is not to be played on one string. Nature does nothing individually. All forces are paired like the sexes, and every particle of matter in the universe has to obey every other particle. When the individual has progressed to a perfect self-interest, there will be over against it, acting and reacting with it, a correspondingly perfect self-interest of the community. Meanwhile, we who are the creators of society have got the times out of joint, because, less experienced than the Creator of the balanced matter of earth, we have given the precedence to the powers on one side. As gods we are but half-grown. For a hundred years or so our economic theory has been one of industrial government by the self-interest of the individual. Political government by the self-interest of the individual we call anarchy. It is one of the paradoxes of public opinion that the people of America, least tolerant of this theory of anarchy in political government, lead in practising it in industry. Politically, we are civilized; industrially, not yet. Our century, given to this *laissez-faire*—"leave the individual alone; he will do what is best for himself, and what is best for him is best for all"— has done one good: it has put society at the mercy of its own ideals, and has produced an actual anarchy in industry which is horrifying us into a change of doctrines.

We have not been able to see the people for the persons in it. But there is a people, and it is as different from a mere juxtaposition of persons as a globe of glass from the handful of sand out of which it was melted. It is becoming, socially, known to itself, with that self-consciousness which distinguishes the quick from the dead and the unborn. Every community, said Pascal, is a man, and every man, said Plato, is a community. There is a new self-interest—that of the "man called million," as Mazzini named him—and with this social motive the other, which has so long had its own way, has now to reckon. Mankind has gone astray following a truth seen only partially, but coronated as a whole truth. Many civilizations must worship good men as gods and follow the divinity of one and another before civilization sees that these are only single stars in a firmament of humanity. Our civilization has followed the self-interest of the individual to learn that it was but one of the complex forces of self-interest.

The true *laissez-faire* is, let the individual do what the individual can do best, and let the community do what the community can do best. The *laissez-faire* of social self-interest, if true, cannot conflict with the individual self-interest, if true, but it must outrank it always. What we have called "free competition" has not been free, only freer than what went before. The free is still to come. The pressure we feel is notice to prepare for it. Civilization—the process of making men citizens in their relations to each other, by exacting of each that he give to all that which he receives from all—has reached only those forms of common effort which, because most general and most vital, first demanded its harmonizing touch. Men joining in the labors of the family, the mutual sacrifices of the club or the church in the union of forces for self-defence and for the gains of co-operation on the largest scale in labors of universal concern, like letter-carrying, have come to be so far civilized.

History is condensed in the catchwords of the people. In the phrases of individual self-interest which have been the shibboleths of the main activities of our last hundred years were prophesied: the filling up of the Mississippi by the forest-destroying, self-seeking lumber companies of the North; the disintegration of the American family—among the rich by too little poverty, and among the poor by too much; the embezzlement of public highways and public franchises into private property; the devolution of the American merchants and manufacturers into the business dependants—and social and political dependants, therefore—of a few men in each great department of trade, from dry-goods to whiskey; the devolution of the free farmer into a tenant, and of the working-man into a fixture of the locomotive or the factory, forbidden to leave except by permission of his employer or the public; and that mêlée of injunctions, bayonets, idle men and idle machinery, rich man's fear of poor man and poor man's fear of starvation, we call trade and industry.

Where the self-interest of the individual is allowed to be the rule both of social and personal action, the level of all is forced down to that of the lowest. Business excuses itself for the things it does—cuts in wages, exactions in hours, tricks of competition—on the plea that the merciful are compelled to follow the cruel. "It is pleaded as an excuse by those" (common carriers) "who desire to obey the" (Interstate Commerce) "law that self-preservation drives them to violate it because other carriers persist in doing so," says Senator Cullom. When the self-interest of society is made the standard the lowest must rise to the average. The one pulls down, the other up. That men's hearts are bad and that bad men will do bad things has a truth in it. But whatever the general average of morals, the anarchy which gives such individuals their head and leaves them to set the pace for all will produce infinitely worse results than a policy which applies mutual checks and inspirations. Bad kings make bad reigns, but monarchy is bad because it is arbitrary power, and that, whether it be political or industrial, makes even good men bad.

A partial truth universally applied as this of self-interest has been is a universal error. Everything goes to defeat. Highways are used to prevent travel and traffic. Ownership of the means of production is sought in order to "shut down" production, and the means of plenty make famine. All follow self-interest to find that though they have created marvellous wealth it is not theirs. We pledge "our lives, our fortunes, and our sacred honor" to establish the rule of the majority, and end by finding that the minority—a minority in morals, money, and men—are our masters whichever way we turn. We agonize over "economy," but sell all our grain and pork and oil and cotton at exchanges where we pay brokerage on a hundred or a thousand barrels or bushels or bales of wind to get one real one sold. These intolerabilities —sweat-shops where model merchants buy and sell the cast-off scarlet-fever skins of the poor, factory and mine where childhood is forbidden to become manhood and manhood is forbidden to die a natural death, mausoleums in which we bury the dead rich, slums in which we bury the living poor, coal pools with their manufacture of artificial winter —all these are the rule of private self-interest arrived at its destination.

A really human life is impossible in our cities, but they cannot be reconstructed under the old self-interest. Chicago was rebuilt wrong after the fire. Able men pointed out the avenues to a wider and better municipal life, but they could not be opened through the private inter-positions that blocked the way. The slaughter of railway men coupling cars was shown, in a debate in the United States Senate, to be twice as great as it would have been if the men were in active service in war. But under the scramble for private gain our society on its railway side cannot develop the energy to introduce the improved appliances ready to hand which would save these lives, all young and vigorous. The cost of the change would be repaid in 100 per-cent. dividends every year by the money value alone to us of the men now killed and wounded. But we shall have to wait for a nobler arithmetic to give us investments so good as that. The lean kine of self-interest devour the fat kine. The railroad stockholder, idolater of self-interest, lets himself

be robbed—like the stockholder of all the railroads in this story—
either because he is too rich to mind, too feeble to make himself heard,
or too much implicated elsewhere as principal in the same kind of
depredation to care or dare to stir what he knows to be a universal
scandal. He has become within himself the battle-ground of a troop of
warring devils of selfishness; his selfishness as a stockholder clutched
at the throat by his selfishness as a parasite, in some "inside deal,"
feeding on the stockholder; some rebate arrangement, fast-freight line,
sleeping-car compay or what not. And, as like as not, upon this one's
back is another devil of depredation from some inner ring within a ring.
Torn at the vitals, the enlightened swinishness of our *leit-motif* is
hastening to throw itself into the sea.

We are very poor. The striking feature of our economic condition
is our poverty, not our wealth. We make ourselves "rich" by appropriating the property of others by methods which lessen the total property
of all. Spain took such riches from America and grew poor. Modern
wealth more and more resembles the winnings of speculators in bread
during famine—worse, for to make the money it makes the famine.
What we call cheapness shows itself to be unnatural fortunes for a
very few, monstrous luxury for them and proportionate deprivation
for the people, judges debauched, trustees dishonored, Congress and
State legislatures insulted and defied, when not seduced, multitudes of
honest men ruined and driven to despair, the common carrier made
a mere instrument for the creation of a new baronage, an example
set to hundreds of would-be Cæsars to repeat this rapine in other
industries and call it "business," a process set in operation all over the
United States for the progressive extinction of the independence of
laboring men, and all business men except the very rich, and their
reduction to a state of vassalage to lords or squires in each department
of trade and industry. All these—tears, ruin, dishonor, and treason—
are the unmarked additions to the "price marked on the goods."

Shall we buy cheap of Captain Kidd, and shut our ears to the agony
that rustles in his silks? Shall we believe that Captain Kidd, who kills
commerce by the act which enables him to sell at half-price, is a
cheapener? Shall we preach and practise doctrines which make the
Black Flag the emblem of success on the high seas of human inter-
change of service, and complain when we see mankind's argosies of
hope and plenty shrink into private hoards of treasure, buried in selfish
sands to be lost forever, even to cupidity? If this be cheapness, it comes

by the grace of the seller, and that is the first shape of dearness, as security in society by the grace of the ruler is the first form of insecurity.

The new wealth now administers estates of fabulous extent from metropolitan bureaus, and all the profits flow to men who know nothing of the real business out of which they are made. Red tape, complication, the hired man, conspiracy have taken the place of the watchful eye of the owner, the old-fashioned hand at the plough that must ' hold or drive." We now have Captains of Industry, with a few aids, rearranging from office chairs this or that industry, by mere contrivances of wit compelling the fruits of the labor of tens of thousands of their fellows, who never saw them, never heard of them, to be every day deposited unwilling and unwitting to their own credit at the bank; setting, as by necromancy, hundreds of properties, large and small, in a score of communities, to flying through invisible ways into their hands; sitting calm through all the hubbub raised in courts, legislatures, and public places, and by dictating letters and whispering words remaining the master magicians of the scene; defying, though private citizens, all the forces and authorities of a whole people; by the mere mastery of compelling brain, without putting hand to anything, opening or closing the earth's treasures of oil or coal or gas or copper or what not; pulling down or putting up great buildings, factories, towns themselves; moving men and their money this way and that; inserting their will as part of the law of life of the people—American, European, and Asiatic—and, against the protest of a whole civilization, making themselves, their methods and principles, its emblematic figures.

Syndicates, by one stroke, get the power of selling dear on one side, and producing cheap on the other. Thus they keep themselves happy, prices high, and the people hungry. What model merchant could ask more? The dream of the king who wished that all his people had but one neck that he might decapitate them at one blow is realized to-day in this industrial garrote. The syndicate has but to turn its screw and every neck begins to break. Prices paid to such intercepters are not an exchange of service; they are ransom paid by the people for their lives. The ability of the citizen to pay may fluctuate; what he must pay remains fixed, or advances like the rent of the Irish tenant to the absentee land- lord until the community interfered. Those who have this power to draw money from the people—from every railroad station, every street-car, every fireplace, every salt-cellar, every bread-pan, wash-board, and coal-scuttle—to their own safes have the further incentive to make this money worth the most possible. By contracting the issue of currency and contracting it again by hoarding it in their banks, safe-deposit vaults, and the government treasury, they can depress the prices of all that belongs to the people. Their own prices are fixed. These are "regular prices," established by price-lists. Given, as a ruling motive, the principles of business—to get the most and give the least; given the legal and economic, physical and mechanical control, possible under our present social arrangements, to the few over the many, and the certain end of all this, if unarrested, unreversed, can be nothing less than a return to chattel slavery. There may be some finer name, but the fact will not be finer. Between our present tolerance and our completed subjection the distance is not so far as that from the equality and simplicity of our Pilgrim Fathers to ourselves.

Everything withers—even charity. Aristocratic benevolence spends a shrunken stream in comparison with democratic benevolence. In an address to the public, soliciting subscriptions, the Committee of the United Hospitals Association of New York said, in December, 1893: "The committee have found that, through the obliteration of old methods of individual competition by the establishment of large corporations and trusts in modern times, the income of such charitable institutions as are supported by the individual gifts of the benevolent has been seriously affected."

Franklin pricked the bubble of the lottery by showing that to buy all the tickets and win all the prizes was to be most surely the loser. Our nascent common sense begins to see that the many must always lose where all spend their lives trying to get more than they give, and that all lose when any lose. The welfare of all is more than the welfare of the many, the few, or the one. If the few or the one are not fine enough to accept this truth from sentiment or conscience, they can find other reasons as convincing, though not as amiable. From the old régime of France, the slave-holders of the South, the death-rate of tyrants, the fear of their brothers which the rich and the great of to-day are printing on their faces, in fugitive-slave treaties with Russia, and in the frowning arsenals and armories building in our cities for "law and order," they can learn how to spell self-interest.

If all will sacrifice themselves, none need be sacrificed. But if one may sacrifice another, all are sacrificed. That is the difference between self-interest and other-self interest. In industry we have been substituting all the mean passions that can set man against man in place of the irresistible power of brotherhood. To tell us of the progressive sway of brotherhood in all human affairs is the sole message of history. "Love thy neighbor as thyself" is not the phrase of a ritual of sentiment for the unapplied emotion of pious hours; it is the exact formula of the force to-day operating the greatest institutions man has established. It is as secular as sacred. Only by each neighbor giving the other every right of free thought, free movement, free representation which he demands for himself; only by calling every neighbor a friend, and literally laying down his life for his friend against foreign invasion or domestic tumult; only by the equalization which gives the vote to all and denies kingship to all, however strong or "fittest"—only thus is man establishing the community, the republic, which, with all its failings, is the highest because the realest application of the spirit of human brotherhood. Wonderful are the dividends of this investment. You are but one, and can give only yourself to America. You give free speech, and 65,000,000 of your countrymen will guard the freedom of your lips. Your single offer of your right arm puts 65,000,000 of sheltering arms about you. Does "business" pay such profits? Wealth will remain a secret unguessed by business until it has reincorporated itself under the law which reckons as the property of each one the total of all the possessions of all his neighbors.

Society could not live a day, the Bishop of Peterborough said, if it put the principles of Christ into practice. There is no rarer gift than that of eyes to see what we see. Society is society, and lives its day solely by virtue of having put into actual routine and matter-of-fact application the principles of Christ and other bringers of the same message. Imperfect and faulty though the execution, it is these principles which are the family, the tribe, the sect, the club, the mutual-benefit society, the State, with their mutual services, forbearance, and guarantees. The principles of Christ are the cause and essence of society. They are not the ideal of which we dream; they are the applied means with which we are working out our real life in "the light of common day." They have not been so much revealed to us by our inspired ones as best seen by them. Insurance for fire, accident, sickness, old age, death—the ills that flesh is heir to—has the same co-operation for its innermost forces. Limited now by the intervention of the selfishness of profit-seeking, it needs only to be freed from this, and added, as in New Zealand, to the growing list of the mutualities of the general welfare operated by the State to be seen as what it is. The golden rule is the original of every political constitution, written and unwritten, and all our reforms are but the pains with which we strive to improve the copy.

In the worst governments and societies that have existed one good can be seen—so good that the horrors of them fall back into secondary places as extrinsic, accidental. That good is the ability of men to lead the life together. The more perfect monopoly makes itself the more does it bring into strong lights the greatest fact of our industry, of far more permanent value than the greed which has for the moment made itself the cynosure of all eyes. It makes this fair world more fair to consider the loyalties, intelligences, docilities of the multitudes who are guarding, developing, operating with the faithfulness of brothers and the keen interest of owners properties and industries in which brotherhood is not known and their title is not more than a tenancy at will. One of the largest stones in the arch of "consolidation," perhaps the keystone, is that men have become so intelligent, so responsive and responsible, so co-operative that they can be entrusted in great masses with the care of vast properties owned entirely by others and with the operation of complicated processes, although but a slender cost of subsistence is awarded them out of fabulous profits. The spectacle of the million and more employees of the railroads of this country despatching trains, maintaining tracks, collecting fares and freights, and turning over hundreds of millions of net profits to the owners, not one in a thousand of whom would know how to do the simplest of these things for himself, is possible only where civilization has reached a high average of morals and culture. More and more the mills and mines and stores, and even the farms and forests, are being administered by others than the owners. The virtue of the people is taking the place Poor Richard thought only the eye of the owner could fill. If mankind, driven by their fears and the greed of others, can do so well, what will be their productivity and cheer when the "interest of all" sings them to their work?

This new morality and new spring of wealth have been seized first by the appropriating ones among us. But, as has been in government, their invention of greed is but a passing phase. Mankind belongs to itself, not to kings or monopolists, and will supersede the one as surely as the other with the institutions of democracy. Yes, Callicles, said Socrates, the greatest are usually the bad, for they have the power. If power could continue paternal and benign, mankind would not be rising through one emancipation after another into a progressive communion of equalities.

The individual and society will always be wrestling with each other in a composition of forces. But to just the extent to which civilization prevails, society will be held as inviolable as the individual; not subordinate —indeed inaudible—as now in the counting-room and corporation-office. We have overworked the self-interest of the individual. The line of conflict between individual and social is a progressive one of the discovery of point after point in which the two are identical. Society thus passes from conflict to harmony, and on to another conflict. Civilization is the unceasing accretion of these social solutions. We fight out to an equilibrium, as in the abolition of human slavery; then upon this new level thus built up we enter upon the struggle for a new equilibrium, as now in the labor movement. The man for himself destroys himself and all men; only society can foster him and them.

The greatest happiness of the greatest number is only the doctrine of self-interest writ large and made more dangerous by multitude. It is the self-interest of the majority, and this has written some of the unloveliest chapters of history. There have never been slaves more miserable than those of Sparta, where the State was the owner. American democracy prepares to repeat these distresses of the selfishness of the many, and gives notice to its railway employés of a new divine right—"the convenience of the public"—to which they must forego every right of manhood. No better definition of slave could be found than one who must work at the convenience of another. This is the position into which recent legal decisions and acts of the Federal executive force railway men. These speak in the name of Interstate Commerce, but their logic can be as easily applied by State judges to State commerce, and all working-men are manifestly as necessary, each in his function, to the convenience of the public as the men of the rail. The greatest happiness of all must be the formula. When Lamennais said, "I love my family more than myself, my village more than my family, my country more than my village, and mankind more than my country," he showed himself not only a good lover, but the only good arithmetician.

Children yet, we run everything we do—love or war, work or leisure, religion or liberty—to excess. Every possibility of body and mind must be played upon till it is torn to pieces, as toys by children. Priests, voluptuaries, tyrants, knights, ascetics—in the long procession of fanatics a new-comer takes his place; he is called "the model merchant"—the cruelest fanatic in history. He is the product of ages given to progressive devotion to "trading." He is the high-priest of the latest idolatry, the self-worship of self-interest. Whirling-dervish of the market, self, friends, and family, body and soul, loves, hopes, and faith, all are sacrificed to seeing how many "turns" he can make before he drops dead. Trade began, Sir Henry Sumner Maine tells us, not within the family or community, but without. Its first appearances are on the neutral borderland between hostile tribes. There, in times of peace, they meet to trade, and think it no sin that "the buyer must beware," since the buyer is an enemy. Trade has spread thence, carrying with itself into family and State the poison of enmity. From the fatherhood of the old patriarchal life, where father and brother sold each other nothing, the world has chaffered along to the anarchy of a "free" trade which sells everything. One thing after another has passed out from under the régime of brotherhood and passed in under that of bargainhood. The ground we move on, the bodies we work with, and the necessaries we live by are all being "exchanged," by "rules fetched with cupidity from heartless schools," into the ownership of the Jacobs of mankind. By these rules the cunning are the good, and the weak and the tender the bad, and the good are to have all the goods and the weak are to have nothing. These rules give one the power to supply or deny work to thousands, and to use the starvation terms of the men he disemploys as the measure of the cost of subsistence of all workmen. This must be near the end. The very churches have become mercantilized, and are markets in which "prophets" are paid fancy prices—"always called of God," as Milton said, "but always to a greater benefice"—and worshippers buy and sell knee-room.

Conceptions of duty take on a correspondingly unnatural complexion. The main exhortations the world gives beginners are how to "get on"— the getting on so ardently inculcated being to get, like the old-man-of-the-sea, on somebody's back. "If war fails you in the country where you are, you must go where there is war," said one of the successful men of the fourteenth century to a young knight who asked him for the Laws of Life. "I shall be perfectly satisfied with you," I heard one of the great business geniuses of America say to his son, "if you will only always go to bed at night worth more than when you got up in the morning." The system grows, as all systems do, more complicated, and gets further away from its first purposes of barter of real things and services. It goes more under the hands of men of apt selfishness, who push it further away from general comprehension and the general good. Tariffs, currencies, finances, freight-rate sheets, the laws, become instruments of privilege, and just in proportion become puzzles no people can decipher. "I have a right to buy my labor where I can buy it cheapest"—beginning as a protest against the selfish exclusions of antiquated trade-guilds by the new times—has at last come to mean, "I have a right to do anything to cheapen the labor I want to buy, even to destroying the family life of the people."

When steaming kettles grew into beasts of burden and public highways dwindled into private property administered by private motives for private ends, all previous tendencies were intensified into a sudden whirl redistributing wealth and labors. It appears to have been the destiny of the railroad to begin and of oil to lubricate to its finish the last stage of this crazy commercialism. Business colors the modern world as war reddened the ancient world. Out of such delirium monsters are bred, and their excesses destroy the system that brought them forth. There is a strong suggestion of moral insanity in the unrelieved sameness of mood and unvarying repetition of one act in the life of the model merchant. Sane minds by an irresistible law alternate one tension with another. Only a lunatic is always smiling or always weeping or always clamoring for dividends. Eras show their last stages by producing men who sum up individually the morbid characteristics of the mass. When the crisis comes in which the gathering tendencies of generations shoot forward in the avalanche, there is born some group of men perfect for their function— good be it or bad. They need to take time for no second thought, and will not delay the unhalting reparations of nature by so much as the time given to one tear over the battle-field or the bargain. With their birth their mission is given them, whether it be the mission of Lucifer or Gabriel. This mission becomes their conscience. The righteous indignation that other men feel against sin these men feel against that which withstands them. Sincere as rattlesnakes, they are selfish with the unconsciousness possible to only the entirely commonplace, without the curiosity to question their times or the imagination to conceive the pain they inflict, and their every ideal is satisfied by the conventionalities of church, parlor, and counting-room. These men are the touchstones to wither the cant of an age.

We preach "Do as you would be done by" in our churches, and "A fair exchange no robbery" in our counting-rooms, and "All citizens are equal as citizens" in courts and Congress. Just as we are in danger of believing that to say these things is to do them and be them, there come unto us these men, practical as granite and gravitation. Taking their cue not from our lips, but from our lives, they better the instruction, and, passing easily to the high seats at every table, prove that we are liars and hypocrites. Their only secret is that they do, better than we, the things we are all trying to do, but of which in our morning and evening prayers, seen of all men, we are continually making believe to pray: Good Lord, deliver us! When the hour strikes for such leaders, they come and pass as by a law of nature to the front. All follow them. It is their fate and ours that they must work out to the end the destiny interwoven of their own insatiate ambition and the false ideals of us who have created them and their opportunity.

If our civilization is destroyed, as Macaulay predicted, it will not be by his barbarians from below. Our barbarians come from above. Our great money-makers have sprung in one generation into seats of power kings do not know. The forces and the wealth are new, and have been the opportunity of new men. Without restraints of culture, experience, the pride, or even the inherited caution of class or rank, these men, intoxicated, think they are the wave instead of the float, and that they have created the business which has created them. To them science is but a never-ending repertoire of investments stored up by nature for the syndicates, government but a fountain of franchises, the nations but customers in squads, and a million the unit of a new arithmetic of wealth written for them. They claim a power without control, exercised through forms which make it secret, anonymous, and perpetual. The possibilities of its gratification have been widening before them without interruption since they began, and even at a thousand millions they will feel no satiation and will see no place to stop. They are gluttons of luxury and power, rough, unsocialized, believing that mankind must be kept terrorized. Powers of pity die out of them, because they work through agents and die in their agents, because what they do is not for themselves.

Of gods, friends, learnings, of the uncomprehended civilization they overrun, they ask but one question: How much? What is a good time to sell? What is a good time to buy? The Church and the Capitol, incarnating the sacrifices and triumphs of a procession of martyrs and patriots since the dawn of freedom, are good enough for a money-changer's shop for them, and a market and shambles. Their heathen eyes see in the law and its consecrated officers nothing but an intelligence-office and hired men to help them burglarize the treasures accumulated for thousands of years at the altars of liberty and justice, that they may burn their marbles for the lime of commerce.

By their windfall of new power they have been forced into the position of public enemies. Its new forms make them seem not to be within the jurisdiction of the social restraints which many ages of suffering have taught us to bind about the old powers of man over man. A fury of rule or ruin has always in the history of human affairs been a characteristic of the "strong men" whose fate it is to be in at the death of an expiring principle. The leaders who, two hundred years ago, would have been crazy with conquest, to-day are crazy with competition. To a dying era some man is always born to enfranchise it by revealing it to itself. Men repay such benefactors by turning to rend them. Most unhappy is the fate of him whose destiny it is to lead mankind too far in its own path. Such is the function of these men, such will be their lot, as that of those for whom they are building up these wizard wealths.

Poor thinking means poor doing. In casting about for the cause of our industrial evils, public opinion has successively found it in "competition," "combination," the "corporations," "conspiracies," "trusts." But competition has ended in combination, and our new wealth takes as it chooses the form of corporation or trust, or corporation again, and with every change grows greater and worse. Under these kaleidoscopic masks we begin at last to see progressing to its terminus a steady consolidation, the end of which is one-man power. The conspiracy ends in one, and one cannot conspire with himself. When this solidification of many into one has been reached, we shall be at last face to face with the naked truth that it is not only the form but the fact of arbitrary power, of control without consent, of rule without representation that concerns us.

Business motivated by the self-interest of the individual runs into monopoly at every point it touches the social life—land monopoly, transportation monopoly, trade monopoly, political monopoly in all its forms, from contraction of the currency to corruption in office. The society in which in half a lifetime a man without a penny can become a hundred times a millionaire is as over-ripe, industrially, as was, politically, the Rome in which the most popular bully could lift himself from the ranks of the legion on to the throne of the Cæsars. Our rising issue is with business. Monopoly is business at the end of its journey. It has got there. The irrepressible conflict is now as distinctly with business as the issue so lately met was with slavery. Slavery went first only because it was the cruder form of business.

Against the principles, and the men embodying them and pushing them to extremes—by which the powers of government, given by all for all, are used as franchises for personal aggrandizement; by which, in the same line, the common toil of all and the common gifts of nature, lands, forces, mines, sites, are turned from service to selfishness, and are made by one and the same stroke to give gluts to a few and impoverishment to the many—we must plan our campaign. The yacht of the millionaire incorporates a a million days' labor which might have been given to abolishing the slums, and every day it runs the labor of hundreds of men is withdrawn from the production of helpful things for humanity, and each of us is equally guilty who directs to his own pleasure the labor he should turn to the wants of others. Our fanatic of wealth reverses the rule that serving mankind is the end and wealth an incident, and has made wealth the end and the service an accident, until he can finally justify crime itself if it is a means to the end—wealth—which has come to be the supreme good; and we follow him.

It is an adjudicated fact of the business and social life of America that to receive the profits of crime and cherish the agents who commit it does not disqualify for fellowship in the most "solid" circles—financial, commercial, religious, or social. It illustrates what Ruskin calls the "morbid" character of modern business that the history of its most brilliant episodes must be studied in the vestibules of the penitentiary. The riches of the combinations are the winnings of a policy which, we have seen, has certain constant features. Property to the extent of uncounted millions has been changed from the possession of the many who owned it to the few who hold it:

1. Without the knowledge of the real owners.
2. Without their consent.
3. With no compensation to them for the value taken.
4. By falsehood, often under oath.
5. In violation of the law.

Our civilization is builded on competition, and competition evolves itself crime—to so acute an infatuation has the lunacy of self-interest carried our dominant opinion. We are hurried far beyond the point of not listening to the new conscience which, pioneering in moral exploration, declares that conduct we think right because called "trade" is really lying, stealing, murder. "The definite result," Ruskin preaches, "of all our modern haste to be rich is assuredly and constantly the murder of a certain number of persons by our hands every year." To be unawakened by this new voice is bad enough, but we shut our ears even against the old conscience.

We cannot deal with this unless we cleanse our hearts of all disordering rage. "The rarer action is in virtue rather than in vengeance." Our tyrants are our ideals incarnating themselves in men born to command. What these men are we have made them. All governments are representative governments; none of them more so than our government of industry. We go hopelessly astray if we seek the solution of our problems in the belief that our business rulers are worse men in kind than ourselves. Worse in degree; yes. It is a race to the bad, and the winners are the worst. A system in which the prizes go to meanness invariably marches with the meanest men at the head. But if any could be meaner than the meanest it would be they who run and fail and rail.

Every idea finds its especially susceptible souls. These men are our most susceptible souls to the idea of individual self-interest. They have believed implicitly what we have taught, and have been the most faithful in trying to make the talent given them grow into ten talents. They rise superior to our half-hearted social corrections: publicity, private competition, all devices of market-opposition, private litigation, public investigation, legislation, and criminal prosecution—all. Their power is greater to-day than it was yesterday, and will be greater to-morrow. The public does not withhold its favor, but deals with them, protects them, refuses to treat their crimes as it treats those of the poor, and admits them to the highest places. The predominant mood is the more or less concealed regret of the citizens that they have not been able to conceive and execute the same lucky stroke or some other as profitable. The conclusion is irresistible that men so given the lead are the representatives of the real "spirit of the age," and that the protestants against them are not representative of our times—are at the best but imitators of times which may be.

Two social energies have been in conflict, and the energy of reform has so far proved the weaker. We have chartered the self-interest of the individual as the rightful sovereign of conduct; we have taught that the scramble for profit is the best method of administering the riches of earth and the exchange of services. Only those can attack this system who attack its central principle, that strength gives the strong in the market the right to destroy his neighbor. Only as we have denied that right to the strong elsewhere have we made ourselves as civilized as we are. And we cannot make a change as long as our songs, customs, catchwords, and public opinions tell all to do the same thing if they can. Society, in each person of its multitudes, must recognize that the same principles of the interest of all being the rule of all, of the strong serving the weak, of the first being the last—"I am among you as one that serves"—which have given us the home where the weakest is the one surest of his rights and of the fullest service of the strongest, and have given us the republic in which all join their labor that the poorest may be fed, the weakest defended, and all educated and prospered, must be applied where men associate in common toil as wherever they associate. Not until then can the forces be reversed which generate those obnoxious persons—our fittest.

Our system, so fair in its theory and so fertile in its happiness and prosperity in its first century, is now, following the fate of systems, becoming artificial, technical, corrupt; and, as always happens in human institutions, after noon, power is stealing from the many to the few. Believing wealth to be good, the people believed the wealthy to be good. But, again in history, power has intoxicated and hardened its possessors, and Pharaohs are bred in counting-rooms as they were in palaces. Their furniture must be banished to the world-garret, where lie the out-worn trappings of the guilds and slavery and other old lumber of human institutions.

VII. INTRODUCTION

The position taken by the Republican wing of the Progressive Party under the leadership of Theodore Roosevelt, who articulated the kind of argument that had been made by Herbert Croly (Reading XI), was that sheer magnitude in economic life was not in itself a relevant consideration. Economic trusts, as Roosevelt understood them, should be condemned not for their size but for their function, should that function seem to violate the national interest. The alternative position, one represented by Woodrow Wilson, was that size itself was a threat to the nature of America's political economy.

One of the most impassioned and learned defenders of Wilson's point of view was Louis D. Brandeis (1856–1941). Known as the "people's attorney," he developed a relatively new kind of legal brief that stressed the social and economic facts relevant to the case under consideration. Appointed by Wilson to the United States Supreme Court in 1916, Brandeis remained allied on the bench with the liberal dissenters, Holmes, Cardozo, and Stone.

Early in the first year of Wilson's administration, Brandeis wrote an article that was published in the *American Legal News* on "Competition," which is reprinted as the following selection. It was Brandeis' opinion, as it was Wilson's, that Theodore Roosevelt's brand of progressivism failed to understand that the magnitude of individual businesses alone constituted a social menace; the Democratic view was that regulated competition was the only sound economic policy for the United States to follow. Brandeis' article was an attempt to demonstrate the error in the position which held that monopoly was the result of natural economic development or that monopoly was created by efficiency. On the contrary, he said, criminal actions were often the cause of success of the largest monopolies and trusts in the nation. The social disadvantages of vast industrial enterprises were spelled out by Brandeis. He felt it was the necessary function of government to preserve competition where it then existed, and to restore it where it had been destroyed by the trusts.

The kind of argument advanced here by Brandeis formed an essential part of Wilson's "New Freedom," and became a crucial ingredient in the continuing American effort to understand the relationship between the state and the economy.

VII.

Louis D. Brandeis

COMPETITION

1913

Practically all Americans agree there is a trust problem; but upon every matter relating to the problem there is the greatest diversity of opinion. In this wide divergence of view, two lines of cleavage may be drawn according as men take one or the other side of the two following important questions:

First, shall the industrial policy of America be that of competition, or that of monopoly?

Second, have we adequate governmental machinery to enforce what-

SOURCE. Louis D. Brandeis, *The Curse of Bigness, Miscellaneous Papers of Louis D. Brandeis,* New York: Viking Press, 1934, pp. 112–124. Copyright 1934 by Louis D. Brandeis, 1962 by Susan Brandeis Gilbert and Elizabeth Brandeis Raushenbush. Reprinted with the permission of The Viking Press, Inc.

ever industrial policy America concludes to adopt, whether that policy be competition or monopoly?

Now, these two questions are frequently confused, but they are entirely distinct. The first is a question of economic policy, the second, the question of governmental machinery.

Some men who believe in competition think we have adequate governmental machinery now to secure competition, and all that is necessary is to enforce the Sherman law as it stands. Other men who believe in competition think we lack governmental machinery necessary to secure and maintain it, and that appropriate machinery should be devised and adopted for regulating competition. Likewise, some men who believe that private monopoly should be permissible think that the public will be best served if we simply repeal the Sherman law and let business take care of itself. Other men who believe in private monopoly think that we should devise and introduce new governmental machinery by which monopoly would be regulated.

Furthermore, there is a division among those who believe in the necessity of additional governmental machinery to enforce the policy either of competition or of monopoly; for they differ widely as to the nature of the machinery to be installed. This difference is not merely a difference in numerous and important details. They differ quite fundamentally as to the nature of the machinery to be employed—some persons maintaining that the new machinery shall be wholly judicial, that is, shall be such as will be enforced only through courts of law; other persons insisting that however much the judicial machinery is improved, there must also be introduced administrative machinery; that is, such as would be applied through some kind of a commission. Such a commission was proposed in the bill introduced by a Democrat, Senator Newlands, on August 21, 1911, under the title of Interstate Trade Commission, and another and more elaborate one was later introduced by a Progressive Republican, Senator La Follette, under the name of Federal Trade Commission, and legislation of this character is strongly urged by the New Party [T. Roosevelt's "Bull Moose" progressives].

For the purpose of this discussion most of the differences of view indicated can be eliminated. The question, "Shall we regulate competition or regulate monopoly?" assumes that there will be some regulation, and it is clear that in order to regulate either, the legal machinery must be greatly improved, and an administrative board of some kind, and with fairly broad powers, must be created to supplement the powers of the courts in dealing with this subject.

The only fundamental difference as between the New Party's program and that of its opponent relates to the economic policy to be enforced. All other differences are differences in degree or of emphasis.

In saying that the New Party stands for monopoly I do not mean that it wants to introduce monopoly generally in private industry, but merely that it accepts private monopoly as permissible, and the trusts as in themselves unobjectionable, requiring only that they be "good." It is prepared to protect existing trusts from dismemberment, if only they will be "good" hereafter, thus leaving them in the possession of the huge profits obtained through violations of law. But once we treat monopoly as permissible, we have given away the whole case of competition, for monopoly is the path of least effort in business, and is sure to be pursued, if opened.

On the other hand those who stand for competition do not advocate what has been frequently described as "unrestricted" or "destructive" competition. They demand a regulated competition or, if one may adopt the phrase, competition which is "good."

Regulation is essential to the preservation of competition and to its best development, just as regulation is necessary to the preservation and development of civil or political liberty. To preserve civil and political liberty to the many we have found it necessary to restrict the liberty of the few. Unlicensed liberty leads necessarily to despotism or oligarchy. Those who are stronger must to some extent be curbed. We curb the physically strong in order to protect those physically weaker. The liberty of the merchant and manufacturer to lie in trade, formerly permissible, and expressed in the fine phrase *caveat emptor,* has yielded largely to the better business ethics supplemented by pure-food laws and postal-fraud prosecution. Formerly the interests of business and of the community were supposed to be best served by letting buyer and seller trade without restriction on native or acquired shrewdness. Those laws present examples of protecting those who, by reason of position or training are, in respect to particular business transactions, the weaker or unable to take care of themselves. Recognizing differences in position of employer and employee, we have similarly restricted theoretically freedom of contract by factory laws which prescribe conditions under which work may be performed and, to some extent, the hours of labor. Experience had shown that under the changed conditions in industry it was necessary, in order that life and liberty of the worker be preserved, to put a restraint upon the theoretical freedom of the individual worker and the employer—the employer and the employee—to do as he chose in that respect.

The right of competition must be similarly limited; for excesses of competition lead to monopoly just as excesses of liberty have led to despotism. It is another case where the extremes meet.

What are those excesses of competition which should be prevented because they lead to monopoly? The answer to that question should be sought—not in theorizing, but in the abundant experiences of the last twenty-five years, during which the trusts have been developed. We have but to study the facts and ascertain:

"How did monopoly, wherever it obtained foothold, acquire its position?"

And we can, in the first place, give the comprehensive answer, which should relieve the doubts and fears of many: no monopoly in private industry in America has yet been attained by efficiency alone. No business has been so superior to its competitors in the processes of manufacture or of distribution as to enable it to control the market solely by reason of its superiority. There is nothing in our industrial history to indicate that there is any need whatever to limit the natural growth of a business in order to preserve competition. We may emphatically declare: "Give fair play to efficiency."

One has heard of late the phrases: "You can't make people compete by law." "Artificial competition is undesirable." These are truisms, but their implication is false. Believers in competition make no suggestion that traders be compelled to compete. They ask merely that no trader should be allowed to kill competition. Competition consists in trying to do things better than someone else; that is, making or selling a better article, or the same article at a lesser cost, or otherwise giving better service. It is not competition to resort to methods of the prize ring, and simply "knock the other man out." That is killing a competitor.

Clearly misleading is the phrase, "Natural monopoly should not be interfered with." There are no natural monopolies in the industrial world. The Oil Trust and the Steel Trust have sometimes been called "natural monopolies," but they are both most unnatural monopolies. The Oil Trust acquired its control of the market by ruthless conduct which was not only a sin against society, but in large part involved flagrant violations of law. Without the aid of criminal rebating the

Standard Oil would not have acquired the vast wealth and power which enabled it to destroy its smaller competitors by price-cutting and similar processes. The course of the Tobacco Trust was similar in character.

The Steel Trust, while apparently free from the coarser forms of suppressing competition, acquired control of the market not through greater efficiency, but by buying up existing plants and particularly ore supplies at fabulous prices, and by controlling strategic transportation systems. A monopoly like the Steel Trust can hardly be called natural, when it resulted in the main by the purchase of a single huge concern —the Carnegie Company—for, at least, $250,000,000 more than its value, thus bribing Mr. Carnegie to retire from the field in which he was master; and by the purchase of its vast ore resources at many times their value.

It will be found that wherever competition has been suppressed it has been due either to resort to ruthless processes, or by improper use of inordinate wealth and power. The attempt to dismember existing illegal trusts is not, therefore, an attempt to interfere in any way with the natural law of business. It is an endeavor to restore health by removing a cancer from the body industrial. It is not an attempt to create competition artificially, but it is the removing of the obstacle to competition. The policy of regulated competition is distinctly a constructive policy. It is the policy of development as distinguished from the destructive policy of private monopoly. It has always in the past and must always in the future paralyze individual effort and initiative and deaden enterprise. Business progress demands that the industrial advance be unobstructed and private monopoly's highways of industrial and commercial development kept open.

Earnest argument is constantly made in support of monopoly by pointing to the wastefulness of competition. Undoubtedly competition involves some waste. What human activity does not? The wastes of democracy are among the greatest obvious wastes, but we have compensations in democracy which far outweigh that waste and make it more efficient than absolutism. So it is with competition. Incentive and development which are incident to the former system of business result in so much achievement that the accompanying waste is relatively insignificant. The margin between that which men naturally do and which they can do is so great that a system which urges men on to action, enterprise, and initiative is preferable in spite of the wastes that necessarily attend that process. I say, "necessarily" because there have been and are today wastes incidental to competition that are unnecessary. Those are the wastes which attend that competition which do not develop, but kill. Those wastes the law can and should eliminate. It may do so by regulating competition.

It is, of course, true that the unit in business may be too small to be efficient. The larger unit has been a common incident of monopoly. But a unit too small for efficiency is by no means a necessary incident of competition. It is also true that the unit in business may be too large to be efficient, and this is no uncommon incident of monopoly. In every business concern there must be a size-limit of greatest efficiency. What that limit is will differ in different businesses and under varying conditions in the same business. But whatever the business or organization there is a point where it would become too large for efficient and economic management, just as there is a point where it would be too small to be an efficient instrument. The limit of efficient size is exceeded when the disadvantages attendant upon size outweigh the advantages, when the centrifugal force exceeds the centripetal. Man's work often outruns the capacity of the individual man; and, no matter what the organization, the capacity of an individual man usually determines the success or failure of a particular enterprise, not only financially to the owners, but in service to the community. Organization can do much to make concerns more efficient. Organization can do much to make larger units possible and profitable. But the efficiency even of organization has its bounds; and organization can never supply the combined judgment, initiative, enterprise, and authority which must come from the chief executive officers. Nature sets a limit to their possible accomplishment. As the Germans say, "Care is taken that the trees do not scrape the skies."

That mere size does not bring success is illustrated by the record of our industrial system during the past ten years. This record, if examined, will show that:

1. Most of the trusts which did not secure monopolistic positions have failed to show marked success as compared with the independent concerns.

This is true of many existing trusts, for instance, of the Newspaper Trust, the Writing Paper Trust, the Upper Leather Trust, the Sole Leather Trust, the Woolen Trust, the Paper Bag Trust, the International Mercantile Marine, and those which have failed, like the Cordage Trust, the Mucilage Trust, the Flour Trust, should not be forgotten.

2. Most of those trusts which have shown marked success secured

monopolistic positions either by controlling the whole business themselves, or by doing so in combination with others. And their success
has been due mainly to their ability to fix prices.

This is true, for instance, of the Standard Oil Trust, the Shoe Machinery Trust, the Tobacco Trust, the Steel Trust, the Pullman Car
Company.

3. Most of the trusts which did not secure for themselves monopoly
in the particular branch of trade, but controlled the situation only through
price agreements with competitors, have been unable to hold their own
share of the market as against the independents.

This is true, for instance, of the Sugar Trust, the Steel Trust, the
Rubber Trust.

4. Most of the efficiently managed trusts have found it necessary to
limit the size of their own units for production and for distribution.

This is true, for instance, of the Tobacco Trust, the Standard Oil
Trust, the Steel Trust.

These general rules are, of course, subject to exceptions due to instances of conspicuous ability on the part of managers or unusual trade
conditions.

Lack of efficiency is ordinarily manifested either (1) in rising cost
of product, (2) in defective quality of goods produced, or (3) in failure
to make positive advances in processes and methods.

The third of these manifestations is the most serious of all. In this
respect monopoly works like poison which infects the system for a long
time before it is discovered, and yet a poison so potent that the best of
management can devise no antidote.

Take the case of the Steel Trust. It inherited through the Carnegie
Company the best organization and the most efficient steel makers in
the world. It has had since its organization exceptionally able management. It has almost inexhaustible resources. It produces on so large a
scale that practically no experimental expense would be unprofitable
if it brought the slightest advance in the art. And yet in only ten years
after its organization, high American authority—the *Engineering News,*
declares:

"We are today something like five years behind Germany in iron
and steel metallurgy, and such innovations as are being introduced by
our iron and steel manufacturers are most of them merely following
the lead set by foreigners years ago.

"We do not believe this is because American engineers are any less

ingenious or original than those of Europe, though they may indeed
be deficient in training and scientific education compared with those of
Germany. We believe the main cause is the wholesale consolidation
which has taken place in American industry. A huge organization is
too clumsy to take up the development of an original idea. With the
market closely controlled and certain of profits by following standard
methods, those who control our trusts do not want the bother of developing anything new.

"We instance metallurgy only by way of illustration. There are
plenty of other fields of industry where exactly the same condition exists.
We are building the same machines and using the same methods as a
dozen years ago, and the real advances in the art are being made by
European inventors and manufacturers."

This judgment is confirmed by the "Menace of the Broken Rail."

The Steel Trust was organized in 1901. It has dominated the steel
trade of America. Its power has been particularly great in respect to
rails, partly because of the system of inter-locking directorates. Steel
Trust directors are also directors in railroad companies, owning more
than one half of the railroad mileage in the United States. Ten years
after the organization of the Steel Trust, the country was aroused by
one or two shocking railroad accidents. The accidents appeared to result
from broken rails. The Interstate Commerce Commission was led to make
an investigation into the general subject and found that whereas in 1902
there were 72 derailments due to broken rails, there were in 1911, 249
derailments due to the same cause. In the past decade—the era of the
Steel Trust—there have been 2,059 derailments due to broken rails,
resulting in 106 killed and injured. Of course, all of these rails were not
made by the Steel Trust, and the strain put upon rails has increased with
the increase in the weight of equipment more than ever before; but the
fact that articles produced by the Steel Trust have failed to keep pace
with the requirements of transportation to such an extent as to require
an investigation by the Government certainly indicates a marked limitation upon the efficiency of the greatest of all industrial units. Another
instance of this character of inefficiency was disclosed recently in the ably
managed Shoe Machinery Trust.

The Shoe Machinery Trust, the result of combining directly and indirectly more than a hundred different concerns, acquired substantially
a monopoly of all the essential machinery used in bottoming boots and
shoes. Its energetic managers were conscious of the constant need of

improving and developing inventions and spent large sums in efforts to do so. Nevertheless, in the year 1910 they were confronted with a competitor so formidable that the Company felt itself obliged to buy him off, though in violation of the law and at a cost of about $5,000,000. That competitor, Thomas G. Plant, a shoe manufacturer who had resented the domination of the trust, developed an extensive system of shoe machinery, which is believed to be superior to the Trust's own system, which represents the continuous development of that Company and its predecessors for nearly half a century.

H. B. Endicott, one of the leading shoe manufacturers of the country, and now a director in the Shoe Machinery Trust, publicly declared, after examining the Plant system: "In my judgment, and that of my experts, what you (Plant) have shown us was by far the most perfect set of working machinery that we had ever seen, or expected to see."

But the efficiency of monopolies, even if established, would not justify their existence unless the community should reap benefit from the efficiency; experience teaches us that whenever trusts have developed efficiency, their fruits have been absorbed almost wholly by the trusts themselves. From such efficiency as they have developed the community has gained substantially nothing. For instance:

The Standard Oil Trust, an efficiently managed monopoly, increased the prices of its principal products (refined oil, naphtha, and paraffin wax) between 1895 and 1898, and 1903 to 1906 by 46 per cent. The profits per gallon on crude oil used increased from 1882 to 1906 from $1.78 per gallon to $3.05 per gallon. The profits of the marketing companies of the Trust increased from 88 cents per gallon of illuminating oil in 1898 to $1.50 per gallon in 1906. The profits on naphtha per gallon nearly doubled between 1898 and 1906.

The Tobacco Trust, an efficiently managed monopoly. Between 1899 and 1907 the selling price (less taxes) on smoking tobacco rose from 21.1 cents per pound to 30.1 cents; the profit per pound from 2.8 cents per pound to 9.8 cents. The selling price of plug tobacco rose from 24.9 cents per pound to 30.4 cents; the profit per pound from 1.9 cents to 8.7 cents.

In the snuff business the Tobacco Trust controlled 96 per cent of the market. The extortion was even greater. The selling price of snuff (less taxes) rose from 29.2 cents per pound in 1900 to 37.1 cents in 1907; whereas the cost decreased from 22.6 cents per pound to 20.8 cents. Thus the profit per pound exacted by the Trust rose from 6.6 cents per pound to 16.3 cents per pound. In other worls, in 1907 on every pound of snuff sold by the Trust there was exacted from the public a profit of about 81 per cent on its cost.

The following statement of the Commissioner of Corporations illustrated the power and disposition of the Trust to absorb whatever profits existed:

"The results of the Spanish War tax upon tobacco products especially illustrate the monopolistic power of the combination. When that tax was imposed in 1898, prices were generally raised. In 1901 and 1902 the tax was reduced to its former basis, but the combination was powerful enough to keep its prices at the higher level. It thus absorbed practically all the benefit of the reduction, adding millions yearly to its income. The episode shows the unforeseen results of fiscal legislation affecting monopolistic conditions not fully recognized. The tax reduction, of course, was intended to benefit the consumers. As a matter of fact, it benefited almost solely the controlling interest in the industry."

The Steel Trust, a corporation of reputed efficiency. The high prices maintained by it in the industry are matters of common knowledge. In less than ten years it accumulated for its shareholders or paid out as dividends on stock representing merely water, over $650,000,000.

Compare with this record of increased or stationary prices and of growing profits, the record of strictly competitive manufacturing businesses where the selling prices have shown a marked tendency to decrease and the ratio of profits has been almost uniformly lessened. For instance:

The Book Paper business furnishes a conspicuous example of this. In important mills the average selling-price of book paper declined from 7.08 cents per pound in 1889 to 4.24 cents in 1899, and to 3.99 in 1910; the ratio of profit per pound declined from 19 per cent on cost in 1889 to 13 per cent in 1899 and 7 per cent in 1910. This reduction is the more noteworthy because the principal raw material used —wood—(like wages) has steadily risen in price during the period.

The proposed Government commission to fix prices would not greatly relieve the evils attendant upon monopoly. It might be effective in preventing private monopoly from taking excessive profits, but Government price-regulation would be powerless to secure to the public the low prices commonly attendant upon competition. In other words, price-fixing might reduce the trust's profits, but it would fail materially to reduce the trust's prices; because the limitation of the monopoly's profits would, by lessening this incentive, surely reduce the monopoly's efficiency.

Capital and property will yield, according to the degree of the judgment and efficiency applied in management, vastly different returns. To secure the successful management of any private business reward must be proportionate to success. The establishment of any rule fixing a maximum return on capital would, by placing a limit upon the fruits of achievement, tend to lessen efficiency. For efficiency is naturally reflected in large net earnings; and as no ready means exists for determining whether greater net earnings are due to greater efficiency in management or to excessive profits, large net earnings would be followed by compulsory reduction of prices, and such reduction by a lessening of effort. To take from a private business the natural fruits of efficiency would create a sense of injustice suffered, which would paralyze effort and individual enterprise, and produce slipshod management. The attempt to secure low prices through price-fixing would prove as impotent as the statutes which have sought to protect the public in respect to railroad rates by limiting the dividends of railroads. The permissible dividends generally exhausted the profits. No selling price for monopoly products could be set constitutionally at a point lower than that which would allow a reasonable return on capital. And in the absence of comparative data from any competing businesses producing the same article at less cost, it would be practically impossible to determine that the cost should be lower.

The success of the Interstate Commerce Commission has been invoked as an argument in favor of licensing monopoly, and regulating it by a similar commission.

If the experience of the Interstate Commerce Commission is carefully inquired into, it will be found to present argument against, rather than in favor of, the proposition that the evils naturally attendant upon industrial private monopolies can be avoided through establishing such an industrial commission.

In the first place, the success of the Interstate Commerce Commission has been effective principally in preventing rate increases and in stopping discrimination. The great reductions in railroad rates which have been made in the last 24 years (during the life of the Commission) have been due, in not rare instances, to action of the Interstate Commerce Commission. In those instances where the Commission has reduced rates (as distinguished from preventing increases) the Commission rested its decision largely on the ground that existing rates amounted to discrimination against particular places or articles, or the lower rates were justified by a comparison with other rates of the same or other companies. Price fixing of that nature applied to industrial trusts would afford little protection to the public.

In the second place, there is a radical difference between attempts to fix rates for transportation and similar public services and fixing prices in industrial businesses. The striking characteristic of the railroad problems of the whole country is their uniformity. Problems of transportation, while varying infinitely in detail, are largely the same throughout the whole country, and they are largely the same yesterday, today, and tomorrow. For this reason the Commission reaches its decision as to the reasonableness of a rate most frequently by a comparison of what is charged upon the same or some other railroad for a similar service. In spite, therefore, of the numerous problems as to the reasonableness of rates with which the Interstate Commerce Commission is confronted, their task would be a relatively simple one as compared with that which would necessarily arise if prices were to be fixed in the field of industry. In industry we have, instead of uniformity, infinite variety; instead of stability, constant change.

In the third place, the problems of the Interstate Commerce Commission, relatively simple as they are by reason of the character of the service to be regulated, already far exceed the capacity of that or any single board. A single question of rates, like that involved in the Spokane and intermountain rate cases has been before the Commission awaiting final adjudication nearly twenty years. Think of the infinite questions which would come before an industrial commission seeking to fix rates, and the suffering of the community from the inability of that body to dispose of them promptly and efficiently. It would require not only one but hundreds of commissioners to protect the American people from the extortions of monopolies, even if protection were possible at all.

Everyone admits that the reasonableness of the railroads' rates is in some degree at least dependent upon the cost of the service. The Commission has been in existence twenty-four years and no data exist today for determining with reasonable accuracy the cost of any service upon the railroads, and indeed none can exist until a valuation of the railroads is made.

Since private monopoly is not beneficial to the community there can remain but two questions:

First, can we preserve competition where it exists?

Second, can we restore competition where it has been suppressed?

To both the answer is, Yes.

Diagnosis shows monopoly to be an artificial, not a natural, product. Competition, therefore, may be preserved by preventing that course of conduct by which in the past monopolies have been established. If we had in the past undertaken by appropriate legal and administrative machinery to prevent our financiers and others from carrying out agreements to form monopolies; if we had seriously attempted to prevent those methods of destructive or unfair competition, as are manifest in "cut-throat competition"—discrimination against customers who will not deal exclusively with the combination; if we had made any persistent, intelligent effort to stop advantages gained by railroad discrimination, espionage, or the practice of establishing "fake independents," or to stop those who have secured control of essential raw material from denying business rivals access to it—few of the trusts, of which we now complain, would have come into existence, or would, at all events, have acquired power to control the market. We made no serious attempt to stop monopoly—certainly no intelligent attempt; partly because we lacked knowledge, partly because we lacked desire; for we had a sneaking feeling that perhaps, after all, a private monopoly might be a good thing, and we had no adequate governmental machinery to employ for this purpose. But in the past twenty-two years we have acquired much experience with trusts. We know their ways. We have learned what the defects in the existing machinery are; and if we will but remedy those defects by appropriate legal and administrative machinery—somewhat on the lines proposed in the La Follette–Stanley and Newlands bills—and supplement the prohibition of monopoly by the regulation of competition, we shall be able, not only to preserve the competition we now enjoy, but gradually regain the free soil upon which private monopoly has encroached, and we may be assured that, despite all industrial changes, the day for industrial liberty has not yet passed.

CHAPTER 2

The Attack on Idealism

One of the dominant characteristics of American thought in the decades around the turn of the century was a deepening rejection of idealism. Many scholars and writers in diverse fields attempted to formulate a "realistic" position that would save them from the presumed pieties and intellectual disabilities of preconceived ideas, of blinding teleologies, of rationalism, and of *a priori* reasoning. This new "realism" was implemented especially in law, social theory, and philosophy.

Oliver Wendell Holmes (1841–1935) was the leading critic of idealism in the law. Appointed to the Supreme Court of the United States by Theodore Roosevelt, Holmes became the dominant spokesman of judicial liberalism. Remaining committed to what he called the "free trade in ideas," Holmes consistently took the position that the Constitution was not intended as an obstacle to necessary or desirable social experiments. His rejection of idealism led him to reject also the common law, which he said was not ". . . a brooding omnipresence in the sky."

When Holmes was still a member of the Supreme Judicial Court of Massachusetts, he delivered an address (reprinted as the following selection) in January, 1897 at the dedication of a building at the Boston University Law School. His legal "realism" led him to distinguish between law and morality. His rejection of eternal legal truth led him to argue that there could be no absolute certainty in the law because the law, as was equally true of other branches of knowledge, was based on human judgment and reason, not on pure logic or scientific accuracy. Social considerations, in his view, were also judicial responsibilities. Displaying the impact of evolutionary thought on the law, Holmes believed that statistics and economics must be brought to bear on the law if the law was to relate to social needs. The presentism of his position flew directly in the face of the legal tradition which had emphasized precedent.

The following essay shows some of the consequences of an application of evolutionary theory and new realism to the law.

VIII.

Oliver Wendell Holmes

THE PATH OF THE LAW

1897

When we study law we are not studying a mystery but a well-known profession. We are studying what we shall want in order to appear before judges, or to advise people in such a way as to keep them out of court. The reason why it is a profession, why people will pay lawyers to argue for them or to advise them, is that in societies like ours the command of the public force is intrusted to the judges in certain cases, and the whole power of the state will be put forth, if necessary, to carry out their judgments and decrees. People want to know under what circumstances and how far they will run the risk of coming against what is so much stronger than themselves, and hence it becomes a business to find out when this danger is to be feared. The object of our study, then, is prediction, the prediction of the incidence of the public force through the instrumentality of the courts.

The means of the study are a body of reports, of treatises, and of statutes, in this country and in England, extending back for six hundred years, and now increasing annually by hundreds. In these sibylline leaves are gathered the scattered prophecies of the past upon the cases in which the axe will fall. These are what properly have been called the oracles of the law. Far the most important and pretty nearly the whole meaning of every new effort of legal thought is to make these prophecies more precise, and to generalize them into a thoroughly connected system. The process is one, from a lawyer's statement of a case, eliminating as it does all the dramatic elements with which his client's story has clothed it, and retaining only the facts of legal import, up to the final analyses and abstract universals of theoretic jurisprudence. The reason why a lawyer does not mention that his client wore a white hat when he made a contract, while Mrs. Quickly would be sure to dwell upon it along with the parcel gilt

SOURCE. Oliver Wendell Holmes, Jr., *Collected Legal Papers,* New York: Harcourt, Brace and Co., 1921, pp. 167–173, 179–181, 184–187, and 194–195. Copyright, 1920, by Harcourt, Brace and World, Inc.; renewed, 1948, by Edward J. Holmes. Reprinted with the permission of the publishers.

goblet and the sea-coal fire, is that he foresees that the public force will act in the same way whatever his client had upon his head. It is to make the prophecies easier to be remembered and to be understood that the teachings of the decisions of the past are put into general propositions and gathered into text-books, or that statutes are passed in a general form. The primary rights and duties with which jurisprudence busies itself again are nothing but prophecies. One of the many evil effects of the confusion between legal and moral ideas, about which I shall have something to say in a moment, is that theory is apt to get the cart before the horse, and to consider the right or the duty as something existing apart from and independent of the consequences of its breach, to which certain sanctions are added afterward. But, as I shall try to show, a legal duty so called is nothing but a prediction that if a man does or omits certain things he will be made to suffer in this or that way by judgment of the court; and so of a legal right.

The number of our predictions when generalized and reduced to a system is not unmanageably large. They present themselves as a finite body of dogma which may be mastered within a reasonable time. It is a great mistake to be frightened by the ever-increasing number of reports. The reports of a given jurisdiction in the course of a generation take up pretty much the whole body of the law, and restate it from the present point of view. We could reconstruct the corpus from them if all that went before were burned. The use of the earlier reports is mainly historical, a use about which I shall have something to say before I have finished.

I wish, if I can, to lay down some first principles for the study of this body of dogma or systematized prediction which we call the law, for men who want to use it as the instrument of their business to enable them to prophesy in their turn, and, as bearing upon the study, I wish to point out an ideal which as yet our law has not attained.

The first thing for a business-like understanding of the matter is to understand its limits, and therefore I think it desirable at once to point out and dispel a confusion between morality and law, which sometimes rises to the height of conscious theory, and more often and indeed constantly is making trouble in detail without reaching the point of consciousness. You can see very plainly that a bad man has as much reason as a good one for wishing to avoid an encounter with the public force, and therefore you can see the practical importance of the distinction between morality and law. A man who cares nothing for an ethical rule which is believed and practised by his neighbors is likely nevertheless to care a good deal to avoid being made to pay money, and will want to keep out of jail if he can.

I take it for granted that no hearer of mine will misinterpret what I have to say as the language of cynicism. The law is the witness and external deposit of our moral life. Its history is the history of the moral development of the race. The practice of it, in spite of popular jests, tends to make good citizens and good men. When I emphasize the difference between law and morals I do so with reference to a single end, that of learning and understanding the law. For that purpose you must definitely master its specific marks, and it is for that I ask you for the moment to imagine yourselves indifferent to other and greater things.

I do not say that there is not a wider point of view from which the distinction between law and morals becomes of secondary or no importance, as all mathematical distinctions vanish in presence of the infinite. But I do say that that distinction is of the first importance for the object which we are here to consider—a right study and mastery of the law as a business with well understood limits, a body of dogma enclosed within definite lines. I have just shown the practical reason for saying so. If you want to know the law and nothing else, you must look at it as a bad man, who cares only for the material consequences which such knowledge enables him to predict, not as a good one, who finds his reasons for conduct, whether inside the law or outside of it, in the vaguer sanctions of conscience. The theoretical importance of the distinction is no less, if you would reason on your subject aright. The law is full of phraseology drawn from morals, and by the mere force of language continually invites us to pass from one domain to the other without perceiving it, as we are sure to do unless we have the boundary constantly before our minds. The law talks about rights, and duties, and malice, and intent, and negligence, and so forth, and nothing is easier, or, I may say, more common in legal reasoning, then to take these words in their moral sense, at some stage of the argument, and so to drop into fallacy. For instance, when we speak of the rights of man in a moral sense, we mean to mark the limits of interference with individual freedom which we think are prescribed by conscience, or by our ideal, however reached. Yet it is certain that many laws have been enforced in the past, and it is likely that some are enforced now, which are condemned by the most enlightened opinion of the time, or which at all events pass the limit of interference as many consciences would draw it. Manifestly, therefore, nothing but confusion of thought can result from assuming that the rights of man in a moral sense are equally rights in the sense of the Constitution and the law. No doubt simple and extreme cases can be put of imaginable laws which the statute-making power would not dare to enact, even in the absence of written constitutional prohibitions, because the community would rise in rebellion and fight; and this gives some plausibility to the proposition that the law, if not a part of morality, is limited by it. But this limit of power is not co-extensive with any system of morals. For the most part it falls far within the lines of any such system, and in some cases may extend beyond them, for reasons drawn from the habits of a particular people at a particular time. I once heard the late Professor Agassiz say that a German population would rise if you added two cents to the price of a glass of beer. A statute in such a case would be empty words, not because it was wrong, but because it could not be enforced. No one will deny that wrong statutes can be and are enforced, and we should not all agree as to which were the wrong ones.

The confusion with which I am dealing besets confessedly legal conceptions. Take the fundamental question, What constitutes the law? You will find some text writers telling you that it is something different from what is decided by the courts of Massachusetts or England, that it is a system of reason, that it is a deduction from principles of ethics or admitted axioms or what not, which may or may not coincide with the decisions. But if we take the view of our friend the bad man we shall find that he does not care two straws for the axioms or deductions, but that he does want to know what the Massachusetts or English courts are likely to do in fact. I am much of his mind. The prophecies of what the courts will do in fact, and nothing more pretentious, are what I mean by the law....

I ... have shown the danger, both to speculation and to practice, of confounding morality with law, and the trap which legal language lays for us on that side of our way. For my own part, I often doubt whether it would not be a gain if every word of moral significance could be banished from the law altogether, and other words adopted which should convey legal ideas uncolored by anything outside the law. We should lose the fossil records of a good deal of history and the majesty got from ethical associations, but by ridding ourselves of an unnecessary confusion we should gain very much in the clearness of our thought.

So much for the limits of the law. The next thing which I wish to consider is what are the forces which determine its content and its growth. You may assume, with Hobbes and Bentham and Austin, that all law emanates from the sovereign, even when the first human being to enunciate it are the judges, or you may think that law is the voice of the Zeitgeist, or what you like. It is all one to my present purpose. Even if every decision required the sanction of an emperor with despotic power and a whimsical turn of mind, we should be interested none the less, still with a view to prediction, in discovering some order, some rational explanation, and some principle of growth for the rules which he laid down. In every system there are such explanations and principles to be found. It is with regard to them that a second fallacy comes in, which I think it important to expose.

The fallacy to which I refer is the notion that the only force at work in the development of the law is logic. In the broadest sense, indeed, that notion would be true. The postulate on which we think about the universe is that there is a fixed quantitative relation between every phenomenon and its antecedents and consequents. If there is such a thing as a phenomenon without these fixed quantitative relations, it is a miracle. It is outside the law of cause and effect, and as such transcends our power of thought, or at least is something to or from which we cannot reason. The condition of our thinking about the universe is that it is capable of being thought about rationally, or, in other words, that every part of it is effect and cause in the same sense in which those parts are with which we are most familiar. So in the broadest sense it is true that the law is a logical development, like everything else. The danger of which I speak is not the admission that the principles of governing other phenomena also govern the law, but the notion that a given system, ours, for instance, can be worked out like mathematics from some general axioms of conduct. This is the natural error of the schools, but it is not confined to them. I once heard a very eminent judge say that he never let a decision go until he was absolutely sure that it was right. So judicial dissent often is blamed, as if it meant simply that one side or the other were not doing their sums right, and, if they would take more trouble, agreement inevitably would come.

This mode of thinking is entirely natural. The training of lawyers is a training in logic. The processes of analogy, discrimination, and deduction are those in which they are most at home. The language of judicial decision is mainly the language of logic. And the logical method and form flatter that longing for certainty and for repose which is in every human mind. But certainty generally is illusion, and repose is not the destiny of man. Behind the logical form lies a judgment as to the relative worth and importance of competing legislative grounds, often an inarticulate and unconscious judgment, it is true, and yet the very root and nerve of the whole proceeding. You can give any conclusion a logical form. You always can imply a condition in a contract. But why do you imply it? It is because of some belief as to the practice of the community or of a class, or because of some opinion as to policy, or, in short, because of some attitude of yours upon a matter not capable of exact quantitative measurement, and therefore not capable of founding exact logical conclusions. Such matters really are battle grounds where the means do not exist for determinations that shall be good for all time, and where the decision can do no more than embody the preference of a given body in a given time and place. We do not realize how large a part of our law is open to reconsideration upon a slight change in the habit of the public mind. No concrete proposition is self evident, no matter how ready we may be to accept it. . . .

I think that the judges themselves have failed adequately to recognize their duty of weighing considerations of social advantage. The duty is inevitable, and the result of the often proclaimed judicial aversion to deal with such considerations is simply to leave the very ground and foundation of judgments inarticulate, and often unconscious, as I have said. When socialism first began to be talked about, the comfortable classes of the community were a good deal frightened. I suspect that this fear has influenced judicial action both here and in England, yet it is certain that it is not a conscious factor in the decisions to which I refer. I think that something similar has led people who no longer hope to control the legislatures to look to the courts as expounders of the Constitutions, and that in some courts new principles have been discovered outside the bodies of those instruments, which may be generalized into acceptance of the economic doctrines which prevailed about fifty years ago, and a wholesale prohibition of what a tribunal of lawyers does not think about right. I cannot but believe that if the training of lawyers led them habitually to consider more definitely and explicitly the social advantage on which the rule they lay down must be justified, they sometimes would hesitate where now they are confident, and see that really they were taking sides upon debatable and often burning questions.

So much for the fallacy of logical form. Now let us consider the present condition of the law as a subject for study, and the ideal toward which it tends. We still are far from the point of view which I desire to see reached. No one has reached it or can reach it as yet. We are only at the beginning of a philosophical reaction, and of a reconsideration of the worth of doctrines which for the most part still are taken for granted without any deliberate, conscious, and systematic questioning of their grounds. The development of our law has gone on for nearly a thousand years, like the development of a plant, each generation taking the inevitable next step, mind, like matter, simply obeying a law of spontaneous growth. It is perfectly natural and right that it should have been so. . . . Most of the things we do, we do for no better reason than that our fathers have done them or that our neighbors do them, and the same is true of a larger part than we suspect of what we think. The reason is a good one, because our short life gives us no time for a better, but it is not the best. It does not follow, because we all are compelled to take on faith at second hand most of the rules on which we base our action and our thought, that each of us may not try to set some corner of his world in the order of reason, or that all of us collectively should not aspire to carry reason as far as it will go throughout the whole domain. In regard to the law, it is true, no doubt, that an evolutionist will hesitate to affirm universal validity for his social ideals, or for the principles which he thinks should be embodied in legislation. He is content if he can prove them best for here and now. He may be ready to admit that he knows nothing about an absolute best in the cosmos, and even that he knows next to nothing about a permanent best for men. Still it is true that a body of law is more rational and more civilized when every rule it contains is referred articulately and definitely to an end which it subserves, and when the grounds for desiring that end are stated or are ready to be stated in words.

At present, in very many cases, if we want to know why a rule of law has taken its particular shape, and more or less if we want to know why it exists at all, we go to tradition. We follow it into the Year Books, and perhaps beyond them to the customs of the Salian Franks, and somewhere in the past, in the German forests, in the needs of Norman kings, in the assumptions of a dominant class, in the absence of generalized ideas, we find out the practical motive for what now best is justified by the mere fact of its acceptance and that men are accustomed to it. The rational study of law is still to a large extent the study of history. History must be a part of the study, because without it we cannot know the precise scope of rules which it is our business to know. It is a part of the rational study, because it is the first step toward an enlightened scepticism, that is, towards a deliberate reconsideration of the worth of those rules. When you get the dragon out of his cave on to the plain and in the daylight, you can count his teeth and claws, and see just what is his strength. But to get him out is only the first step. The next is either to kill him, or to tame him and make him a useful animal. For the rational study of the law the black-letter man may be the man of the present, but the man of the future is the man of statistics and the master of economics. It is revolting to have no better reason for a rule of law than that so it was laid down in the time of Henry IV. It is still more revolting if the grounds upon which it was laid down have vanished long since, and the rule simply persists from blind imitation of the past. . .

. . . Our only interest in the past is for the light it throws upon the present. I look forward to a time when the part played by history in the explanation of dogma shall be very small, and instead of ingenious research we shall spend our energy on a study of the ends sought to be attained and the reasons for desiring them. As a step toward that ideal it seems to me that every lawyer ought to seek an understanding of economics. The present divorce between the schools of political economy and law seems to me an evidence of how much progress in philosophical study still remains to be made. In the present state of political economy, indeed, we come again upon history on a larger scale, but there we are called on to consider and weigh the ends of legislation, the means of attaining them, and the cost. We learn that for everything we have we give up something else, and we are taught to set the advantage we gain against the other advantage we lose, and to know what we are doing when we elect.

IX. INTRODUCTION

William James (1842–1910) was the most powerful critic of idealism of his time. Raised in the atmosphere of the New England Transcendentalists, he had absorbed the idealism of Emerson both directly and through his father. He made his way from painting to medicine, to psychology, and finally to philosophy; throughout his entire career, William James was in search of an alternative to philosophical idealism.

James was introduced early to the supercharged mysticism of Swedenborg by his father. The gentle and pervasive pieties of his father's house, coupled with the Emersonian ideas of universal essences and blendings, undoubtedly contributed to his decision to explore *The Varieties of Religious Experience,* a selection from which follows.

Plurality and diversity of religions was not a regrettable fact for James. It was an axiom of his that different problems require different solutions, and religious problems were not exceptional. Insisting throughout his life that religion was a real fact, James did not abandon his attack on idealism, but was rather asserting the reality of individual and private perception. He was willing to admit that private realities were private but, nonetheless, real. Should science ignore or deny those realities, a vital aspect of the human condition would be missed. He asserted, in direct contrast to Rauschenbusch (Reading V), that individualism was the essence of religion. Feeling and conduct, rather than formal theology, were crucial to religion. He was, however, willing to concede that there was a creed common to most of the world's religions. One of James's essential tasks in the work from which the following selection is taken was to define the "spiritual sphere," to which all of the world's religions pointed, and with which all of the world's religions describe some kind of union. The reality of God, in James's view, was demonstrated not as a result of the essential nature of the Godhead, but rather because the idea of God produced real energy, which produced real effects in the real world, as Henry Adams was to say of the Virgin (Reading XIV). It was characteristic of James to undertake an investigation of the religious mood and temper in order to advance his general rejection of philosophical and theological idealism.

IX.
William James
THE VARIETIES OF RELIGIOUS EXPERIENCE
1902

. . . Summing up in the broadest possible way the characteristics of the religious life, . . . it includes the following beliefs:

1. That the visible world is part of a more spiritual universe from which it draws its chief significance;

2. That union or harmonious relation with that higher universe is our true end;

3. That prayer or inner communion with the spirit thereof—be that spirit 'God' or 'law'—is a process wherein work is really done, and spiritual energy flows in and produces effects, psychological or material, within the phenomenal world.

SOURCE. William James, *The Varieties of Religious Experience,* New York: Longmans, Green and Co., 1902, pp. 485–519.

Religion includes also the following psychological characteristics:

4. A new zest which adds itself like a gift to life, and takes the form either of lyrical enchantment or of appeal to earnestness and heroism.

5. An assurance of safety and a temper of peace, and, in relation to others, a preponderance of loving affections.

In illustrating these characteristics by documents, we have been literally bathed in sentiment. In re-reading my manuscript, I am almost appalled at the amount of emotionality which I find in it. After so much of this, we can afford to be dryer and less sympathetic in the rest of the work that lies before us. . . .

Ought it to be assumed that in all men the mixture of religion with other elements should be identical? Ought it, indeed, to be assumed that the lives of all men should show identical religious elements? In other words, is the existence of so many religious types and sects and creeds regrettable?

To these questions I answer 'No' emphatically. And my reason is that I do not see how it is possible that creatures in such different positions and with such different powers as human individuals are, should have exactly the same functions and the same duties. No two of us have identical difficulties, nor should we be expected to work out identical solutions. Each, from his peculiar angle of observation, takes in a certain sphere of fact and trouble, which each must deal with in a unique manner. One of us must soften himself, another must harden himself; one must yield a point, another must stand firm,—in order the better to defend the position assigned him. If an Emerson were forced to be a Wesley, or a Moody forced to be a Whitman, the total human consciousness of the divine would suffer. The divine can mean no single quality, it must mean a group of qualities, by being champions of which in alternation, different men may all find worthy missions. Each attitude being a syllable in human nature's total message, it takes the whole of us to spell the meaning out completely. So a 'god of battles' must be allowed to be the god for one kind of person, a god of peace and heaven and home, the god for another. We must frankly recognize the fact that we live in partial systems, and that parts are not interchangeable in the spiritual life. If we are peevish and jealous, destruction of the self must be an element of our religion; why need it be one if we are good and sympathetic from the outset? If we are sick souls, we require a religion of deliverance; but why think so much of deliverance, if we are healthy-minded? Unquestionably, some men have the completer experience and the higher vocation, here just as in the social world; but for each man to stay in his own experience, whate'er it be, and for others to tolerate him there, is surely best.

But, you may now ask, would not this one-sidedness be cured if we should all espouse the science of religions as our own religion? In answering this question I must open again the general relations of the theoretic to the active life.

Knowledge about a thing is not the thing itself. You remember . . . that to understand the causes of drunkenness, as a physician understands them, is not to be drunk. A science might come to understand everything about the causes and elements of religion, and might even decide which elements were qualified, by their general harmony with other branches of knowledge, to be considered true; and yet the best man at this science might be the man who found it hardest to be personally devout. *Tout savoir c'est tout pardonner.* The name of Renan would doubtless occur to many persons as an example of the way in which breadth of knowledge may make one only a dilettante in possibilities, and blunt the acuteness of one's living faith. If religion be a function by which either God's cause or man's cause is to be really advanced, then he who lives the life of it, however narrowly, is a better servant than he who merely knows about it, however much. Knowledge about life is one thing; effective occupation of a place in life, with its dynamic currents passing through your being, is another.

For this reason, the science of religions may not be an equivalent for living religion; and if we turn to the inner difficulties of such a science, we see that a point comes when she must drop the purely theoretic attitude, and either let her knots remain uncut, or have them cut by active faith. To see this, suppose that we have our science of religions constituted as a matter of fact. Suppose that she has assimilated all the necessary historical material and distilled out of it as its essence the same conclusions which I myself a few moments ago pronounced. Suppose that she agrees that religion, wherever it is an active thing, involves a belief in ideal presences, and a belief that in our prayerful communion with them, work is done, and something real comes to pass. She has now to exert her critical activity, and to decide how far, in the light of other sciences and in that of general philosophy, such beliefs can be considered *true.*

Dogmatically to decide this is an impossible task. Not only are the other sciences and the philosophy still far from being completed, but in their present state we find them full of conflicts. The sciences of nature know nothing of spiritual presences, and on the whole hold no practical commerce whatever with the idealistic conceptions towards which general philosophy inclines. The so-called scientist is, during his scientific hours at least, so materialistic that one may well say that on the whole the influence of science goes against the notion that religion should be recognized at all. And this antipathy to religion finds an echo within the very science of religions itself. The cultivator of this science has to become acquainted with so many groveling and horrible superstitions that a presumption easily arises in his mind that any belief that is religious probably is false. In the 'prayerful communion' of savages with such mumbo-jumbos of deities as they acknowledge, it is hard for us to see what genuine spiritual work—even though it were work relative only to their dark savage obligations—can possibly be done.

The consequence is that the conclusions of the science of religions are as likely to be adverse as they are to be favorable to the claim that the essence of religion is true. There is a notion in the air about us that religion is probably only an anachronism, a case of 'survival,' an atavistic relapse into a mode of thought which humanity in its more enlightened examples has outgrown; and this notion our religious anthropologists at present do little to counteract.

This view is so widespread at the present day that I must consider it with some explicitness before I pass to my own conclusions. Let me call it the 'Survival theory,' for brevity's sake.

The pivot round which the religious life . . . revolves, is the interest of the individual in his private personal destiny. Religion, in short, is a monumental chapter in the history of human egotism. The gods believed in—whether by crude savages or by men disciplined intellectually—agree with each other in recognizing personal calls. Religious thought is carried on in terms of personality, this being, in the world of religion, the one fundamental fact. To-day, quite as much as at any previous age, the religious individual tells you that the divine meets him on the basis of his personal concerns.

Science, on the other hand, has ended by utterly repudiating the personal point of view. She catalogues her elements and records her laws indifferent as to what purpose may be shown forth by them, and constructs her theories quite careless of their bearing on human anxieties and fates. Though the scientist may individually nourish a religion, and be a theist in his irresponsible hours, the days are over when it could be said that for Science herself the heavens declare the glory of God and the firmament showeth his handiwork. Our solar system, with its harmonies, is seen now as but one passing case of a certain sort of moving equilibrium in the heavens, realized by a local accident in an appalling wilderness of worlds where no life can exist. In a span of time which as a cosmic interval will count but as an hour, it will have ceased to be. The Darwinian notion of chance production, and subsequent destruction, speedy or deferred, applies to the largest as well as to the smallest facts. It is impossible, in the present temper of the scientific imagination, to find in the driftings of the cosmic atoms, whether they work on the universal or on the particular scale, anything but a kind of aimless weather, doing and undoing, achieving no proper history, and leaving no result. Nature has no one distinguishable ultimate tendency with which it is possible to feel a sympathy. In the vast rhythm of her processes, as the scientific mind now follows them, she appears to cancel herself. The books of natural theology which satisfied the intellects of our grandfathers seem to us quite grotesque, representing, as they did, a God who conformed the largest things of nature to the paltriest of our private wants. The God whom science recognizes must be a God of universal laws exclusively, a God who does a wholesale, not a retail business. He cannot accommodate his processes to the convenience of individuals. The bubbles on the foam which coats a stormy sea are floating episodes, made and unmade by the forces of the wind and water. Our private selves are like those bubbles,—epiphenomena . . . ; their destinies weigh nothing and determine nothing in the world's irremediable currents of events.

You see how natural it is, from this point of view, to treat religion as a mere survival, for religion does in fact perpetuate the traditions of the most primeval thought. To coerce the spiritual powers, or to square them and get them on our side, was, during enormous tracts of time, the one great object in our dealings with the natural world. For our ancestors, dreams, hallucinations, revelations, and cock-and-bull stories were inextricably mixed with facts. Up to a comparatively recent date such distinctions as those between what has been verified and what is only conjectured, between the impersonal and the personal aspects of existence, were hardly suspected or conceived. Whatever you imagined in a lively manner, whatever you thought fit to be true, you affirmed confidently; and whatever you affirmed, your comrades believed. Truth was what had not yet been contradicted, most things were taken into the mind from the point of view of their human suggestiveness, and the attention confined itself exclusively to the æsthetic and dramatic aspects of events.

How indeed could it be otherwise? The extraordinary value, for explanation and prevision, of those mathematical modes of conception which science uses, was a result that could not possibly have been expected in advance. Weight, movement, velocity, direction, position, what thin, pallid, uninteresting ideas! How could the richer animistic aspects of Nature, the peculiarities and oddities that make phenomena picturesquely striking or expressive, fail to have been first singled out and followed by philosophy as the more promising avenue to the knowledge of Nature's life? Well, it is still in these richer animistic and dramatic aspects that religion delights to dwell. It is the terror and beauty of phenomena, the 'promise' of the dawn and of the rainbow, the 'voice' of the thunder, the 'gentleness' of the summer rain, the 'sublimity' of the stars, and not the physical laws which these things follow, by which the religious mind still continues to be most impressed; and just as of yore, the devout man tells you that in the solitude of his room or of the fields he still feels the divine presence, that inflowings of help come in reply to his prayers, and that sacrifices to this unseen reality fill him with security and peace.

Pure anachronism! says the survival-theory;—anachronism for which deanthropomorphization of the imagination is the remedy required. The less we mix the private with the cosmic, the more we dwell in universal and impersonal terms, the truer heirs of Science we become.

In spite of the appeal which this impersonality of the scientific attitude makes to a certain magnanimity of temper, I believe it to be shallow, and I can now state my reason in comparatively few words. That reason is that, so long as we deal with the cosmic and the general, we deal only with the symbols of reality, but *as soon as we deal with private and personal phenomena as such, we deal with realities in the completest sense of the term.* I think I can easily make clear what I mean by these words.

The world of our experience consists at all times of two parts, an objective and a subjective part, of which the former may be incalculably more extensive than the latter, and yet the latter can never be omitted or suppressed. The objective part is the sum total of whatsoever at any given time we may be thinking of, the subjective part is the inner 'state' in which the thinking comes to pass. What we think of may be enormous,—the cosmic times and spaces, for example,—whereas the inner state may be the most fugitive and paltry activity of mind. Yet the cosmic objects, so far as the experience yields them, are but ideal pictures of something whose existence we do not inwardly possess but only point at outwardly, while the inner state is our very experience itself; its reality and that of our experience are one. A conscious field *plus* its object as felt or thought of *plus* an attitude towards the object *plus* the sense of a self to whom the attitude belongs—such a concrete bit of personal experience may be a small bit, but it is a solid bit as long as it lasts; not hollow, not a mere abstract element of experience, such as the 'object' is when taken all alone. It is a *full* fact, even though it be an insignificant fact; it is of the *kind* to which all realities whatsoever must belong; the motor currents of the world run through the like of it; it is on the line connecting real events with real events. That unsharable feeling which each one of us has of the pinch of his individual destiny as he privately feels it rolling out on fortune's wheel may be disparaged for its egotism, may be sneered at as unscientific, but it is the one thing that fills up the measure of our concrete actuality, and any would-be existent that should lack such a feeling, or its analogue, would be a piece of reality only half made up.

If this be true, it is absurd for science to say that the egotistic elements of experience should be suppressed. The axis of reality runs solely through the egotistic places,—they are strung upon it like so many beads. To describe the world with all the various feelings of the individual pinch of destiny, all the various spiritual attitudes, left out from the description— they being as describable as anything else—would be something like offering a printed bill of fare as the equivalent for a solid meal. Religion makes no such blunder. The individual's religion may be egotistic, and those private realities which it keeps in touch with may be narrow enough; but at any rate it always remains infinitely less hollow and abstract, as far as it goes, than a science which prides itself on taking no account of anything private at all.

A bill of fare with one real raisin on it instead of the word 'raisin,' with one real egg instead of the word 'egg,' might be an inadequate meal, but it would at least be a commencement of reality. The contention of the survival-theory that we ought to stick to non-personal elements exclusively seems like saying that we ought to be satisfied forever with reading the naked bill of fare. I think, therefore, that however particular questions connected with our individual destinies may be answered, it is only by acknowledging them as genuine questions, and living in the sphere of thought which they open up, that we become profound. But to live thus is to be religious; so I unhesitatingly repudiate the survival-theory of religion, as being founded on an egregious mistake. It does not follow, because our ancestors made so many errors of fact and mixed them with their religion, that we should therefore leave off being religious at all. By being religious we establish ourselves in possession of ultimate reality at the only points at which reality is given us to guard. Our responsible concern is with our private destiny, after all.

You see now why I have been so individualistic throughout these lectures, and why I have seemed so bent on rehabilitating the element of feeling in religion and subordinating its intellectual part. Individuality is founded in feeling; and the recesses of feeling, the larger, blinder strata of character, are the only places in the world in which we catch real fact in the making, and directly perceive how events happen, and how work is actually done. Compared with this world of living individualized feelings, the world of generalized objects which the intellect contemplates is without solidity or life. As in stereoscopic or kinetoscopic pictures seen outside the instrument, the third dimension, the movement, the vital element, are not there. We get a beautiful picture of an express train supposed to be moving, but where in the picture, as I have heard a friend say, is the energy or the fifty miles an hour?

Let us agree, then, that Religion, occupying herself with personal destinies and keeping thus in contact with the only absolute realities which we know, must necessarily play an eternal part in human history. The next thing to decide is what she reveals about those destinies, or whether indeed she reveals anything distinct enough to be considered a general message to mankind. We have done as you see, with our preliminaries, and our final summing up can now begin.

I am well aware that after all the palpitating documents which I have quoted, and all the perspectives of emotion-inspiring institution and belief that my previous lectures have opened, the dry analysis to which I now advance may appear to many of you like an anti-climax, a tapering-off and flattening out of the subject, instead of a crescendo of interest and result. I said awhile ago that the religious attitude of Protestants appears poverty-stricken to the Catholic imagination. Still more poverty-stricken, I fear, may my final summing up of the subject appear at first to some of you. On which account I pray you now to bear this point in mind, that in the present part of it I am expressly trying to reduce religion to its lowest admissible terms, to that minimum, free from individualistic excrescences, which all religions contain as their nucleus, and on which it may be hoped that all religious persons may agree. That established, we should have a result which might be small, but would at least be solid; and on it and round it the ruddier additional beliefs on which the different individuals make their venture might be grafted, and flourish as richly as you please. I shall add my own over-belief (which will be, I confess, of a somewhat pallid kind, as befits a critical philosopher), and you will, I hope, also add your over-beliefs, and we shall soon be in the varied world of concrete religious constructions once more. For the moment, let me dryly pursue the analytic part of the task.

Both thought and feeling are determinants of conduct, and the same conduct may be determined either by feeling or by thought. When we survey the whole field of religion, we find a great variety in the thoughts that have prevailed there; but the feelings on the one hand and the conduct on the other are almost always the same, for Stoic, Christian, and Buddhist saints are practically indistinguishable in their lives. The theories which Religion generates, being thus variable, are secondary; and if you wish to grasp her essence, you must look to the feelings and the conduct as being the more constant elements. It is between these two elements that the short circuit exists on which she carries on her principal business, while the ideas and symbols and other institutions form loop-lines which may be perfections and improvements, and may even some day all be united into one harmonious system, but which are not to be regarded as organs with an indispensable function, necessary at all times for religious life to go on. This seems to me the first conclusion which we are entitled to draw from the phenomena we have passed in review.

The next step is to characterize the feelings. To what psychological order do they belong?

The resultant outcome of them is in any case what Kant calls a 'sthenic' affection, an excitement of the cheerful, expansive, 'dynamogenic' order which, like any tonic, freshens our vital powers. In almost every lecture . . . we have seen how this emotion overcomes temperamental melancholy and imparts endurance to the Subject, or a zest, or a meaning, or an enchantment and glory to the common objects of life. The name of 'faith-state,' . . . is a good one. It is a biological as well as a psychological condition, and Tolstoy is absolutely accurate in classing faith among the forces *by which men live.* The total absence of it, anhedonia, means collapse.

The faith-state may hold a very minimum of intellectual content. We saw examples of this in . . . sudden raptures of the divine presence, or in . . . mystical seizures. . . . It may be a mere vague enthusiasm, half spiritual, half vital, a courage, and a feeling that great and wondrous things are in the air.

When, however, a positive intellectual content is associated with a faith-state, it gets invincibly stamped in upon belief, and this explains the passionate loyalty of religious persons everywhere to the minutest details of their so widely differing creeds. Taking creeds and faith-state together, as forming 'religions,' and treating these as purely subjective phenomena, without regard to the question of their 'truth,' we are obliged, on account of their extraordinary influence upon action and endurance, to class them amongst the most important biological functions of mankind. Their stimulant and anæsthetic effect is so great that . . . so long as men can *use* their God, they care very little who he is, or even whether he is at all. . . .

At this purely subjective rating, therefore, Religion must be considered vindicated in a certain way from the attacks of her critics. It would seem that she cannot be a mere anachronism and survival, but must exert a permanent function, whether she be with or without intellectual content, and whether, if she have any, it be true or false.

We must next pass beyond the point of view of merely subjective utility, and make inquiry into the intellectual content itself.

First, is there, under all the discrepancies of the creeds, a common nucleus to which they bear their testimony unanimously?

And second, ought we to consider the testimony true?

I will take up the first question first, and answer it immediately in the affirmative. The warring gods and formulas of the various religions do indeed cancel each other, but there is a certain uniform deliverance in which religions all appear to meet. It consists of two parts: (1) an uneasiness and (2) its solution.

1. The uneasiness, reduced to its simplest terms, is a sense that there is *something wrong about us* as we naturally stand.

2. The solution is a sense that *we are saved from the wrongness* by making proper connection with the higher powers.

In those more developed minds which alone we are studying, the wrongness takes a moral character, and the salvation takes a mystical tinge. I think we shall keep well within the limits of what is common to all such minds if we formulate the essence of their religious experience in terms like these:

The individual, so far as he suffers from his wrongness and criticises it, is to that extent consciously beyond it, and in at least possible touch with something higher, if anything higher exist. Along with the wrong part there is thus a better part of him, even though it may be but a most helpless germ. With which part he should identify his real being is by no means obvious at this stage; but when stage 2 (the stage of solution or salvation) arrives, the man identifies his real being with the germinal higher part of himself; and does so in the following way. He becomes

conscious that this higher part is conterminous and continuous with a
MORE of the same quality, which is operative in the universe outside of
him, and which he can keep in working touch with, and in a fashion get
on board of and save himself when all his lower being has gone to pieces
in the wreck.

It seems to me that all the phenomena are accurately describable in
these very simple general terms. They allow for the divided self and the
struggle; they involve the change of personal centre and the surrender of
the lower self; they express the appearance of exteriority of the helping
power and yet account for our sense of union with it; and they fully justify
our feelings of security and joy. There is probably no autobiographic document, among all those which I have quoted, to which the description will
not well apply. One need only add such specific details as will adapt it to
various theologies and various personal temperaments, and one will then
have the various experiences reconstructed in their individual forms.

So far, however, as this analysis goes, the experiences are only psychological phenomena. They possess, it is true, enormous biological worth.
Spiritual strength really increases in the subject when he has them, a new
life opens for him, and they seem to him a place of conflux where the
forces of two universes meet; and yet this may be nothing but his subjective way of feeling things, a mood of his own fancy, in spite of the
effects produced. I now turn to my second question: What is the objective
'truth' of the content?

The part of the content concerning which the question of truth most
pertinently arises is that 'MORE of the same quality' with which our own
higher self appears in the experience to come into harmonious working
relation. Is such a 'more' merely our own notion, or does it really exist?
If so, in what shape does it exist? Does it act, as well as exist? And in
what form should we conceive of that 'union' with it of which religious
geniuses are so convinced?

It is in answering these questions that the various theologies perform
their theoretic work, and that their divergencies most come to light. They
all agree that the 'more' really exists; though some of them hold it to exist
in the shape of a personal god or gods, while others are satisfied to conceive it as a stream of ideal tendency embedded in the eternal structure of
the world. They all agree, moreover, that it acts as well as exists, and that
something really is effected for the better when you throw your life into
its hands. It is when they treat of the experience of 'union' with it that
their speculative differences appear most clearly. Over this point pantheism

and theism, nature and second birth, works and grace and karma, immortality and reincarnation, rationalism and mysticism, carry on inveterate disputes.

At the end of my lecture on Philosophy I held out the notion that an impartial science of religions might sift out from the midst of their discrepancies a common body of doctrine which she might also formulate in terms to which physical science need not object. This, I said, she might adopt as her own reconciling hypothesis, and recommend it for general belief. I also said that in my last lecture I should have to try my own hand at framing such an hypothesis.

The time has now come for this attempt. Who says 'hypothesis' renounces the ambition to be coercive in his arguments. The most I can do is, accordingly, to offer something that may fit the facts so easily that your scientific logic will find no plausible pretext for vetoing your impulse to welcome it as true.

The 'more,' as we called it, and the meaning of our 'union' with it, form the nucleus of our inquiry. Into what definite description can these words be translated and for what definite facts do they stand? It would never do for us to place ourselves offhand at the position of a particular theology, the Christian theology, for example, and proceed immediately to define the 'more' as Jehovah, and the 'union' as his imputation to us of the righteousness of Christ. That would be unfair to other religions, and, from our present standpoint at least, would be an over-belief.

We must begin by using less particularized terms; and, since one of the duties of the science of religions is to keep religion in connection with the rest of science, we shall do well to seek first of all a way of describing the 'more,' which psychologists may also recognize as real. The *subconscious self* is nowadays a well-accredited psychological entity; and I believe that in it we have exactly the mediating term required. Apart from all religious considerations, there is actually and literally more life in our total soul than we are at any time aware of. . . .

Let me then propose, as an hypothesis, that whatever it may be on its *farther* side, the 'more' with which in religious experience we feel ourselves connected is on its *hither* side the subconscious continuation of our conscious life. Starting thus with a recognized psychological fact as our basis, we seem to preserve a contact with 'science' which the ordinary theologian lacks. At the same time the theologian's contention that the religious man is moved by an external power is vindicated, for it is one of the peculiarities of invasions from the subconscious region to take on objective appearances, and to suggest to the Subject an external control. In the religious life the control is felt as 'higher'; but since on our hypothesis it is primarily the higher faculties of our own hidden mind which are controlling, the sense of union with the power beyond us is a sense of something, not merely apparently, but literally true.

This doorway into the subject seems to me the best one for a science of religions, for it mediates between a number of different points of view. Yet it is only a doorway, and difficulties present themselves as soon as we step through it, and ask how far our transmarginal consciousness carries us if we follow it on its remoter side. Here the over-beliefs begin: here mysticism and the conversion-rapture and Vedantism and transcendental idealism bring in their monistic interpretations and tell us that the finite self rejoins the absolute self, for it was always one with God and identical with the soul of the world. Here the prophets of all the different religions come with their visions, voices, raptures, and other openings, supposed by each to authenticate his own peculiar faith.

Those of us who are not personally favored with such specific revelations must stand outside of them altogether and, for the present at least, decide that, since they corroborate incompatible theological doctrines, they neutralize one another and leave no fixed result. If we follow any one of them, or if we follow philosophical theory and embrace monistic pantheism on non-mystical grounds, we do so in the exercise of our individual freedom, and build out our religion in the way most congruous with our personal susceptibilities. Among these susceptibilities intellectual ones play a decisive part. Although the religious question is primarily a question of life, of living or not living in the higher union which opens itself to us as a gift, yet the spiritual excitement in which the gift appears a real one will often fail to be aroused in an individual until certain particular intellectual beliefs or ideas which, as we say, come home to him, are touched. These ideas will thus be essential to that individual's religion;—which is as much as to say that over-beliefs in various directions are absolutely indispensable, and that we should treat them with tenderness and tolerance so long as they are not intolerant themselves. As I have elsewhere written, the most interesting and valuable things about a man are usually his over-beliefs.

Disregarding the over-beliefs, and confining ourselves to what is common and generic, we have in *the fact that the conscious person is continuous with a wider self through which saving experiences come,* a positive content of religious experience which, it seems to me, *is literally and objectively true as far as it goes.* If I now proceed to state my own hypothesis about the farther limits of this extension of our personality, I shall be offering my own over-belief—though I know it will appear a sorry under-belief to some of you—for which I can only bespeak the same indulgence which in a converse case I should accord to yours.

The further limits of our being plunge, it seems to me, into an altogether other dimension of existence from the sensible and merely 'understandable' world. Name it the mystical region, or the supernatural region, whichever you choose. So far as our ideal impulses originate in this region (and most of them do originate in it, for we find them possessing us in a way for which we cannot articulately account), we belong to it in a more intimate sense than that in which we belong to the visible world, for we belong in the most intimate sense wherever our ideals belong. Yet the unseen region in question is not merely ideal, for it produces effects in this world. When we commune with it, work is actually done upon our finite personality, for we are turned into new men, and consequences in the way of conduct follow in the natural world upon our regenerative change. But that which produces effects within another reality must be termed a reality itself, so I feel as if we had no philosophic excuse for calling the unseen or mystical world unreal.

God is the natural appellation, for us Christians at least, for the supreme reality, so I will call this higher part of the universe by the name of God. We and God have business with each other; and in opening ourselves to his influence our deepest destiny is fulfilled. The universe, at those parts of it which our personal being constitutes, takes a turn genuinely for the worse or for the better in proportion as each one of us fulfills or evades God's demands. As far as this goes, I probably have you with me, for I only translate into schematic language what I may call the instinctive belief of mankind: God is real since he produces real effects.

The real effects in question, so far as I have as yet admitted them, are exerted on the personal centres of energy of the various subjects, but the spontaneous faith of most of the subjects is that they embrace a wider sphere than this. Most religious men believe (or 'know,' if they be mystical) that not only they themselves, but the whole universe of beings to whom the God is present, are secure in his parental hands.

There is a sense, a dimension, they are sure, in which we are *all* saved, in spite of the gates of hell and all adverse terrestrial appearances. God's existence is the guarantee of an ideal order that shall be permanently preserved. This world may indeed, as science assures us, some day burn up or freeze; but if it is part of his order, the old ideals are sure to be brought elsewhere to fruition, so that where God is, tragedy is only provisional and partial, and shipwreck and dissolution are not the absolutely final things. Only when this farther step of faith concerning God is taken, and remote objective consequences are predicted, does religion, as it seems to me, get wholly free from the first immediate subjective experience, and bring a *real hypothesis* into play. A good hypothesis in science must have other properties than those of the phenomenon it is immediately invoked to explain, otherwise it is not prolific enough. God, meaning only what enters into the religious man's experience of union, falls short of being an hypothesis of this more useful order. He needs to enter into wider cosmic relations in order to justify the subject's absolute confidence and peace.

That the God with whom, starting from the hither side of our own extra-marginal self, we come at its remoter margin into commerce should be the absolute world-ruler, is of course a very considerable over-belief. Over-belief as it is, though, it is an article of almost every one's religion. Most of us pretend in some way to prop it upon our philosophy, but the philosophy itself is really propped upon this faith. What is this but to say that Religion, in her fullest exercise of function, is not a mere illumination of facts already elsewhere given, not a mere passion, like love, which views things in a rosier light. It is indeed that, as we have seen abundantly. But it is something more, namely a postulator of new *facts* as well. The world interpreted religiously is not the materialistic world over again, with an altered expression; it must have, over and above the altered expression, a natural constitution different at some point from that which a materialistic world would have. It must be such that different events can be expected in it, different conduct must be required.

This thoroughly 'pragmatic' view of religion has usually been taken as a matter of course by common men. They have interpolated divine miracles into the field of nature, they have built a heaven out beyond the grave. It is only transcendentalist metaphysicians who think that, without adding any concrete details to Nature, or subtracting any, but simply calling it the expression of absolute spirit, you make it more divine just as it stands. I believe the pragmatic way of taking religion to be the deeper way. It gives it body as well as soul, it makes it claim, as everything real must claim, some characteristic realm of fact as its very own. What the more characteristically divine facts are, apart from the actual inflow of energy in the faith-state and the prayer-state, I know not. But the over-belief on which I am ready to make my personal venture is that they exist. The whole drift of my education goes to persuade me that the world of our present consciousness is only one out of many worlds of consciousness that exist, and that those other worlds must contain experiences which have a meaning for our life also; and that although in the main their experiences and those of this world keep discrete, yet the two become continuous at certain points, and higher energies filter in. By being faithful in my poor measure to this over-belief, I seem to myself to keep more sane and true. I *can,* of course, put myself into the sectarian scientist's attitude, and imagine vividly that the world of sensations and of scientific laws and objects may be all. But whenever I do this, I hear that inward monitor . . . whispering the word 'bosh!' Humbug is humbug, even though it bear the scientific name, and the total expression of human experience, as I view it objectively, invincibly urges me beyond the narrow 'scientific' bounds. Assuredly, the real world is of a different temperament,—more intricately built than physical science allows. So my objective and my subjective conscience both hold me to the over-belief which I express. Who knows whether the faithfulness of individuals here below to their own poor over-beliefs may not actually help God in turn to be more effectively faithful to his own greater tasks?

X. INTRODUCTION

The intellectual system of Charles Saunders Peirce constituted an important advance in the long philosophical tradition behind pragmatism. The several hypotheses formulated by Peirce became the heart of the argument pragmatists were to make for the next generation. According to Peirce, whether or not knowledge had validity could be finally answered inductively, in a scientific way. He felt it was the community of investigators, rather than any single individual, that would validate the experimental method; the thought of the intellectual community was the collective mind that perceived the reality of the external object. Mathematical logic was to take the place of philosophical idealism; mathematical philosophy must become practical and seek to prove the reality of the intellectual community that was the basis of Peirce's vision.

William James could and did learn much from Peirce, but he could learn from no man to abandon his almost instinctive acceptance of individualism. Always at the center of what James was saying, one could find a sovereign individual whose singularity was much more vital than incidental membership in any group. Naturally enough, Peirce repudiated James's individualism.

In his characteristically uncluttered prose, James, in the following essay, shows why that system of thought called pragmatism must turn away from abstractions and *a priori* reasoning, from verbal solutions, first principles, and pretended absolutes. Pragmatism, he announced, must turn to facts, action, and power. Rejecting closed systems, James was obviously obliged to announce that pragmatism itself was a method not a system, a technique not a result, a genetic theory of truth. Theories therefore were useful as tools, not as ends. There is a complete rejection of transcendental idealism in the following essay, except insofar as such a system would give comfort to a certain class of minds, a class whose minds were given a brutal blow by Darwin's implied suggestion about the absence of design in nature. This essay is a convenient summary of the central tenets of this characteristically American philosophy.

X.

William James

WHAT PRAGMATISM MEANS

1907

Some years ago, being with a camping party in the mountains, I returned from a solitary ramble to find every one engaged in a ferocious metaphysical dispute. The *corpus* of the dispute was a squirrel—a live squirrel supposed to be clinging to one side of a tree-trunk; while over against the tree's opposite side a human being was imagined to stand. This human witness tries to get sight of the squirrel by moving rapidly round the tree, but no matter how fast he goes, the squirrel moves as

SOURCE. William James, *Pragmatism*, New York: Longmans, Green and Co., 1907, pp. 43–81. Copyright 1907 by William James. Reprinted by permission of Paul R. Reynolds Inc., 599 Fifth Avenue, New York 17, N.Y.

fast in the opposite direction, and always keeps the tree between himself and the man, so that never a glimpse of him is caught. The resultant metaphysical problem now is this: *Does the man go round the squirrel or not?* He goes round the tree, sure enough, and the squirrel is on the tree; but does he go round the squirrel? In the unlimited leisure of the wilderness, discussion had been worn threadbare. Every one had taken sides, and was obstinate; and the numbers on both sides were even. Each side, when I appeared therefore appealed to me to make it a majority. Mindful of the scholastic adage that whenever you meet a contradiction you must make a distinction, I immediately sought and found one, as follows: "Which party is right," I said, "depends on what you *practically mean* by 'going round' the squirrel. If you mean passing from the north of him to the east, then to the south, then to the west, and then to the north of him again, obviously the man does go round him, for he occupies these successive positions. But if on the contrary you mean being first in front of him, then on the right of him, then behind him, then on his left, and finally in front again, it is quite as obvious that the man fails to go round him, for by the compensating movements the squirrel makes, he keeps his belly turned towards the man all the time, and his back turned away. Make the distinction, and there is no occasion for any farther dispute. You are both right and both wrong according as you conceive the verb 'to go round' in one practical fashion or the other."

Although one or two of the hotter disputants called my speech a shuffling evasion, saying they wanted no quibbling or scholastic hairsplitting, but meant just plain honest English 'round,' the majority seemed to think that the distinction had assuaged the dispute.

I tell this trivial anecdote because it is a peculiarly simple example of what I wish now to speak of as *the pragmatic method*. The pragmatic method is primarily a method of settling metaphysical disputes that otherwise might be interminable. Is the world one or many?—fated or free?—material or spiritual?—here are notions either of which may or may not hold good of the world; and disputes over such notions are unending. The pragmatic method in such cases is to try to interpret each notion by tracing its respective practical consequences. What difference would it practically make to any one if this notion rather than that notion were true? If no practical difference whatever can be traced, then the alternatives mean practically the same thing, and all dispute is idle. Whenever a dispute is serious, we ought to be able to show some practical difference that must follow from one side or the other's being right.

A glance at the history of the idea will show you still better what pragmatism means. The term is derived from the same Greek word πράγμα, meaning action, from which our words 'practice' and 'practical' come. It was first introduced into philosophy by Mr. Charles Peirce in 1878. In an article entitled 'How to Make Our Ideas Clear,' in the *Popular Science Monthly* for January of that year Mr. Peirce, after pointing out that our beliefs are really rules for action, said that, to develop a thought's meaning, we need only determine what conduct it is fitted to produce: that conduct is for us its sole significance. And the tangible fact at the root of all our thought-distinctions, however subtle, is that there is no one of them so fine as to consist in anything but a possible difference of practice. To attain perfect clearness in our thoughts of an object, then, we need only consider what conceivable effects of a practical kind the object may involve—what sensations we are to expect from it, and what reactions we must prepare. Our conception of these effects, whether immediate or remote, is then for us the whole of our conception of the object, so far as that conception has positive significance at all.

This is the principle of Peirce, the principle of pragmatism. It lay entirely unnoticed by any one for twenty years, until I, in an address before Professor Howison's philosophical union at the university of California, brought it forward again and made a special application of it to religion. By that date (1898) the times seemed ripe for its reception. The word 'pragmatism' spread, and at present it fairly spots the pages of the philosophic journals. On all hands we find the 'pragmatic movement' spoken of, sometimes with respect, sometimes with contumely, seldom with clear understanding. It is evident that the term applies itself conveniently to a number of tendencies that hitherto have lacked a collective name, and that it has 'come to stay.'

To take in the importance of Peirce's principle, one must get accustomed to applying it to concrete cases. I found a few years ago that Ostwald, the illustrious Leipzig chemist, had been making perfectly distinct use of the principle of pragmatism in his lectures on the philosophy of science, though he had not called it by that name.

"All realities influence our practice," he wrote me, "and that influence is their meaning for us. I am accustomed to put questions to my classes in this way: In what respects would the world be different if this alternative or that were true? If I can find nothing that would become different, then the alternative has no sense."

That is, the rival views mean practically the same thing, and meaning, other than practical, there is for us none. Ostwald in a published lecture gives this example of what he means. Chemists have long wrangled over the inner constitution of certain bodies called 'tautomerous.' Their properties seemed equally consistent with the notion that an instable hydrogen atom oscillates inside of them, or that they are instable mixtures of two bodies. Controversy raged, but never was decided. "It would never have begun," says Ostwald, "if the combatants had asked themselves what particular experimental fact could have been made different by one or the other view being correct. For it would then have appeared that no difference of fact could possibly ensue; and the quarrel was as unreal as if, theorizing in primitive times about the raising of dough by yeast, one party should have invoked a 'brownie,' while another insisted on an 'elf' as the true cause of the phenomenon."

It is astonishing to see how many philosophical disputes collapse into insignificance the moment you subject them to this simple test of tracing a concrete consequence. There can *be* no difference anywhere that doesn't *make* a difference elsewhere—no difference in abstract truth that doesn't express itself in a difference in concrete fact and in conduct consequent upon that fact, imposed on somebody, somehow, somewhere, and somewhen. The whole function of philospohy ought to be to find out what definite difference it will make to you and me, at definite instants of our life, if this world-formula or that world-formula be the true one.

There is absolutely nothing new in the pragmatic method. Socrates was an adept at it. Aristotle used it methodically. Locke, Berkeley, and Hume made momentous contributions to truth by its means. Shadworth Hodgson keeps insisting that realities are only what they are 'known as.' But these forerunners of pragmatism used it in fragments: they were preluders only. Not until in our time has it generalized itself, become conscious of a universal mission, pretended to a conquering destiny. I believe in that destiny, and I hope I may end by inspiring you with my belief.

Pragmatism represents a perfectly familiar attitude in philosophy, the empiricist attitude, but it represents it, as it seems to me, both in a more radical and in a less objectionable form than it has ever yet assumed. A pragmatist turns his back resolutely and once for all upon a lot of inveterate habits dear to professional philosophers. He turns away from abstraction and insufficiency, from verbal solutions, from bad *a priori* reasons, from fixed principles, closed systems, and pretended absolutes and origins. He turns towards concreteness and adequacy, towards facts, towards action and towards power. That means the empiricist temper regnant and the rationalist temper sincerely given up. It means the open air and possibilities of nature, as against dogma, artificiality, and the pretence of finality in truth.

At the same time it does not stand for any special results. It is a method only. But the general triumph of that method would mean an enormous change in what I called in my last lecture the 'temperament' of philosophy. Teachers of the ultrarationalistic type would be frozen out, much as the courtier type is frozen out in republics, as the ultramontane type of priest is frozen out in Protestant lands. Science and metaphysics would come much nearer together, would in fact work absolutely hand in hand.

Metaphysics has usually followed a very primitive kind of quest. You know how men have always hankered after unlawful magic, and you know what a great part in magic *words* have always played. If you have his name, or the formula of incantation that binds him, you can control the spirit, genie, afrite, or whatever the power may be. Solomon knew the names of all the spirits, and having their names, he held them subject to his will. So the universe has always appeared to the natural mind as a kind of enigma, of which the key must be sought in the shape of some illuminating or power-bringing word or name. That word names the universe's *principle,* and to possess it is after a fashion to possess the universe itself. 'God,' 'Matter,' 'Reason,' 'the Absolute,' 'Energy,' are so many solving names. You can rest when you have them. You are at the end of your metaphysical quest.

But if you follow the pragmatic method, you cannot look on any such word as closing your quest. You must bring out of each word its practical cash-value, set it at work within the stream of your experience. It appears less as a solution, then, than as a program for more work, and more particularly as an indication of the ways in which existing realities may be *changed.*

Theories thus become instruments, not answers to enigmas, in which we can rest. We don't lie back upon them, we move forward, and, on occasion, make nature over again by their aid. Pragmatism unstiffens all our theories, limbers them up and sets each one at work. Being nothing essentially new, it harmonizes with many ancient philosophic tendencies. It agrees with nominalism for instance, in always appealing to particulars; with utilitarianism in emphasizing practical aspects; with positivism in its disdain for verbal solutions, useless questions and metaphysical abstractions.

All these, you see, are *anti-intellectualist* tendencies. Against rationalism as a pretension and a method pragmatism is fully armed and militant. But, at the outset, at least, it stands for no particular results. It has no dogmas, and no doctrines save its method. As the young Italian pragmatist Papini has well said, it lies in the midst of our theories, like a corridor in a hotel. Innumerable chambers open out of it. In one you may find a man writing an atheistic volume; in the next some one on his knees praying for faith and strength; in a third a chemist investigating a body's properties. In a fourth a system of idealistic metaphysics is being excogitated; in a fifth the impossibility of metaphysics is being shown. But they all own the corridor, and all must pass through it if they want a practicable way of getting into or out of their respective rooms.

No particular results then, so far, but only an attitude of orientation, is what the pragmatic method means. *The attitude of looking away from first things, principles, 'categories,' supposed necessities; and of looking towards last things, fruits, consequences, facts.*

So much for the pragmatic method! You may say that I have been praising it rather than explaining it to you, but I shall presently explain it abundantly enough by showing how it works on some familiar problems. Meanwhile the word pragmatism has come to be used in a still wider sense, as meaning also a certain *theory of truth.* . . .

One of the most successfully cultivated branches of philosophy in our time is what is called inductive logic, the study of the conditions under which our sciences have evolved. Writers on this subject have begun to show a singular unanimity as to what the laws of nature and elements of fact mean, when formulated by mathematicians, physicists and chemists. When the first mathematical, logical, and natural uniformities, the first *laws*, were discovered, men were so carried away by the clearness, beauty and simplification that resulted, that they believed themselves to have deciphered authentically the eternal thoughts of the Almighty. His mind also thundered and reverberated in syllogisms. He also thought in conic sections, squares and roots and ratios, and geometrized like Euclid. He made Kepler's laws for the planets to follow; he made velocity increase proportionately to the time in falling bodies; he made the law of the sines for light to obey when refracted; he established the classes, orders, families and genera of plants and animals, and fixed the distances between them. He thought the archetypes of all things and devised their variations; and when we rediscover any one of these his wondrous institutions, we seize his mind in its very literal intention.

But as the sciences have developed farther, the notion has gained ground that most, perhaps all, of our laws are only approximations. The laws themselves, moreover, have grown so numerous that there is no counting them; and so many rival formulations are proposed in all the branches of science that investigators have become accustomed to the notion that no theory is absolutely a transcript of reality, but that any one of them may from some point of view be useful. Their great use is to summarize old facts and to lead to new ones. They are only a man-made language, a conceptual shorthand, as some one calls them, in which we write our reports of nature; and languages, as is well known, tolerate much choice of expression and many dialects.

Thus human arbitrariness has driven divine necessity from scientific logic. If I mention the names of Sigwart, Mach, Ostwald, Pearson, Milhaud, Poincaré, Duhem, Ruyssen, those of you who are students will easily identify the tendency I speak of, and will think of additional names.

Riding now on the front of this wave of scientific logic Messrs. Schiller and Dewey appear with their pragmatistic account of what truth everywhere signifies. Everywhere, these teachers say, 'truth' in our ideas and beliefs means the same thing that it means in science. It means, they say, nothing but this, *that ideas (which themselves are but parts of our experience) become true just in so far as they help us to get into satisfactory relation with other parts of our experience,* to summarize them and get about among them by conceptual short-cuts instead of following the interminable succession of particular phenomena. Any idea upon which we can ride, so to speak; any idea that will carry us prosperously from any one part of our experience to any other part, linking things satisfactorily, working securely, simplifying, saving labor; is true for just so much, true in so far forth, true *instrumentally.* This is the 'instrumental' view of truth taught so successfully at Chicago, the view that truth in our ideas means their power to 'work,' promulgated so brilliantly at Oxford.

Messrs. Dewey, Schiller and their allies, in reaching this general conception of all truth, have only followed the example of geologists, biologists and philologists. In the establishment of these other sciences, the successful stroke was always to take some simple process actually observable in operation—as denudation by weather, say, or variation from parental type, or change of dialect by incorporation of new words and pronunciations—and then to generalize it, making it apply to all times, and produce great results by summating its effects through the ages.

The observable process which Schiller and Dewey particularly singled out for generalization is the familiar one by which any individual settles into *new opinions*. The process here is always the same. The individual has a stock of old opinions already, but he meets a new experience that puts them to a strain. Somebody contradicts them; or in a reflective moment he discovers that they contradict each other; or he hears of facts with which they are incompatible; or desires arise in him which they cease to satisfy. The result is an inward trouble to which his mind till then had been a stranger, and from which he seeks to escape by modifying his previous mass of opinions. He saves as much of it as he can, for in this matter of belief we are all extreme conservatives. So he tries to change first this opinion, and then that (for they resist change very variously), until at last some new idea comes up which he can graft upon the ancient stock with a minimum of disturbance of the latter, some idea that mediates between the stock and the new experience and runs them into one another most felicitously and expediently.

This new idea is then adopted as the true one. It preserves the older stock of truths with a minimum of modification, stretching them just enough to make them admit the novelty, but conceiving that in ways as familiar as the case leaves possible. An *outrée* explanation, violating all our preconceptions, would never pass for a true account of a novelty. We should scratch round industriously till we found something less excentric. The most violent revolutions in an individual's beliefs leave most of his old order standing. Time and space, cause and effect, nature and history, and one's own biography remain untouched. New truth is always a go-between, a smoother-over of transitions. It marries old opinion to new fact so as ever to show a minimum of jolt, a maximum of continuity. We hold a theory true just in proportion to its success in solving this 'problem of maxima and minima.' But success in solving this problem is eminently a matter of approximation. We say this theory solves it on the whole more satisfactorily than that theory; but that means more satisfactorily to ourselves, and individuals will emphasize their points of satisfaction differently. To a certain degree, therefore, everything here is plastic.

The point I now urge you to observe particularly is the part played by the older truths. Failure to take account of it is the source of much of the unjust criticism levelled against pragmatism. Their influence is absolutely controlling. Loyalty to them is the first principle—in most cases it is the only principle; for by far the most usual way of handling phenomena so novel that they would make for a serious rearrangement of our preconception is to ignore them altogether, or to abuse those who bear witness for them.

You doubtless wish examples of this process of truth's growth, and the only trouble is their superabundance. The simplest case of new truth is of course the mere numerical addition of new kinds of facts, or of new single facts of old kinds, to our experience—an addition that involves no alteration in the old beliefs. Day follows day, and its contents are simply added. The new contents themselves are not true, they simply *come* and *are.* Truth is *what we say about* them, and when we say that they have come, truth is satisfied by the plain additive formula.

But often the day's contents oblige a rearrangement. If I should now utter piercing shrieks and act like a maniac on this platform, it would make many of you revise your ideas as to the probable worth of my philosophy. 'Radium' came the other day as part of the day's content, and seemed for a moment to contradict our ideas of the whole order of nature, that order having come to be identified with what is called the conservation of energy. The mere sight of radium paying heat away indefinitely out of its own pocket seemed to violate that conservation. What to think? If the radiations from it were nothing but an escape of unsuspected 'potential' energy, pre-existent inside of the atoms, the principle of conservation would be saved. The discovery of 'helium' as the radiation's outcome, opened a way to this belief. So Ramsay's view is generally held to be true, because, although it extends our old ideas of energy, it causes a minimum of alteration in their nature.

I need not multiply instances. A new opinion counts as 'true' just in proportion as it gratifies the individual's desire to assimilate the novel in his experience to his beliefs in stock. It must both lean on old truth and grasp new fact; and its success (as I said a moment ago) in doing this, is a matter for the individual's appreciation. When old truth grows, then, by new truth's addition, it is for subjective reasons. We are in the process and obey the reasons. That new idea is truest which performs most felicitously its function of satisfying our double urgency. It makes itself true, gets itself classed as true, by the way it works; grafting itself then upon the ancient body of truth, which thus grows much as a tree grows by the activity of a new layer of cambium.

Now Dewey and Schiller proceed to generalize this observation and to apply it to the most ancient parts of truth. They also once were plastic. They also were called true for human reasons. They also mediated between still earlier truths and what in those days were novel observations. Purely objective truth, truth in whose establishment the function of giving human satisfaction in marrying previous parts of experience with newer parts played no role whatever, is nowhere to be found. The reasons why we call things true is the reason why they *are* true, for 'to be true' *means* only to perform this marriage-function.

The trail of the human serpent is thus over everything. Truth independent; truth that we *find* merely; truth no longer malleable to human need; truth incorrigible, in a word; such truth exists indeed superabundantly—or is supposed to exist by rationalistically minded thinkers; but then it means only the dead heart of the living tree, and its being there means only that truth also has its paleontology, and its 'prescription,' and may grow stiff with years of veteran service and petrified in men's regard by sheer antiquity. But how plastic even the oldest truths nevertheless really are has been vividly shown in our day by the transformation of logical and mathematical ideas, a transformation which seems even to be invading physics. The ancient formulas are reinterpreted as special expressions of much wider principles, principles that our ancestors never got a glimpse of in their present shape and formulation.

Mr. Schiller still gives to all this view of truth the name of 'Humanism,' but, for this doctrine too, the name of pragmatism seems fairly to be in the ascendant, so I will treat it under the name of pragmatism in these lectures.

Such then would be the scope of pragmatism—first, a method,

and second, a genetic theory of what is meant by truth. And these two things must be our future topics.

What I have said of the theory of truth will, I am sure, have appeared obscure and unsatisfactory to most of you by reason of its brevity. I shall make amends for that hereafter. In a lecture on 'common sense' I shall try to show what I mean by truths grown petrified by antiquity. In another lecture I shall expatiate on the idea that our thoughts become true in proportion as they successfully exert their go-between function. In a third I shall show how hard it is to discriminate subjective from objective factors in Truth's development. You may not follow me wholly in these lectures; and if you do, you may not wholly agree with me. But you will, I know, regard me at least as serious, and treat my effort with respectful consideration.

You will probably be surprised to learn, then, that Messrs. Schiller's and Dewey's theories have suffered a hailstorm of contempt and ridicule. All rationalism has risen against them. In influential quarters Mr. Schiller, in particular, has been treated like an impudent schoolboy who deserves a spanking. I should not mention this, but for the fact that it throws so much sidelight upon that rationalistic temper to which I have opposed the temper of pragmatism. Pragmatism is uncomfortable away from facts. Rationalism is comfortable only in the presence of abstractions. This pragmatist talk about truths in the plural, about their utility and satisfactoriness, about the success with which they 'work,' etc., suggests to the typical intellectualist mind a sort of coarse lame second-rate makeshift article of truth. Such truths are not real truth. Such tests are merely subjective. As against this, objective truth must be something non-utilitarian, haughty, refined, remote, august, exalted. It must be an absolute correspondence of our thoughts with an equally absolute reality. It must be what we *ought* to think unconditionally. The conditioned ways in which we *do* think are so much irrelevance and matter for psychology. Down with psychology, up with logic, in all this question!

See the exquisite contrast of the types of mind! The pragmatist clings to facts and concreteness, observes truth at its work in particular cases, and generalizes. Truth, for him, becomes a class-name for all sorts of definite working-values in experience. For the rationalist it remains a pure abstraction, to the bare name of which we must defer. When the pragmatist undertakes to show in detail just *why* we must defer, the rationalist is unable to recognize the concretes from which his own abstraction is taken. He accuses us of *denying* truth; whereas we have only sought to trace exactly why people follow it and always ought to follow it. Your typical ultra-abstractionist fairly shudders at concreteness: other things equal, he positively prefers the pale and spectral. If the two universes were offered, he would always choose the skinny outline rather than the rich thicket of reality. It is so much purer, clearer, nobler.

I hope that as these lectures go on, the concreteness and closeness to facts of the pragmatism which they advocate may be what approves itself to you as its most satisfactory peculiarity. It only follows here the example of the sister-sciences, interpreting the unobserved by the observed. It brings old and new harmoniously together. It converts the absolutely empty notion of a static relation of 'correspondence' . . . between our minds and reality, into that of a rich and active commerce (that any one may follow in detail and understand) between particular thoughts of ours, and the great universe of other experiences in which they play their parts and have their uses.

But enough of this at present! The justification of what I say must be postponed. I wish now to add a word in further explanation of the claim I made at our last meeting, that pragmatism may be a happy harmonizer of empiricist ways of thinking with the more religious demands of human beings.

Men who are strongly of the fact-loving temperament, you may remember me to have said, are liable to be kept at a distance by the small sympathy with facts which that philosophy from the present-day fashion of idealism offers them. It is far too intellectualistic. Old fashioned theism was bad enough, with its notion of God as an exalted monarch, made up of a lot of unintelligible or preposterous 'attributes'; but, so long as it held strongly by the argument from design, it kept some touch with concrete realities. Since, however, Darwinism has once for all displaced design from the minds of the 'scientific,' theism has lost that foothold; and some kind of an immanent or pantheistic deity working *in* things rather than above them is, if any, the kind recommended to our contemporary imagination. Aspirants to a philosophic religion turn, as a rule, more hopefully nowadays towards idealistic pantheism than towards the older dualistic theism, in spite of the fact that the latter still counts able defenders.

But . . . the brand of pantheism offered is hard for them to assimilate if they are lovers of facts, or empirically minded. It is the absolutistic brand, spurning the dust and reared upon pure logic. It keeps no connexion whatever with concreteness. Affirming the Absolute Mind, which is its substitute for God, to be the rational presupposition of all particulars of fact, whatever they may be, it remains supremely indifferent to what the particular facts in our world actually are. Be they what they may, the Absolute will father them. Like the sick lion in Esop's fable, all footprints lead into his den, but *nulla vestigia retrorsum.* You cannot redescend into the world of particulars by the Absolute's aid, or deduce any necessary consequences of detail important for your life from your idea of his nature. He gives you indeed the assurance that all is well with *Him,* and for his eternal way of thinking; but thereupon he leaves you to be finitely saved by your own temporal devices.

Far be it from me to deny the majesty of this conception, or its capacity to yield religious comfort to a most respectable class of minds. But from the human point of view, no one can pretend that is doesn't suffer from the faults of remoteness and abstractness. It is eminently a product of what I have ventured to call the rationalistic temper. It disdains empiricism's needs. It substitutes a pallid outline for the real world's richness. It is dapper, it is noble in the bad sense, in the sense in which to be noble is to be inapt for humble service. In this real world of sweat and dirt, it seems to me that when a view of things is 'noble,' that ought to count as a presumption against its truth, and as a philosophic disqualification. The prince of darkness may be a gentleman, as we are told he is, but whatever the God of earth and heaven is, he can surely be no gentleman. His menial services are needed in the dust of our human trials, even more than his dignity is needed in the empyrean.

Now pragmatism, devoted though she be to facts, has no such materialistic bias as ordinary empiricism labors under. Moreover, she has no objection whatever to the realizing of abstractions, so long as you get about among particulars with their aid and they actually carry you somewhere. Interested in no conclusions but those which our minds and our experiences work out together, she has no *a priori* prejudices against theology. *If theological ideas prove to have a value for concrete life, they will be true, for pragmatism, in the sense of being good for so much. For how much more they are true, will depend entirely on their relations to the other truths that also have to be acknowledged.*

What I said just now about the Absolute of transcendental idealism, is a case in point. First, I called it majestic and said it yielded religious comfort to a class of minds, and then I accused it of remoteness and sterility. But so far as it affords such comfort, it surely is not sterile;

it has that amount of value; it performs a concrete function. As a good pragmatist, I myself ought to call the Absolute true 'in so far forth,' then; and I unhesitatingly now do so.

But what does *true in so far forth* mean in this case? To answer, we need only apply the pragmatic method. What do believers in the Absolute mean by saying that their belief affords them comfort? They mean that since, in the Absolute finite evil is 'overruled' already, we may, therefore, whenever we wish, treat the temporal as if it were potentially the eternal, be sure that we can trust its outcome, and, without sin, dismiss our fear and drop the worry of our finite responsibility. In short, they mean that we have a right ever and anon to take a moral holiday, to let the world wag in its own way, feeling that its issues are in better hands than ours and are none of our business.

The universe is a system of which the individual members may relax their anxieties occasionally, in which the don't-care mood is also right for men, and moral holidays in order,—that, if I mistake not, is part, at least, of what the Absolute is 'known-as,' that is the great difference in our particular experiences which his being true makes, for us, that is his cash-value when he is pragmatically interpreted. Farther than that the ordinary lay-reader in philosophy who thinks favorably of absolute idealism does not venture to sharpen his conceptions. He can use the Absolute for so much, and so much is very precious. He is pained at hearing you speak incredulously of the Absolute, therefore, and disregards your criticisms because they deal with aspects of the conception that he fails to follow.

If the Absolute means this, and means no more than this, who can possibly deny the truth of it? To deny it would be to insist that men should never relax, and that holidays are never in order.

I am well aware how odd it must seem to some of you to hear me say that an idea is 'true' so long as to believe it is profitable to our lives. That it is *good,* for as much as it profits, you will gladly admit. If what we do by its aid is good, you will allow the idea itself to be good in so far forth, for we are the better for possessing it. But is it not a strange misuse of the word 'truth,' you will say, to call ideas also 'true' for this reason?

To answer this difficulty fully is impossible at this stage of my account. . . . Let me now say only this, that truth is *one species of good,* and not, as is usually supposed, a category distinct from good, and coordinate with it. *The true is the name of whatever proves itself to be good in the way of belief, and good, too, for definite, assignable reasons.* Surely you must admit this, that if there were *no* good for life in true ideas, or if the knowledge of them were positively disadvantageous and false ideas the only useful ones, then the current notion that truth is divine and precious, and its pursuit a duty, could never have grown up or become a dogma. In a world like that, our duty would be to *shun* truth, rather. But in this world, just as certain foods are not only agreeable to our taste, but good for our teeth, our stomach, and our tissues; so certain ideas are not only agreeable to think about, or agreeable as supporting other ideas that we are fond of, but they are also helpful in life's practical struggles. If there be any life that it is really better we should lead, and if there be any idea which, if believed in, would help us to lead that life, then it would be really *better for us* to believe in that idea, *unless, indeed, belief in it incidentally clashed with other greater vital benefits.*

'What would be better for us to believe'! This sounds very like a definition of truth. It comes very near to saying 'what we *ought* to believe': and in *that* definition none of you would find any oddity. Ought we ever not to believe what it is *better for us* to believe? And can we then keep the notion of what is better for us, and what is true for us, permanently apart?

Pragmatism says no, and I fully agree with her. Probably you also agree, so far as the abstract statement goes, but with a suspicion that if we practically did believe everything that made for good in our own personal lives, we should be found indulging all kinds of fancies about this world's affairs, and all kinds of sentimental superstitions about a world hereafter. Your suspicion here is undoubtedly well founded, and it is evident that something happens when you pass from the abstract to the concrete that complicates the situation.

I said just now that what is better for us to believe is true *unless the belief incidentally clashes with some other vital benefit.* Now in real life what vital benefits is any particular belief of ours most liable to clash with? What indeed except the vital benefits yielded by *other beliefs* when these prove incompatible with the first ones? In other words, the greatest enemy of any one of our truths may be the rest of our truths. Truths have once for all this desperate instinct of self-preservation and of desire to extinguish whatever contradicts them. My belief in the Absolute, based on the good it does me, must run the gauntlet of all my other beliefs. Grant that it may be true in giving me a moral holiday. Nevertheless, as I conceive it,—and let me speak now confidentially, as it were, and merely in my own private person,—it clashes with other truths of mine whose benefits I hate to give up on its account. It happens to be associated with a kind of logic of which I am the enemy, I find that it entangles me in metaphysical paradoxes that are inacceptable, etc., etc. But as I have enough trouble in life already without adding the trouble of carrying these intellectual inconsistencies, I personally just give up the Absolute. I just *take* my moral holidays; or else as a professional philosopher, I try to justify them by some other principle.

If I could restrict my notion of the Absolute to its bare holiday-giving value, it wouldn't clash with my other truths. But we can not easily thus restrict our hypotheses. They carry supernumerary features, and these it is that clash so. My disbelief in the Absolute means then disbelief in those other supernumerary features, for I fully believe in the legitimacy of taking moral holidays.

You see by this what I meant when I called pragmatism a mediator and reconciler and said, borrowing the word from Papini, that she 'unstiffens' our theories. She has in fact no prejudices whatever, no obstructive dogmas, no rigid canons of what shall count as proof. She is completely genial. She will entertain any hypothesis, she will consider any evidence. It follows that in the religious field she is at a great disadvantage both over positivistic empiricism, with its anti-theological bias, and over religious rationalism, with its exclusive interest in the remote, the noble, the simple, and the abstract in the way of conception.

In short, she widens the field of search for God. Rationalism sticks to logic and the empyrean. Empiricism sticks to the external senses. Pragmatism is willing to take anything, to follow either logic or the senses and to count the humblest and most personal experiences. She will count mystical experiences if they have practical consequences. She will take a God who lives in the very dirt of private fact—if that should seem a likely place to find him.

Her only test of probable truth is what works best in the way of leading us, what fits every part of life best and combines with the collectivity of experience's demands, nothing being omitted. If theological ideas should do this, if the notion of God, in particular, should prove to do it, how could pragmatism possibly deny God's existence? She could see no meaning in treating as 'not true' a notion that was pragmatically so successful. What other kind of truth could there be, for her, than all this agreement with concrete reality?

. . . But you see already how democratic she [pragmatism] is. Her manners are as various and flexible, her resources as rich and endless, and her conclusions as friendly as those of mother nature.

XI. INTRODUCTION

The attack on idealism in social theory is exemplified in the work of Herbert Croly (1869–1930). In *The Promise of American Life,* 1909, Croly spelled out an important thought that was a result of his own recoil from what he believed to be traditional American idealism. The combination of optimism and fatalism that Croly believed to be characteristic of American life had led inevitably, in his view, to social conservatism. He was persuaded that indigenous optimism had led Americans to think in terms of an inevitable and manifest destiny which would come to pass because Americans were Americans. Such faith in the future, according to Croly, could only destroy the most desirable future. Jeffersonianism—the national illusion and delusion— had led Americans to stress individualism and weak government. Moral preachment and sentimentalism could not compete with the efficiency and power of the political boss or with that of the captain of industry.

The restoration of individualism was not the cure for the evils that individualism had created. Old laws were no answer to problems which were in part created by those laws. Reform would have to be national in scope, and only a strong and vigorous national government could undertake that reform. The new community of America required a new conception of the public interest, as opposed to the private rights of individuals, and demanded a new role for the national government. Individualism had to be subordinated to the welfare of the community. In the shorthand of American political history, Croly said that the cure would be a democratized Hamiltonianism.

Hard social analysis, coupled with an understanding of power—not the kind of blind faith typical of Jesus and Tolstoy—was the means to the end as Croly envisaged it. The rejection of truths that Americans had taken to be self-evident was essential to Croly's blueprint for social change. His tough realism and celebration of national power recommended his analysis to Theodore Roosevelt. Providing an important part of the intellectual background of Roosevelt's "new nationalism," Croly's book, a selection from which is presented here, was an influential and pithy contribution to American thought about the political economy.

XI.

Herbert Croly

THE PROMISE OF AMERICAN LIFE
1909

The changes which have been taking place in industrial and political and social conditions have all tended to impair the consistency of feeling characteristic of the first phase of American national democracy. Americans are divided from one another much more than they were during the Middle Period by differences of interest, of intellectual outlook, of moral and technical standards, and of manner of life. Grave inequalities of power and deep-lying differences of purpose have developed in relation of the several primary American activities. The millionaire, the "Boss," the union laborer, and the lawyer, have all taken advantage of the loose American political organization to promote somewhat unscrupulously their own interests, and to obtain special sources of power and profit at the expense of a wholesome national balance. But the foregoing examples of specialized organization and purposes do not stand alone. They are the most conspicuous and the most troublesome because of the power wielded by those particular classes, and because they can claim for their purposes the support of certain aspects of the American national tradition. Yet the same process has been taking place in all the other departments of American social and intellectual life. Technical experts of all kinds— engineers, men of letters, and artists—have all of them been asserting much more vigorously their own special interests and purposes. In so asserting themselves they cannot claim the support of the American national democratic convention. On the contrary, the proclamation of high technical standards and of insistent individual purposes is equivalent to a revolt from the traditions of the Middle Period, which were all in favor of cheap work and the average worker. But different as is the situation of these technical experts, the fundamental meaning of their self-assertion is analogous to that of the millionaire and the "Boss." The vast incoherent mass of the American people is falling into definite social

SOURCE. Herbert Croly, *The Promise of American Life,* New York: The Macmillan Co., 1909, pp. 138–140, 148–154, and 281–284. Reprinted with the permission of The Macmillan Co. Copyright 1909, The Macmillan Co.

groups, which restrict and define the mental outlook and social experience of their members. The all-round man of the innocent Middle Period has become the exception. The earlier homogeneity of American society has been impaired, and no authoritative and edifying, but conscious, social ideal has as yet taken its place.

The specialized organization of American industry, politics, and labor, and the increasingly severe special discipline imposed upon the individual, are not to be considered as evils. On the contrary, they are indications of greater practical efficiency, and they contain a promise of individual moral and intellectual emancipation. But they have their serious and perilous aspects, because no sufficient provision has been made for them in the national democratic tradition. What it means is that the American nation is being confronted by a problem which the earlier national democracy expected to avoid—the social problem. By the social problem is usually meant the problem of poverty; but grave inequalities of wealth are merely the most dangerous and distressing expression of fundamental differences among the members of a society of interest and of intellectual and moral standards. In its deepest aspect, consequently, the social problem is the problem of preventing such divisions from dissolving the society into which they enter—of keeping such a highly differentiated society fundamentally sound and whole.

In this country the solution of the social problem demands the substitution of a conscious social ideal for the earlier instinctive homogeneity of the American nation. That homogeneity has disappeared never to return. We should not want it to return, because it was dependent upon too many sacrifices of individual purpose and achievement. But a democracy cannot dispense with the solidarity which it imparted to American life, and in one way or another such solidarity must be restored. There is only one way in which it can be restored, and that is by means of a democratic social ideal, which shall give consistency to American social life, without entailing any essential sacrifice of desirable individual and class distinctions. I have used the word "restoration" to describe this binding and healing process; but the consistency which would result from the loyal realization of a comprehensive coherent democratic social ideal would differ radically from the earlier American homogeneity of feeling. The solidarity which it would impart to American society would have its basis in feeling and its results in good fellowship; but it must always remain a promise and constructive ideal rather than a finished performance. The social problem must, as long as societies continue to endure, be solved afresh by almost every generation; and the one chance of progress depends both upon an invincible loyalty to a constructive social ideal and upon a correct understanding by the new generation of the actual experience of its predecessors. . . .

The prevailing preconception of the reformers, that the existing evils and abuses have been due chiefly to the energy and lack of scruple with which business men and politicians have taken advantage of the good but easy-going American, and that a general increase of moral energy, assisted by some minor legal changes, will restore the balance,—such a conception of the situation is less than half true. No doubt, the "plain people" of the United States have been morally indifferent, and have allowed unscrupulous special interests to usurp too much power; but that is far from being the whole story. The unscrupulous energy of the "Boss" or the "tainted" millionaire is vitally related to the moral indifference of the "plain people." Both of them have been encouraged to believe by the nature of our traditional ideas and institutions that a man could be patriotic without being either public-spirited or disinterested. The democratic state has been conceived as a piece of political machinery, which existed for the purpose of securing certain individual rights and opportunities—the expectation being that the greatest individual happiness would be thereby promoted, and one which harmonized with the public interest. Consequently when the "Boss" and the "tainted" millionaire took advantage of this situation to secure for themselves an unusually large amount of political and economic power, they were putting into practice an idea which traditionally had been entirely respectable, and which during the pioneer period had not worked badly. On the other hand, when the mass of American voters failed to detect the danger of such usurpation until it had gone altogether too far, they, too, were not without warrant for their lethargy and callousness. They, too, in a smaller way had considered the American political and economic system chiefly as a system framed for their individual benefit, and it did not seem sportsmanlike to turn and rend their more successful competitors, until they were told that the "trusts" and the "Bosses" were violating the sacred principle of equal rights. Thus the abuses of which we are complaining are not weeds which have been allowed to spring up from neglect, and which can be eradicated by a man with a hoe. They are cultivated plants, which, if not precisely specified in the plan of the American political and economic garden, have at least been encouraged by traditional methods of cultivation.

The fact that this dangerous usurpation of power has been accomplished partly by illegal methods has blinded many reformers to two considerations, which have a vital relation to both the theory and the practice of reform. Violation of the law was itself partly the result of conflicting and unwise state legislation, and for this reason did not seem very heinous either to its perpetrators or to public opinion. But even if the law had not been violated, similar results would have followed. Under the traditional American system, with the freedom permitted to the individual, with the restriction placed on the central authority, and with its assumption of a substantial identity between the individual and the public interest—under such a system unusually energetic and unscrupulous men were bound to seize a kind and an amount of political and economic power which was not entirely wholesome. They had a license to do so; and if they had failed to take advantage thereof, their failure would have been an indication, not of disinterestedness or moral impeccability, but of sheer weakness and inefficiency.

How utterly confusing it is, consequently, to consider reform as equivalent merely to the restoration of the American democracy to a former condition of purity and excellence! Our earlier political and economic condition was not at its best a fit subject for any great amount of complacency. It cannot be restored, even if we would; and the public interest has nothing to gain by its restoration. The usurpation of power by "trusts" and "Bosses" is more than anything else an expression of a desirable individual initiative and organizing ability—which have been allowed to become dangerous and partly corrupt, because of the incoherence and the lack of purpose and responsibility in the traditional American political and economic system. A "purification" might well destroy the good with the evil; and even if it were successful in eradicating certain abuses, would only prepare the way for the outbreak in another form of the tendency towards individual aggrandizement and social classification. No amount of moral energy, directed merely towards the enforcement of the laws, can possibly avail to accomplish any genuine or lasting reform. It is the laws themselves which are partly at fault, and still more at fault is the group of ideas and traditional practices behind the laws.

Reformers have failed for the most part to reach a correct diagnosis of existing political and economic abuses, because they are almost as much the victim of perverted, confused, and routine habits of political thought as the ordinary politician. They have eschewed the tradition of partisan conformity in reference to controverted political questions, but they have not eschewed a still more insidious tradition of conformity— the tradition that a patriotic American citizen must not in his political thinking go beyond the formulas consecrated in the sacred American writings. They adhere to the stupefying rule that the good Fathers of the Republic relieved their children from the necessity of vigorous, independent, or consistent thinking in political matters,—that it is the duty of their loyal children to repeat the sacred words and then await a miraculous consummation of individual and social prosperity. Accordingly, all the leading reformers begin by piously reiterating certain phrases about equal rights for all and special privileges for none, and of government of the people, by the people, and for the people. Having in this way proved their fundamental political orthodoxy, they proceed to interpret the phrases according to their personal, class, local, and partisan preconceptions and interests. They have never stopped to inquire whether the principle of equal rights in its actual embodiment in American institutional and political practice has not been partly responsible for some of the existing abuses, whether it is either a safe or sufficient platform for a reforming movement, and whether its continued proclamation as the fundamental political principle of a democracy will help or hinder the higher democratic consummation. Their unquestioning orthodoxy in this respect has made them faithless both to their own personal interest as reformers and to the cause of reform. Reform exclusively as a moral protest and awakening is condemned to sterility. Reformers exclusively as moral protestants and purifiers are condemned to misdirected effort, to an illiberal puritanism, and to personal self-stultification. Reform must necessarily mean an intellectual as well as a moral challenge; and its higher purposes will never be accomplished unless it is accompanied by a masterful and jubilant intellectual awakening.

All Americans, whether they are professional politicians or reformers, "predatory" millionaires or common people, political philosophers or schoolboys, accept the principle of "equal rights for all and special privileges for none" as the absolutely sufficient rule of an American democratic political system. The platforms of both parties testify on its behalf. Corporation lawyers and their clients appear frequently to believe in it. Tammany offers tribute to it during every local political campaign in New York. A Democratic Senator, in the intervals between his votes for increased duties on the products of his state, declares it to be the summary of all political wisdom. The fact that Mr. Bryan incorporates it in most of his speeches does not prevent Mr. Hearst from keeping it standing in type for the purpose of showing how very American the *American* can be. The fact that Mr. Hearst has appropriated it with the American flag as belonging peculiarly to himself has not prevented Mr. Roosevelt from explaining the whole of his policy of reform as at bottom an attempt to restore a "Square Deal"—that is, a condition of equal rights and non-existing privileges. More radical reformers find the same principle equally useful for their own purposes. Mr. Frederic C. Howe, in his "Hope of Democracy," bases an elaborate scheme of municipal socialism exclusively upon it. Mr. William Smythe, in his "Constructive Democracy," finds warrant in the same principle for the immediate purchase by the central government of the railway and "trust" franchises. Mr. Henry George, Jr., in his "Menace of Privilege," asserts that the plain American citizen can never enjoy equality of rights as long as land, mines, railroad rights of way and terminals, and the like remain in the hands of private owners. The collectivist socialists are no less certain that the institution of private property necessarily gives some men an unjust advantage over others. There is no extreme of radicalism or conservatism, of individualism or socialism, of Republicanism or Democracy, which does not rest its argument on this one consummate principle.

In this respect the good American finds himself in a situation similar to that with which he was confronted before the Civil War. At that time, also, Abolitionist and slave-holder, Republican and pioneer Democrat, each of them declared himself to be the interpreter of the true democratic doctrine; and no substantial progress could be made towards the settlement of the question, until public opinion had been instructed as to the real meaning of democracy in relation to the double-headed problem of slavery and states' rights. It required the utmost intellectual courage and ability to emancipate the conception of democracy from the illusions and confusions of thought which enabled Davis, Douglas, and Garrison all to pose as impeccable democrats; and at the present time reformers need to devote as much ability and more courage to the task of framing a fitting creed for a reformed and reforming American democracy.

The political lessons of the anti-slavery and states' rights discussions may not be of much obvious assistance in thinking out such a creed; but they should at least help the reformers to understand the methods whereby the purposes of a reformed democracy can be achieved. No progress was made towards the solution of the slavery question until the question itself was admitted to be national in scope, and its solution a national responsibility. No substantial progress had been made in the direction of reform until it began to be understood that here, also, a national responsibility existed, which demanded an exercise of the powers of the central government. Reform is both meaningless and powerless unless the Jeffersonian principle of non-interference is abandoned. The experience of the last generation plainly shows that the American economic and social system cannot be allowed to take care of itself, and that the automatic harmony of the individual and the public interest, which is the essence of the Jeffersonian democratic creed, has proved to be an illusion. Interference with the natural course of individual and popular action there must be in the public interest; and such interference must at least be sufficient to accomplish its purposes. The house of the American democracy is again by way of being divided against itself, because the national interest has not been consistently asserted as against special and local interests; and again, also, it can be reunited only by being partly reconstructed on better foundations. If reform does not and cannot mean restoration, it is bound to mean reconstruction.

The reformers have come partly to realize that the Jeffersonian policy of drift must be abandoned. They no longer expect the American ship of state by virtue of its own righteous framework to sail away to a safe harbor in the Promised Land. They understand that there must be a vigorous and conscious assertion of the public as opposed to private and special interests, and that the American people must to a greater extent than they have in the past subordinate the latter to the former. They behave as if the American ship of state will hereafter require careful steering; and a turn or two at the wheel has given them some idea of the course they must set. On the other hand, even the best of them have not learned the name of its ultimate destination, the full difficulties of the navigation, or the stern discipline which may eventually be imposed upon the ship's crew. They do not realize, that is, how thoroughly Jeffersonian individualism must be abandoned for the benefit of a genuinely individual and social consummation; and they do not realize how dangerous and fallacious a chart their cherished principle of equal rights may well become. In reviving the practice of vigorous national action for the achievement of a national purpose, the better reformers have, if they only knew it, been looking in the direction of a much more trustworthy and serviceable political principle. The assumption of such a responsibility implies the rejection of a large part of the Jeffersonian creed, and a renewed attempt to establish in its place the popularity of its Hamiltonian rival.

On the other hand, it involves no less surely the transformation of Hamiltonianism into a thoroughly democratic political principle. None of these interferences have, however, as yet been generally drawn, and no leading reformer has sought to give reform its necessary foundation of positive political principle.

Only a very innocent person will expect reformers to be convinced of such a novel notion of reform by mere assertion, no matter how emphatic, or by argument, no matter how conclusive. But if, as I have said, reform actually implies a criticism of traditional American ideas, and a more responsible and more positive conception of democracy, these implications will necessarily be revealed in the future history of the reforming agitation. The reformers who understand will be assisted by the logic of events, whereas those who cannot and will not understand will be thwarted by the logic of events. Gradually (it may be anticipated) reformers, who dare to criticise and who are not afraid to reconstruct will be sharply distinguished from reformers who believe reform to be a species of higher conservatism. The latter will be forced where they belong into the ranks of the supporters and beneficiaries of the existing system; and the party of genuine reform will be strengthened by their departure. On the other hand, the sincere and thorough-going reformers can hardly avoid a division into two divergent groups. One of these groups will stick faithfully to the principle of equal rights and to the spirit of the true Jeffersonian faith. It will seek still further to undermine the representative character of American institutions, to deprive official leadership of any genuine responsibility, and to cultivate individualism at the expense of individual and national integrity. The second group, on the other hand, may learn from experience that the principle of equal rights is a dangerous weapon in the hands of factious and merely revolutionary agitators, and even that such a principle is only a partial and poverty-stricken statement of the purpose of a democratic polity. The logic of its purposes will compel it to favor the principle of responsible representative government, and it will seek to forge institutions which will endow responsible political government with renewed life. Above all, it may discover that the attempt to unite the Hamiltonian principle of national political responsibility and efficiency with a frank democratic purpose will give a new meaning to the Hamiltonian system of political ideas and a new power to democracy.

One would hardly dare to assert that such a future for the reforming agitation is already prophesied by the history of reform; but the divergence between different classes of the reformers is certainly widening, and some such alignment can already be distinguished. . . .

Undesirable and inadequate forms of democracy always seek to dispense in one way or another with [the] . . . tedious process of achieving a morally authoritative Sovereign will. We Americans have identified democracy with certain existing political and civil rights, and we have, consequently, tended to believe that the democratic consummation was merely a matter of exercising and preserving those rights. The grossest form of this error was perpetrated when Stephen A. Douglas confused authoritative popular Sovereignty with the majority vote of a few hundred "squatters" in a frontier state, and asserted that on democratic principles such expressions of the popular will should be accepted as final. But an analogous mistake lurks in all static forms of democracy. The bestowal and the exercise of political and civil rights are merely a method of organization, which if used in proper subordination to the ultimate democratic purpose, may achieve in action something of the authority of a popular Sovereign will. But to cleave to the details of such an organization as the very essence of democracy is utterly to pervert the principle of national democratic Sovereignty. From this point of view, the Bourbon who wishes the existing system with its maladaptations and contradictions preserved in all its lack of integrity, commits an error analogous to that of the radical, who wishes by virtue of a majority vote immediately to destroy some essential part of the fabric. Both of them conceive that the whole moral and national authority of the democratic principle can be invoked in favor of institutions already in existence or of purposes capable of immediate achievement.

On the other hand, there are democrats who would seek a consummate democracy without the use of any political machinery. The idea that a higher type of associated life can be immediately realized by a supreme act of faith must always be tempting to men who unite social aspirations with deep religious faith. It is a more worthy and profound conception of democracy than the conventional American one of a system of legally constituted and equally exercised rights, fatally resulting in material prosperity. Before any great stride can be made towards a condition of better democracy, the constructive democratic movement must obtain more effective support both from scientific discipline and religious faith. Nevertheless, the triumph of Tolstoyan democracy at the present moment would be more pernicious in its results than the triumph of Jeffersonian Democracy. Tolstoy has merely given a fresh and exalted version of the old doctrine of non-resistance, which, as it was proclaimed by Jesus, referred in the most literal way to another world. In this world faith cannot dispense with power and organization. The sudden and immediate conversion of unregenerate men from a condition of violence, selfishness, and sin into a condition of beatitude and brotherly love can obtain even comparative permanence only by virtue of exclusiveness. The religious experience of our race has sufficiently testified to the permanence of the law. One man can be evangelized for a lifetime. A group of men can be evangelized for many years. Multitudes of men can be evangelized only for a few hours. No faith can achieve comparatively stable social conquests without being established by habit, defined by thought, and consolidated by organization. Usually the faith itself subsequently sickens of the bad air it breathes in its own house. Indeed, it is certain to lose initiative and vigor, unless it can appeal intermittently to some correlative source of enthusiasm and devotion. But with the help of efficient organization it may possibly survive, whereas in the absence of such a worldly body, it must in a worldly sense inevitably perish. Democracy as a living movement in the direction of human brotherhood has required, like other faiths, an efficient organization and a root in ordinary human nature; and it obtains such an organization by virtue of the process of national development—on condition, of course, that the nation is free to become a genuine and thorough-going democracy.

A democracy organized into a nation, and imbued with the national spirit, will seek by means of experimentation and discipline to reach the object which Tolstoy would reach by an immediate and a miraculous act of faith. The exigencies of such schooling frequently demand severe coercive measures, but what schooling does not? A nation cannot merely discharge its unregenerate citizens; and the best men in a nation or in any political society cannot evade the responsibility which the fact of human unregeneracy places upon the whole group. After men had reached a certain stage of civilization, they frequently began to fear that the rough conditions of political association excluded the highest and most fruitful forms of social life; and they sought various ways of improving the quality of the association by narrowing its basis. They tried to found small communities of saints who were connected exclusively by moral and religious bonds, and who in this way freed themselves from the hazards, the distraction, and the violence inseparable from political association. Such communities have made at different times great successes; but their success has not been permanent. The political aspect of associated life is not to be evaded. In proportion as political organization gained in prosperity, efficiency, and dignity, special religious associations lost their independence and power. Even the most powerful religious association in the world, the Catholic Church, has been fighting a losing battle with political authority, and it is likely in the course of time to occupy in relation to the political powers a position analogous to that of the Greek or the English church. The ultimate power to command must rest with that authority which, if necessary, can force people to obey; and any plan of association which seeks to ignore the part which physical force plays in life is necessarily incomplete. Just as formerly the irresponsible and meaningless use of political power created the need of special religious associations, independent of the state, so now the responsible, the purposeful, and the efficient use of physical force, characteristic of modern nations, has in its turn made such independence less necessary, and tends to attach a different function to the church. A basis of association narrower than the whole complex of human powers and interests will not serve. National organization provides such a basis. The perversity of human nature may cause its ultimate failure; but it will not fail because it omits any essential constituent in the composition of a permanent and fruitful human association. So far as it fulfills its responsibilities, it guarantees protection against predatory powers at home and abroad. It provides in appropriate measure for individual freedom, for physical, moral, and intellectual discipline, and for social consistency. It has prizes to offer as well as coercion to exercise; and with its foundations planted firmly in the past, its windows and portals look out towards a better future. The tendency of its normal action is continually if very slowly, to diminish the distance between the ideal of human brotherhood, and the political, economic, and social conditions, under which at any one time men manage to live together.

That is the truth to which the patriotic Americans should firmly cleave. The modern nation, particularly in so far as it is constructively democratic, constitutes the best machinery as yet developed for raising the level of human association. It really teaches men how they must feel, what they must think, and what they must do, in order that they may live together amicably and profitably. The value of this school for its present purposes is increased by its very imperfections, because its imperfections issue inevitably from the imperfections of human nature. Men being as unregenerate as they are, all worthy human endeavor involves consequences of battle and risk. The heroes of the struggle must maintain their achievements and at times even promote their objects by compulsion. The policeman and the soldier will continue for an indefinite period to be guardians of the national schools, and the nations have no reason to be ashamed of this fact. It is merely symbolic of the very comprehensiveness of their responsibilities—that they have to deal with the problem of human inadequacy and unregeneracy in all its forms,—that they cannot evade this problem by allowing only the good boys to attend school—that they cannot even mitigate it by drawing too sharp a distinction between the good boys and the bad. Such indiscriminate attendance in these national schools, if it is to be edifying, involves one practical consequence of dominant importance. Everybody within the schoolhouse—masters, teachers, pupils and janitors, old pupils and young, good pupils and bad, must feel one to another an indestructible loyalty. Such loyalty is merely the subjective aspect of their inevitable mutual association; it is merely the recognition that as a worldly body they must all live or die and conquer or fail together.

XII. INTRODUCTION

Following William James, but yet committed to the social situation, was John Dewey (1859–1952). As one scholar put it, "Dewey had been from the beginning preoccupied with the logic of practice and had discovered in James's *Psychology* the instrumentalist logic that revolutionized his own ethical theory." Dewey worked out a double-pronged system of ethics stressing both psychological and social dimensions. The "Chicago school" of instrumentalism was based on that ethical system.

The characteristic function of the human mind, according to Dewey, was to change activity by predicting the consequences of that activity. Mind was therefore the instrument by which man could test and feel his way in the natural and human world. Consistently seeking ways by which the mind could be free to follow its own prediction of consequences, Dewey addressed himself not only to problems in epistemology and metaphysics but to questions of education and social policy. Throughout his long and productive life, Dewey applied his instrumentalism to a vast array of questions.

The following chapter from a popular book of his shows more of Dewey's method than of his conclusions; it displays his basic view of the relationship of ideas to the social milieu in which they originated; and it shows, once again, the enormity of Darwin's impact on American thought.

XII.

John Dewey

THE SCIENTIFIC FACTOR IN RECONSTRUCTION OF PHILOSOPHY 1920

Philosophy starts from some deep and wide way of responding to the difficulties life presents, but it grows only when material is at hand for making this practical response conscious, articulate and communicable. Accompanying the economic, political and ecclesiastical changes . . . was a scientific revolution enormous in scope and leaving unchanged almost no detail of belief about nature, physical and human. In part this scientific transformation was produced by just the change in practical attitude and temper. But as it progressed, it furnished that change an appropriate vocabulary, congenial to its needs, and made it articulate. The advance of science in its larger generalizations and in its specific detail of fact supplied precisely that intellectual equipment of ideas and concrete fact that was needed in order to formulate, precipitate, communicate and propagate the new disposition. Today, accordingly, we shall deal with those contrasting conceptions of the structure and constitution of Nature, which when they are accepted on the authority of science (alleged or real), form the intellectual framework of philosophy.

Contrasting conceptions of ancient and modern science have been selected. For I see no way in which the truly philosophic import of the picture of the world painted by modern science can be appreciated except to exhibit it in contrast with that earlier picture which gave classic metaphysics its intellectual foundation and confirmation. The world in which philosophers once put their trust was a closed world, a world consisting internally of a limited number of fixed forms, and having definite boundaries externally. The world of modern science is an open world, a world varying indefinitely without the possibility of assignable limit in its internal make-up, a world stretching beyond any assignable bounds externally. Again, the world in which even the most intelligent men of olden times thought they lived was a fixed world, a realm where changes went on only within immutable limits of rest and permanence, and a world where the fixed and unmoving was, as we have already noted, higher in quality and authority than the moving and altering. And in the third place, the world which men once saw with their eyes, portrayed in their imaginations and repeated in their plans of conduct, was a world of a limited number of classes, kinds, forms, distinct in quality (as kinds and species must be distinct) and arranged in a graded order of superiority and inferiority.

It is not easy to recall the image of the universe which was taken for granted in the world tradition. In spite of its dramatic rendering (as in Dante), of the dialectical elaborations of Aristotle and St. Thomas, in spite of the fact that it held men's minds captive until the last three hundred years, and that its overthrow involved a religious upheaval, it is already dim, faded and remote. Even as a separate and abstract thing of theory it is not easy to recover.

As something pervasive, interwoven with all the details of reflection and observation, with the plans and rules of behavior, it is impossible to call it back again. Yet, as best we can, we need to put before our minds a definitely enclosed universe, something which can be called a universe in a literal and visible sense, having the earth at its fixed and unchanging centre and at a fixed circumference the heavenly arch of fixed stars moving in an eternal round of divine ether, hemming in all things and keeping them forever at one and in order. The earth, though at the centre, is the coarsest, grossest, most material, least significant and good (or perfect) of the parts of this closed world. It is the scene of maximum fluctuation and vicissitude. It is the least rational, and therefore the least notable, or knowable; it offers the least to reward contemplation, provoke admiration and govern conduct. Between this grossly material centre and the immaterial, spiritual and eternal heavens lie a series of regions of moon, planets, sun, etc., each of which gains in rank, value, rationality and true being as it is farther from earth and nearer the heavens. Each of these regions is composed of its own appropriate stuff of earth, water, air, fire in its own dominant degree, until we reach the heavenly firmament which transcends all these principles, being constituted, as was just said, of that immaterial, inalterable energy called ether.

Within this tight and pent in universe, changes take place of course. But they are only of a small number of fixed kinds; and they operate only within fixed limits. Each kind of stuff has its own appropriate motion. It is the nature of earthly things to be heavy, since they are gross, and hence to move downward. Fire and superior things are light and hence move upward to their proper place; air rises only to the plane of the planets, where it then takes its back and forth motion which naturally belongs to it, as is evident in the winds and in respiration. Ether being the highest of all physical things has a purely circular movement. The daily return of the fixed stars is the closest possible approximation to eternity, and to the self-involved revolution of mind upon its own ideal axis of reason. Upon the earth in virtue of its earthly nature—or rather its lack of virtue—is a scene of mere change. Mere flux, aimless and meaningless, starts at no definite point and arrives at nothing, amounts to nothing. Mere changes of quantity, all purely mechanical changes, are of this kind. They are like the shiftings of the sands by the sea. They may be sensed, but they cannot be "noted" or understood; they lack fixed limits which govern them. They are contemptible. They are casual, the sport of accident.

Only changes which lead to some defined or fixed outcome of form are of any account and can have any account—any *logos* or reason—made of them. The growth of plants and animals illustrates the highest kind of change which is possible in the sublunary or mundane sphere. They go from one definite fixed form to another. Oaks generate only oaks, oysters only oysters, man only man. The material factor of mechanical production enters in, but enters in as accident to prevent the full consummation of the type of the species, and to bring about the meaningless variations which diversify various oaks or oysters from one another, or in extreme cases to produce freaks, sports, monsters, three-handed or four-toed men. Aside from accidental and undesirable variations, each individual has a fixed career to pursue, a fixed path in which to travel. Terms which sound modern, words like potentiality and development abound in Aristotelian thought, and have misled some into reading into his thought modern meanings. But the significance of these words in classic and medieval thought is rigidly determined by their context. Development holds merely of the course of changes which takes place within a particular member of the species. It is only a name for the predetermined movement from the acorn to the oak tree. It takes place not in things generally but only in some one of the numerically insignificant members of the oak species. Development, evolution, never means, as in modern science, origin of new forms, a mutation from an old species, but only the monotonous traversing of a previously plotted cycle of change. So potentiality never means, as in modern life, the possibility of novelty, of invention, of radical deviation, but only that principle in virtue of which the acorn becomes the oak. Technically, it is the capacity for movement between opposites. Only the cold can become hot; only the dry can become wet; only the babe can become a man; the seed the full-grown wheat and so on. Potentiality instead of implying the emergence of anything novel means merely the facility with which a particular thing repeats the recurrent processes of its kind, and thus becomes a specific case of the eternal forms in and through which all things are constituted.

In spite of the almost infinite numerical diversity of individuals, there are only a limited number of species, kinds or sorts. And the world is essentially a world which falls into sorts; it is pre-arranged into distinct classes. Moreover, just as we naturally arrange plants and animals into series, ranks and grades, from the lower to the highest, so with all things in the universe. The distinct classes to which things belong by their very nature form a hierarchical order. There are castes in nature. The universe is constituted on an aristocratic, one can truly say a feudal, plan. Species, classes do not mix or overlap—except in cases of accident, and to the result of chaos. Otherwise, everything belongs in advance to a certain class, and the class has its own fixed place in the hierarchy of Being. The universe is indeed a tidy spot whose purity is interfered with only by those irregular changes in individuals which are due to the presence of an obdurate matter that refuses to yield itself wholly to rule and form. Otherwise it is a universe with a fixed place for everything and where everything knows its place, its station and class, and keeps it. Hence what are known technically as final and formal causes are supreme, and efficient causes are relegated to an inferior place. The so-called final cause is just a name for the fact that there is some fixed form characteristic of a class or sort of things which governs the changes going on, so that they tend toward it as their end and goal, the fulfilment of their true nature. The supralunar region is the end or final cause of the proper movements of air and fire; the earth of the motions of crass, heavy things; the oak of the acorn; the mature form in general of the germinal.

The "efficient cause," that which produces and instigates a movement is only some external change as it accidentally gives a kind of push to an immature, imperfect being and starts it moving toward its perfected or fulfilled form. The final cause is the perfected form regarded as the *explanation or reason* of prior changes. When it is not taken in reference to the changes completed and brought to rest in it, but in itself it is the "formal cause": The inherent *nature* or character which "makes" or constitutes a thing *what it is* so far as it truly *is*, namely, what it is so far as it does not change. Logically and practically all of the traits which have been enumerated cohere. Attack one and you attack all. When any one is undermined, all go. This is the reason why the intellectual modification of the last few centuries may truly be called a revolution. It has substituted a conception of the world differing at every point. It makes little matter at what point you commence to trace the difference, you find yourself carried into all other points.

Instead of a closed universe, science now presents us with one infinite in space and time, having no limits here or there, at this end, so to speak, or at that, and as infinitely complex in internal structure as it is infinite in extent. Hence it is also an open world, an infinitely variegated one, a world which in the old sense can hardly be called a universe at all; so multiplex and far-reaching that it cannot be summed up and grasped in any one formula. And change rather than fixity is now a measure of "reality" or energy of being; change is omnipresent. The laws in which the modern man of science is interested are laws of motion, of generation and consequence. He speaks of law where the ancients spoke of kind and essence, because what he wants is a correlation of changes, an ability to detect one change occurring in correspondence with another. He does not try to define and delimit something remaining constant *in* change. He tries to describe a constant order *of* change. And while the word "constant" appears in both statements, the meaning of the word is not the same. In one case, we are dealing with something constant in *existence*, physical or metaphysical; in the other case, with something constant in *function* and operation. One is a form of independent being; the other is a formula of description and calculation of interdependent changes.

In short, classic thought accepted a feudally arranged order of classes or kinds, each "holding" from a superior and in turn giving the rule of conduct and service to an inferior. . . . We have a fairly definite notion of society as organized upon the feudal basis. The family principle, the principle of kinship is strong, and especially is this true as we ascend in the social scale. At the lower end, individuals may be lost more or less in the mass. Since all are parts of the common herd, there is nothing especial to distinguish their birth. But among the privileged and ruling class the case is quite different. The tie of kinship at once marks a group off externally and gives it distinction, and internally holds all its members together. Kinship, kind, class, genus are synonymous terms, starting from social and concrete facts and going to the technical and abstract. For kinship is a sign of a common nature, of something universal and permanent running through all particular individuals, and giving them a real and objective unity. Because such and such persons are kin they are *really*, and not merely conventionally, marked off into a class having something unique about it. All contemporary members are bound into an objective unity which includes ancestors and descendants and excludes all who belong to another kin or kind. Assuredly this parcelling out of the world into separate kinds, each having its qualitatively distinct nature in contrast with other species, binding numerically distinct individuals together, and preventing their diversities from exceeding fixed bounds, may without exaggeration be called a projection of the family principle into the world at large.

In a feudally organized society, moreover, each kinship group or species occupies a definite place. It is marked by the possession of a specific *rank* higher or lower with respect to other grades. This position confers upon it certain privileges, enabling it to enforce certain claims upon those lower in the scale and entailing upon it certain services and homage to be rendered to superiors. The relationship of causation, so to speak, is up and down. Influence, power, proceeds from above to below; the activities of the inferior are performed with respect, quite literally, to what is above. Action and reaction are far from being equal and in opposite directions. All action is of one sort, of the nature of lordship, and proceeds from the higher to the lower. Reaction is of the nature of subjection and deference and proceeds from lower to higher. The classic theory of the constitution of the world corresponds point by point to this ordering of classes in a scale of dignity and power.

A third trait assigned by historians to feudalism is that the ordering of ranks centres about armed service and the relationship of armed defense and protection. I am afraid that what has already been said about the parallelism of ancient cosmology with social organization may seem a fanciful analogy; and if a comparison is also drawn in this last regard, there will be no doubt in your minds that a metaphor is being forced. Such is truly the case if we take the comparison too literally. But not so, if we confine our attention to the notion of rule and command implied in both. Attention has already been called to the meaning that is now given the term law—a constant relationship among changes. Nevertheless, we often hear about laws which "govern" events, and it often seems to be thought that phenomena would be utterly disorderly were there not laws to keep them in order. This way of thinking is a survival of reading social relationships into nature—not necessarily a feudal relationship, but the relation of ruler and ruled, sovereign and subject. Law is assimilated to a command or order. If the factor of personal will is eliminated (as it was in the best Greek thought) still the idea of law or universal is impregnated with the sense of a guiding and ruling influence exerted from above on what is naturally inferior to it. The universal governs as the end and model which the artisan has in mind "governs" his movements. The Middle Ages added to this Greek idea of control the idea of a command proceeding from a superior will; and hence thought of the operations of nature as if they were a fulfilment of a task set by one who had authority to direct action.

The traits of the picture of nature drawn by modern science fairly spring by contrast into high relief. Modern science took its first step when daring astronomers abolished the distinction of high, sublime and ideal forces operating in the heavens from lower and material forces actuating terrestrial events. The supposed heterogeneity of substances and forces between heaven and earth was denied. It was asserted that the same laws hold everywhere, that there is homogeneity of material and process everywhere throughout nature. The remote and esthetically sublime is to be scientifically described and explained in terms of homely familiar events and forces. The material of direct handling and observation is that of which we are surest; it is the better known. Until we can convert the grosser and more superficial observations of far-away things in the heavens into elements identical with those of things directly at hand, they remain blind and not understood. Instead of presenting superior worth, they present only problems. They are not means of enlightenment but challenges. The earth is not superior in rank to sun, moon and stars, but it is equal in dignity, and its occurrences give the key to the understanding of celestial existences. Being *at* hand, they are also capable of being brought *under* our hand; they can be manipulated, broken up, resolved into elements which can be managed, combined at will in old and new forms. The net result may be termed, I think, without any great forcing, the substitution of a democracy of individual facts equal in rank for the feudal system of an ordered gradation of general classes of unequal rank.

One important incident of the new science was the destruction of the idea that the earth is the centre of the universe. When the idea of a fixed centre went, there went with it the idea of a closed universe and a circumscribing heavenly boundary. To the Greek sense, just because its theory of knowing was dominated by esthetic considerations, the finite was the perfect. Literally, the finite was the finished, the ended, the completed, that with no ragged edges and unaccountable operations. The infinite or limitless was lacking in character just because it was in-finite. Being every-thing, it was nothing. It was unformed and chaotic, uncontrolled and unruly, the source of incalculable deviations and accidents. Our present feeling that associates infinity with boundless power, with capacity for expansion that knows no end, with the delight in a progress that has no external limit, would be incomprehensible were it not that interest has shifted from the esthetic to the practical; from interest in beholding a harmonious and complete scene to interest in transforming an inhar-monious one. One has only to read the authors of the transition period, say Giordano Bruno, to realize what a pent-in, suffocating sensation they associated with a closed, finite world, and what a feeling of exhilaration, expansion and boundless possibility was aroused in them by the thought of a world infinite in stretch of space and time, and composed internally of infinitesimal infinitely numerous elements. That which the Greeks with-drew from with repulsion they welcomed with an intoxicated sense of adventure. The infinite meant, it was true, something forever untraversed even by thought, and hence something forever unknown—no matter how great attainment in learning. But this "forever unknown" instead of being chilling and repelling was now an inspiring challenge to ever-renewed inquiry, and an assurance of inexhaustible possibilities of progress.

The student of history knows well that the Greeks made great prog-ress in the science of mechanics as well as of geometry. At first sight, it appears strange that with this advance in mechanics so little advance was made in the direction of modern science. The seeming paradox impels us to ask why it was that mechanics remained a separate science, why it was not used in description and explanation of natural phenomena after the manner of Galileo and Newton. The answer is found in the social paral-lelism already mentioned. Socially speaking, machines, tools, were devices employed by artisans. The science of mechanics had to do with the kind of things employed by human mechanics, and mechanics were base fel-lows. They were at the lower end of the social scale, and how could light on the heavens, the highest, be derived from them? The application of considerations of mechanics to natural phenomena would moreover have implied an interest in the practical control and utilization of phenomena which was totally incompatible with the importance attached to final causes as fixed determiners of nature. All the scientific reformers of the sixteenth and seventeenth centuries strikingly agree in regarding the doc-trine of final causes as *the* cause of the failure of science. Why? Because this doctrine taught that the processes of nature are held in bondage to certain fixed ends which they must tend to realize. Nature was kept in leading strings; it was cramped down to production of a limited number of stereotyped results. Only a comparatively small number of things could be brought into being, and these few must be similar to the ends which similar cycles of change had effected in the past. The scope of inquiry and understanding was limited to the narrow round of processes eventuating in the fixed ends which the observed world offered to view. At best, invention and production of new results by use of machines and tools must be restricted to articles of transient dignity and bodily, not intellectual, use.

When the rigid clamp of fixed ends was taken off from nature, observation and imagination were emancipated, and experimental control for scientific and practical purposes enormously stimulated. Because natural processes were no longer restricted to a fixed number of immovable ends or results, anything might conceivably happen. It was only a question of what elements could be brought into juxtaposition so that they would work upon one another. Immediately, mechanics ceased to be a separate science and became an organ for attacking nature. The mechanics of the lever, wheel, pulley and inclined plane told accurately what happens when things in space are used to move one another during definite periods of time. The whole of nature became a scene of pushes and pulls, of cogs and levers, of motions of parts or elements to which the formulae of movements produced by well-known machines were directly applicable.

The banishing of ends and forms from the universe has seemed to many an ideal and spiritual impoverishment. When nature was regarded as a set of mechanical interactions, it apparently lost all meaning and purpose. Its glory departed. Elimination of differences of quality deprived it of beauty. Denial to nature of all inherent longings and aspiring tendencies toward ideal ends removed nature and natural science from contact with poetry, religion and divine things. There seemed to be left only a harsh, brutal despiritualized exhibition of mechanical forces. As a consequence, it has seemed to many philosophers that one of their chief problems was to reconcile the existence of this purely mechanical world with belief in objective rationality and purpose—to save life from a degrading materialism. Hence many sought to re-attain by way of an analysis of the process of knowing, or epistemology, that belief in the superiority of Ideal Being which had anciently been maintained on the basis of cosmology. But when it is recognized that the mechanical view is determined by the requirements of an experimental control of natural energies, this problem of reconciliation no longer vexes us. Fixed forms and ends, let us recall, mark fixed limits to change. Hence they make futile all human efforts to produce and regulate change except within narrow and unimportant limits. They paralyze constructive human inventions by a theory which condemns them in advance to failure. Human activity can conform only to ends already set by nature. It was not till ends were banished from nature that purposes became important as factors in human minds capable of reshaping existence. A natural world that does not subsist for the sake of realizing a fixed set of ends is relatively malleable and plastic; it may be used for this end *or* that. That nature can be known through the application of mechanical formulae is the prime condition of turning it to human account. Tools, machines are means to be utilized. Only when nature is regarded as mechanical, is systematic invention and construction of machines relevant to nature's activities. Nature is subdued to human purpose because it is no longer the slave of metaphysical and theological purpose.

Bergson has pointed out that man might well be called *Home Faber.* He is distinguished as the tool-making animal. This has held good since man was man; but till nature was construed in mechanical terms, the making of tools with which to attack and transform nature was sporadic and accidental. Under such circumstances it would not have occurred even to a Bergson that man's tool-making capacity was so important and fundamental that it could be used to define him. The very things that make the nature of the mechanical-physical scientist esthetically blank and dull are the things which render nature amenable to human control. When qualities were subordinated to quantitative and mathematical relationships, color, music and form disappeared from the object of the scientist's inquiry as such. But the remaining properties of weight, extension, numerable velocity of movement and so on were just the qualities which lent themselves to the substitution of one thing for another, to the conversion of one form of energy into another; to the effecting of transformations. When chemical fertilizers can be used in place of animal manures, when improved grain and cattle can be purposefully bred from inferior animals and grasses, when mechanical energy can be converted into heat and electricity into mechanical energy, man gains power to manipulate nature. Most of all he gains power to frame *new* ends and aims and to proceed in regular system to their actualization. Only indefinite substitution and convertibility regardless of quality render nature manageable. The mechanization of nature is the condition of a practical and progressive idealism in action.

It thus turns out that the old, old dread and dislike of matter as something opposed to mind and threatening it, to be kept within the narrowest bounds of recognition; something to be denied so far as possible lest it encroach upon ideal purposes and finally exclude them from the real world, is as absurd practically as it was impotent intellectually. Judged from the only scientific standpoint, what it does and how it functions, matter means conditions. To respect matter means to respect the conditions of achievement; conditions which hinder and obstruct and which have to be changed, conditions which help and further and which can be used to modify obstructions and attain ends. Only as men have learned to pay sincere and persistent regard to matter, to the conditions upon which depends negatively and positively the success of all endeavor, have they shown sincere and fruitful respect for ends and purposes. To profess to have an aim and then neglect the means of its execution is self-delusion of the most dangerous sort. Education and morals will begin to find themselves on the same road of advance that say chemical industry and medicine have found for themselves when they too learn fully the lesson of wholehearted and unremitting attention to means and conditions—that is, to what mankind so long despised as material and mechanical. When we take means for ends we indeed fall into moral materialism. But when we take ends without regard to means we degenerate into sentimentalism. In the name of the ideal we fall back upon mere luck and chance and magic or exhortation and preaching; or else upon a fanaticism that will force the realization of preconceived ends at any cost.

I have touched in this lecture upon many things in a cursory way. Yet there has been but one point in mind. The revolution in our conceptions of nature and in our methods of knowing it has bred a new temper of imagination and aspiration. It has confirmed the new attitude generated by economic and political changes. It has supplied this attitude with definite intellectual material with which to formulate and justify itself.

In the first lecture it was noted that in Greek life prosaic matter of fact or empirical knowledge was at a great disadvantage as compared with the imaginative beliefs that were bound up with special institutions and moral habitudes. Now this empirical knowledge has grown till it has broken its low and limited sphere of application and esteem. It has itself become an organ of inspiring imagination through introducing ideas of boundless possibility, indefinite progress, free movement, equal opportunity irrespective of fixed limits. It has reshaped social institutions, and in so far developed a new morale. It has achieved ideal values. It is convertible into creative and constructive philosophy.

Convertible, however, rather than already converted. When we consider how deeply embedded in customs of thought and action the classic philosophy came to be and how congenial it is to man's more spontaneous beliefs, the throes that attended its birth are not to be wondered at. We should rather wonder that a view so upsetting, so undermining, made its way without more persecutions, martyrdoms and disturbances. It certainly is not surprising that its complete and consistent formulation in philosophy has been long delayed. The main efforts of thinkers were inevitably directed to minimizing the shock of change, easing the strains of transition, mediating and reconciling. When we look back upon almost all of the thinkers of the seventeenth and eighteenth centuries, upon all excepting those who were avowedly sceptical and revolutionary, what strikes us is the amount of traditional subject-matter and method that is to be found even among those who were regarded as most advanced. Men cannot easily throw off their old habits of thinking, and never can throw off all of them at once. In developing, teaching and receiving new ideas we are compelled to use some of the old ones as tools of understanding and communication. Only piecemeal, step-by-step, could the full import of the new science be grasped. Roughly speaking, the seventeenth century witnessed its application in astronomy and general cosmology; the eighteenth century in physics and chemistry; the nineteenth century undertook an application in geology and the biological sciences.

It was said that it has now become extremely difficult to recover the view of the world which universally obtained in Europe till the seventeenth century. Yet after all we need only recur to the science of plants and animals as it was before Darwin and to the ideas which even now are dominant in moral and political matters to find the older order of conceptions in full possession of the popular mind. Until the dogma of fixed unchangeable types and species, of arrangement in classes of higher and lower, of subordination of the transitory individual to the universal or kind had been shaken in its hold upon the science of life, it was impossible that the new ideas and method should be made at home in social and moral life. Does it not seem to be the intellectual task of the twentieth century to take this last step? When this step is taken the circle of scientific development will be rounded out and the reconstruction of philosophy be made an accomplished fact.

CHAPTER 3

The Republic of Letters

A. Cynicism

XIII. INTRODUCTION

When Ambrose Bierce (1842–1914[?]) defined impunity as wealth and the African as "a nigger that votes our way," the depth of his cynicism was perfectly apparent.

Born in Ohio, raised in Indiana, wounded twice in the Civil War, Bierce settled in San Francisco in 1876 where he remained for twenty years. In 1913 he went to Mexico and disappeared without leaving any trace.

As his personal bitterness became more acute, he expected his fame to be finally realized in the work of his pupils, the two most promising of whom committed suicide. His generalized disgust and gift for the epigram can be illustrated with hundreds of examples, from which the following was taken: "Heaven is a prophecy uttered by the lips of despair, but Hell is an inference from analogy."

The world, in Bierce's squinting eye, appeared to be rotten and could only become worse. He despised puritanism, the American commitment to the idea of progress, and socialism. He hated the great rich of his time as well as the restricted world of San Francisco where he chose to live.

Bierce's significance in American intellectual history is that almost alone he represents the American strain of the European *fin de siècle*. Wedded to estheticism and dandyism, to an aristocratic conception of the republic of letters, Bierce seems somehow not to fit into the mainstream of American development. But his flagrant war with American society was felt to be real by men who fought with different weapons and in different arenas. A growing number of writers and scholars in America at the turn of the century also felt that the materialism, empty optimism, faith in a fatalistic progress, and physical ugliness of America would destroy any intelligent and sensitive man.

167

In the following fantasy, Bierce shows most of the aspects of American society that he found offensive. His sardonic style and intense loathing of America joined to keep him from a wider audience.

XIII.

Ambrose Bierce

ASHES OF THE BEACON

1909

AN HISTORICAL MONOGRAPH WRITTEN IN 4930

Of the many causes that conspired to bring about the lamentable failure of "self-government" in ancient America the most general and comprehensive was, of course, the impracticable nature of the system itself. In the light of modern culture, and instructed by history, we readily discern the folly of those crude ideas upon which the ancient Americans based what they knew as "republican institutions," and maintained, as long as maintenance was possible, with something of a religious fervor, even when the results were visibly disastrous.

To us of to-day it is clear that the word "self-government" involves a contradiction, for government means control by something other than the thing to be controlled. When the thing governed is the same as the thing governing there is no government, though for a time there may be, as in the case under consideration there was, a considerable degree of forbearance, giving a misleading appearance of public order. This, however, soon must, as in fact it soon did, pass away with the delusion that gave it birth. The habit of obedience to written law, inculcated by generations of respect for actual government able to enforce its authority, will persist for a long time, with an ever lessening power upon the imagination of the people; but there comes a time when the tradition is forgotten and the delusion exhausted. When men perceive that nothing is restraining them but their consent to be restrained, then at last there is nothing to obstruct the free play of that selfishness which is the dominant characteristic and fundamental motive of human nature and human action respectively.

SOURCE. Ambrose Bierce, *Works,* Volume I, New York: The Neale Publishing Co., 1909, pp. 17–22, 30–34, 40–41, 50–52, 58–59, 61–63, 68–71, 77, and 82–84. Reprinted from *The Collected Writings of Ambrose Bierce* (1943) with the permission of The Citadel Press, New York.

Politics, which may have had something of the character of a contest of principles, becomes a struggle of interests, and its methods are frankly serviceable to personal and class advantage. Patriotism and respect for law pass like a tale that is told. Anarchy, no longer disguised as "government by consent," reveals his hidden hand, and in the words of our greatest living poet,

> lets the curtain fall,
> And universal darkness buries all!

The ancient Americans were a composite people; their blood was a blend of all the strains known in their time. Their government, while they had one, being merely a loose and mutable expression of the desires and caprices of the majority—that is to say, of the ignorant, restless and reckless—gave the freest rein and play to all the primal instincts and elemental passions of the race. In so far and for so long as it had any restraining force, it was only the restraint of the present over the power of the past— that of a new habit over an old and insistent tendency ever seeking expression in large liberties and indulgences impatient of control. In the history of that unhappy people, therefore, we see unveiled the workings of the human will in its most lawless state, without fear of authority or care of consequence. Nothing could be more instructive.

Of the American form of government, although itself the greatest of evils afflicting the victims of those that it entailed, but little needs to be said here; it has perished from the earth, a system discredited by an unbroken record of failure in all parts of the world, from the earliest historic times to its final extinction. Of living students of political history not one professes to see in it anything but a mischievous creation of theorists and visionaries—persons whom our gracious sovereign has deigned to brand for the world's contempt as "dupes of hope purveying to sons of greed." The political philosopher of to-day is spared the trouble of pointing out the fallacies of republican government, as the mathematician is spared that of demonstrating the absurdity of the convergence of parallel lines; yet the ancient Americans not only clung to their error with a blind, unquestioning faith, even when groaning under its most insupportable burdens, but seem to have believed it of divine origin. It was thought by them to have been established by the god Washington, whose worship, with that of such *dii minores* as Gufferson, Jaxon and Lincon (identical probably with the Hebru Abrem) runs like a shining thread through all the warp and woof of the stuff that garmented their moral nakedness.

Some stones, very curiously incribed in many tongues, were found by the explorer Droyhors in the wilderness bordering the river Bhitt (supposed by him to be the ancient Potomac) as lately as the reign of Barukam IV. These stones appear to be fragments of a monument or temple erected to the glory of Washington in his divine character of Founder and Preserver of republican institutions. If this tutelary deity of the ancient Americans really invented representative government they were not the first by many to whom he imparted the malign secret of its inauguration and denied that of its maintenance.

Although many of the causes which finally, in combination, brought about the downfall of the great American republic were in operation from the beginning—being, as has been said, inherent in the system—it was not until the year 1995 (as the ancients for some reason not now known reckoned time) that the collapse of that vast, formless fabric was complete. In that year the defeat and massacre of the last army of law and order in the lava beds of California extinguished the final fires of enlightened patriotism and quenched in blood the monarchical revival. Thenceforth armed opposition to anarchy was confined to desultory and insignificant warfare waged by small gangs of mercenaries in the service of wealthy individuals and equally feeble bands of proscripts fighting for their lives. In that year, too, "the Three Presidents" were driven from their capitals, Cincinnati, New Orleans and Duluth, their armies dissolving by desertion and themselves meeting death at the hands of the populace.

The turbulent period between 1920 and 1995, with its incalculable waste of blood and treasure, its dreadful conflicts of armies and more dreadful massacres by passionate mobs, its kaleidoscopic changes of government and incessant effacement and redrawing of boundaries of states, its interminable tale of political assassinations and proscriptions—all the horrors incident to intestinal wars of a naturally lawless race—had so exhausted and dispirited the surviving protagonists of legitimate government that they could make no further head against the inevitable, and were glad indeed and most fortunate to accept life on any terms that they could obtain.

But the purpose of this sketch is not bald narration of historic fact, but examination of antecedent germinal conditions; not to recount calamitous events familiar to students of that faulty civilization, but to trace, as well as the meager record will permit, the genesis and development of the causes that brought them about. . . .

No improvement in the fortunes of the original anarchists through immigration to what was then called the New World would have made them good citizens. From centuries of secret war against particular forms of authority in their own countries they had inherited a bitter antagonism to all authority, even the most beneficent. In their new home they were worse than in their old. In the sunshine of opportunity the rank and sickly growth of their perverted natures became hardy, vigorous, bore fruit. They surrounded themselves with proselytes from the ranks of the idle, the vicious, the unsuccessful. They stimulated and organized discontent. Every one of them became a center of moral and political contagion. To those as yet unprepared to accept anarchy was offered the milder dogma of Socialism, and to those even weaker in the faith something vaguely called Reform. Each was initiated into that degree to which the induration of his conscience and the character of his discontent made him eligible, and in which he could be most serviceable, the body of the people still cheating themselves with the false sense of security begotten of the belief that they were somehow exempt from the operation of all agencies inimical to their national welfare and integrity. Human nature, they thought, was different in the West from what it was in the East: in the New World the old causes would not have the old effects: a republic had some inherent vitality of its own, entirely independent of any action intended to keep it alive. They felt that words and phrases had some talismanic power, and charmed themselves asleep by repeating "liberty," "all men equal before the law," "dictates of conscience," "free speech" and all manner of such incantation to exorcise the spirits of the night. And when they could no longer close their eyes to the dangers environing them; when they saw at last that what they had mistaken for the magic power of their form of government and its assured security was really its radical weakness and subjective peril— they found their laws inadequate to repression of the enemy, the enemy too strong to permit the enactment of adequate laws. The belief that a malcontent armed with freedom of speech, a newspaper, a vote and a rifle is less dangerous than a malcontent with a still tongue in his head, empty hands and under police surveillance was abandoned, but all too late. From its fatuous dream the nation was awakened by the noise of arms, the shrieks of women and the red glare of burning cities. . . .

In turning from this branch of our subject to consider the causes of the failure and bloody disruption of the great American republic other than those inherent in the form of government, it may not be altogether unprofitable to glance briefly at what seems to a superficial view the inconsistent phenomenon of great material prosperity. It is not to be denied that this unfortunate people was at one time singularly prosperous, in so far as national wealth is a measure and proof of prosperity. Among nations it was the richest nation. But at how great a sacrifice of better things was its wealth obtained! By the neglect of all education except that crude, elementary sort which fits men for the coarse delights of business and affairs but confers no capacity of rational enjoyment; by exalting the worth of wealth and making it the test and touchstone of merit; by ignoring art, scorning literature and despising science, except as these might contribute to the glutting of the purse; by setting up and maintaining an artificial standard of morals which condoned all offenses against the property and peace of every one but the condoner; by pitilessly crushing out of their natures every sentiment and aspiration unconnected with accumulation of property, these civilized savages and commercial barbarians attained their sordid end. . . .

In the higher courts of the land, where juries were unknown and appointed judges held their seats for life . . . Justice might have been content to dwell, and there she actually did sometimes set her foot. Unfortunately, the great judges had the consciences of their education. They had crept to place through the slime of the lower courts and their robes of office bore the damnatory evidence. Unfortunately, too, the attorneys, the jury habit strong upon them, brought into the superior tribunals the moral characteristics and professional methods acquired in the lower. Instead of assisting the judges to ascertain the truth and the law, they cheated in argument and took liberties with fact, deceiving the court whenever they deemed it to the interest of their cause to do so, and as willingly won by a technicality or a trick as by the justice of their contention and their ability in supporting it. Altogether, the entire judicial system of the Connected States of America was inefficient, disreputable, corrupt.

The result might easily have been foreseen and doubtless was predicted by patriots whose admonitions have not come down to us. Denied protection of the law, neither property nor life was safe. Greed filled his coffers from the meager hoards of Thrift, private vengeance took the place of legal redress, mad multitudes rioted and slew with virtual immunity from punishment or blame, and the land was red with crime. . . .

The game of insurance, as practiced by the ancient Americans (and, as Gakler conjectures, by some of the tribesmen of Europe), was gambling, pure and simple, despite the sentimental character that its proponents sought to impress upon some forms of it for the greater prosperity of their dealings with its dupes. Essentially, it was a bet between the insurer and the insured. The number of ways in which the wager was made—all devised by the insurer—was almost infinite, but in none of them was there a departure from the intrinsic nature of the transaction as seen in its simplest, frankest form, which we shall here expound.

To those unlearned in the economical institutions of antiquity it is necessary to explain that in ancient America, long prior to the disastrous Japanese war, individual ownership of property was unrestricted; every person was permitted to get as much as he was able, and hold it as his own without regard to his needs, or whether he made any good use of it or not. By some plan of distribution not now understood even the habitable surface of the earth, with the minerals beneath, was parceled out among the favored few, and there was really no place except at sea where children of the others could lawfully be born. Upon a part of the dry land that he had been able to acquire, or had leased from another for the purpose, a man would build a house worth, say, ten thousand *drusoes*. (The ancient unit of value was the "dollar," but nothing is now known as to its actual worth.) Long before the building was complete the owner was beset by "touts" and "cappers" of the insurance game, who poured into his ears the most ingenious expositions of the advantages of betting that it would burn down—for with incredible fatuity the people of that time continued, generation after generation, to build inflammable habitations. The persons whom the capper represented—they called themselves an "insurance company"—stood ready to accept the bet, a fact which seems to have generated no suspicion in the mind of the house-owner. Theoretically, of course, if the house did burn payment of the wager would partly or wholly recoup the winner of the bet for the loss of his house, but in fact the result of the transaction was commonly very different. For the privilege of betting that his property would be destroyed by fire the owner had to pay to the gentleman betting that it would not be, a certain percentage of its value every year, called a "premium." The amount of this was determined by the company, which employed statisticians and actuaries to fix it at such a sum that, according to the law of probabilities, long before the house was "due to burn," the company would have received more than the value of it in premiums. In other words, the owner of the house would himself supply the money to pay his bet, and a good deal more. . . .

A remarkable feature of the crude and primitive civilization of the Americans was their religion. This was polytheistic, as is that of all backward peoples, and among their minor deities were their own women. This has been disputed by respectable authorities, among them Gunkux and the younger Kekler, but the weight of archæological testimony is against them, for, as Sagab-Joffy ingeniously points out, none of less than divine rank would by even the lowest tribes be given unrestricted license to kill. Among the Americans woman, as already pointed out, indubitably had that freedom, and exercised it with terrible effect, a fact which makes the matter of their religion pertinent to the purpose of this monograph. If ever an American woman was punished by law for murder of a man no record of the fact is found; whereas, such American literature as we possess is full of the most enthusiastic adulation of the impossible virtues and imaginary graces of the human female. One writer even goes to the length of affirming that respect for the sex is the foundation of political stability, the cornerstone of civil and religious liberty! After the breakup of the republic and the savage intertribal wars that followed, Gyneolatry was an exhausted cult and woman was relegated to her old state of benign subjection. . . .

Great Britain had a government that governed; America had not. Happily for humanity, the kind of government that does not govern, self-government, "government of the people, by the people and for the people" (to use a meaningless paradox of that time) has perished from the face of the earth.

An inherent weakness in republican government was that it assumed the honesty and intelligence of the majority, "the masses," who were neither honest nor intelligent. It would doubtless have been an excellent government for a people so good and wise as to need none. In a country having such a system the leaders, the politicians, must necessarily all be demagogues, for they can attain to place and power by no other method than flattery of the people and subserviency to the will of the majority. In all the ancient American political literature we look in vain for a single utterance of truth and reason regarding these matters. In none of it is a hint that the multitude was ignorant and vicious, as we know it to have been, and as it must necessarily be in any country, to whatever high average of intelligence and morality the people attain; for "intelligence" and "morality" are comparative terms, the standard of comparison being the intelligence and morality of the wisest and best, who must always be the few. Whatever general advance is made, those not at the head are behind —are ignorant and immoral according to the new standard, and unfit to control in the higher and broader policies demanded by the progress made. Where there is true and general progress the philosopher of yesterday would be the ignoramus of to-day, the honorable of one generation the vicious of another. The peasant of our time is incomparably superior to the statesman of ancient America, yet he is unfit to govern, for there are others more fit.

That a body of men can be wiser than its wisest member seems to the modern understanding so obvious and puerile an error that it is inconceivable that any people, even the most primitive, could ever have entertained it; yet we know that in America it was a fixed and steadfast political faith. The people of that day did not, apparently, attempt to explain how the additional wisdom was acquired by merely assembling in council, as in their "legislatures"; they seem to have assumed that it was so, and to have based their entire governmental system upon that assumption, with never a suspicion of its fallacy. It is like assuming that a mountain range is higher than its highest peak. In the words of Golpek, "The early Americans believed that units of intelligence were addable quantities," or as Soseby more wittily puts it, "They thought that in a combination of idiocies they had the secret of sanity."

The Americans, as has been said, never learned that even among themselves majorities ruled, not because they ought, but because they could —not because they were wise, but because they were strong. The count of noses determined, not the better policy, but the more powerful party. The weaker submitted, as a rule, for it had to or risk a war in which it would be at a disadvantage. Yet in all the early years of the republic they seem honestly to have dignified their submission as "respect for the popular verdict." They even quoted from the Latin language the sentiment that "the voice of the people is the voice of God." And this hideous blasphemy was as glib upon the lips of those who, without change of mind, were defeated at the polls year after year as upon those of the victors. . . .

But how, it may be asked, could people so misgoverned get on, even as well as they did?

From the records that have come down to us it does not appear that they got on very well. They were preyed upon by all sorts of political adventurers, whose power in most instances was limited only by the contemporaneous power of other political adventurers equally unscrupulous. A full half of the taxes wrung from them was stolen. Their public lands, millions of square miles, were parceled out among banded conspirators. Their roads and the streets of their cities were nearly impassable. Their public buildings, conceived in abominable taste and representing enormous sums of money, which never were used in their construction, began to tumble about the ears of the workmen before they were completed. The most delicate and important functions of government were intrusted to men with neither knowledge, heart nor experience, who by their corruption imperiled the public interest and by their blundering disgraced the national name. In short, all the train of evils inseparable from government of any kind beset this unhappy people with tenfold power, together with hundreds of worse ones peculiar to their own faulty and unnatural system. It was thought that their institutions would give them peace, yet in the first three-quarters of a century of their existence they fought three important wars: one of revenge, one of aggression and one—the bloodiest and most wasteful known up to that time—among themselves. And before a century and a half had passed they had the humiliation to see many of their seaport cities destroyed by the Emperor of Japan in a quarrel which they had themselves provoked by their greed of Oriental dominion.

By far the most important factor concerned in bringing about the dissolution of the republic and the incredible horrors that followed it was what was known as "the contest between capital and labor." This momentous struggle began in a rather singular way through an agitation set afoot by certain ambitious women who preached at first to inattentive and inhospitable ears, but with ever increasing acceptance, the doctrine of equality of the sexes, and demanded the "emancipation" of woman. True, woman was already an object of worship and had, as noted before, the right to kill. She was treated with profound and sincere deference, because of certain humble virtues, the product of her secluded life. Men of that time appear to have felt for women, in addition to religious reverence, a certain sentiment known as "love." The nature of this feeling is not clearly known to us, and has been for ages a matter of controversy evolving more heat than light. This much is plain: it was largely composed of good will, and had its root in woman's dependence. Perhaps it had something of the character of the benevolence with which we regard our slaves, our children and our domestic animals—everything, in fact, that is weak, helpless and inoffensive.

Woman was not satisfied; her superserviceable advocates taught her to demand the right to vote, to hold office, to own property, to enter into employment in competition with man. Whatever she demanded she eventually got. With the effect upon her we are not here concerned; the predicted gain to political purity did not ensue, nor did commercial integrity receive any stimulus from her participation in commercial pursuits. What indubitably did ensue was a more sharp and bitter competition in the industrial world through this increase of more than thirty per cent. in its wage-earning population. In no age nor country has there ever been sufficient employment for those requiring it. The effect of so enormously increasing the already disproportionate number of workers in a single generation could be no other than disastrous. Every woman employed displaced or excluded some man, who, compelled to seek a lower employment, displaced another, and so on, until the least capable or most unlucky of the series became a tramp—a nomadic mendicant criminal! The number of these dangerous vagrants in the beginning of the twentieth century of their era has been estimated by Holobom at no less than seven and a half *blukuks!* Of course, they were as tow to the fires of sedition, anarchy and insurrection. . . .

Naturally combinations of labor entailed combinations of capital. These were at first purely protective. They were brought into being by the necessity of resisting the aggressions of the others. But the trick of combination once learned, it was seen to have possibilities of profit in directions not dreamed of by its early promoters; its activities were not long confined to fighting the labor unions with their own weapons and with superior cunning and address. The shrewd and energetic men whose capacity and commercial experience had made them rich while the laborers remained poor were not slow to discern the advantages of coöperation over their own former method of competition among themselves. They continued to fight the labor unions, but ceased to fight one another. The result was that in the brief period of two generations almost the entire business of the country fell into the hands of a few gigantic corporations controlled by bold and unscrupulous men, who, by daring and ingenious methods, made the body of the people pay tribute to their greed. . . .

With the formation of powerful and unscrupulous trusts of both labor and capital to subdue each other the possibilities of combination were not exhausted; there remained the daring plan of combining the two belligerents! And this was actually effected. The laborer's demand for an increased wage was always based upon an increased cost of living, which was itself chiefly due to increased cost of production from reluctant concessions of his former demands. But in the first years of the twentieth century observers noticed on the part of capital a lessening reluctance. More frequent and more extortionate and reasonless demands encountered a less bitter and stubborn resistance; capital was apparently weakening just at the time when, with its strong organizations of trained and willing strike-breakers, it was most secure. Not so; an ingenious malefactor, whose name has perished from history, had thought out a plan for bringing the belligerent forces together to plunder the rest of the population. In the accounts that have come down to us details are wanting, but we know that, little by little, this amazing project was accomplished. Wages rose to incredible rates. The cost of living rose with them, for employers—their new allies wielding in their service the weapons previously used against them, intimidation, the boycott, and so forth—more than recouped themselves from the general public. Their employees got rebates on the prices of products, but for consumers who were neither laborers nor capitalists there was no mercy. Strikes were a thing of the past; strike-breakers threw themselves gratefully into the arms of the unions; "industrial discontent" vanished, in the words of a contemporary poet, "as by the stroke of an enchanter's wand." All was peace, tranquillity and order! Then the storm broke.

A man in St. Louis purchased a sheep's kidney for seven-and-a-half dollars. In his rage at the price he exclaimed: "As a public man I have given twenty of the best years of my life to bringing about a friendly understanding between capital and labor. I have succeeded, and may God have mercy on my meddlesome soul!"

The remark was resented, a riot ensued, and when the sun went down that evening his last beams fell upon a city reeking with the blood of a hundred millionaires and twenty thousand citizens and sons of toil!

Students of the history of those troublous times need not to be told what other and more awful events followed that bloody reprisal. Within forty-eight hours the country was ablaze with insurrection, followed by intestinal wars which lasted three hundred and seventy years and were marked by such hideous barbarities as the modern historian can hardly bring himself to relate. The entire stupendous edifice of popular government, temple and citadel of fallacies and abuses, had crashed to ruin. For centuries its fallen columns and scattered stones sheltered an ever diminishing number of skulking anarchists, succeeded by hordes of skin-clad savages subsisting on offal and raw flesh—the race-remnant of an extinct civilization. All finally vanished from history into a darkness impenetrable to conjecture.

B. The Woman and Democracy

XIV. INTRODUCTION

The *Education* of Henry Adams (1838–1918) is an American classic whose erudition, sensitivity, and subtlety created reverberations in many different areas of society. The following selection emphasizes two major problems of American society in the early twentieth century: the problem of power and the problem of the status of sex.

In 1879 Adams published an anonymous novel called *Democracy*, in which he analyzed the defeminization of his heroine:

"In her own mind . . . she frowned on the idea of seeking for men. What she wished to see, she thought, was the clash of interests, the interests of forty millions of people and a whole continent, centering at Washington; guided, restrained, controlled, or unrestrained and uncontrollable, by men of ordinary mould; the tremendous forces of government, and the machinery of society, at work. What she wanted was POWER. Perhaps the force of the engine was a little confused in her mind with that of the engineer, the power with the men who wielded it. Perhaps the human interest of politics was after all what really attracted her, and, however strongly she might deny it, the passion for exercising power, for its own sake, might dazzle and mislead a woman who had exhausted all the ordinary feminine resources."

In terms of his philosophy of history, Henry Adams intended to measure the change from the thirteenth to the twentieth century. His *Mont-St.-Michel and Chartres* was his attempt to fix a point of departure from which he could measure change; his *Education* was intended as the terminal point. His brother, Brooks Adams, explained that the role of sex, personified by the Virgin, was crucial to Adams' historical vision. (Adams viewed the Virgin as a symbol of womanhood and the power of sex.)

"As Henry neared the end of his application of the development of the 13th century according to scientific and historical theory, in 'Mont St. Michel and Chartres,' he turned more and more toward his next step in the 'Reformation,' on which he constantly talked with me. He found the 'Reformation' most antagonistic, chiefly, I think, because of the Puritan attack on women; for it was during the Reformation that the Virgin was dethroned and, according to his theory . . . that the degradation of woman began."

The power of sex, as exemplified in the worship of the Virgin, according to Adams, was the living force behind the intellectual and

artistic creations of the thirteenth century. The twentieth century replaced the earlier worship of the Woman with the impersonal and
silent force of the "dynamo." The Woman could not be present in
sexless America, and therefore the power that had built the cathedral
of Chartres was unavailable in America. The measure of the change in
the source of social power could be made precise through an analysis of
the intellectual and artistic creations of contemporary America.

Adams' own pessimism and dense humanism was, at least in part, a
result of his view that America had fled in fright and fear from the
power of sex. The following selection is his most explicit statement of
these issues.

XIV.

Henry Adams
THE DYNAMO AND THE VIRGIN
1900

Until the Great Exposition of 1900 [in Paris] closed its doors in
November, Adams haunted it, aching to absorb knowledge, and helpless
to find it. He would have liked to know how much of it could have been
grasped by the best-informed man in the world. While he was thus
meditating chaos, [Samuel P.] Langley [a scientist] came by, and showed
it to him. At Langley's behest, the Exhibition dropped its superfluous
rags and stripped itself to the skin, for Langley knew what to study, and
why, and how; while Adams might as well have stood outside in the
night, staring at the Milky Way. Yet Langley said nothing new, and
taught nothing that one might not have learned from Lord Bacon,
three hundred years before; but though one should have known the
"Advancement of Science" as well as one knew the "Comedy of Errors,"
the literary knowledge counted for nothing until some teacher should
show how to apply it. Bacon took a vast deal of trouble in teaching
King James I and his subjects, American or other, towards the year
1620, that true science was the development or economy of forces;
yet an elderly American in 1900 knew neither the formula nor the

SOURCE. Henry Adams, *The Education of Henry Adams,* Boston: Houghton
Mifflin, 1918, pp. 379–390. Copyright 1946 by Charles F. Adams. Reprinted
with the permission of the publisher, Houghton Mifflin Company.

forces; or even so much as to say to himself that his historical business in the Exposition concerned only the economies or developments of force since 1893, when he began the study at [a world's fair in] Chicago.

Nothing in education is so astonishing as the amount of ignorance it accumulates in the form of inert facts. Adams had looked at most of the accumulations in the storehouses called Art Museums; yet he did not know how to look at the art exhibits of 1900. He had studied Karl Marx and his doctrines of history with profound attention, yet he could not apply them at Paris. Langley, with the ease of a great master of experiment, threw out of the field every exhibit that did not reveal a new application of force, and naturally threw out, to begin with, almost the whole art exhibit. Equally, he ignored almost the whole industrial exhibit. He led his pupil directly to the forces. His chief interest was in new motors to make his airship feasible, and he taught Adams the astonishing complexities of the new Daimler motor, and of the automobile, which, since 1893, had become a nightmare at a hundred kilometres an hour, almost as destructive as the electric tram which was only ten years older; and threatening to become as terrible as the locomotive steam-engine itself, which was almost exactly Adams's own age.

Then he showed his scholar the great hall of dynamos, and explained how little he knew about electricity or force of any kind, even of his own special sun, which spouted heat in inconceivable volume, but which, as far as he knew, might spout less or more, at any time, for all the certainty he felt in it. To him, the dynamo itself was but an ingenious channel for conveying somewhere the heat latent in a few tons of poor coal hidden in a dirty engine-house carefully kept out of sight; but to Adams the dynamo became a symbol of infinity. As he grew accustomed to the great gallery of machines, he began to feel the forty-foot dynamos as a moral force, much as the early Christians felt the Cross. The planet itself seemed less impressive, in its old-fashioned, deliberate, annual or daily revolution, than this huge wheel, revolving within arm's-length at some vertiginous speed, and barely murmuring—scarcely humming an audible warning to stand a hair's-breadth further for respect of power—while it would not wake the baby lying close against its frame. Before the end, one began to pray to it; inherited instinct taught the natural expression of man before silent and infinite force. Among the thousand symbols of ultimate energy, the dynamo was not so human as some, but it was the most expressive.

Yet the dynamo, next to the steam-engine, was the most familiar of exhibits. For Adams's objects its value lay chiefly in its occult mechanism. Between the dynamo in the gallery of machines and the engine-house outside, the break of continuity amounted to abysmal fracture for a historian's objects. No more relation could he discover between the steam and the electric current than between the Cross and the cathedral. The forces were interchangeable if not reversible, but he could see only an absolute *fiat* in electricity as in faith. Langley could not help him. Indeed, Langley seemed to be worried by the same trouble, for he constantly repeated that the new forces were anarchical, and especially that he was not responsible for the new rays, that were little short of parricidal in their wicked spirit towards science. His own rays, with which he had doubled the solar spectrum, were altogether harmless and beneficent; but Radium denied its God—or, what was to Langley the same thing, denied the truths of his Science. The force was wholly new.

A historian who asked only to learn enough to be as futile as Langley or Kelvin, made rapid progress under this teaching, and mixed himself up in the tangle of ideas until he achieved a sort of Paradise of ignorance vastly consoling to his fatigued senses. He wrapped himself in vibrations and rays which were new, and he would have hugged Marconi and Branly had he met them, as he hugged the dynamo; while he lost his arithmetic in trying to figure out the equation between the discoveries and the economies of force. The economies, like the discoveries, were absolute, supersensual, occult; incapable of expression in horse-power. What mathematical equivalent could he suggest as the value of a Branly coherer? Frozen air, or the electric furnace, had some scale of measurement, no doubt, if somebody could invent a thermometer adequate to the purpose; but X-rays had played no part whatever in man's consciousness, and the atom itself had figured only as a fiction of thought. In these seven years man had translated himself into a new universe which had no common scale of measurement with the old. He had entered a supersensual world, in which he could measure nothing except by chance collisions of movements imperceptible to his senses, perhaps even imperceptible to his instruments, but perceptible to each other, and so to some known ray at the end of the scale. Langley seemed prepared for anything, even for an indeterminable number of universes interfused—physics stark mad in metaphysics.

Historians undertake to arrange sequences,—called stories, or histories—assuming in silence a relation of cause and effect. These assumptions, hidden in the depths of dusty libraries, have been astounding, but commonly unconscious and childlike; so much so, that if any captious critic were to drag them to light, historians would probably reply, with one voice, that they had never supposed themselves required to know what they were talking about. Adams, for one, had toiled in vain to find out what he meant. He had even published a dozen volumes of American history for no other purpose than to satisfy himself whether, by the severest process of stating, with the least possible comment, such facts as seemed sure, in such order as seemed rigorously consequent, he could fix for a familiar moment a necessary sequence of human movement. The result had satisfied him as little as at Harvard College. Where he saw sequence, other men saw something quite different, and no one saw the same unit of measure. He cared little about his experiments and less about his statesmen, who seemed to him quite as ignorant as himself and, as a rule, no more honest; but he insisted on a relation of sequence, and if he could not reach it by one method, he would try as many methods as science knew. Satisfied that the sequence of men led to nothing and that the sequence of their society could lead no further, while the mere sequence of time was artificial, and the sequence of thought was chaos, he turned at last to the sequence of force; and thus it happened that, after ten years' pursuit, he found himself lying in the Gallery of Machines at the Great Exposition of 1900, his historical neck broken by the sudden irruption of forces totally new.

Since no one else showed much concern, an elderly person without other cares had no need to betray alarm. The year 1900 was not the first to upset schoolmasters. Copernicus and Galileo had broken many professorial necks about 1600; Columbus had stood the world on its head towards 1500; but the nearest approach to the revolution of 1900 was that of 310, when Constantine set up the Cross. The rays that Langley disowned, as well as those which he fathered, were occult, supersensual, irrational; they were a revelation of mysterious energy like that of the Cross; they were what, in terms of mediæval science, were called immediate modes of the divine substance.

The historian was thus reduced to his last resources. Clearly if he was bound to reduce all these forces to a common value, this common value could have no measure but that of their attraction on his own mind. He must treat them as they had been felt; as convertible, reversible, interchangeable attractions on thought. He made up his mind to venture it; he would risk translating rays into faith. Such a reversible process would vastly amuse a chemist, but the chemist could not deny that he, or some of his fellow physicists, could feel the force of both. When Adams was a boy in Boston, the best chemist in the place had probably never heard of Venus except by way of scandal, or of the Virgin except as idolatry; neither had he heard of dynamos or automobiles or radium; yet his mind was ready to feel the force of all, though the rays were unborn and the women were dead.

Here opened another totally new education, which promised to be by far the most hazardous of all. The knife-edge along which he must crawl, like Sir Lancelot in the twelfth century, divided two kingdoms of force which had nothing in common but attraction. They were as different as a magnet is from gravitation, supposing one knew what a magnet was, or gravitation, or love. The force of the Virgin was still felt at Lourdes, and seemed to be as potent as X-rays; but in America neither Venus nor Virgin ever had value as force—at most as sentiment. No American had ever been truly afraid of either.

This problem in dynamics gravely perplexed an American historian. The Woman had once been supreme; in France she still seemed potent, not merely as a sentiment, but as a force. Why was she unknown in America? For evidently America was ashamed of her, and she was ashamed of herself, otherwise they would not have strewn fig-leaves so profusely all over her. When she was a true force, she was ignorant of fig-leaves, but the monthly-magazine-made American female had not a feature that would have been recognized by Adam. The trait was notorious, and often humorous, but any one brought up among Puritans knew that sex was sin. In any previous age, sex was strength. Neither art nor beauty was needed. Every one, even among Puritans, knew that neither Diana of the Ephesians nor any of the Oriental goddesses was worshipped for her beauty. She was goddess because of her force; she was the animated dynamo; she was reproduction—the greatest and most mysterious of all energies; all she needed was to be fecund. . . . All this was to American thought as though it had never existed. The true American knew something of the facts, but nothing of the feelings; he read the letter, but he never felt the law. Before this historical chasm, a mind like that of Adams felt itself helpless; he turned from the Virgin to the Dynamo as though he were a Branly coherer. On one side, at the Louvre and at Chartres, as he knew by the record of work actually done and still before his eyes, was the highest energy ever known to man, the creator of four-fifths of his noblest art, exercising vastly more attraction over the human mind than all the steam-engines and dynamos ever dreamed of; and yet this energy was unknown to the American mind. An American Virgin would never dare command; an American Venus would never dare exist.

The question, which to any plain American of the nineteenth century seemed as remote as it did to Adams, drew him almost violently to study, once it was posed; and on this point Langleys were as useless as though they were Herbert Spencers or dynamos. The idea survived only as art. There one turned as naturally as though the artist were himself a woman. Adams began to ponder, asking himself whether he knew of any American artist who had ever insisted on the power of sex, as every classic had always done; but he could think only of Walt Whitman; Bret Harte, as far as the magazines would let him venture; and one or two painters, for the flesh-tones. All the rest had used sex for sentiment, never for force; to them, Eve was a tender flower, and Herodias an unfeminine horror. American art, like the American language and American education, was as far as possible sexless. Society regarded this victory over sex as its greatest triumph, and the historian readily admitted it, since the moral issue, for the moment, did not concern one who was studying the relations of unmoral force. He cared nothing for the sex of the dynamo until he could measure its energy.

Vaguely seeking a clue, he wandered through the art exhibit, and, in his stroll, stopped almost every day before St. Gaudens's General Sherman, which had been given the central post of honor. St. Gaudens himself was in Paris, putting on the work his usual interminable last touches, and listening to the usual contradictory suggestions of brother sculptors. Of all the American artists who gave to American art whatever life it breathed in the seventies, St. Gaudens was perhaps the most sympathetic, but certainly the most inarticulate. General Grant or Don Cameron had scarcely less instinct of rhetoric than he. All the others— the Hunts, Richardson, John La Farge, Stanford White—were exuberant; only St. Gaudens could never discuss or dilate on an emotion, or suggest artistic arguments for giving to his work the forms that he felt. He never laid down the law, or affected the despot, or became brutalized like Whistler by the brutalities of his world. He required no incense; he was no egoist; his simplicity of thought was excessive; he could not imitate, or give any form but his own to the creations of his hand. No one felt more strongly than he the strength of other men, but the idea that they could affect him never stirred an image in his mind.

This summer his health was poor and his spirits were low. For such a temper, Adams was not the best companion, since his own gaiety was not *folle;* but he risked going now and then to the studio on Mont Parnasse to draw him out for a stroll in the Bois de Boulogne, or dinner as pleased his moods, and in return St. Gaudens sometimes let Adams go about in his company.

Once St. Gaudens took him down to Amiens, with a party of Frenchmen, to see the cathedral. Not until they found themselves actually studying the sculpture of the western portal did it dawn on Adams's mind that, for his purposes, St. Gaudens on that spot had more interest to him than the cathedral itself. Great men before great monuments express great truths, provided they are not taken too solemnly. Adams never tired of quoting the supreme phrase of his idol Gibbon, before the Gothic cathedrals: "I darted a contemptuous look on the stately monuments of superstition." Even in the footnotes of his history, Gibbon had never inserted a bit of humor more human than this, and one would have paid largely for a photograph of the fat little historian, on the background of Notre Dame of Amiens, trying to persuade his readers—perhaps himself—that he was darting a contemptuous look on the stately monument, for which he felt in fact the respect which every man of his vast study and active mind always feels before objects worthy of it; but besides the humor, one felt also the relation. Gibbon ignored the Virgin, because in 1789 religious monuments were out of fashion. In 1900 his remark sounded fresh and simple as the green fields to ears that had heard a hundred years of other remarks, mostly no more fresh and certainly less simple. Without malice, one might find it more instructive than a whole lecture of Ruskin. One sees what one brings, and at that moment Gibbon brought the French Revolution. Ruskin brought reaction against the Revolution. St. Gaudens had passed beyond all. He liked the stately monuments much more than he liked Gibbon or Ruskin; he loved their dignity; their unity; their scale; their lines; their lights and shadows; their decorative sculpture; but he was even less conscious than they of the force that created it all —the Virgin, the Woman—by whose genius "the stately monuments of superstition" were built, through which she was expressed. He would have seen more meaning in Isis with the cow's horns, at Edfoo, who expressed the same thought. The art remained, but the energy was lost even upon the artist.

Yet in mind and person St. Gaudens was a survival of the 1500;

he bore the stamp of the Renaissance, and should have carried an image of the Virgin round his neck, or stuck in his hat, like Louis XI. In mere time he was a lost soul that had strayed by chance into the twentieth century, and forgotten where it came from. He writhed and cursed at his ignorance, much as Adams did at his own, but in the opposite sense. St. Gaudens was a child of Benvenuto Cellini, smothered in an American cradle. Adams was a quintessence of Boston, devoured by curiosity to think like Benvenuto. St. Gaudens's art was starved from birth, and Adams's instinct was blighted from babyhood. Each had but half of a nature, and when they came together before the Virgin of Amiens they ought both to have felt in her the force that made them one; but it was not so. To Adams she became more than ever a channel of force; to St. Gaudens she remained as before a channel of taste.

For a symbol of power, St. Gaudens instinctively preferred the horse, as was plain in his horse and Victory of the Sherman monument. Doubtless Sherman also felt it so. The attitude was so American that, for at least forty years, Adams had never realized that any other could be in sound taste. How many years had he taken to admit a notion of what Michael Angelo and Rubens were driving at? He could not say; but he knew that only since 1895 had he begun to feel the Virgin or Venus as force, and not everywhere even so. At Chartres—perhaps at Lourdes—possibly at Cnidos if one could still find there the divinely naked Aphrodite of Praxiteles—but otherwise one must look for force to the goddesses of Indian mythology. The idea died out long ago in the German and English stock. St. Gaudens at Amiens was hardly less sensitive to the force of the female energy than Matthew Arnold at the Grande Chartreuse. Neither of them felt goddesses as power—only as reflected emotion, human expression, beauty, purity, taste, scarcely even as sympathy. They felt a railway train as power; yet they, and all other artists, constantly complained that the power embodied in a railway train could never be embodied in art. All the steam in the world could not, like the Virgin, build Chartres.

Yet in mechanics, whatever the mechanicians might think, both energies acted as interchangeable forces on man, and by action on man all known force may be measured. Indeed, few men of science measured force in any other way. After once admitting that a straight line was the shortest distance between two points, no serious mathematician cared to deny anything that suited his convenience, and rejected no symbol, unproved or unproveable, that helped him to accomplish work.

The symbol was force, as a compass-needle or a triangle was force, as the mechanist might prove by losing it, and nothing could be gained by ignoring their value. Symbol or energy, the Virgin had acted as the greatest force the Western world ever felt, and had drawn man's activities to herself more strongly than any other power, natural or supernatural, had ever done; the historian's business was to follow the track of the energy; to find where it came from and where it went to; its complex source and shifting channels; its values, equivalents, conversions. It could scarcely be more complex than radium; it could hardly be deflected, diverted, polarized, absorbed more perplexingly than other radiant matter. Adams knew nothing about any of them, but as a mathematical problem of influence on human progress, though all were occult, all reacted on his mind, and he rather inclined to think the Virgin easiest to handle.

The pursuit turned out to be long and tortuous, leading at last into the vast forests of scholastic science. From Zeno to Descartes, hand in hand with Thomas Aquinas, Montaigne, and Pascal, one stumbled as stupidly as though one were still a German student of 1860. Only with the instinct of despair could one force one's self into this old thicket of ignorance after having been repulsed at a score of entrances more promising and more popular. Thus far, no path had led anywhere, unless perhaps to an exceedingly modest living. Forty-five years of study had proved to be quite futile for the pursuit of power; one controlled no more force in 1900 than in 1850, although the amount of force controlled by society had enormously increased. The secret of education still hid itself somewhere behind ignorance, and one fumbled over it as feebly as ever. In such labyrinths, the staff is a force almost more necessary than the legs; the pen becomes a sort of blind-man's dog, to keep him from falling into the gutters. The pen works for itself, and acts like a hand, modelling the plastic material over and over again to the form that suits it best. The form is never arbitrary, but it is a sort of growth like crystallization, as any artist knows too well; for often the pencil or pen runs into side-paths and shapelessness, loses its relations, stops or is bogged. Then it has to return on its trail, and recover, if it can, its line of force. The result of a year's work depends more on what is struck out than on what is left in; on the sequence of the main lines of thought, than on their play or variety. Compelled once more to lean heavily on this support, Adams covered more thousands of pages with figures as formal as though they were algebra, laboriously striking out, altering, burning, experimenting, until the year had expired, the Exposition had long been closed, and winter drawing to its end, before he sailed from Cherbourg, on January 19, 1901, for home.

XV. INTRODUCTION

Henry James (1843–1916), the brother of William James, was the most accomplished artist that America had yet produced. No selection from his work can give a fair idea of the wealth of his mind or the success of his art, and needless to say, is no substitute for the great novels. He must, of course, first be appreciated as a creative writer. The chapter reprinted here does, however, exemplify his mature literary style, the acuity of his perception, as well as the subtlety and sophistication of his mind.

After several trips to Europe, and partly as a result of his growing sense of the aridity and flatness of the American physical, intellectual, and social landscapes, James became an exile in 1875, settling finally and permanently in London the following year. He had already decided that the American background was uncongenial to his art, as he tried to explain in a private letter written before his exile:

"Looking about for myself, I conclude that the face of nature and civilization in this our country is to a certain point a very sufficient literary field. But it will yield its secrets only to a really grasping *imagination. . . .* To write well and worthily of American things one need even more than elsewhere to be a *master.* But unfortunately one is less!"

Always in search of density and resonance, James could not for very long keep his inner eye away from the American scene. His great novels are international in plot, whose characters personify, at least on the most superficial level, the conflict between the old world and the new.

For James, as for Henry Adams, the stature and behavior of the American woman was a major problem. Of what precisely did the Americanism of his major heroines consist? In the following selection from his volume of observations, *The American Scene,* one comes as close as possible to an explicit statement of his views of the woman in America.

It is instructive that a discussion of the city of Washington, D. C., was the occasion for his analysis of the sexual nature of American society. Because American men devoted their whole energy to business, all other affairs in America had been by default turned over to the woman. Seizing the opportunity, she pretended the situation was normal.

The uniqueness of women in America was the result of their special training in freedom; their audacity was the result of their social security. Washington, alone among the American cities, took on a more normal aspect, at least from the European point of view, with men engaging in spheres other than business, participating in the ubiquitous conversation of Washington. It was therefore, according to James, only in Washington that men existed socially. Because of that fact, women in Washington seemed to fit with greater proportion into the total scene, as if their sisters elsewhere in America had taken too much on when their men abdicated.

When James contemplated the monumental aspect of the city of Washington, another American question obtruded itself: Can money produce an interesting and graceful city? He concluded tentatively that there was not enough American history, outside of economic history, to go around. But yet some of the monuments of the capital city, the White House and the Capitol, were able to evoke the past of the democratic man in America, and it was entirely appropriate that James should brood about James Fenimore Cooper's solitary heroes in the shadows of the buildings of state.

XV.

Henry James
WASHINGTON
1907

Washington . . . had struck me from the first as presenting two distinct faces; the more obvious of which was the public and official, the monumental, with features all more or less majestically playing the great administrative, or, as we nowadays put it, Imperial part. This clustered, yet at the same time oddly scattered, city, a general impression of high granite steps, of light gray corniced colonnades, rather harmoniously low, contending for effect with slaty mansard roofs and masses of iron excrescence, a general impression of somewhat vague, empty, sketchy, fundamentals, however expectant, however spacious, overweighted by a single Dome and overaccented by a single Shaft—this loose congregation

SOURCE. Henry James, *The American Scene,* New York: Harper and Brothers, 1907, pp. 326–350. Copyright 1907 by Henry James. Reprinted by permission of Paul R. Reynolds Inc., 599 Fifth Avenue, New York 17, N.Y.

of values seemed, strangely, a matter disconnected and remote, though remaining in its way portentous and bristling all incoherently at the back of the scene. The back of the scene, indeed, to one's quite primary sense, might have been but an immense painted, yet unfinished cloth, hung there to a confessedly provisional end and marked with the queerness, among many queernesses, of looking always the same; painted once for all in clear, bright, fresh tones, but never emerging from its flatness, after the fashion of other capitals, into the truly, the variously, modelled and rounded state. (It appeared provisional therefore because looking as if it might have been unhooked and removed as a whole; because any one object in it so treated would have made the rest also come off.) The foreground was a different thing, a thing that, ever so quaintly, seemed to represent the force really in possession; though consisting but of a small company of people engaged perpetually in conversation and (always, I repeat, for the rank outsider) singularly destitute of conspicuous marks or badges. This little society easily became, for the detached visitor, the city itself, *the* national capital and the greater part of the story; and that, ever, in spite of the comparatively scant intensity of its political permeation. The political echo was of course to be heard in it, and the public character, in its higher forms, to be encountered—though only in "single spies," not in battalions; but there was something that made it much more individual than any mere predominance of political or administrative color would have made it; leaving it in that case to do no more than resemble the best society in London, or that in best possession of the field in Paris.

Two sharp signs my remoter remembrance had shown me the then Washington world, and the first met, as putting forth; one of these the fact of its being extraordinarily easy and pleasant, and the other that of one's appearing to make out in it not more than half a dozen members of the Lower House and not more than a dozen of the Upper. This kept down the political permeation, and was bewildering, if one was able to compare, in the light of the different London condition, the fact of the social ubiquity there of the acceptable M.P. and that of the social frequency even of his more equivocal hereditary colleague. A London nestling under the towers of Westminster, yet practically void of members of the House of Commons, and with the note of official life far from exclusively sounding, that might have been in those days the odd image of Washington, had not the picture been stamped with other variations still. These were a whole cluster, not instantly to be made out, but constituting the unity of the place as soon as perceived; representing that finer extract or essence which the self-respecting observer is never easy till he be able to shake up and down in bottled form. The charming company of the foreground then, which referred itself so little to the sketchy back-scene, the monstrous Dome and Shaft, figments of the upper air, the pale colonnades and mere myriad-windowed Buildings, was the second of the two faces, and the more one lived with it the more, up to a certain point, one lived away from the first. In time, and after perceiving *how* it was what it so agreeably was, came the recognition of common ground; the recognition that, in spite of strange passages of the national life, liable possibly to recur, during which the President himself was scarce thought to be in society, the particular precious character that one had apprehended could never have ripened without a general consensus. One had put one's finger on it when one had seen disengage itself from many anomalies, from not a few drolleries, the superior, the quite majestic fact of the City of Conversation pure and simple, and positively of the only specimen, of any such intensity, in the world.

That had remained for me, from the other time, the properest name of Washington, and nothing could so interest me, on a renewal of acquaintance, too long postponed and then too woefully brief, as to find my description wholly justified. If the emphasis added by "pure and simple" be invariably retained, the description will continue, I think, to embrace and exhaust the spectacle, while yet leaving it every inch of its value. Clearly quite immeasurable, on American ground, the value of such an assertion of a town-type directly opposed to the unvarying American, and quite unique, on any ground, so organized a social indifference to the vulgar vociferous Market. Washington may of course *know* more than she confesses—no community could perhaps really be as ignorant as Washington used at any rate to look, of this particular thing, of "goods" and shares and rises and falls and all such sordidities; but she knows assuredly still the very least she can get off with, and nothing even yet pleases her more than to forget what she does know. She unlearns, she turns her back, while London, Paris, Berlin, Rome, in their character of political centres, strike us as, on the contrary, feverishly learning, trying more and more to do the exact opposite. (I speak, naturally, as to Washington, of knowing actively and interestedly, in the spirit of gain—not merely of the enjoyed lights of political and administrative science, doubtless as abundant there as anywhere else). It might fairly have been, I used to think, that the charming place—charming in the particular connection I speak of—had on its conscience to make one forget for an hour the colossal greed of New York. Nothing, in fact, added more to its charm than its appearing virtually to invite one to impute to it some such vicarious compunction.

If I be reminded, indeed, that the distinction I here glance at is negative, and be asked what then (if she knew nothing of the great American interest) Washington did socially know, my answer, I recognize, has at once to narrow itself, and becomes perhaps truly the least bit difficult to utter. It none the less remains distinct enough that, the City of Conversation being only in question, and a general subject of all the conversation having thereby to be predicated, our responsibility is met as soon as we are able to say what Washington mainly talks, and appears always to go mainly talking, about. Washington talks about herself, and about almost nothing else; falling superficially indeed, on that ground, but into line with the other capitals. London, Paris, Berlin, Rome, goodness knows, talk about themselves: that is each member of this sisterhood talks, sufficiently or inordinately, of the great number of divided and differing selves that form together her controlling identity. London, for instance, talks of everything in the world without thereby for a moment, as it were, ceasing to be egotistical. It has taken everything in the world to make London up, so that she is in consequence simply doomed never to get away from herself. Her conversation is largely, I think, the very effort to do that; but she inevitably figures in it but as some big buzzing insect which keeps bumping against a treacherous mirror. It is in positive quest of an identity of some sort, much rather—an identity other than merely functional and technical—that Washington goes forth, encumbered with no ideal of avoidance or escape: it is about herself *as* the City of Conversation precisely that she incessantly converses; adorning the topic, moreover, with endless ingenuity and humor. But that, absolutely, remains the case; which thus becomes one of the most thorough, even if probably one of the most natural and of the happiest, cases of collective self-consciousness that one knows. The spectacle, as it at first met my senses, was that of a numerous community in ardent pursuit of some workable conception of its social self, and trying meanwhile intelligently to talk itself, and even this very embarrassment, into a *subject* for conversation. Such a picture might not seem purely pleasing, on the side of variety of appeal, and I admit one may have had one's reserves about it; reserves sometimes reflected, for example, in dim inward speculation—one of the effects of the Washington air I have already glanced at—as to the amount of response it might evoke in the diplomatic body. It may have been on my part a morbid obsession, but the diplomatic body was liable to strike one there as more characteristically "abysmal" than elsewhere, more impenetrably bland and inscrutably blank; and it was obvious, certainly, that their concern to help the place intellectually to find itself was not to be expected to approach in intensity the concern even of a repatriated absentee. You were concerned only if you had, by your sensibility, a stake in the game; which was the last thing a foreign representative would wish to confess to, this being directly opposed to all his enjoined duties. It is no part of the office of such personages to assist the societies to which they are accredited to find themselves—it is much more their mission to leave all such vaguely and, so far as may be, grotesquely groping: so apt are societies, in finding themselves, to find other things too. This detachment from the whole mild convulsion of effort, the considerate pretence of not being too aware of it, combined with latent probabilities of alarm about it no less than of amusement, represented, to the unquiet fancy, much more the spirit of the old-time Legations.

What *was*, at all events, better fun, of the finer sort, than having one's self a stake in the outcome?—what helped the time (so much of it as there was!) more to pass than just to join in the so fresh experiment of constitutive, creative talk? The boon, it should always be mentioned, meanwhile went on not in the least in the tone of solemnity. That would have been fatal, because probably irritating, and it was where the good star of Washington intervened. The tone was, so to speak, of *conscious* self-consciousness, and the highest genius for conversation doubtless dwelt in the fact that the ironic spirit was ready always to give its very self away, fifty times over, for the love, or for any quickening, of the theme. The foundation for the whole happy predicament remained, moreover, of the firmest, and the essence of the case was to be as easily stated as the great social fact is, in America, whether through exceptions or aggravations, everywhere to be stated. Nobody was in "business"—that was the sum and substance of it; and for the one large human assemblage on the continent of which this was true the difference made was huge. Nothing could strike one more than that it was the only way in which, over the land, a difference *could* be made, and than how, in our vast commercial democracy, almost any difference—by which I mean almost any exception—promptly acquires prodigious relief. The value here was at once that the place could offer to view a society, the

only one in the country, in which Men existed, and that that rich little
fact became the key to everything. Superficially taken, I recognize, the
circumstance fails to look portentous; but it looms large immediately,
gains the widest bearing, in the light of any direct or extended
acquaintance with American conditions. From the moment it is
adequately borne in mind that the business-man, in the United States,
may, with no matter what dim struggles, gropings, yearnings, never
hope to be anything *but* a business-man, the size of the field he so
abdicates is measured, as well as the fact of the other care to which his
abdication hands it over. It lies there waiting, pleading from all its pores,
to be occupied—the lonely waste, the boundless gaping void of "society";
which is but a rough name for all the *other* so numerous relations with
the world he lives in that are imputable to the civilized being. Here
it is then that the world he lives in accepts its doom and becomes, by
his default, subject and plastic to his mate; his default having made,
all around him, the unexampled opportunity of the woman—which
she would have been an incredible fool not to pounce upon. It needs
little contact with American life to perceive how she *has* pounced, and
how, outside business, she has made it over in her image. She has been,
up to now, on the vast residual tract, in peerless possession, and is
occupied in developing and extending her wonderful conquest, which
she appreciates to the last inch of its extent.

She has meanwhile probably her hours of amazement at the size
of her windfall; she cannot quite live without wonder at the oddity of
her so "sleeping" partner, the strange creature, by her side, with his values
and his voids, but who is best known to her as having yielded what she
would have clutched to the death. Yet these are mere mystic, inscrutable
possibilities—dreams, for us, of her hushed, shrouded hours: the face
she shows, on all the facts, is that of mere unwinking tribute to the
matter of course. The effect of these high signs of assurance in her
has been—and it is really her master-stroke—to represent the situation
as perfectly normal. Her companion's attitude, totally destitute of high
signs, does everything it can to further this feat; so that, as disposed
together in the American picture, they testify, extraordinarily, to the
successful rupture of a universal law, the sight is at first, for observation,
most mystifying. Then the impunity of the whole thing gains upon us;
the equilibrium strikes us, however strangely, as at least provisionally
stable; we see that a society in many respects workable would seem to
have been arrived at, and that we shall in any case have time to study it.

The phenomenon may easily become, for a spectator, the sentence written largest in the American sky: when he is in search of the characteristic, what else so plays the part? The woman is two-thirds of the apparent life —which means that she is absolutely all of the social; and, as this is nowhere else the case, the occasion is unique for seeing what such a situation may make of her. The result elsewhere, in Europe generally, of conditions in which men have actively participated and to which, throughout, they personally contribute, she has only the old story to tell, and keeps telling it after her fashion. The woman produced by a women-made society alone has obviously quite a new story—to which it is not for a moment to be gainsaid that the world at large has, for the last thirty years in particular, found itself lending an attentive, at times even a charmed, ear. The extent and variety of this attention have been the specious measure of the personal success of the type in question, and are always referred to when its value happens to be challenged. "The American woman?—why, she has beguiled, she has conquered, the globe: look at her fortune everywhere and fail to accept her if you can."

She has been, accordingly, about the globe, beyond all doubt, a huge success of curiosity; she has at her best—and far beyond any consciousness and intention of her own, lively as these for the most part usually are—infinitely amused the nations. It has been found among them that, for more reasons than we can now go into, her manner of embodying and representing her sex has fairly made of her a new human convenience, not unlike fifty of the others, of a slightly different order, the ingenious mechanical appliances, stoves, refrigerators, sewing-machines, type-writers, cash-registers, that have done so much, in the household and the place of business, for the American name. By which I am of course far from meaning that the revelation has been of her utility as a domestic drudge; it has been much rather in the fact that the advantages attached to her being a woman at all have been so happily combined with the absence of the drawbacks, for persons intimately dealing with her, traditionally suggested by that condition. The corresponding advantages, in the light of almost any old order, have always seemed inevitably paid for by the drawbacks; but here, unmistakably, was a case in which—as at first appeared, certainly—they were to be enjoyed very nearly for nothing. What it came to, evidently, was that she had been grown in an air in which a hundred of the "European" complications and dangers didn't exist, and in which also she had had to take upon herself a certain training for freedom. It was not that she had had, in the vulgar sense, to "look out" for herself, inasmuch as it was of the very essence of her position not to be threatened or waylaid; but that she could develop her audacity on the basis of her security, just as she could develop her "powers" in a medium from which criticism was consistently absent. Thus she arrived, full-blown, on the general scene, the least criticised object, in proportion to her importance, that had ever adorned it. It would take long to say why her situation, under this retrospect, may effect the inner fibre of the critic himself as one of the most touching on record; he may merely note his perception that she was to have been after all but the sport of fate. For why need she originally, he wonders, have embraced so confidently, so gleefully, yet so unguardedly, the terms offered her to an end practically so perfidious? Why need she, unless in the interest of her eventual discipline, have turned away with so light a heart after watching the Man, the deep American man, retire into his tent and let down the flap? She had her "paper" from him, their agreement signed and sealed; but would she not, in some other air and under some other sky, have been visited by a saving instinct? Would she not have said, "No, this is too unnatural; there must be a trap in it somewhere—it's addressed really, in the long run, to making a fool of me?" It is impossible, of course, to tell; and her case, as it stands for us, at any rate, is that she showed no doubts. It is not on the American scene and in the presence of mere American phenomena that she is even yet to be observed as showing them; but does not my digression find itself meanwhile justified by the almost clear certainty that the first symptoms of the revulsion—of the *con*vulsion, I am tempted to say—must break out in Washington?

For here—and it is what I have been so long in coming to—here alone in the American world, do we catch the other sex not observing the agreement. I have described this anomaly, at Washington, as that of Man's socially "existing"; since we have seen that his fidelity to his compact throughout the country in general has involved his not doing so. What has happened, obviously, has been that his reasons, at a stroke, have dropped, and that he finds himself, without them, a different creature. He has discovered that he *can* exist in other connections than that of the Market, and that all he has therefore to settle is the question of whether he may. The most delicate interest of Washington is the fact that it is quite practically *being* settled there—in the practical way which is yet also the dramatic. *Solvitur ambulando;* it is being settled—that is the charm—as it goes, settled without discussion. It would be awkward and gross to say that Man has dealt any conscious blow at the monopoly of his companion, or that her prestige, as mistress of the situation, has suffered in any manner a noted abatement. Yet none the less, as he has there, in a degree, socially found himself and, allured by the new sense, is evidently destined to seek much further still, the sensible effect, the change of impression on one's coming from other places, is of the most marked. Man is solidly, vividly present, and the presence of Woman has consequently, for the proposed intensity, to reckon with it. The omens on behalf of the former appearance are just now strikingly enhanced, as happens, by the accident of the rare quality, as it were, of the particular male presence supremely presiding there; and it would certainly be strange that this idea of the recommittal to masculine hands of some share at least in the interests of civilization, some part of the social property and social office, should not, from so high an example, have received a new impulse and a new consecration. Easily enough, if we had space here to consider it, might come up the whole picture of the new indications thus afforded, the question of the degree in which a sex capable, in the American air, of having so despoiled itself may really be capable of retracing its steps and repairing its mistake. It would appear inevitable to ask whether such a mistake on such a scale *can* prove effectively reparable—whether ground so lost can be effectively recovered. Has not the American woman, with such a start, gained such an irreducible advance, on the whole high plane of the amenities, that her companion will never catch up with her? This last is an inquiry that I must, alas, brush aside, though feeling it, as I have already noted, *the* most oddly interesting that the American spectacle proposes to us; only saying, provisionally, that the aspect of manners through the nation at large offers no warrant whatever for any prompt "No" to it.

It is not, however, of the nation at large I here speak; the case is of the extremely small, though important and significant, fraction of the whole represented by the Washington group—which thus shows us the Expropriated Half in the very act of itself pondering that issue. Is the man "up to it," up to the major heritage, the man who *could,* originally, so inconceivably, and for a mere mess of pottage if there ever was one, let it go? "Are we up to it, really, at this time of day, and what on earth will awfully become of us if the question, once put to the test, shall have to be decided against us?" I think it not merely fanciful to say that some dim, distressful interrogative sound of that sort frequently reached, in the Washington air, the restless analyst—though not to any quickening of his own fear. With a perfect consciousness that it was still early to say, that the data are as yet insufficient and that the missing quantity must absolutely be found before it can be weighed and valued, he was none the less struck with the felicity of many symptoms and would fairly have been able to believe at moments that the character hitherto so effaced has but to show the confidence of taking itself for granted. That act of itself reveals, restores, reinstates and completes this character. Is it not, for that matter, essentially implied in our recognition of the place as the City of Conversation? The victim of effacement, the outcast at the door, has, all the while we have been talking of him *talked himself* back; and if anything could add to this happy portent it would be another that had scarcely less bearing. Nowhere more than in Washington, positively, were the women to have struck me as naturally and harmoniously in the social picture—as happily, soothingly, proportionately, and no more than proportionately, participant and ministrant. Hence the irresistible conclusion that with the way really shown them they would only ask to take it; the way being their assent to the truth that the abdication of the Man proves ever (after the first flush of their triumph) as bad really for their function as for his. Hence, in fine, the appearance that, with the proportions re-established, they will come to recognize their past world as a fools' paradise, and their present, and still more their future, as much more made to endure. They could not, one reasoned, have been, in general, so perfectly agreeable unless they had been pleased, and they could not have been pleased without the prospect of gaining, by the readjusted relation, more, on the whole, than they were to lose; without the prospect even again perhaps of truly and insidiously gaining more than the other beneficiary. That *would* be, I think, the feminine conception of a readministered justice. Washington, at such a rate, in any case, might become to them as good as "Europe," and a Europe of their own would obviously be better than a Europe of other people's. There are, after all, other women on other continents.

One might have been sure in advance that the character of a democracy would nowhere more sharply mark itself than in the democratic substitute for a court city, and Washington is cast in the mould that expresses most the absence of salient social landmarks and constituted features. Here it is that conversation, as the only invoked presence, betrays a little its inadequacy to the furnishing forth, all by itself, of an outward view. It tells us it must be there, since in all the wide empty vistas nothing else is, and the general elimination *can* but have left it. A pleading, touching effect, indeed, lurks in this sense of it as seated, at receipt of custom, by any decent door of any decent domicile and watching the vacancy for reminder and appeal. It is left to conversation alone to people the scene with accents; putting aside two or three objects to be specified, there is *never* an accent in it, up and down, far and wide, save such as fall rather on the ear of the mind; those projected by the social spirit starved for the sense of an occasional emphasis. The White House is an accent—one of the lightest, sharpest possible; and the Capitol, of course, immensely, another; though the latter falls on the exclusively political page, as to which I have been waiting to say a word. It should meanwhile be mentioned that we are promised these enhancements, these illustrations, of the great general text, on the most magnificent scale; a splendid projected and announced Washington of the future, with approaches even now grandly outlined and massively marked; in face of which one should perhaps confess to the futility of any current estimate. If I speak thus of the Capitol, however, let me not merely brush past the White House to get to it—any more than feel free to pass into it without some preliminary stare at that wondrous Library of Congress which glitters in fresh and almost unmannerly emulation, almost frivolous irrelevance of form, in the neighborhood of the greater building. About the ingenuities and splendors of this last costly structure, a riot of rare material and rich ornament, there would doubtless be much to say—did not one everywhere, on all such ground, meet the open eye of criticism simply to establish with it a private intelligence, simply to respond to it by a deprecating wink. The guardian of that altar, I think, is but too willing, on such a hint, to let one pass without the sacrifice.

It is a case again here, as on fifty other occasions, of the tribute instantly paid by the revisiting spirit; but paid, all without question, to the general *kind* of presence for which the noisy air, over the land, feels so sensibly an inward ache—the presence that corresponds there, no matter how loosely, to that of the housing and harboring European Church in the ages of great disorder. The Universities and the greater Libraries (the smaller, for a hundred good democratic reasons, are another question), repeat, in their manner, to the imagination, East and West, the note of the old thick-walled convents and quiet cloisters: they are large and charitable, they are sturdy, often proud and often rich, and they have the incalculable value that they represent the only intermission to inordinate rapacious traffic that the scene offers to view. With the suggestion of sacred ground they play even upon the most restless of analysts as they will, making him face about, with ecstasy, any way they seem to point; so that he feels it his business much less to count over their shortcomings than to proclaim them places of enchantment. They are better at their worst than anything else at its best, and the comparatively sweet sounds that stir their theoretic stillness are for him as echoes of the lyre of Apollo. The Congressional Library is magnificent, and would become thus a supreme sanctuary even were it ten times more so: there would seem to be nothing then but to pronounce it a delight and have done with it—or let the appalled imagination, in other words, slink into it and stay there. But here is pressed precisely, with particular force, the spring of the question that takes but a touch to sound: is the case of this remarkable creation, by exception, a case in which the violent waving of the pecuniary wand *has* incontinently produced interest? The answer can only be, I feel, a shy assent—though shy indeed only till the logic of the matter is apparent. This logic is that, though money alone can gather in on such a scale the treasures of knowledge, these treasures, in the form of books and documents, themselves organize and furnish their world. They appoint and settle the proportions, they thicken the air, they people the space, they create and consecrate all their relations, and no one shall say that, where they scatter life, which they themselves in fact *are,* history does not promptly attend. Emphatically yes, therefore, the great domed and tiered, galleried and statued central hall of the Congressional, the last word of current constructional science and artistic resource, already crowns itself with that grace.

The graceful thing in Washington beyond any other, none the less, is the so happily placed and featured White House, the late excellent extensions and embellishments of which have of course represented expenditure—but only of the refined sort imposed by some mature portionless gentlewoman on relatives who have accepted the principle of making her, at a time of life, more honorably comfortable. The whole ample precinct and margin formed by the virtual continuity of its grounds with those expanses in which the effect of the fine Washington Obelisk rather spends or wastes itself (not a little as if some loud monosyllable had been uttered, in a preoccupied company, without a due production of sympathy or sense)—the fortunate isolation of the White House, I say, intensifies its power to appeal to that musing and mooning visitor whose perceptions alone, in all the conditions, I hold worthy of account. Hereabouts, beyond doubt, history had from of old seemed to me insistently seated, and I remember a short spring-time of years ago when Lafayette Square itself, contiguous to the Executive Mansion, could create a rich sense of the past by the use of scarce other witchcraft than its command of that pleasant perspective and its possession of the most prodigious of all Presidential effigies, Andrew Jackson, as archaic as a Ninevite king, prancing and rocking through the ages. If that atmosphere, moreover, in the fragrance of the Washington April, was even a quarter of a century since as a liquor of bitter-sweet taste, overflowing its cup, what was the ineffable mixture now, with all the elements further distilled, all the life further sacrificed, to make it potent? One circled about the place as for meeting the ghosts, and one paused, under the same impulse, before the high palings of the White House drive, as if wondering at haunted ground. There the ghosts stood in their public array, spectral enough and clarified; yet scarce making it easier to "place" the strange, incongruous blood-drops, as one looked through the rails, on that revised and freshened page. But one fortunately has one's choice, in all these connections, as one turns away; the mixture, as I have called it, is really here so fine. General Jackson, in the centre of the Square, still rocks his hobby and the earth; but the fruit of the interval, to my actual eyes, hangs nowhere brighter than in the brilliant memorials lately erected to Lafayette and to Rochambeau. Artful, genial, expressive, the tribute of French talent, these happy images supply, on the spot, the note without which even the most fantasticating sense of our national past would feel itself rub forever against mere brown homespun. Everything else gives way, for me, I confess, as I again stand before them; everything, whether as historic fact, or present *agrément,* or future possibility, yields to this one high luxury of our old friendship with France.

The "artistic" Federal city already announced spreads itself then before us, in plans elaborated even to the finer details, a city of palaces and monuments and gardens, symmetries and circles and far radiations, with the big Potomac for water-power and water-effect and the recurrent Maryland spring, so prompt and so full-handed, for a perpetual benediction. This imagery has, above all, the value, for the considering mind, that it presents itself as under the wide-spread wings of the general Government, which fairly make it figure to the rapt vision as the object caught up in eagle claws and lifted into fields of air that even the high brows of the municipal boss fail to sweep. The wide-spread wings affect us, in the prospect, as great fans that, by their mere tremor, will blow the work, at all steps and stages, clean and clear, disinfect it quite ideally of any germ of the job, and prepare thereby for the American voter, on the spot and in the pride of possession, quite a new kind of civic consciousness. The scheme looms largest, surely, as a demonstration of the possibilities of that service to him, and nothing about it will be more interesting than to measure—though this may take time—the nature and degree of his alleviation. Will the new pride I speak of sufficiently inflame him? Will the taste of the new consciousness, finding him so fresh to it, prove the right medicine? One can only regret that we must still rather indefinitely wait to see—and regret it all the more that there is always, in America, yet another lively source of interest involved in the execution of such designs, and closely involved just in proportion as the high intention, the formal majesty, of the thing seems assured. It comes back to what we constantly feel, throughout the country, to what the American scene everywhere depends on for half its appeal or its effect; to the fact that the social conditions, the material, pressing and pervasive, make the particular experiment or demonstration, whatever it may pretend to, practically a new and incalculable thing. This general Americanism is often the one tag of character attaching to the case after every other appears to have abandoned it. The thing is happening, or will have to happen, in the American way—that American way which is more different from all other native ways, taking country with country, than any of these latter are different from each other; and the question is of how, each time, the American way will see it through.

The element of suspense—beguilement, ever, of the sincere observer—is provided for by the fact that, though this American way never fails to come up, he has to recognize as by no means equally true that it never fails to succeed. It is inveterately applied, but with consequences bewilderingly various; which means, however, for our present moral, but that the certainty of the *determined* American effect is an element to attend quite especially such a case as the employment of the arts of design, on an unprecedented scale, for public uses, the adoption on this scale of the whole æsthetic law. Encountered in America, phenomena of this order strike us mostly as occurring in the historic void, as having to present themselves in the hard light of that desert, and as needing to extort from it, so far as they can, something of the shading of their interest. Encountered in older countries, they show, on the contrary, as taking up the references, as consenting perforce to the relations, of which the air is already full, and as having thereby much rather to get themselves expressive by charm than to get themselves expressive by weight. The danger "in Europe" is of their having too many things to say, and too many others to distinguish these from; the danger in the States is of their not having things enough—with enough tone and resonance furthermore to give them. What therefore will the multitudinous and elaborate forms of the Washington to come have to "say," and what, above all, besides gold and silver, stone and marble and trees and flowers, will they be able to say it *with?* That is one of the questions in the mere phrasing of which the restless analyst finds a thrill. There is a thing called interest that has to be produced for him—positively as if he were a rabid usurer with a clutch of his imperilled bond. He has seen again and again how the most expensive effort often fails to lead up to interest, and he has seen how it may bloom in soil of no more worth than so many layers of dust and ashes. He has learnt in fact—he learns greatly in America— to mistrust any plea for it *directly* made by money, which operates too often as the great puffing motor-car framed for whirling him, in his dismay, quite away from it. And he has inevitably noted, at the same time, from how comparatively few other sources this rewarding dividend on his invested attention may be drawn. He thinks of these sources as few, that is, because he sees the same ones, which are the references by which interest is fed, used again and again, with a desperate economy; sees the same ones, even as the human heroes, celebrities, extemporized lions or scape-goats, required social and educational figure-heads and "values," having to serve in *all* the connections and adorn all the tales. That is one of the liveliest of his American impressions. He has at moments his sense that, in presence of such vast populations and instilled, emulous demands, there is not, outside the mere economic, enough native history, recorded or current, to go round.

It seemed to me on the spot, moreover, that such reflections were rather more than less pertinent in face of the fact that I was again to find the Capitol, whenever I approached, and above all whenever I entered it, a vast and many-voiced creation. The thing depends of course somewhat on the visitor, who will be the more responsive, I think, the further back into the "origins" of the whole American spectacle his personal vision shall carry him; but this hugest, as I suppose it, of all the homes of debate only asks to put forth, on opportunity, an incongruous, a various, an inexhaustible charm. I may as well say at once that I found myself from the first adoring the Capitol, though I may not pretend here to dot all the i's of all my reasons—since some of these might appear below the dignity of the subject and others alien to its simplicity. The ark of the American covenant may strike one thus, at any rate, as a compendium of all the national ideals, a museum, crammed full, even to overflowing, of all the national terms and standards, weights and measures and emblems of greatness and glory, and indeed as a builded record of half the collective vibrations of a people; their conscious spirit, their public faith, their bewildered taste, their ceaseless curiosity, their arduous and interrupted education. Such were to my vision at least some of its aspects, but the place had a hundred sides, and if I had had time to look for others still I felt I should have found them. What it comes to —whereby the "pull," in America, is of the greatest—is that association really reigns there, and in the richest, and even again and again in the drollest, forms; it is thick and vivid and almost gross, it assaults the wondering mind. The labyrinthine pile becomes thus inordinately *amusing*—taking the term in its finer modern sense. The analogy may seem forced, but it affected me as playing in Washington life very much the part that St. Peter's, of old, had seemed to me to play in Roman: it offered afternoon entertainment, at the end of a longish walk, to any spirit in the humor for the uplifted and flattered vision—and this without suggesting that the sublimities in the two cases, even as measured by the profanest mind, tend at all to be equal. The Washington dome is indeed capable, in the Washington air, of admirable, of sublime, effects; and there are cases in which, seen at a distance above its yellow Potomac, it varies but by a shade from the sense—yes, absolutely the divine campagna-sense—of St. Peter's and the like-colored Tiber.

But the question is positively of the impressiveness of the great terraced Capitol hill, with its stages and slopes, staircases and fountains, its general presentation of its charge. And if the whole mass and prospect "amuse," as I say, from the moment they are embraced, the visitor curious of the *democratic assimilation* of the greater dignities and majesties will least miss the general logic. That is the light in which the whole thing is supremely interesting; the light of the fact, illustrated at every turn, that the populations maintaining it deal with it so directly and intimately, so sociably and humorously. We promptly take in that, if ever we are to commune in a concentrated way with the sovereign people, and see their exercised power raise a side-wind of irony for forms and arrangements other than theirs, the occasion here will amply serve. Indubitably, moreover, at a hundred points, the irony operates, and all the more markedly under such possible interference; the interference of the monumental spittoons, that of the immense amount of vulgar, of barbaric, decoration, that of the terrible artistic tributes from, and scarce less to, the different States—the unassorted marble mannikins in particular, each a portrayal by one of the commonwealths of her highest worthy, which make the great Rotunda, the intended Valhalla, resemble a stone-cutter's collection of priced sorts and sizes. Discretion exists, throughout, only as a flower of the very first or of these very latest years; the large middle time, corresponding, and even that unequally, with the English Victorian, of sinister memory, was unacquainted with the name, and waits there now, in its fruits, but for a huge sacrificial fire, some far-flaring act-of-faith of the future: a tribute to the æsthetic law which one already feels stirring the air, so that it may arrive, I think, with an unexampled stride. Nothing will have been more interesting, surely, than so public a wiping-over of the æsthetic slate, with all the involved collective compunctions and repudiations, the general exhibition of a colossal conscience, a conscience proportionate to the size and wealth of the country. To such grand gestures does the American scene lend itself!

The elements in question are meanwhile there, in any case, just as the sovereign people are there, "going over" their property; but we are aware none the less of impressions—that of the ponderous proud Senate, for instance, so sensibly massive; that of the Supreme Court, so simply, one almost says so chastely, yet, while it breathes supremacy, so elegantly, so all intellectually, in session—under which the view, taking one extravagance with another, recurs rather ruefully to glimpses elsewhere caught, glimpses of authority emblazoned, bewigged, bemantled, bemarshalled, in almost direct defeat of its intention of gravity. For the reinstated absentee, in these presences, the mere recovery of native privilege was at all events a balm—after too many challenged appeals and abused patiences, too many hushed circuitous creepings, among the downtrodden, in other and more bristling halls of state. The sense of a certain large, final benignity in the Capitol comes then, I think, from this impression that the national relation to it is that of a huge flourishing Family to the place of business, the estate-office, where, in a myriad open ledgers, which offer no obscurity to the hereditary head for figures, the account of their colossal revenue is kept. They meet there in safe sociability, as all equally initiated and interested—not as in a temple or a citadel, but by the warm domestic hearth of Columbia herself; a motherly, chatty, clear-spectacled Columbia, who reads all the newspapers, knows, to the last man, every one of her sons by name, and, to the last boy, even her grandsons, and is fenced off, at the worst, but by concentric circles of rocking-chairs. It is impossible, as I say, not to be fondly conscious of her welcome—unless again, and yet again, I read into the general air, confusedly, too much of the happy accident of the basis of my introduction. But if my sensibility responds with intensity to this, so much the better; for what were such felt personal aids and influences, after all, but cases and examples, embodied expressions, of character, type, distinction, products of the *working* of the whole thing?—specimens, indeed, highly concentrated and refined, and made thereby, I admit, more charming and insidious.

It must also be admitted that to exchange the inner aspects of the vast monument for the outer is to be reminded with some sharpness of a Washington in which half the sides that have held our attention drop, as if rather abashed, out of sight. Not its pleasant brightness as of a winter watering-place, not its connections, however indirect, with the older, but those with the newer, the newest, civilization, seem matter of recognition for its various marble fronts; it rakes the prospect, it rakes the continent, to a much more sweeping purpose, and is visibly concerned but in immeasurable schemes of which it can consciously remain the centre. Here, in the vast spaces—mere empty light and air, though such pleasant air and such pretty light as yet—the great Federal future seems, under vague bright forms, to hover and to stalk, making the horizon recede to take it in, making the terraces too, below the long colonnades, the admirable stand-points, the sheltering porches, of political philosophy. The comparatively new wings of the building filled me, whenever I walked there, with thanksgiving for their large and perfect elegance: so, in Paris, might the wide mated fronts that are of such a noble effect on either side of the Rue Royale shine in multiplied majesty and recovered youth over an infinite Place de la Concorde. These parts of the Capitol, on their Acropolis height, are ideally constructed for "raking," and for this suggestion of their dominating the American scene in playhouse gallery fashion. You are somehow possessed of it *all* while you tread them—their marble embrace appears so the complement of the vast democratic lap. Though I had them in general, for contemplation, quite to myself, I met one morning a trio of Indian braves, braves dispossessed of forest and prairie, but as free of the builded labyrinth as they had ever been of these; also arrayed in neat pot-hats, shoddy suits and light overcoats, with their pockets, I am sure, full of photographs and cigarettes: circumstances all that quickened their resemblance, on the much bigger scale, to Japanese celebrities, or to specimens, on show, of what the Government can do with people with whom it is supposed able to do nothing. They seemed just then and there, for a mind fed betimes on the Leatherstocking Tales, to project as in a flash an image in itself immense, but foreshortened and simplified—reducing to a single smooth stride the bloody footsteps of time. One rubbed one's eyes, but there, at its highest polish, shining in the beautiful day, was the brazen face of history, and there, all about one, immaculate, the printless pavements of the State.

C. The Challenge

XVI. INTRODUCTION

The challenge to established American patterns of thought resulted, naturally enough, in an attack by the young on the faith of their fathers. It fell to Randolph Bourne (1886–1918), a pathetically misshapen man who is best remembered for his rejection of the aims and spirit of America in World War I, to make the clearest renunciation of the ideas and ideals of the generation that had educated and trained him. Truths, Bourne said, which were once considered obvious no longer could be. The middle class, small town, still Puritan America, according to Bourne and his colleagues, had become intellectually irrelevant to the younger generation, especially because of the older generation's continued belief in a superannuated individualism. The quaint "belief that social ills may be cured by personal virtue," typical of the best of that older America, was the old ideological springboard that in Bourne's view could no longer function. But the individualism of the old generation manifested itself in religious, political, and economic terms only. Intellectually that older generation had not been individualistic enough to suit Bourne. The rigidity of the social structure, the support given to industrial capitalism by an individualistically oriented Christianity, meant that, among other things, the older generation had not truly understood the democratic ethic.

The challenge that Bourne threw in the face of traditional America called for radical social reform, whose success would depend upon the intellectual freedom and literary accomplishments of America's young intellectuals. Suffocated by the heavy atmosphere of late-Victorian America, Bourne and the rest of the young radicals hoped that their manifestoes of the pre-war period would contribute in a significant way to throwing open the doors to a brighter, freer, and more excellent tomorrow.

XVI.

Randolph S. Bourne
THIS OLDER GENERATION
1915

I read with ever-increasing wonder the guarded defenses and discreet apologies for the older generation which keep filtering through the essays of the *Atlantic*. I can even seem to detect a growing decision of tone, a definite assurance of conviction, which seems to imply that a rally has been undertaken against the accusations which the younger generation, in its self-assurance, its irreverence for the old conventions and moralities, its passion for the novel and startling, seemed to be bringing against them. The first faint twinges of conscience felt by the older generation have given place to renewed homily. There is an evident anxiety to get itself put on record as perfectly satisfied with its world, and desirous that its sons and daughters should learn anew of those peculiar beauties in which it has lived. Swept off its feet by the call to social service and social reform, it is slowly regaining its foundation, and, slightly flushed, and with garments somewhat awry, it proclaims again its belief in the eternal verities of Protestant religion and conventional New England morality.

It is always an encouraging sign when people are rendered self-conscious and are forced to examine the basis of their ideals. The demand that they explain them to skeptics always makes for clarity. When the older generation is put on the defensive, it must first discover what convictions it has, and then sharpen them to their finest point in order to present them convincingly. There are always too many unquestioned things in the world, and for a person or class to have to scurry about to find reasons for its prejudices is about as healthy an exercise as one could wish for either of them. To be sure, the reasons are rarely any more than

SOURCE. Randolph S. Bourne, "This Older Generation," *The Atlantic Monthly,* Vol. 116, No. 3 (Sept., 1915), pp. 385–391. Copyright 1915, by The Atlantic Monthly Company, Boston, Mass. Reprinted with the permission of The Atlantic Monthly Company.

ex post facto excuses,—supports and justifications for the prejudices rather than the causes thereof. Reason itself is very seldom more than that. The important point is that one should feel the need of a reason. This always indicates that something has begun to slide, that the world is no longer so secure as it was, that obvious truths no longer are obvious, that the world has begun to bristle with question marks.

One of the basic grievances of this older generation against the younger of to-day, with its social agitation, its religious heresy, its presumptive individuality, its economic restlessness, is that all this makes it uncomfortable. When you have found growing older to be a process of the reconciliation of the spirit to life, it is decidedly disconcerting to have some youngster come along and point out the irreconcilable things in the universe. Just as you have made a tacit agreement to call certain things non-existent, it is highly discommoding to have somebody shout with strident tones that they are very real and significant. When, after much struggling and compromise, you have got your world clamped down, it is discouraging to have a gale arise which threatens to blow over all your structure. Through so much of the current writing runs this quiet note of disapprobation. These agnostic professors who unsettle the faith of our youth, these 'intellectuals who stick a finger in everybody's pie in the name of social justice,' these sensation-mongers who unveil great masses of political and social corruption, these remorseless scientists who would reveal so many of our reticences—why can't they let us alone? Can they not see that God's in his heaven, all's right with the world?

Now I know this older generation, which doth protest so much. I have lived with it for the last fifteen years, ever since I began to wonder whether all was for the best in the best of all possible worlds. I was educated by it, grew up with it. I doubt if any generation ever had a more docile pupil than I. What they taught me, I find they still believe, or at least so many of them as have not gone over to the enemy or been captured by the militant youth of to-day. Or, as seems rather likely, they no longer precisely believe, but they want their own arguments to convince themselves. It is probable that when we really believe a thing with all our hearts, we do not attempt to justify it. Justification comes only when we are beginning to doubt it.

By this older generation I mean, of course, the mothers and fathers and uncle and aunts of the youth of both sexes between twenty and thirty who are beginning their professional or business life. And I refer of course to the comfortable or fairly comfortable American middle class. Now this older generation has had a religion, a metaphysics, an ethics, and a political and social philosophy, which have reigned practically undisputed until the appearance of the present generation. It has at least never felt called upon to justify itself. It has never been directly challenged, as it is to-day. In order to localize this generation still further, we must see it in its typical setting of the small town or city, clustered about the institutions of church and family. If we have any society which can be called 'America,' it is this society. Its psychology is American psychology; its soul is America's soul.

This older generation, which I have known so well for fifteen years, has a religion which is on the whole as pleasant and easy as could be devised. Though its members are the descendants of the stern and rugged old Puritans, who wrestled with the devil and stripped their world of all that might seduce them from the awful service of God, they have succeeded in straining away by a long process all the repellent attitudes in the old philosophy of life. It is unfair to say that the older generation believes in dogmas and creeds. It would be more accurate to say that it does not disbelieve. It retains them as a sort of guaranty of the stability of the faith, but leaves them rather severely alone. It does not even make more than feeble efforts to reinterpret them in the light of modern knowledge. They are useless, but necessary.

The foundation of this religion may be religious, but the superstructure is almost entirely ethical. Most sermons of to-day are little more than pious exhortations to good conduct. By good conduct is meant that sort of action which will least disturb the normal routine of modern middle-class life: common honesty in business life, faithfulness to duty, ambition in business and profession, filial obligation, the use of talents, and always and everywhere simple human kindness and love. The old Puritan ethics, which saw in the least issue of conduct a struggle between God and the devil, has become a mere code for facilitating the daily friction of conventional life.

Now one would indeed be churlish to find fault with this devout belief in simple goodness, which characterizes the older generation. It is only when these humble virtues are raised up into an all-inclusive programme for social reform and into a philosophy of life, that one begins to question, and to feel afar the deep hostility of the older generation to the new faith.

Simple kindness, common honesty, filial obedience, it is evidently still felt, will solve all the difficulties of personal and social life. The most popular novels of the day are those in which the characters do the most good to each other. The enormous success with the older generation of *The Inside of the Cup, Queed,* and *V.V.'s Eyes,* is based primarily on the fact that these books represent a sublimated form of the good old American melodramatic moral sense. And now comes along Mr. Gerald Stanley Lee with his *Crowds,*—what a funny, individualized, personal-responsibility crowd he gives us, to be sure,—and his panacea for modern social ills by the old solution of applied personal virtue. Never a word about removing the barriers of caste and race and economic inequality, but only an urging to step over them. Never a trumpet-call to level the ramparts of privilege, or build up the heights of opportunity, but only an appeal to extend the charitable hand from the ramparts of heaven, or offer the kindly patronage to the less fortunate, or—most dazzling of all—throw away, in a frenzy of abandonment, life and fortune. Not to construct a business organization where dishonesty would be meaningless, but to be utopianly honest against the business world. In other words, the older generation believes in getting all the luxury of the virtue of goodness, while conserving all the advantages of being in a vicious society.

If there is any one characteristic which distinguishes the older generation, it is this belief that social ills may be cured by personal virtue. Its highest moral ideas are sacrifice and service. But the older generation can never see how intensely selfish these ideals are, in the most complete sense of the word selfish. What they mean always is, 'I sacrifice myself for you,' 'I serve you,' not, 'We cooperate in working ceaselessly toward an ideal where all may be free and none may be served or serve.' These ideals of sacrifice and service are utterly selfish, because they take account only of the satisfaction and moral consolation of the doer. They enhance his moral value; but what of the person who is served or sacrificed for? What of the person who is done good to? If the feelings of sacrifice and service were in any sense altruistic, the moral enhancement of the receiver would be the object sought. But can it not be said that for every individual virtuous merit secured by an act of sacrifice or service on the part of the doer, there is a corresponding depression on the part of the receiver? Do we not universally recognize this by calling a person who is not conscious of this depression, a parasite, and the person who is no longer capable of depression, a pauper? It is exactly those free gifts, such as schools, libraries, and so forth, which are impersonal or social, that we can accept gratefully and gladly; and it is exactly because the ministrations of a Charity Organization Society are impersonal and businesslike that they can be received willingly and without moral depression by the poor.

The ideal of duty is equally open to attack. The great complaint of the younger against the older generation has to do with the rigidity of the social relationships into which the younger find themselves born. The world seems to be full of what may be called canalized emotions. One is 'supposed' to love one's aunt or one's grandfather in a certain definite way, at the risk of being 'unnatural.' One gets almost a sense of the quantitative measurement of emotion. Perhaps the greatest tragedy of family life is the useless energy that is expended by the dutiful in keeping these artificial channels open, and the correct amount of current running. It is exactly this that produces most infallibly the rebellion of the younger generation. To hear that one ought to love this or that person; or to hear loyalty spoken of, as the older generation so often speaks of it, as if it consisted in an allegiance to something which one no longer believes in,—this is what soonest liberates those forces of madness and revolt which bewilder spiritual teachers and guides. It is those dry channels of duty and obligation through which no living waters of emotion flow that it is the ideal of the younger generation to break up. They will have no network of emotional canals which are not brimming, no duties which are not equally loves.

But when they are loves, you have duty no longer meaning very much. Duty, like sacrifice and service, always implies a personal relation of individuals. You are always doing your duty to somebody or something. Always the taint of inequality comes in. You are morally superior to the person who has duty done to him. If that duty is not filled with good-will and desire, it is morally hateful, or at very best, a necessary evil,—one of those compromises with the world which must be made in order to get through it at all. But duty without good-will is a compromise with our present state of inequality, and to raise duty to the level of a virtue is to consecrate that state of inequality forevermore.

It is the same thing with service. The older generation has attempted an insidious compromise with the new social democracy by combining the words 'social' and 'service.' Under cover of the ideal of service it tries to appropriate to itself the glory of social work, and succeeds in almost convincing itself and the world that its Christianity has always held the same ideal. The faithful are urged to extend their activities. The assumption is that, by doing good to more individuals, you are thereby becoming social. But to speak of 'social democracy,' which of course means a freely cooperating, freely reciprocating society of equals, and 'service,' together, is a contradiction of terms. For, when you serve people or do good to them, you thereby render yourself unequal with them. You insult the democratic ideal. If the service is compulsory, it is menial and you are inferior. If voluntary, you are superior. The difference, however, is only academic. The entire Christian scheme is a clever but unsuccessful attempt to cure the evils of inequality by transposing the values. The slave serves gladly instead of servilely. That is, he turns his master into a slave. That is why good Christian people can never get over the idea that Socialism means simply the triumph of one class over another. To-day the proletarian is down, the capitalist up. To-morrow the proletarian will be up and the capitalist down. To pull down the mighty from their seats and exalt them of low degree is the highest pitch to which Christian ethics ever attained. The failure of the older generation to recognize a higher ethic, the ethic of democracy, is the cause of all the trouble.

The notorious Victorian era, which in its secret heart this older generation still admires so much, accentuated all the latent individualism of Christian ethics, and produced a code which, without the rebellion of the younger generation, would have spiritually guaranteed forever all moral caste divisions and inequalities of modern society. The Protestant Church, in which this exaggerated ethic was enshrined, is now paying heavily the price of this debauch of ethical power. Its rapidly declining numbers show that human nature has an invincible objection to being individually saved. The Catholic Church, which saves men as members of the Beloved Community, and not as individuals, flourishes. When one is saved by Catholicism, one becomes a democrat, and not a spiritual snob and aristocrat, as one does through Calvinism. The older generation can never understand that superb loyalty which is loyalty to a community,—a loyalty which, paradoxical as it may seem, nourishes the true social personality in proportion as the individual sense is lessened. The Protestant Church in its tenacious devotion to the personal idea of a Divine Master—the highest and most popular Christian ideal of to-day—shows how very far it still is away from the ideals and ethics of a social democracy, a life lived in the Beloved Community.

The sense of self-respect is the very keystone of the personality in whose defense all this individualistic philosophy has been carefully built up. The Christian virtues date from ages when there was a vastly greater number of morally depressed people than there is now. The tenacious survival of these virtues can be due only to the fact that they were valuable to the moral prestige of some class. Our older generation, with its emphasis on duty, sacrifice, and service, shows us very clearly what those interests were. I deliberately accuse the older generation of conserving and greatly strengthening these ideals, as a defensive measure. Morals are always the product of a situation; they reflect a certain organization of human relations which some class or group wishes to preserve. A moral code or set of ideals is always the invisible spiritual sign of a visible social grace. In an effort to retain the *status quo* of that world of inequalities and conventions in which they most comfortably and prosperously live, the older generation has stamped, through all its agencies of family, church, and school, upon the younger generation, just those seductive ideals which would preserve its position. These old virtues upon which, however, the younger generation is already making guerilla warfare are simply the moral support with which the older generation buttresses its social situation.

The natural barriers and prejudices by which our elders are cut off from a freely flowing democracy are thus given a spiritual justification, and there is added for our elders the almost sensual luxury of leaping, by free grace, the barriers and giving themselves away. But the price has to be paid. Just as profits, in the socialist philosophy, are taken to be an abstraction from wages, through the economic power which one class has over another, so the virtues of the older generation may be said to be an abstraction from the virtue of other classes less favorably situated from a moral or personal point of view. Their swollen self-respect is at the expense of others.

How well we know the type of man in the older generation who has been doing good all his life! How his personality has thrived on it! How he has ceaselessly been storing away moral fat in every cranny of his soul! His goodness has been meat to him. The need and depression of other people has been, all unconsciously to him, the air which he has breathed. Without their compensating misfortune or sin, his goodness would have wilted and died. If good people would earnestly set to work to make the world uniformly healthy, courageous, beautiful, and prosperous, the field of their vocation would be constantly limited, and finally destroyed. That they so stoutly resist all philosophies and movements which have these ends primarily in view is convincing evidence of the fierce and jealous egoism which animates their so plausibly altruistic spirit. One suspects that the older generation does not want its vocation destroyed. It takes an heroic type of goodness to undermine all the foundations on which our virtue rests.

If then I object to the ethical philosophy of the older generation on the ground that it is too individualistic, and, under the pretense of altruism, too egoistic, I object to its general intellectuality as not individual enough. Intellectually the older generation seems to me to lead far too vegetative a life. It may be that this life has been lived on the heights, that these souls have passed through fires and glories, but there is generally too little objective evidence of this subjective fact. If the intuition which accompanies experience has verified all the data regarding God, the soul, the family, and so forth,—to quote one of the staunchest defenders of the generation,—this verification seems to have been obtained rather that the issues might be promptly disposed of and forgotten. Certainly the older generation is rarely interested in the profounder issues of life. It never speaks of death,—the suggestion makes it uncomfortable. It shies in panic at hints of sex-issues. It seems resolute to keep life on as objective a plane as possible. It is no longer curious about the motives and feelings of people. It seems singularly to lack the psychological sense. If it gossips, it recounts actions, effects; it rarely seeks to interpret. It tends more and more to treat human beings as moving masses of matter instead of as personalities filled with potent influence, or as absorbingly interesting social types, as I am sure the younger generation does.

The older generation seems no longer to generalize, although it gives every evidence of having once prodigiously generalized, for its world is all hardened and definite. There are the good and the criminal, and the poor, the people who can be called nice, and the ordinary people. The world is already plotted out. Now I am sure that the generalizations of the truly philosophical mind are very fluid and ephemeral. They are no sooner made than the mind sees their insufficiency and has to break them up. A new cutting is made, only in turn to be shaken and rearranged. This keeps the philosopher thinking all the time, and it makes his world a very uncertain place. But he at least runs no risk of hardening, and he has his eyes open to most experience.

I am often impressed with the fact that the older generation has grown weary of thinking. It has simply put up the bars in its intellectual shop-windows and gone off home to rest. It may well be that this is because it has felt so much sorrow that it does not want to talk about sorrow, or so much love that to interpret love tires it, or repulsed so many rude blows of destiny that it has no interest in speaking of destiny. Its flame may be low for the very reason that it has burned so intensely. But how many of the younger generation would eagerly long for such interpretations if the older would only reveal them! And how little plausible is that experience when it is occasionally interpreted! No, enthusiasm, passion for ideas, sensuality, religious fervor,—all the heated weapons with which the younger generation attacks the world, seem only to make the older generation uneasy. The spirit, in becoming reconciled to life, has lost life itself.

As I see the older generation going through its daily round of business, church, and family life, I cannot help feeling that its influence is profoundly pernicious. It has signally failed to broaden its institutions for the larger horizon of the time. The church remains a private club of comfortable middle-class families, while outside there grows up without spiritual inspiration a heterogeneous mass of people without ties, roots, or principles. The town changes from a village to an industrial centre, and church and school go through their time-honored and listless motions. The world widens, society expands, formidable crises appear, but the older generation does not broaden, or if it does, the broadening is in no adequate proportion to our needs. The older generation still uses the old ideas for the new problem. Whatever new wine it finds must be poured into the old bottles.

Where are the leaders among the older generation in America who, with luminous faith and intelligence, are rallying around them the disintegrated numbers of idealistic youth, as Bergson and Barrès and Jaurès have done in France? A few years ago there seemed to be a promise of a forward movement toward Democracy, led by battled veterans in a war against privilege. But how soon the older generation became wearied in the march! What is left now of that shining army and its leader? Must the younger generation eternally wait for the sign?

The answer is, of course, that it will not wait. It must shoulder the gigantic task of putting into practice its ideals and revolutionary points of view as wholeheartedly and successfully as our great-grandfathers applied theirs and tightened the philosophy of life which imprisons the older generation. The shuddering fear that we in turn may become weary, complacent, evasive, should be the best preventive of that stagnation. We shall never have done looking for the miracle, that it shall be given us to lighten, cheer, and purify our 'younger generation,' even as our older has depressed and disintegrated us.

D. The Twenties

XVII. INTRODUCTION

It is not helpful to think of World War I as the cause of the disillusion-ment so characteristic of the scholars and writers of the 1920's. An important strain of the literary mentality in America, at least since the Civil War (and before too, for that matter), had found nourishment in its rejection of the dominant patterns of American society. The war, however, did help to solidify the literary response to the nation by demonstrating to some the stupidity and horror that supposedly resulted from the idealism of traditional America. Woodrow Wilson's idealism served as a symbol to the post-war generation, as both the President and the war itself were cited as proof of the position taken by the alienated writers of the pre-war period. Both the danger of optimism and the shallowness of idealism, a hundred voices of the post-war generation tried to explain, had now—presumably—been made perfectly clear.

The intellectual life of the 1920's moved in several directions simul-taneously. A lingering disgust with the war led a number of intellectuals to reject politics and indeed even society altogether. A similar revulsion, however, led others, usually social scientists, to attempt to find a new basis for social action, a new program for political reconstruction. In social terms, a significant dimension of the 1920's was the attempt to purge American society of the strange and foreign ingredients which seemed not to have a place in a Protestant and rural America. Prohibi-tion, the Red scare, immigration restriction, the Scopes trial, the relative isolationism of America's foreign policy, the reemergence of the Ku Klux Klan, were all attempts to return to a known, and therefore presumably more secure, past.

In more purely literary terms, the 1920's were remarkable for the spirit of experimentation. The rejection of old standards and values led, in the work of Gertrude Stein and E. E. Cummings, among others, to an attack on language itself. The rejection of politics seemed to make it possible for a number of writers of the time to rediscover the individual, as exemplified in the work of Fitzgerald and Hemingway. The rhetoric of Freud, accessible for the first time to a wide circle of writers, facili-tated the expression of discontent in purely modern terms. Alienation and unhappiness became an integral part of the modern scene.

No American writer of the decade enjoyed the acclaim offered to Sinclair Lewis (1885–1951). At the time, his novels seemed to constitute a multifaceted attack on the smugness, provincialism, and meanness of

American life. It is now clear that Lewis stood in a double relationship to his subjects. For instance, it is apparent that Gopher Prairie, with its ignorance and bigotry, made poor Carol Kennicott desperately unhappy, but it is equally true that her bleeding-heart do-goodism was more than a trifle silly. Lewis' presumed assault on small-town America achieved its success partly because that America had virtually entered into Lewis' own bloodstream. Nonetheless, Lewis' portrait of Main Street was an early barrage of the 1920's against established America. In the following selection, which is Carol Kennicott's impressions of her first walk down Main Street, one can already sense the "revolt from the village" that was to become increasingly important throughout the decade.

XVII.

Sinclair Lewis

MAIN STREET

1920

When Carol had walked for thirty-two minutes she had completely covered the town, east and west, north and south; and she stood at the corner of Main Street and Washington Avenue and despaired.

Main Street with its two-story brick shops, its story-and-a-half wooden residences, its muddy expanse from concrete walk to walk, its huddle of Fords and lumber-wagons, was too small to absorb her. The broad, straight, unenticing gashes of the streets let in the grasping prairie on every side. She realized the vastness and the emptiness of the land. The skeleton iron windmill on the farm a few blocks away, at the north end of Main Street, was like the ribs of a dead cow. She thought of the coming of the Northern winter, when the unprotected houses would crouch together in terror of storms galloping out of that wild waste. They were so small and weak, the little brown houses. They were shelters for sparrows, not homes for warm laughing people.

She told herself that down the street the leaves were a splendor. The maples were orange; the oaks a solid tint of raspberry. And the lawns had been nursed with love. But the thought would not hold. At

SOURCE. Sinclair Lewis, *Main Street,* New York: Harcourt, Brace and Co., 1920, pp. 33–38. Copyright, 1920, by Harcourt, Brace & World, Inc.; renewed, 1948, by Sinclair Lewis. Reprinted with the permission of the publishers.

best the trees resembled a thinned woodlot. There was no park to rest the eyes. And since not Gopher Prairie but Wakamin was the county-seat, there was no court-house with its grounds.

She glanced through the fly-specked windows of the most pretentious building in sight, the one place which welcomed strangers and determined their opinion of the charm and luxury of Gopher Prairie—the Minniemashie House. It was a tall lean shabby structure, three stories of yellow-streaked wood, the corners covered with sanded pine slabs purporting to symbolize stone. In the hotel office she could see a stretch of bare unclean floor, a line of rickety chairs with brass cuspidors between, a writing-desk with advertisements in mother-of-pearl letters upon the glass-covered back. The dining-room beyond was a jungle of stained table-cloths and catsup bottles.

She looked no more at the Minniemashie House.

A man in cuffless shirt-sleeves with pink arm-garters, wearing a linen collar but no tie, yawned his way from Dyer's Drug Store across to the hotel. He leaned against the wall, scratched a while, sighed, and in a bored way gossiped with a man tilted back in a chair. A lumber-wagon, its long green box filled with large spools of barbed-wire fencing, creaked down the block. A Ford, in reverse, sounded as though it were shaking to pieces, then recovered and rattled away. In the Greek candy-store was the whine of a peanut-roaster, and the oily smell of nuts.

There was no other sound nor sign of life.

She wanted to run, fleeing from the encroaching prairie, demanding the security of a great city. Her dreams of creating a beautiful town were ludicrous. Oozing out from every drab wall, she felt a forbidding spirit which she could never conquer.

She trailed down the street on one side, back on the other, glancing into the cross streets. It was a private Seeing Main Street tour. She was within ten minutes beholding not only the heart of a place called Gopher Prairie, but ten thousand towns from Albany to San Diego:

Dyer's Drug Store, a corner building of regular and unreal blocks of artificial stone. Inside the store, a greasy marble soda-fountain with an electric lamp of red and green and curdled-yellow mosaic shade. Pawed-over heaps of toothbrushes and combs and packages of shaving-soap. Shelves of soap-cartons, teething-rings, garden-seeds, and patent medicines in yellow packages—nostrums for consumption, for "women's diseases"—notorious mixtures of opium and alcohol, in the very shop to which her husband sent patients for the filling of prescriptions.

From a second-story window the sign "W. P. Kennicott, Phys. & Surgeon," gilt on black sand.

A small wooden motion-picture theater called "The Rosebud Movie Palace." Lithographs announcing a film called "Fatty in Love."

Howland & Gould's Grocery. In the display window, black, overripe bananas and lettuce on which a cat was sleeping. Shelves lined with red crêpe paper which was now faded and torn and concentrically spotted. Flat against the wall of the second story the signs of lodges—the Knights of Pythias, the Maccabees, the Woodmen, the Masons.

Dahl & Oleson's Meat Market—a reek of blood.

A jewelry shop with tinny-looking wrist-watches for women. In front of it, at the curb, a huge wooden clock which did not go.

A fly-buzzing saloon with a brilliant gold and enamel whisky sign across the front. Other saloons down the block. From them a stink of stale beer, and thick voices bellowing pidgin German or trolling out dirty songs—vice gone feeble and unenterprising and dull—the delicacy of a mining-camp minus its vigor. In front of the saloons, farmwives sitting on the seats of wagons, waiting for their husbands to become drunk and ready to start home.

A tobacco shop called "The Smoke House," filled with young men shaking dice for cigarettes. Racks of magazines, and pictures of coy fat prostitutes in striped bathing-suits.

A clothing store with a display of "ox-blood-shade Oxfords with bull-dog toes." Suits which looked worn and glossless while they were still new, flabbily draped on dummies like corpses with painted cheeks.

The Bon Ton Store—Haydock & Simons'—the largest shop in town. The first-story front of clear glass, the plates cleverly bound at the edges with brass. The second story of pleasant tapestry brick. One window of excellent clothes for men, interspersed with collars of floral piqué which showed mauve daisies on a saffron ground. Newness and an obvious notion of neatness and service. Haydock & Simons. Haydock. She had met a Haydock at the station; Harry Haydock; an active person of thirty-five. He seemed great to her, now, and very like a saint. His shop was clean!

Axel Egge's General Store, frequented by Scandinavian farmers. In the shallow dark window-space heaps of sleazy sateens, badly woven gala-teas, canvas shoes designed for women with bulging ankles, steel and red glass buttons upon cards with broken edges, a cottony blanket, a granite-ware frying-pan reposing on a sun-faded crêpe blouse.

Sam Clark's Hardware Store. An air of frankly metallic enterprise.

Guns and churns and barrels of nails and beautiful shiny butcher knives.

Chester Dashaway's House Furnishing Emporium. A vista of heavy oak rockers with leather seats, asleep in a dismal row.

Billy's Lunch. Thick handleless cups on the wet oilcloth-covered counter. An odor of onions and the smoke of hot lard. In the doorway a young man audibly sucking a toothpick.

The warehouse of the buyer of cream and potatoes. The sour smell of a dairy.

The Ford Garage and the Buick Garage, competent one-story brick and cement buildings opposite each other. Old and new cars on grease-blackened concrete floors. Tire advertisements. The roaring of a tested motor; a racket which beat at the nerves. Surly young men in khaki union-overalls. The most energetic and vital places in town.

A large warehouse for agricultural implements. An impressive barricade of green and gold wheels, of shafts and sulky seats, belonging to machinery of which Carol knew nothing—potato-planters, manure-spreaders, silage-cutters, disk-harrows, breaking-plows.

A feed store, its windows opaque with the dust of bran, a patent medicine advertisement painted on its roof.

Ye Art Shoppe, Prop. Mrs. Mary Ellen Wilks, Christian Science Library open daily free. A touching fumble at beauty. A one-room shanty of boards recently covered with rough stucco. A show-window delicately rich in error: vases starting out to imitate tree-trunks but running off into blobs of gilt—an aluminum ash-tray labeled "Greetings from Gopher Prairie"—a Christian Science magazine—a stamped sofa-cushion portraying a large ribbon tied to a small poppy, the correct skeins of embroidery-silk lying on the pillow. Inside the shop, a glimpse of bad carbon prints of bad and famous pictures, shelves of phonograph records and camera films, wooden toys, and in the midst an anxious small woman sitting in a padded rocking chair.

A barber shop and pool room. A man in shirt sleeves, presumably Del Snafflin the proprietor, shaving a man who had a large Adam's apple.

Nat Hick's Tailor Shop, on a side street off Main. A one-story building. A fashion-plate showing human pitchforks in garments which looked as hard as steel plate.

On another side street a raw red-brick Catholic Church with a varnished yellow door.

The post-office—merely a partition of glass and brass shutting off the rear of a mildewed room which must once have been a shop. A tilted writing-shelf against a wall rubbed black and scattered with official notices and army recruiting-posters.

The damp, yellow-brick schoolbuilding in its cindery grounds.

The State Bank, stucco masking wood.

The Farmer's National Bank. An Ionic temple of marble. Pure, exquisite, solitary. A brass plate with "Ezra Stowbody, Pres't."

A score of similar shops and establishments.

Behind them and mixed with them, the houses, meek cottages or large, comfortable, soundly uninteresting symbols of prosperity.

In all the town not one building save the Ionic bank which gave pleasure to Carol's eyes; not a dozen buildings which suggested that, in the fifty years of Gopher Prairie's existence, the citizens had realized that it was either desirable or possible to make this, their common home, amusing or attractive.

It was not only the unsparing unapologetic ugliness and the rigid straightness which overwhelmed her. It was the planlessness, the flimsy temporariness of the buildings, their faded unpleasant colors. The street was cluttered with electric-light poles, telephone poles, gasoline pumps for motor cars, boxes of goods. Each man had built with the most valiant disregard of all the others. Between a large new "block" of two-story brick shops on one side, and the fire-brick Overland garage on the other side, was a one-story cottage turned into a millinery shop. The white temple of the Farmers' Bank was elbowed back by a grocery of glaring yellow brick. One store-building had a patchy galvanized iron cornice; the building beside it was crowned with battlements and pyramids of brick capped with blocks of red sandstone.

She escaped from Main Street, fled home.

She wouldn't have cared, she insisted, if the people had been comely. She had noted a young man loafing before a shop, one unwashed hand holding the cord of an awning; a middle-aged man who had a way of staring at women as though he had been married too long and too prosaically; an old farmer, solid, wholesome, but not clean—his face like a potato fresh from the earth. None of them had shaved for three days.

"If they can't build shrines, out here on the prairie, surely there's nothing to prevent their buying safety-razors!" she raged.

She fought herself: "I must be wrong. People do live here. It *can't* be as ugly as—as I know it is! I must be wrong. But I can't do it. I can't go through with it."

She came home too seriously worried for hysteria; and when she found

Kennicott waiting for her, and exulting, "Have a walk? Well, like the town? Great lawns and trees, eh?" she was able to say, with a self-protective maturity new to her, "It's very interesting."

XVIII. INTRODUCTION

One increasingly characteristic response to an unacceptable America was exile. The literary exodus to European centers of civilization, usually Paris, was typically undertaken with great zest: the literary rebels seem always delighted—delighted with their unhappiness with America, and delighted with the fact of exile. For the best, however, expatriation was not a simple matter. Men fled to Europe in order to write about America and Americans.

The following essay by Edmund Wilson (born in 1895) captures the ambivalence of the expatriate. Wilson spoke for a large and articulate American contingent in Europe when he explained that it was necessary to go to Europe where truth was sought and beauty appreciated. But the real fight, as Wilson understood "real," was constantly with the America he had left. It was precisely the magnitude of American barbarity that made resistance to it seem heroic. Demonstrating, in the following selection, the extent of his own Americanism, Wilson explained that it was the American future, not its past, that was truly significant—an idea with which so American a type as Henry Ford could agree. The optimism of Wilson's essay could hardly be contained, as he asserted that reason would win in America because of the natural freshness, zest, and freedom of the country. And yet, the necessary bifocal vision demanded that America be viewed from the neighborhood of Notre Dame.

XVIII.

Edmund Wilson

NIGHT THOUGHTS IN PARIS
1922

Here one no longer has the heart to cheer for a new battle: this gentle and gracious land is the scene of too many defeats. Who can think seriously of taking up arms to crusade for an old truth? In France all the truths are old and are therefore banalities and platitudes. Though they be the bringers of life itself, they have lost too many times. One grows sophisticated about truths that seem never to change the face of life. The most they can do has been done—and left still the ruin of the battlefield, the people ignorant and starved, the sharpers always in power.—They pay dear for their manners and beauty; their heirlooms oppress them like a load. The dry, tempered fields of Champagne, ploughed over with so many conflicts, the dense gray façades of Paris with their seriousness and their richness, with their inlaid acanthus-topped columns of a faded and abolished magnificence, the yellow long-windowed châteaux sunk deep in the countryside, all these are a part of the burden that these people must always drag with them, of the all-dominating mountain in whose shadow they must always live.

No wonder Futurism was born in Italy, where the weight of the past lies heaviest—where the young man, opening his eyes, looking out for new fabrics and forms, is confronted with a monstrous mirror, wrought elaborately of Venetian silver, which floridly reflects in turn the forms of the ancient world. No wonder he smashes the mirror, refusing to copy a copy. No wonder he would blast a soil overlaid and smothered with richness, where no new little weed can pierce through the gorgeousness of crops long dead. At least, he thinks, a locomotive has no nonsense of culture about it—it is swift, it is accurate, it is powerful, it makes men swifter and more powerful, and all this it does without having learned what Lorenzo learned from Politian, what Politian learned from Plato, what Plato learned from Parmenides; it feels under no obligation to look

SOURCE. Edmund Wilson, "Night Thoughts in Paris," *New Republic,* Vol. XXX (March 15, 1922), pp. 75–77. Reprinted with the permission of Edmund Wilson.

like a cathedral; it is not compelled, through veneration, to measure its whistle by Bach. What a vital and care-free creature a locomotive appears! It is as indifferent and destructive to tradition as one would like, oneself, to be. Can one do better than to imitate its shafts, its wheels, its angles, its shrieks and its grinding?

But *I* can scarcely adore the locomotive. I know it all too well. Machines are not novelties to me, as they are to Signor Marinetti. I come from the land of machines and have been bored to death by too many of them. Why then—like Signor Marinetti, turning in impatience from Europe—do I dream of my native America as of something beautiful and free? America, as everyone knows, is not especially beautiful or free. We live and build without taste; our towns are like rubbish-heaps, we abjectly suffer to be stifled; we have not even our original rights; we are a people all alike, uniformly mediocre. When I shall see New York again, like a blank and barren mountain, between the hard steel-gray of the water and the hard steel-gray of the sky—when I see even the black and white planes, stiffly plumed with smoke, become pitilessly distinct in the raw October light; the docks raying out like cogs; the National Biscuit Company—what high excitement will lift my heart as if before the curtain of a drama? . . . {*sic*}

It is a drama which derives its force from the odds against the hero. It is precisely the barbarity of the background which gives dignity to those who struggle against it. The very fact that their enlightenment is so awkward and so uncertain only makes our poets and saints more heroic figures: what bitter and terrific cost for a few commonplaces! They have all the world against them as far as their eyes can reach; they get no support from their kindred or from their predecessors. They come to consciousness and sometimes perish in a consciousnessless sea. In Europe there are certain feats which have already been accomplished: beauty has come to be recognized; ideas are understood. But in America, as yet, all this is still to do. On the continent, having won these things, men have grown indifferent to them: familiar with all ideas, they no longer receive them as revelations; long skilful at works of art, they have finally become tired of them and, contemptuous of perfection, because everyone has learned the trick, they turn with feverish zest to the clumsy, the strident and the crude. But in America, the humblest harmony is still an incredible dream. Among us, even a decent novel takes on the air of a miracle. In that prosperous, unphilosophical world of commerce and manufacture, a suggestion that any other aim may concern a serious man seems fanciful and absurd, completely out of touch with reality—to behold such a purpose arise and assert itself against reality—to become a reality itself—makes one catch one's breath with wonder, as if it were a story-book come true. To hear authentic fancies and ideas clothe themselves in our barbarous tongue—in that sprawling, square-syllabled speech where the words seem to lie like frame-houses strewn loosely and colorlessly on the unfenced outskirts of a town—which seems fit only for a prosaic trade and a plebeian extravagance and irony—is like seeing old pieces of string woven into a firm fabric. The struggle of reason and art takes on Promethean proportions. It has almost the thrill of the revival of learning at the end of the Middle Ages: a new kind of darkness has whelmed mankind and again they must fight to the surface. As Plato came to the ignorance of Europe, so Bernard Shaw comes to us! Felix Fays and Carol Kennicotts, reading *Man and Superman* in remote farms and dreary towns of the vast desert of the West, seem to hear a terrible voice that wakes them with words of fire. It exhorts them to be up, to learn how to think and live, to cast off their locust-shells for the flaming garb of the divine! But they can never stand free in that dress; they must bear their shells always with them. At most, they may chirp a little, move faintly their atrophied wings.

When I think of Greenwich Village, it is almost with tears. For there this battered battalion dress their guns against a whole nation. Where the traffic, gnashing iron teeth, no longer oppresses the pavement, where the toned red bricks of low houses still front an open square, where the soft moans and hoots of the shipping wash the island from either shore, from the darkest corners of the country they have fled for comfort and asylum. You may think them feeble and ridiculous—but feebleness is always relative. It may require as much force of character and as much independent thought for one of these to leave his Kansas home and espouse the opinions of Freud as for Wagner to achieve new harmonies or Einstein to conceive a finite universe. The thought of them makes me respond with a sharp gust of sympathy, precisely because they *are* ridiculous and yet stand for something noble. And one is touched by something like reverence when one finds among this strange indifferent people, to whom the rest of the world is a newspaper story, history a tedious legend and abstract thought a form of insanity, a man who really knows on what stage he is playing, for what drama he has been cast. By his realization he makes us realize, too, for what drama our setting is the setting: for the drama of humanity, in a sense, no setting can be trivial or mean. Gopher Prairie itself, in all its ludicrousness and futility, when the human spirit rears itself there, has its importance and its dignity.

And now that a breach has been made what a flood might sweep off the dam!—what a thundering torrent of energy, of enthusiasm, of life! Things are always beginning in America; we are always on the verge of great adventures. History seems to lie before us instead of behind. Intoxicated with the sun, we perform wildly the dismalest tasks. We are driven by the pressure of energy as if by an exalting purpose to the accomplishment of gigantic labors without importance or point. To think even of the stupidest and vulgarest of our national occupations—of our movies, our manufacturing and our hideous advertisements—is to be infected with a sort of exhilaration at their very momentum and bulk. Shall we always, like Niagara Falls, go on crashing down our cataract with the sole result that, as a by-product, we manufacture breakfast-food?—No! Voice is added to voice. The opposition is rising. The first barrage has been fired; already the ramparts quake! Our enemy offers huger bulk than the enemy in Europe, but he is much less firmly rooted. Two generations might rout him. To arms then! Let me return; I shall not cease from mental fight nor shall my sword rest in my hand till intolerance has been stricken from the laws, till the time-clock has been beaten to a punch-bowl!

—Here in Paris, as I lie in bed and hear the brief whistle of locomotives, I think of hospital-trains in the Vosges unloading in the thin gray dawn, of characters in Henry James crossing to Lucerne or Venice, of Maupassant travelling to Cannes, of Verlaine on the road to Brussels, of Voltaire fleeing down from Prussia embroiled at his Frankfort inn, of Charles VIII descending on Italy, of Dante coming up to Paris, of Saint Louis on his doomed crusade, of Charlemagne lost in the Pyrenees—old wanderings, old agonies, old battles, that have worn the old highways to grooves, that have scarred and made venerable the land with the marks of their noble disasters.—In my bed in New Jersey I shall lie and hear prolonged more thrilling shouts, the wild distant wailing of the trains that rush swift and far across the country—to New York, to Baltimore, to Richmond; to Chicago, to Galveston, to Detroit; to Seattle and San Francisco; to Halifax and Mexico City. They bring no echoes of famous poetry; their cities have no names of distinction. They scotch a wake of soot and smoke through a land already sooty and smoky, over low interminable prairies, through a scattered and unwieldy world. But where there is a petulance and a sadness in the piping of the French engines, I shall hear

in the American ones an eagerness and a zest: they have elbow-room here
for their racing; they can drive on as far as they like; they have an unknown country to explore, a country that no one has ever heard of.—
What sort of men are these who live in nameless towns? At a distance,
they seem neither intelligent nor colorful nor fine—scarcely members of
the same race as the beings who have built civilization. But I know that
in the wide spaces of that wilderness, in the life of that loose abundant
world, for all the reign of mediocrity and the tyranny of intolerance, there
is a new freshness and freedom to be brought to the function of mankind
—the function which, in the long run, we shall never be able to get out
of: staring out in wonder and dismay at the mysterious shapes of the
world, either to ask ourselves what laws move them or, combining those
shapes anew, to make shift to create a nobler world in which our souls
may find a home.

XIX. INTRODUCTION

In a sense, Ernest Hemingway (1899–1961) joined the attack on language of the 1920's. The celebrated sparseness of his style, the search for
simplicity, and, most important, the attempt to use gesture as a substitute for language shows how much Hemingway learned from Gertrude Stein. His rejection of the old idealism, his discomfort with ideas
like patriotism and nobility, as well as most other abstractions, led him,
as one critic has well said, to create heroes to whom things happen. The
following bullfight scenes from Hemingway's first novel exemplify these
stylistic innovations so inextricably associated with the intellectual life
of the 1920's.

XIX.

Ernest Hemingway
THE SUN ALSO RISES
1926

The bull-fight on the second day was much better than on the first. Brett sat between Mike and me at the barrera, and Bill and Cohn went up above. Romero was the whole show. I do not think Brett saw any other bull-fighter. No one else did either, except the hard-shelled technicians. It was all Romero. There were two other matadors, but they did not count. I sat beside Brett and explained to Brett what it was all about. I told her [Brett] about watching the bull, not the horse, when the bulls charged the pica-dors, and got her to watching the picador place the point of his pic so that she saw what it was all about, so that it became more something that was going on with a definite end, and less of a spectacle with unexplained horrors. I had her watch how Romero took the bull away from a fallen horse with his cape, and how he held him with the cape and turned him, smoothly and suavely, never wasting the bull. She saw how Romero avoided every brusque movement and saved his bulls for the last when he wanted them, not winded and discomposed but smoothly worn down. She saw how close Romero always worked to the bull, and I pointed out to her the tricks the other bull-fighters used to make it look as though they were working closely. She saw why she liked Romero's cape-work and why she did not like the others.

Romero never made any contortions, always it was straight and pure and natural in line. The others twisted themselves like corkscrews, their elbows raised, and leaned against the flanks of the bull after his horns had passed, to give a faked look of danger. Afterward, all that was faked turned bad and gave an unpleasant feeling. Romero's bull-fighting gave real emotion, because he kept the absolute purity of line in his movements and always quietly and calmly let the horns pass him close each time. He did not have to emphasize their closeness. Brett saw how something that was beautiful done close to the bull was ridiculous if it were done a little way

SOURCE. Ernest Hemingway, *The Sun Also Rises,* New York: Charles Scribner's Sons, 1926, pp. 173–174 and 224–230. Copyright 1926 Charles Scribner's Sons; renewal copyright 1954 Ernest Hemingway. Reprinted with the permission of Charles Scribner's Sons.

off. I told her how since the death of Joselito all the bull-fighters had been developing a technic that simulated this appearance of danger in order to give a fake emotional feeling, while the bull-fighter was really safe. Romero had the old thing, the holding of his purity of line through the maximum of exposure, while he dominated the bull by making him realize he was unattainable, while he prepared him for the killing. . . .

Pedro Romero had the greatness. He loved bull-fighting, and I think he loved the bulls, and I think he loved Brett. Everything of which he could control the locality he did in front of her all that afternoon. Never once did he look up. He made it stronger that way, and did it for himself, too, as well as for her. Because he did not look up to ask if it pleased he did it all for himself inside, and it strengthened him, and yet he did it for her, too. But he did not do it for her at any loss to himself. He gained by it all through the afternoon.

His first "quite" was directly below us. The three matadors take the bull in turn after each charge he makes at a picador. Belmonte was the first, Marcial was the second. Then came Romero. The three of them were standing at the left of the horse. The picador, his hat down over his eyes, the shaft of his pic angling sharply toward the bull, kicked in the spurs and held them and with the reins in his left hand walked the horse forward toward the bull. The bull was watching. Seemingly he watched the white horse, but really he watched the triangular steel point of the pic. Romero, watching, saw the bull start to turn his head. He did not want to charge. Romero flicked his cape so the color caught the bull's eye. The bull charged with the reflex, charged, and found not the flash of color but a white horse, and a man leaned far over the horse, shot the steel point of the long hickory shaft into the hump of muscle on the bull's shoulder, and pulled his horse sideways as he pivoted on the pic, making a wound, enforcing the iron into the bull's shoulder, making him bleed for Belmonte.

The bull did not insist under the iron. He did not really want to get at the horse. He turned and the group broke apart and Romero was taking him out with his cape. He took him out softly and smoothly, and then stopped and, standing squarely in front of the bull, offered him the cape. The bull's tail went up and he charged, and Romero moved his arms ahead of the bull, wheeling, his feet firmed. The dampened, mud-weighted cape swung open and full as a sail fills, and Romero pivoted with it just ahead of the bull. At the end of the pass they were facing each other again. Romero smiled. The bull wanted it again, and Romero's cape filled again, this time on the other side. Each time he let the bull pass so close that the man and the bull and the cape that filled and pivoted ahead of the bull were all one sharply etched mass. It was all so slow and so controlled. It was as though he were rocking the bull to sleep. He made four veronicas like that, and finished with a half-veronica that turned his back on the bull and came away toward the applause, his hand on his hip, his cape on his arm, and the bull watching his back going away.

In his own bulls he was perfect. His first bull did not see well. After the first two passes with the cape Romero knew exactly how bad the vision was impaired. He worked accordingly. It was not brilliant bull-fighting. It was only perfect bull-fighting. The crowd wanted the bull changed. They made a great row. Nothing very fine could happen with a bull that could not see the lures, but the President would not order him replaced.

"Why don't they change him?" Brett asked.

"They've paid for him. They don't want to lose their money."

"It's hardly fair to Romero."

"Watch how he handles a bull that can't see the color."

"It's the sort of thing I don't like to see."

It was not nice to watch if you cared anything about the person who was doing it. With the bull who could not see the colors of the capes, or the scarlet flannel of the muleta, Romero had to make the bull consent with his body. He had to get so close that the bull saw his body, and would start for it, and then shift the bull's charge to the flannel and finish out the pass in the classic manner. The Biarritz crowd did not like it. They thought Romero was afraid, and that was why he gave that little sidestep each time as he transferred the bull's charge from his own body to the flannel. They preferred Belmonte's imitation of himself or Marcial's imitation of Belmonte. There were three of them in the row behind us.

"What's he afraid of the bull for? The bull's so dumb he only goes after the cloth."

"He's just a young bull-fighter. He hasn't learned it yet."

"But I thought he was fine with the cape before."

"Probably he's nervous now."

Out in the centre of the ring, all alone, Romero was going on with the same thing, getting so close that the bull could see him plainly, offering the body, offering it again a little closer, the bull watching dully, then so close that the bull thought he had him, offering again and finally drawing the charge and then, just before the horns came, giving the bull the red cloth to follow with that little, almost imperceptible, jerk that so offended the critical judgment of the Biarritz bull-fight experts.

"He's going to kill now," I said to Brett. "The bull's still strong. He wouldn't wear himself out."

Out in the centre of the ring Romero profiled in front of the bull, drew the sword out from the folds of the muleta, rose on his toes, and sighted along the blade. The bull charged as Romero charged. Romero's left hand dropped the muleta over the bull's muzzle to blind him, his left shoulder went forward between the horns as the sword went in, and for just an instant he and the bull were one, Romero way out over the bull, the right arm extended high up to where the hilt of the sword had gone in between the bull's shoulders. Then the figure was broken. There was a little jolt as Romero came clear, and then he was standing, one hand up, facing the bull, his shirt ripped out from under his sleeve, the white blowing in the wind, and the bull, the red sword hilt tight between his shoulders, his head going down and his legs settling.

"There he goes," Bill said.

Romero was close enough so the bull could see him. His hand still up, he spoke to the bull. The bull gathered himself, then his head went forward and he went over slowly, then all over, suddenly, four feet in the air.

They handed the sword to Romero, and carrying it blade down, the muleta in his other hand, he walked over to in front of the President's box, bowed, straightened, and came over to the barrera and handed over the sword and muleta.

"Bad one," said the sword-handler.

"He made me sweat," said Romero. He wiped off his face. The sword-handler handed him the water-jug. Romero wiped his lips. It hurt him to drink out of the jug. He did not look up at us.

Marcial had a big day. They were still applauding him when Romero's last bull came in. It was the bull that had sprinted out and killed the man in the morning running.

During Romero's first bull his hurt face had been very noticeable. Everything he did showed it. All the concentration of the awkwardly delicate working with the bull that could not see well brought it out. The fight with Cohn had not touched his spirit but his face had been smashed and his body hurt. He was wiping all that out now. Each thing that he did with this bull wiped that out a little cleaner. It was a good bull, a big bull, and with horns, and it turned and recharged easily and surely. He was what Romero wanted in bulls.

When he had finished his work with the muleta and was ready to kill, the crowd made him go on. They did not want the bull killed yet, they did not want it to be over. Romero went on. It was like a course in bull-fighting. All the passes he linked up, all completed, all slow, templed and smooth. There were no tricks and no mystifications. There was no brusqueness. And each pass as it reached the summit gave you a sudden ache inside. The crowd did not want it ever to be finished.

The bull was squared on all four feet to be killed, and Romero killed directly below us. He killed not as he had been forced to by the last bull, but as he wanted to. He profiled directly in front of the bull, drew the sword out of the folds of the muleta and sighted along the blade. The bull watched him. Romero spoke to the bull and tapped one of his feet. The bull charged and Romero waited for the charge, the muleta held low, sighting along the blade, his feet firm. Then without taking a step forward, he became one with the bull, the sword was in high between the shoulders, the bull had followed the low-swung flannel, that disappeared as Romero lurched clear to the left, and it was over. The bull tried to go forward, his legs commenced to settle, he swung from side to side, hesitated, then went down on his knees, and Romero's older brother leaned forward behind him and drove a short knife into the bull's neck at the base of the horns. The first time he missed. He drove the knife in again, and the bull went over, twitching and rigid. Romero's brother, holding the bull's horn in one hand, the knife in the other, looked up at the President's box. Handkerchiefs were waving all over the bull-ring. The President looked down from the box and waved his handkerchief. The brother cut the notched black ear from the dead bull and trotted over with it to Romero. The bull lay heavy and black on the sand, his tongue out. Boys were running toward him from all parts of the arena, making a little circle around him. They were starting to dance around the bull.

Romero took the ear from his brother and held it up toward the President. The President bowed and Romero, running to get ahead of the crowd, came toward us. He leaned up against the barrera and gave the ear to Brett. He nodded his head and smiled. The crowd were all about him. Brett held down the cape.

"You liked it?" Romero called.

Brett did not say anything. They looked at each other and smiled. Brett had the ear in her hand.

"Don't get bloody," Romero said, and grinned.

XX. INTRODUCTION

The disaffection and humanistic pessimism of the mind of the 1920's was most beautifully caught by Joseph Wood Krutch (born in 1893) in *The Modern Temper,* at the close of the decade. Providing a dramatic contrast to the optimism of Wilson's essay (Reading XVIII), Krutch's essay was a gentle and felicitous dirge sung over the corpse of the human spirit.

Krutch felt that it was no longer necessary to do battle in the name of naturalism, because he took that position virtually for granted; such an assumption is perhaps the most noteworthy characteristic of his essay. That nature had no goal, that man was alone in a purposeless and essentially hostile world meant, for Krutch, that a patternless reality had obtruded itself into modern experience and had destroyed the sustaining illusions of the past, including the illusion of God. Alienation had become a fact of the modern world because there was no longer a moral or ethical authority left. Man's knowledge and his desire were always and everywhere in conflict. The hard and tough rationalism of science and industry would perhaps create an antiseptic and dehumanized future that, Krutch felt, would simply amount to extinction.

Krutch's book was the capstone of the skepticism of the decade. His position was more than a sophisticated yawn, more than mere detachment from the materialism of the decade, because he had absorbed the implications of both Darwin and Freud, and his essay was an attempt really to confront the tragedy of contemporary existence.

The following selection is "The Genesis of a Mood," the first chapter of Krutch's book.

XX.

Joseph Wood Krutch
THE MODERN TEMPER
1929

The world which any consciousness inhabits is a world made up in part of experience and in part of fancy. No experience, and hence no knowledge, is complete, but the gaps which lie between the solid fragments are filled in with shadows. Connections, explanations, and reasons are supplied by the imagination, and thus the world gets its patterned completeness from material which is spun out of the desires. But as time goes on and experience accumulates there remains less and less scope for the fancy. The universe becomes more and more what experience has revealed, less and less what imagination has created, and hence, since it was not designed to suit man's needs, less and less what he would have it be. With increasing knowledge his power to manipulate his physical environment increases, but in gaining the knowledge which enables him to do so he surrenders insensibly the power which in his ignorance he had to mold the universe. The forces of nature obey him, but in learning to master them he has in another sense allowed them to master him. He has exchanged the universe which his desires created, the universe made for man, for the universe of nature of which he is only a part. Like the child growing into manhood, he passes from the world which is fitted to him into a world for which he must fit himself.

If, then, the world of poetry, mythology, and religion represents the world as a man would like to have it, while science represents the world as he gradually comes to discover it, we need only compare the two to realize how irreconcilable they appear. For the cozy bowl of the sky arched in a protecting curve above him he must exchange the cold immensities of space, and, for the spiritual order which he has designed, the chaos of nature. God he had loved *because* God was anthropomorphic, because He was made in man's own image, with purposes and desires which were human and hence understandable. But Nature's purpose, if purpose she can

SOURCE. Joseph Wood Krutch, *The Modern Temper,* New York: Harcourt, Brace and Co., 1929, pp. 7–26. Copyright 1929 Harcourt, Brace and World, Inc.; renewed 1957 by Joseph Wood Krutch. Reprinted with permission of the publishers.

be said to have, is no purpose of his and is not understandable in his terms. Her desire merely to live and to propagate in innumerable forms, her ruthless indifference to his values, and the blindness of her irresistible will strike terror to his soul, and he comes in the fullness of his experience to realize that the ends which he proposes to himself—happiness and order and reason—are ends which he must achieve, if he achieve them at all, in her despite. Formerly he had believed in even his darkest moments that the universe was rational if he could only grasp its rationality, but gradually he comes to suspect that rationality is an attribute of himself alone and that there is no reason to suppose that his own life has any more meaning than the life of the humblest insect that crawls from one annihilation to another. Nature, in her blind thirst for life, has filled every possible cranny of the rotting earth with some sort of fantastic creature, and among them man is but one—perhaps the most miserable of all, because he is the only one in whom the instinct of life falters long enough to enable it to ask the question "Why?" As long as life is regarded as having been created, creating may be held to imply a purpose, but merely to have come into being is, in all likelihood, merely to go out of it also.

Fortunately, perhaps, man, like the individual child, was spared in his cradle the knowledge which he could not bear. Illusions have been lost one by one. God, instead of disappearing in an instant, has retreated step by step and surrendered gradually his control of the universe. Once he decreed the fall of every sparrow and counted the hairs upon every head; a little later he became merely the original source of the laws of nature, and even today there are thousands who, unable to bear the thought of losing him completely, still fancy that they can distinguish the uncertain outlines of a misty figure. But the rôle which he plays grows less and less, and man is left more and more alone in a universe to which he is completely alien. His world was once, like the child's world, three-quarters myth and poetry. His teleological concepts molded it into a form which he could appreciate and he gave to it moral laws which would make it meaningful, but step by step the outlines of nature have thrust themselves upon him, and for the dream which he made is substituted a reality devoid of any pattern which he can understand.

In the course of this process innumerable readjustments have been made, and always with the effort to disturb as little as possible the myth which is so much more full of human values than the fact which comes in some measure to replace it. Thus, for example, the Copernican theory of astronomy, removing the earth from the center of the universe and assigning it a very insignificant place among an infinitude of whirling motes, was not merely resisted as a fact, but was, when finally accepted, accepted as far as possible without its implications. Even if taken entirely by itself and without the whole system of facts of which it is a part, it renders extremely improbable the assumption, fundamental in most human thought, that the universe has man as its center and is hence understandable in his terms, but this implication was disregarded just as, a little later, the implications of the theory of evolution were similarly disregarded. It is not likely that if man had been aware from the very beginning that his world was a mere detail in the universe, and himself merely one of the innumerable species of living things, he would ever have come to think of himself, as he even now tends to do, as a being whose desires must be somehow satisfiable and whose reason must be matched by some similar reason in nature. But the myth, having been once established, persists long after the assumptions upon which it was made have been destroyed, because, being born of desire, it is far more satisfactory than any fact.

Unfortunately, perhaps, experience does not grow at a constant, but at an accelerated, rate. The Greeks who sought knowledge, not through the study of nature, but through the examination of their own minds, developed a philosophy which was really analogous to myth, because the laws which determined its growth were dictated by human desires, and they discovered few facts capable of disturbing the pattern which they devised. The Middle Ages retreated still further into themselves, but with the Renaissance man began to surrender himself to nature, and the sciences, each nourishing the other, began their iconoclastic march. Three centuries lay between the promulgation of the Copernican theory and the publication of the *Origin of Species*, but in sixty-odd years which have elapsed since that latter event the blows have fallen with rapidity which left no interval for recovery. The structures which are variously known as mythology, religion, and philosophy, and which are alike in that each has as its function the interpretation of experience in terms which have human values, have collapsed under the force of successive attacks and shown themselves utterly incapable of assimilating the new stores of experience which have been dumped upon the world. With increasing completeness science maps out the pattern of nature, but the latter has no relation to the pattern of human needs and feelings.

Consider, for example, the plight of ethics. Historical criticism having destroyed what used to be called by people of learning and intelligence "Christian Evidences," and biology having shown how unlikely it is that man is the recipient of any transcendental knowledge, there remains no foundation in authority for ideas of right and wrong; and if, on the other hand, we turn to the traditions of the human race, anthropology is ready to prove that no consistent human tradition has ever existed. Custom has furnished the only basis which ethics have ever had, and there is no conceivable human action which custom has not at one time justified and at another condemned. Standards are imaginary things, and yet it is extremely doubtful if man can live well, either spiritually or physically, without the belief that they are somehow real. Without them society lapses into anarchy and the individual becomes aware of an intolerable disharmony between himself and the universe. Instinctively and emotionally he is an ethical animal. No known race is so low in the scale of civilization that it has not attributed a moral order to the world, because no known race is so little human as not to suppose a moral order so innately desirable as to have an inevitable existence. It is man's most fundamental myth, and life seems meaningless to him without it. Yet, as that systematized and cumulative experience which is called science displaces one after another the myths which have been generated by need, it grows more and more likely that he must remain an ethical animal in a universe which contains no ethical element.

Mystical philosophers have sometimes said that they "accepted the universe." They have, that is to say, formed of it some conception which answered the emotional needs of their spirit and which brought them a sense of being in harmony with its aims and processes. They have been aware of no needs which nature did not seem to supply and of no ideals which she too did not seem to recognize. They have felt themselves one with her because they have had the strength of imagination to make her over in their own image, and it is doubtful if any man can live at peace who does not thus feel himself at home. But as the world assumes the shape which science gives it, it becomes more and more difficult to find such emotional correspondences. Whole realms of human feeling, like the realm of ethics, find no place for themselves in the pattern of nature and generate needs for which no satisfaction is supplied. What man knows is everywhere at war with what he wants.

In the course of a few centuries his knowledge, and hence the universe of which he finds himself an inhabitant, has been completely revolutionized, but his instincts and his emotions have remained, relatively at least, unchanged. He is still, as he always was, adjusted to the orderly, purposeful, humanized world which all peoples unburdened by experience have figured to themselves, but that world no longer exists. He has the same sense of dignity to which the myth of his descent from the gods was designed to minister, and the same innate purposefulness which led him to attribute a purpose to nature, but he can no longer think in terms appropriate to either. The world which his reason and his investigation reveal is a world which his emotions cannot comprehend.

Casually he accepts the spiritual iconoclasm of science, and in the detachment of everyday life he learns to play with the cynical wisdom of biology and psychology, which explain away the awe of emotional experience just as earlier science explained away the awe of conventional piety. Yet, under the stress of emotional crises, knowledge is quite incapable of controlling his emotions or of justifying them to himself. In love, he calls upon the illusions of man's grandeur and dignity to help him accept his emotions, and faced with tragedy he calls upon illusion to dignify his suffering; but lyric flight is checked by the rationality which he has cultivated, and in the world of metabolism and hormones, repressions and complexes, he finds no answer for his needs. He is feeling about love, for example, much as the troubadour felt, but he thinks about it in a very different way. Try as he may, the two halves of his soul can hardly be made to coalesce, and he cannot either feel as his intelligence tells him that he should feel or think as his emotions would have him think, and thus he is reduced to mocking his torn and divided soul. In the grip of passion he cannot, as some romanticist might have done, accept it with a religious trust in the mystery of love, nor yet can he regard it as a psychiatrist, himself quite free from emotion, might suggest—merely as an interesting specimen of psychical botany. Man *qua* thinker may delight in the intricacies of psychology, but man *qua* lover has not learned to feel in its terms; so that, though complexes and ductless glands may serve to explain the feelings of another, one's own still demand all these symbols of the ineffable in which one has long ceased to believe.

Time was when the scientist, the poet, and the philosopher walked hand in hand. In the universe which the one perceived the other found himself comfortably at home. But the world of modern science is one in which the intellect alone can rejoice. The mind leaps, and leaps perhaps with a sort of elation, through the immensities of space, but the spirit, frightened and cold, longs to have once more above its head the inverted bowl beyond which may lie whatever paradise its desires may create. The lover who surrendered himself to the Implacable Aphrodite or who fancied his foot upon the lowest rung of the Platonic ladder of love might retain his self-respect, but one can neither resist nor yield gracefully to a carefully catalogued psychosis. A happy life is a sort of poem, with a poem's elevation and dignity, but emotions cannot be dignified unless they are first respected. They must seem to correspond with, to be justified by, something in the structure of the universe itself; but though it was the function of religion and philosophy to hypostatize some such correspondence, to project a humanity upon nature, or a least to conceive of a humane force above and beyond her, science finds no justification for such a process and is content instead to show how illusions were born.

The most ardent love of truth, the most resolute determination to follow nature no matter to what black abyss she may lead, need not blind one to the fact that many of the lost illusions had, to speak the language of science, a survival value. Either individuals or societies whose life is imbued with a cheerful certitude, whose aims are clear, and whose sense of the essential rightness of life is strong, live and struggle with an energy unknown to the skeptical and the pessimistic. Whatever the limitations of their intellects as instruments of criticism, they possess the physical and emotional vigor which is, unlike critical intelligence, analogous to the processes of nature. They found empires and conquer wildernesses, and they pour the excess of their energy into works of art which the intelligence of more sophisticated peoples continue to admire even though it has lost the faith in life which is requisite for the building of a Chartres or the carving of a Venus de Milo. The one was not erected to a law of nature or the other designed to celebrate the *libido*, for each presupposed a sense of human dignity which science nowhere supports.

Thus man seems caught in a dilemma which his intellect has devised. Any deliberately managed return to a state of relative ignorance, however desirable it might be argued to be, is obviously out of the question. We cannot, as the naive proponents of the various religions, new and old, seem to assume, believe one thing and forget another merely because we happen to be convinced that it would be desirable to do so; and it is worth observing that the new psychology, with its penetrating analysis of the influence of desire upon belief, has so adequately warned the reason of the tricks which the will can play upon it that it has greatly decreased the possibility of beneficent delusion and serves to hold the mind in a steady contemplation of that from which it would fain escape. Weak and uninstructed intelligences take refuge in the monotonous repetition of once living creeds, or are even reduced to the desperate expedient of going to sleep amid the formulae of the flabby pseudo-religions in which the modern world is so prolific. But neither of these classes affords any aid to the robust but serious mind which is searching for some terms upon which it may live.

And if we are, as by this time we should be, free from any teleological delusion, if we no longer make the unwarranted assumption that every human problem is somehow of necessity solvable, we must confess it may be that for the sort of being whom we have described no survival is possible in any form like that which his soul has now taken. He is a fantastic thing that has developed sensibilities and established values beyond the nature which gave him birth. He is of all living creatures the one to whom the earth is the least satisfactory. He has arrived at a point where he can no longer delude himself as to the extent of his predicament, and should he either become modified or disappear the earth would continue to spin and the grass to grow as it has always done. Of the thousands of living species the vast majority would be as unaware of his passing as they are unaware now of his presence, and he would go as a shadow goes. His arts, his religions, and his civilizations—these are fair and wonderful things, but they are fair and wonderful to him alone. With the extinction of his poetry would be extinguished also the only sensibility for which it has any meaning, and there would remain nothing capable of feeling a loss. Nothing would be left to label the memory of his discontent "divine," and those creatures who find in nature no lack would resume their undisputed possession of the earth.

Anthropoid in form some of them might continue to be, and possessed as well of all of the human brain that makes possible a cunning adaption to the conditions of physical life. To them nature might yield up subtler secrets than any yet penetrated; their machines might be more wonderful and their bodies more healthy than any yet known—even though there had passed away, not merely all myth and poetry, but the need for them as well. Cured of his transcendental cravings, content with things as they are, accepting the universe as experience had shown it to be, man would be freed of his soul and, like the other animals, either content or at least desirous of nothing which he might not hope ultimately to obtain.

Nor can it be denied that certain adumbrations of this type have before now come into being. Among those of keener intellect there are scientists to whom the test tube and its contents are all-sufficient, and among those of coarser grain, captains of finance and builders of mills, there are those to whom the acquirement of wealth and power seems to constitute a life in which no lack can be perceived. Doubtless they are not new types;

doubtless they have always existed; but may they not be the strain from which Nature will select the coming race? Is not their creed the creed of Nature, and are they not bound to triumph over those whose illusions are no longer potent because they are no longer really believed? Certain philosophers, clinging desperately to the ideal of a humanized world, have proposed a retreat into the imagination. Bertrand Russell in his popular essay, *A Free Man's Worship*, Unamuno and Santayana *passim* throughout their works, have argued that the way of salvation lay in a sort of ironic belief, in a determination to act as though one still believed the things which once were really held true. But is not this a desperate expedient, a last refuge likely to appeal only to the leaders of a lost cause? Does it not represent the last, least substantial, phase of fading faith, something which borrows what little substance it seems to have from a reality of the past? If it seems half real to the sons of those who lived in the spiritual world of which it is a shadow, will it not seem, a little further removed, only a faint futility? Surely it has but little to oppose to those who come armed with the certitudes of science and united with, not fleeing from, the nature amid which they live.

And if the dilemma here described is itself a delusion it is at least as vividly present and as terribly potent as those other delusions which have shaped or deformed the human spirit. There is no significant contemporary writer upon philosophy, ethics, or esthetics whose speculations do not lead him to it in one form or another, and even the less reflective are aware of it in their own way. Both our practical morality and our emotional lives are adjusted to a world which no longer exists. In so far as we adhere to a code of conduct, we do so largely because certain habits still persist, not because we can give any logical reason for preferring them, and in so far as we indulge ourselves in the primitive emotional satisfactions—romantic love, patriotism, zeal for justice, and so forth—our satisfaction is the result merely of the temporary suspension of our disbelief in the mythology upon which they are founded. Traditionalists in religion are fond of asserting that our moral codes are flimsy because they are rootless; but, true as this is, it is perhaps not so important as the fact that our emotional lives are rootless too.

If the gloomy vision of a dehumanized world which has just been evoked is not to become a reality, some complete readjustment must be made, and at least two generations have found themselves unequal to the task. The generation of Thomas Henry Huxley, so busy with destruction as never adequately to realize how much it was destroying, fought with such zeal against frightened conservatives that it never took time to do more than assert with some vehemence that all would be well, and the generation that followed either danced amid the ruins or sought by various compromises to save the remains of a few tottering structures. But neither patches nor evasions will serve. It is not a changed world but a new one in which man must henceforth live if he lives at all, for all his premises have been destroyed and he must proceed to new conclusions. The values which he thought established have been swept away along with the rules by which he thought they might be attained.

To this fact many are not yet awake, but our novels, our poems, and our pictures are enough to reveal that a generation aware of its predicament is at hand. It has awakened to the fact that both the ends which its fathers proposed to themselves and the emotions from which they drew their strength seem irrelevant and remote. With a smile, sad or mocking, according to individual temperament, it regards those works of the past in which were summed up the values of life. The romantic ideal of a world well lost for love and the classic ideal of austere dignity seem equally ridiculous, equally meaningless when referred, not to the temper of the past, but to the temper of the present. The passions which swept through the once major poets no longer awaken any profound response, and only in the bleak, torturous complexities of a T. S. Eliot does it find its moods given adequate expression. Here disgust speaks with a robust voice and denunciation is confident, but ecstasy, flickering and uncertain, leaps fitfully up only to sink back among the cinders. And if the poet, with his gift of keen perceptions and his power of organization, can achieve only the most momentary and unstable adjustments, what hope can there be for those whose spirit is a less powerful instrument?

And yet it is with such as he, baffled, but content with nothing which plays only upon the surface, that the hope for a still humanized future must rest. No one can tell how many of the old values must go or how new the new will be. Thus, while under the influence of the old mythology the sexual instinct was transformed into romantic love and tribal solidarity into the religion of patriotism, there is nothing in the modern consciousness capable of effecting these transmutations. Neither the one nor the other is capable of being, as it once was, the *raison d'être* of a life or the motif of a poem which is not, strictly speaking, derivative and anachronistic. Each is fading, each becoming as much a shadow as devotion to the cult of purification through self-torture. Either the instincts upon which they are founded will achieve new transformations or they will remain merely instincts, regarded as having no particular emotional significance in a spiritual world which, if it exists at all, will be as different from the spiritual world of, let us say, Robert Browning as that world is different from the world of Cato the Censor.

As for this present unhappy time, haunted by ghosts from a dead world and not yet at home in its own, its predicament is not . . . unlike the predicament of the adolescent who has not yet learned to orient himself without reference to the mythology amid which his childhood was passed. He still seeks in the world of his experience for the values which he had found there, and he is aware only of a vast disharmony. But boys—most of them, at least—grow up, and the world of adult consciousness has always held a relation to myth intimate enough to make readjustment possible. The finest spirits have bridged the gulf, have carried over with them something of a child's faith, and only the coarsest have grown into something which was no more than finished animality. Today the gulf is broader, the adjustment more difficult, than ever it was before, and even the possibility of an actual human maturity is problematic. There impends for the human spirit either extinction or a readjustment more stupendous than any made before.

CHAPTER 4

Depression Realism

A. The Meaning of the Economy

XXI. INTRODUCTION

In at least one sense the Depression of the 1930's did not profoundly alter the nature or quality of American thought. The "realistic" recoil from idealism was intensified in that decade, along with the deepening conviction that ways had to be found to contain unregulated individualism. Earlier analytical modes and moods were followed by scholars and writers of the depression with, however, a new sense of urgency required by the magnitude of the emergency. But it is true that the retreat from politics that had characterized much of the intellectual life of the 1920's was now abandoned; it is equally true that the apparent rediscovery of the individual of the twenties was now similarly rejected. But the lines of skepticism and realism of the previous decade remained as primary anterior assumptions in the work of many social analysts during the New Deal.

It was obviously important to understand the nature and function of the American economy. It was important to understand the relationship between the state and the economy and between the individual and his society. A major forward step was taken by Adolf A. Berle, Jr. (born in 1895) and Gardiner C. Means (born in 1896) in their now classic work, *The Modern Corporation and Private Property*, 1932. It was their intention to provide a morphology of the American economy with the purpose of understanding the nature of power. American industrial capitalism, as they analyzed it, had created a situation in which a very few men could direct and control the material resources of the nation. Since that was a fact, Berle and Means wrote, realistic political and economic thought would have to confront it. America was not what men dreamed, was not the home of the independent entrepreneur, and the usual discussions of competition were applicable, therefore, to a world which no longer existed, if in fact it ever did. On the basis of the data they collected, and the generalizations at which they arrived, the older vision of the Muckrakers seemed now to be vindicated through the use of social science.

The following selection is from the third chapter, "The Concentration of Economic Power" of *The Modern Corporation and Private Property*.

XXI.

Adolf A. Berle, Jr. and Gardiner C. Means

THE MODERN CORPORATION AND
PRIVATE PROPERTY
1932

The corporate system has done more than evolve a norm by which business is carried on. Within it there exists a centripetal attraction which draws wealth together into aggregations of constantly increasing size, at the same time throwing control into the hands of fewer and fewer men. The trend is apparent; and no limit is as yet in sight. Were it possible to say that circumstances had established the concentration, but that there was no basis to form an opinion as to whether the process would continue, the whole problem might be simplified. But this is not the case. So far as can be seen, every element which favored concentration still exists, and the only apparent factor which may end the tendency is the limit in the ability of a few human beings effectively to handle the aggregates of property brought under their control.

The size of the modern giant corporation is difficult to grasp. Many people would consider large a corporation having assets of a million dollars or an income of $50,000. Measured by the average corporation this idea would be justified. In 1927 two-thirds of all corporations reporting net incomes earned less than $5,000 each. The average non-banking corporation in that year had an income of only $22,000, and gross assets of but $570,000. In comparison with the average corporation the million dollar company would be large. But in comparison to the

SOURCE. Adolf A. Berle, Jr. and Gardiner C. Means, *The Modern Corporation and Private Property*, New York: Commerce Clearing House, 1932, pp. 18–19, 24–35, and 38–46. Copyright 1932 by The Macmillan Co., renewed 1960 by A. A. Berle and G. C. Means. Reprinted with the permission of The Macmillan Company.

great modern corporation both are pigmies. On the basis of assets, the American Telephone and Telegraph Company would be equivalent to over 8,000 average sized corporations, and both the United States Steel Corporation and the Pennsylvania Railroad Company to over 4,000. A hundred million dollar company would be equivalent in assets to nearly 200 average corporations. Clearly such great organisms are not to be thought of in the same terms as the average company. Already the Telephone Company controls more wealth than is contained within the borders of twenty-one of the states in the country.

The great extent to which economic activity is today carried on by such large enterprises is clearly indicated by the . . . list of the two hundred largest non-banking corporations, compiled as of January 1, 1930. Nearly all of these companies had assets of over one hundred million dollars, and fifteen had assets of over a billion dollars. Their combined assets amounted to eighty-one billions of dollars or, as we shall see, nearly half of all corporate wealth in the United States. . . .

These great companies form the very framework of American industry. The individual must come in contact with them almost constantly. He may own an interest in one or more of them, he may be employed by one of them, but above all he is continually accepting their service. If he travels any distance he is almost certain to ride on one of the great railway systems. The engine which draws him has probably been constructed by the American Locomotive Company or the Baldwin Locomotive Works; the car in which he rides is likely to have been made by the American Car and Foundry Company or one of its subsidiaries, unless he is enjoying the services of the Pullman Company. The rails have almost certainly been supplied by one of the eleven steel companies on the list; and coal may well have come from one of the four coal companies, if not from a mine owned by the railroad itself. Perhaps the individual travels by automobile—in a car manufactured by the Ford, General Motors, Studebaker, or Chrysler Companies, on tires supplied by Firestone, Goodrich, Goodyear, or the United States Rubber Company. He may choose among the brands of gas furnished by one of the twenty petroleum companies all actively seeking his trade. Should he pause to send a telegram or to telephone, one of the listed companies would be sure to fill his need.

Perhaps, on the other hand, the individual stays in his own home in comparative isolation and privacy. What do the two hundred largest companies mean to him there? His electricity and gas are almost sure to be furnished by one of these public utility companies: the aluminum of his kitchen utensils by the Aluminum Co. of America. His electric refrigerator may be the product of General Motors Co., or of one of the two great electric equipment companies, General Electric and Westinghouse Electric. The chances are that the Crane Company has supplied his plumbing fixtures, the American Radiator and Standard Sanitary Corp. his heating equipment. He probably buys at least some of his groceries from the Great Atlantic and Pacific Tea Co.—a company that expected to sell one-eighth of all the groceries in the country in 1930 —and he secures some of his drugs, directly or indirectly, from the United Drug Company. The cans which contain his groceries may well have been made by the American Can Company; his sugar has been refined by one of the major companies, his meat has probably been prapared by Swift, Armour, or Wilson, his crackers put up by the National Biscuit Company. The newspaper which comes to his door may be printed on International Paper Company paper or on that of the Crown Zellerbach Corporation; his shoes may be one of the International Shoe Company's makes; and although his suit may not be made of American Woolen Company cloth, it has doubtless been stitched on a Singer sewing machine.

If he seeks amusement through a radio he will almost of necessity use a set made under a license of the Radio Corporation of America. When he steps out to the movies he will probably see a Paramount, Fox, or Warner Brothers' picture (taken on Eastman Kodak film) at a theatre controlled by one of these producing groups. No matter which of the alluring cigarette advertisements he succumbs to he is almost sure to find himself smoking one of the many brands put out by the "big four" tobacco companies, and he probably stops to buy them at the United Cigar store on the corner.

Even where the individual does not come in direct contact, he cannot escape indirect contact with these companies, so ubiquitous have they become. There are few articles of consumption to whose production one of the big companies has not to some extent contributed. The International Harvester Company and the Deere Company, plowmakers, have aided in the production of most of the bread that the American eats, to much of the cotton he wears and to many of the other agricultural products he consumes. It is almost impossible to obtain electric power from a local utility without receiving service from generating equipment supplied by one of the two big electric equipment companies. Few industrial products are made without the aid at some point in the process of steel derived from one of the big companies. And nearly every article involves transportation by one of the big railroads, either in the state of a raw material or that of a finished product.

While these companies play an integral part in the business of the country, their dominant position becomes apparent only when we seek to examine their importance in relation to the whole of the American economy. Here we must turn to the tool of statistics for only thus can we grasp the picture of our economic life as a whole. . . .

In seeking to present a picture of the relative positions of these large corporations, four economic areas will be examined: (1) the New York stock market; (2) all corporate wealth; (3) all business wealth; and (4) the national wealth.

In the New York stock market there can be no question of the dominant position of the large corporation. Taking the list of stocks published weekly by the "Commercial and Financial Chronicle" and covering all but the most inactive stocks traded on the New York Stock Exchange in a normal week, 130 out of the 573 independent American corporations represented can be classed as huge companies, each reporting assets of over one hundred million dollars. These 130 companies controlled more than 80 per cent of the assets of all the companies represented. In Table 1 these corporations are grouped by size showing the total assets held by each group and the per cent which this represents of the assets of all the corporations covered.

TABLE 1

Size Measured by Gross Assets	Number of Companies	Gross Assets Held by Group	Per Cent of Total Assets Represented
Under $50,000,000	372	$ 7,325,000,000	10.9
$50–$100,000,000	71	4,950,000,000	7.4
Over $100,000,000	130	54,714,000,000	81.7
Total	573	$66,989,000,000	100.0

Besides showing the overwhelming importance of the huge corporation, this table shows what is perhaps of even greater significance, the relative unimportance of the medium-sized corporation having assets between $50,000,000 and $100,000,000 and as a group controlling less than 8 per cent of the total assets represented. The small corporations —and in this day of industrial giants the reader must not be shocked by the reference to all corporations with assets less than $50,000,000 as small—though numerous, do not hold an important position. It is noteworthy, however, that practically half the corporations included had less than $30,000,000 assets and as a group controlled less than 6 per cent of the total.

When we compare the combined assets of the two hundred largest non-banking corporations with the assets of all non-banking corporations, their dominant role is further emphasized. These companies, 42 railroads, 52 public utilities, and 106 industrials, each with assets over ninety million dollars, had combined assets at the beginning of 1930 of $81,074,000,000. According to an estimate based on Income Tax figures, the total assets of all non-banking corporations at the beginning of 1930 amounted to $165,000,000,000. Thus the two hundred big companies controlled 49.2 per cent or nearly half of all non-banking corporate wealth, while the remaining half was owned by the more than 300,000 smaller companies.

The same dominant position of the large companies is shown when we compare the net income of the largest companies with the net income of all corporations. In 1929, the most recent year for which Income Tax statistics have been published, the largest two hundred non-banking corporations, each with an income of over $5,000,000, received 43.2 per cent of the income of all non-banking corporations.

Even this figure, however, tends to minimize the importance of the big companies. To a very considerable extent the Income Tax statistics, on which it is based, fail to include as part of the income of a big company all the income derived from property under its control. In compiling the figures of income the Treasury Department has tabulated as separate corporations all companies filing separate Income Tax returns, even when they were actually controlled by other companies. Since any subsidiary company controlled through ownership of less than 95 per cent of its stock (or of the voting stock) was required to file a separate return—and any subsidiary could file a separate return if it so desired— many companies are included as separate when actually they were controlled by other compannes and for the present purpose should have their earnings consolidated with the latter.

For instance, the American Telephone and Telegraph Company was presumably represented in Income Tax returns as at least four companies, the parent company with assets over $3,000 million in 1928, the Pacific Telephone and Telegraph Company with assets over $379 million, the New England Telephone and Telegraph Company with $268 million assets and the Mountain States Telephone and Telegraph Company with $80 million assets. Even dividends received from these subsidiaries were not included in the statutory net income of the parent. Many other large corporations were in the same situation. For this reason the earned incomes reported by the large companies are frequently less than the earnings of property under their control.

A second factor tending to minimize the apparent importance of the large corporation, is the greater proportion of its income which is paid out as interest and therefore is not included as "statutory net income." It is fairly certain that large companies, particularly railroad and public utilities, tend to have a larger indebtedness in proportion to their size than small companies. If the net income of all subsidiary corporations had been included in the net income of parents, and if income had included income represented by amounts paid out as interest, it is probable that the two hundred largest would have received well over 45 per cent of the net income of all corporations. This figure would therefore tend to give support to the figure derived on the basis of gross assets.

The income figures also indicated that the medium-sized corporation is not a particularly important factor. The 800 non-financial corporations next in size (according to net income) after the largest 200, received only 19.3 per cent of the net income of all corporations. This figure covers all corporations reporting income of over one million dollars and less than four and one-half million dollars, incomes representing assets ranging roughly from 18 to 80 million dollars. If all corporations had filed consolidated income accounts, the 800 corporations would have reported a still smaller proportion of corporate income since that of many important corporations would have been shifted into the higher group and only a slight balancing would come through addition from below.

In contrast to the medium-sized, the small corporation, reporting an income under one million dollars, makes an important showing. Such corporations accounted for 37.5 per cent of all corporate income, due, in large measure, to the sheer weight of numbers among the smallest units. This would seem to indicate that the bulk of corporate wealth was represented either by huge units having assets running into the hundreds of millions or by relatively small corporations having assets under four million dollars.

When we seek to compare the wealth of the big companies with that of all industry we get into difficulty since there appears to be no adequate basis for estimating the total business wealth in the country. A very rough estimate, however, indicates that at least 78 per cent and probably a larger proportion of American business wealth is corporate wealth. Since the two hundred largest corporations controlled approximately 49 per cent of all corporate wealth, the rough calculation would indicate that they controlled 38 per cent or more of all business wealth.

When we come to national wealth, we are necessarily dealing with estimates which can at best be only most approximate. The National Industrial Conference Board has estimated that the national wealth at the end of 1928 amounted to $360,062,000,000. If we assume an increase equal to the average of the previous six years we should have $367,000,000,000 as the national wealth in 1929. Since the total assets of the two hundred big companies in that year amounted to $81,077,000,000, they controlled roughly 22 per cent of the total wealth of the country. The lower relative importance of the large corporation in comparison to the national wealth is in large measure due to the importance of agricultural land and improvements, residential real estate, personal property including automobiles, and the large volume of government property.

To recapitulate . . . Table 2 gives the results of the foregoing analysis. It is apparent from these figures that a very considerable portion

TABLE 2. RELATIVE IMPORTANCE OF LARGE CORPORATIONS
(On or about January 1, 1930)

	Results Obtained by Actual Computation	Probable Limits
Proportion of corporate wealth (other than banking) controlled by the 200 largest corporations	49.2%	45–53%
Proportion of business wealth (other than banking) controlled by the 200 largest corporations	38.0%	35–45%
Proportion of national wealth controlled by the 200 largest corporations	22.0%	15–25%

of the industrial wealth of the country has been concentrated under the control of a relatively few huge units. There were over 300,000 non-financial corporations in the country in 1929. Yet 200 of these, or less than seven-hundredths of one per cent, control nearly half the corporate wealth.

It must further be remembered that the influence of one of these huge companies extends far beyond the assets under its direct control. Smaller companies which sell to or buy from the larger companies are likely to be influenced by them to a vastly greater extent than by other smaller companies with which they might deal. In many cases the continued prosperity of the smaller company depends on the favor of the larger and almost inevitably the interests of the latter become the interests of the former. The influence of the larger company on prices is often greatly increased by its mere size, even though it does not begin to approach a monopoly. Its political influence may be tremendous. Therefore, if roughly half of corporate wealth is controlled by two hundred large corporations and half by smaller companies, it is fair to assume that very much more than half of industry is dominated by these great units. This concentration is made even more significant when it is recalled that as a result of it, approximately 2,000 individuals out of a population of one hundred and twenty-five million are in a position to control and direct half of industry.

The actual extent to which the concentration of power has progressed is striking enough. More striking still, however, is the pace at which it is proceeding. In 1909, the assets of the 200 then largest non-banking corporations amounted to only $26.0 billion. By 1919 they had reached $43.7 billion, an increase of 68 per cent in ten years. In the next ten years from 1919 to 1929 they increased to $81.1 billion, an increase of 85 per cent.

The growth of 150 identical corporations included in the largest 200 companies in both 1919 and 1928 is given in Table 3.

The assets of 44 identical railroads increased from $18 billion in 1919 to $23 billion in 1928 or 24 per cent; 71 identical industrial corporations increased from $14 billion to $23 billion in the same period, a growth of approximately 58 per cent in nine years. In the public utility field, as is well known, the rate has been vastly more rapid. In the same nine years the assets of 35 identical utilities grew from $6 billion to $18 billion, or nearly three times. The more rapid growth of the utilities approximately compensates for the slow growth

TABLE 3. GROSS ASSETS OF 150 IDENTICAL CORPORATIONS COMMON TO
BOTH 1919 AND 1928 LIST OF 200 LARGEST AMERICAN CORPORATIONS
(Gross Assets as of Dec. 31 in Million Dollars)

Year	44 Railroads	71 Industrials	35 Public Utilities	150 Corporations
1919	18,480	14,288	6,017	38,785
1920	20,535	16,186	6,393	43,114
1921	20,186	15,590	6,745	42,521
1922	20,643	15,962	7,757	44,362
1923	20,409	17,174	8,749	46,332
1924	20,839	17,703	9,814	48,356
1925	21,272	19,111	11,508	51,891
1926	21,881	20,569	13,562	56,012
1927	22,462	21,154	15,580	59,192
1928	23,026	22,675	17,703	63,404
Increase 1919–1928	24%	58%	194%	63%
Annual Rate of Growth 1919–1928	2.4%	5.2%	12.3%	5.6%
Increase 1924–1928	9%	9%	80%	31%
Annual Rate of Growth 1924–1928	2.3%	6.0%	15.9%	7.0%

of the railroads, and the total for the 150 corporations shows a growth
from $39 billion to $63 billion, or an increase of practically 63 per cent.

Though the growth of the large corporations shown in these tables
is rapid, it is truly significant only if it has been more rapid than the
growth of all industrial wealth. . . . When the rates of growth of the
wealth of all non-financial corporations and of the assets of the 200
largest corporations are thus compared, they show the large corporations
as a group to be growing very much more rapidly than all corporations.
For the period from 1909 to 1928 their annual rate of growth has
been 5.4 per cent, while that of all corporations (assuming the
estimates are reliable) has amounted to only 3.6 per cent, and for corporations other than the largest 200 only 2.0 per cent. The large
corporations would thus appear to be increasing in wealth over 50 per
cent faster than all corporations or over two and one-half times as

fast as smaller corporations. From 1921 to 1928 the annual rate of growth of the large corporations has been 6.1 per cent compared with 4.4 per cent for all corporations or 3.1 per cent for the smaller companies. From 1924 to 1928, a period of most rapid growth, the annual rates were respectively 7.7 per cent for the large, 4.9 per cent for all, and only 2.6 per cent for corporations other than the largest 200, indicating that the large corporations were growing more than half again as fast as all corporations and three times as fast as smaller corporations. . . .

This increase in the proportion [of net income] received by the large companies could theoretically be explained on two grounds other than the actual growth of the large corporations. If they had obtained an increasing rate of return on their capital in comparison with the smaller companies, the increase in the proportion of income could be explained. It could likewise be explained on the ground that for a large number of subsidiary corporations the net income was not consolidated with the parent in the earlier years and was so consolidated in the later years. This latter explanation, however, could at most account for only a very small part of the increase, since approximately the same proportion of all non-financial corporate dividends were reported as received by non-financial corporations in 1927 as in 1922, indicating that subsidiaries were reported as separate corporations to approximately the same extent throughout the period.

It is quite conceivable that an important part of the increase is explained by the greater profitableness of large corporations; but the fact that the change coincides roughly with the change shown for corporate wealth tends to strengthen the conclusion that the large corporations have increased greatly both their proportion of the wealth and their proportion of the income of all corporations.

Though it is not possible to obtain figures for the growth of industrial wealth, we have already seen that the corporation has become increasingly important in industry after industry. Presumably a constantly increasing proportion of all industrial wealth has come under corporate sway. If that be the fact, the proportion of industrial wealth controlled by the 200 corporations has been increasing at a rate even more rapid than their proportion of all corporate wealth.

The relative growth of the wealth of the large corporations and the national wealth can only be very roughly calculated. As we have indicated, national wealth is a difficult concept to define, and all estimates of national wealth must be, at best, approximate; so that too much reliance should not be placed on any comparison of the growth of corporate wealth with that of national wealth. Between 1922 and 1928 the estimates by the National Industrial Conference Board indicate a growth in national wealth of 12.5 per cent compared with the growth in assets of the 200 largest corporations of 45.6 per cent, or annual rates of growth of 2.0 per cent and 6.3 per cent respectively. While the estimates based on the 1930 census figures may be considerably higher than those of the Conference Board, the estimates of the latter for 1928 would have to be increased by over 30 per cent to make the rate of increase in the national wealth equal to that of the 200 corporations. There can, therefore, be little doubt that the wealth of the large corporations has been increasing at a very much more rapid rate than the total national wealth.

To summarize the conclusions with relation to growth:

1. On the basis of gross assets, the large corporations appear to have been growing between two and three times as fast as all other non-financial corporations.

2. This conclusion is supported by the figures of corporate income.

3. Since an increased proportion of industrial wealth presumably continues to come under corporate sway, the proportion of industrial wealth controlled by the large corporations has been increasing at a rate even faster than the proportion of corporate wealth controlled by them.

4. Since estimates of national wealth are extremely approximate it is not possible to determine the growth in the proportion of national wealth controlled by the large corporations, but there can be little question that the proportion has been increasing at a rapid rate.

Just what does this rapid growth of the big companies promise for the future? Let us project the trend of the growth of recent years. If the wealth of the large corporations and that of all the corporations should each continue to increase for the next twenty years at its average annual rate for the twenty years from 1909 to 1929, 70 per cent of all corporate activity would be carried on by two hundred corporations by 1950. If the more rapid rates of growth from 1924 to 1929 were maintained for the next twenty years 85 per cent of corporate wealth would be held by two hundred huge units. It would take only forty years at the 1909–1929 rates or only thirty years at the 1924–1929 rates for all corporate activity and practically all industrial activity to be absorbed by two hundred giant companies. If the indicated growth of the large corporations and of the national wealth were to be effective from now until 1950, half of the national wealth would be under the control of big companies at the end of that period.

Whether the future will see any such complete absorption of economic activity into a few great enterprises it is not possible to predict . . . [because] the rate of growth has not been uniform. The years from 1921 through 1923 showed little more growth by the large corporations than by all, though this slackening may reflect only a breathing spell after the excessive growth of the war years. One would expect, moreover, that the rate of concentration would slacken as a larger and larger proportion of industry became absorbed and less remained to be added. The trend of the recent past indicates, however, that the great corporation, already of tremendous importance today, will become increasingly important in the future.

This conclusion is still further confirmed when we examine the ways in which the growth of the large companies takes place and compare their growth by each method with that of other companies. A given corporation can increase the wealth under its control in three major ways: by reinvesting its earnings, by raising new capital through the sale of securities in the public markets, and by acquiring control of other corporations by either purchase or exchange of securities. While there are numerous other ways by which an increase could take place, such as private sale of securities to individuals, these three so far outweigh other methods that they alone need to be considered.

A comparison of the savings of large corporations with those of all corporations indicates that the big companies as a group save a larger proportion of their net income. In the six-year period from 1922 to 1927 inclusive, 108 corporations (all of the 200 largest for which consolidated statements could be obtained for each year) saved 38.5 per cent of their net income available for dividends. In the same period, all corporations combined saved only 29.4 per cent of their net income. Since the earnings of the large corporations are included as an important proportion in the earnings of all corporations and since these large companies saved a larger than average percentage of earnings, the remaining corporations, mainly smaller companies, must have saved a proportion very much smaller than average, probably less than 25 per cent of their earnings. The importance of this method of growth is indicated by the fact that roughly a quarter of the growth of the large corporations was derived from earnings between 1922 and 1927.

Of much greater importance as a source of relative expansion has been the second method—the raising of new capital in the public markets. Over 55 per cent of the growth of the large companies has been made possible by the public offering of additional securities, a fact which particularly concerns us here since these offerings are all made to the public investor, and since the dependence of these corporations on new capital is undoubtedly one of the strongest factors determining the relation between those who control the corporations and their investing stockholders. Here again the large corporation increases the wealth under its control by this means of expansion to a much greater extent than the smaller companies. From 1922 to 1927 inclusive, a sample study indicates that two-thirds of all public offerings of new securities (as reported by the "Commercial and Financial Chronicle"—excluding banking companies) were made by the two hundred largest companies or their subsidiaries.

The third and more spectacular method of growth of the large corporations is by consolidation or merger. Within the eleven years, 1919 through 1929, no less than 49 corporations recorded among the largest two hundred at one time or another during the period have disappeared by merging with other large companies on the list. . . . Roughly 20 per cent of the growth of the largest companies which we have been observing can be attributed to additions through merger, a growth which effects a reduction in the corporate wealth lying outside the control of the largest group.

The growth in the assets of the two hundred largest corporations in the six-year period from 1922 to 1927 inclusive is given in Table 4, as well as estimates of the manner of growth.

TABLE 4

Estimated savings out of earnings	$5,748,000,000	26.5%
Estimated new capital from sale of securities	11,813,000,000	55.0%
Estimated growth as a result of mergers	4,000,000,000	18.5%
	$21,561,000,000	100.0%
Estimated reduction from reappraisals, etc., and error in estimates	$ 2,000,000,000	
Net growth in assets, 1922–1927, inclusive	19,561,000,000	

One question yet remains—are these companies likely to survive? It is sometimes said that consolidations of great magnitude sooner or later, more often sooner, go into a period of decline,—that beyond a certain point the organization breaks down, and the whole falls of its own weight. There appears, however, to be little foundation for such a suggestion. Examination of the condition in 1928 of the two hundred companies which were largest in 1919 shows the following.

Of the 200 largest corporations in 1919:—

23	merged with larger companies.
154	were included in list of largest 200 corporations in 1928.
21	remained large and active concerns though 7 of them went through reorganization.
2	liquidated or the equivalent.
200	

This table shows 25 companies actually disappearing in nine years, or a rate of disappearance of 1.4 per cent a year. If this were the normal rate of disappearance it would indicate an average expectancy of over 70 years of further life. At the same time the disappearance of a corporation through merger does not indicate that its organization has broken down and that it is about to fall into dissolution; it passes, but does not die. If we regard the two liquidated companies as the only ones which actually disappeared, we would have a dissolution rate of 1 per cent in nine years or an average expectancy of 900 years of life, either as an independent concern or as an integral part of a larger enterprise. On the other hand if we apply the rates of merger and of dissolution simultaneously they indicate that at the end of 360 years sixteen of the two hundred companies would have disappeared through dissolution and all the remaining companies would have merged into a single corporation having a life expectancy of over 1000 years. Furthermore, if the changes in the nine years are a promise of the future, half of the companies included in the 1919 list of 200 companies will also be represented in a list of the largest 200 compiled a century hence, 10 directly and 90 as absorbed units in these 10.

These figures are, of course, an unwarranted extension into the future of the trend of the nine years from 1919 to 1928. They serve, however, to indicate that there is little in the history of the 200 companies in the nine-year period considered to suggest that the large corporation has a short life cycle ending in dissolution.

In conclusion, then, the huge corporation, the corporation with $90,000,000 of assets or more, has come to dominate most major industries if not all industry in the United States. A rapidly increasing proportion of industry is carried on under this form of organization. There is apparently no immediate limit to its increase. It is coming more and more to be the industrial unit with which American economic, social, and political life must deal. The implications of this fact challenge many of the basic assumptions of current thought.

1. Most fundamental of all, it is now necessary to think, to a very important extent, in terms of these huge units rather than in terms of the multitude of small competing elements of private enterprise. The emphasis must be shifted to that very great proportion of industry in the hands of a relatively few units, units which can be studied individually and concretely. Such studies will reveal the operation of half of industry and what is more important, that half which is likely to be more typical of the industry of the future.

2. Competition has changed in character and the principles applicable to present conditions are radically different from those which apply when the dominant competing units are smaller and more numerous. The principles of duopoly have become more important than those of free competition.

3. An increasing proportion of production is carried on for use and not for sale. With the increase in the large companies, a larger proportion of goods are consumed by the producing organization in the process of making further goods. To this extent the calculus of cost versus quality would presumably be solved in the interest of producing a product which would yield the maximum use per unit of cost rather than the maximum profit per unit of investment. Under the latter incentive the consumer is only incidentally offered the product which will give him the most use per unit of cost unless he himself is easily able to measure usefulness. Adulteration, shoddy goods, and goods of lower quality than would be economically desirable are frequent under the incentive for profit. To the extent that production is for use by the producing organization there is no such incentive.

4. The nature of capital has changed. To an increasing extent it is composed not of tangible goods, but of organizations built in the past and available to function in the future. Even the value of tangible goods tends to become increasingly dependent upon their organized relationship to other tangible goods composing the property of one of these great units.

5. Finally, a society in which production is governed by blind economic forces is being replaced by one in which production is carried on under the ultimate control of a handful of individuals. The economic power in the hands of the few persons who control a giant corporation is

a tremendous force which can harm or benefit a multitude of individuals, affect whole districts, shift the currents of trade, bring ruin to one community and prosperity to another. The organizations which they control have passed far beyond the realm of private enterprise—they have become more nearly social institutions.

Such is the character of the corporate system—dynamic, constantly building itself into greater aggregates, and thereby changing the basic conditions which the thinking of the past has assumed.

XXII. INTRODUCTION

Eight months after Franklin Roosevelt was inaugurated, Rexford G. Tugwell (born in 1891) gave a speech at Columbia University on "The Economics of the Recovery Program." He was an early member of Roosevelt's brain trust, as well as an official of the administration. In one sense Tugwell's speech was merely a defense of the administration's program, as that had emerged in the "hundred days." But it was also more than that. He attempted to explain the basic economic assumptions of the New Dealers, and to make the logic of the administration's attack on the depression explicit. Somehow, according to Tugwell—and to F. D. R. too—the nation had to be made into a community whose concerted action was essential if the depression were to be ended or even eased. The details of Tugwell's economic analysis show that the New Deal had absorbed a significant part of Keynesian economics, that the "seamless web," as Roosevelt had put it, of the American economy required a total, rather than a piecemeal, assault on the various sectors of the economy.

Tugwell was explicit about the need for intellectuals to adjust their thinking to new conditions if they would be of service to the nation. The intimate relationship between politics and the economy, according to Tugwell, was yet not properly understood by academics.

It is a curious fact of the intellectual life of the 1930's that optimism and buoyancy returned. The crisis of vast physical deprivation meant, at least, an end to boredom. The civilized and sometimes elegant alienation of the 1920's was replaced with a commitment to the task at hand. In Tugwell's speech, which follows, the sparks of optimism and vigor, coupled with a sense of the magnitude and difficulty of the problem, light up his analysis of the social problem.

XXII.

Rexford G. Tugwell

THE ECONOMICS OF THE RECOVERY PROGRAM 1933

In the midst of the cross currents of activity in Washington, it is necessary from time to time to stand apart and recall the general outline of the program which is expressing itself in a day-to-day detailed activity. Only as it is considered as a whole will the apparent paradoxes be reconciled and the total effort be comprehended.

The general objective is clear and easily stated—to restore a workable exchangeability among the separate parts of our economic machine and to set it to functioning again; and beyond this to perfect arrangements which may prevent its future disorganization. This means that we must insure adequate income to the farmers, adequate wages to the workers, an adequate return to useful capital, and an adequate remuneration to management. What we want, really, is to provide the opportunity for every individual and every group to work and to be able to consume the product of others' work. This involves a creation of buying power which is coordinate with the creation of goods. We shall not rest nor be diverted to lesser things until that minimum is achieved.

But to outline an objective in such broad terms does not take us far in understanding specific undertakings. What constitutes a workable relationship among income to farmers, wages to workers, and a return to useful capital? Here is a question which we can answer only when we have considered why they are now inadequate.

That they are less than our productive capacity entitles us to, there can be no doubt. Consider what our economic machine could have produced if it had been working in the last four years at the same rate as in 1928 and 1929. If all the labor and equipment which have been idle during the depression could have been converted into houses, every second family in the country could have had a brand new $5,000 house; or we could have scrapped the whole American railroad system and rebuilt it three times

SOURCE. Rexford Guy Tugwell, *The Battle for Democracy,* New York: Columbia University Press, 1935, pp. 78–96. Reprinted with the permission of Columbia University Press.

over. Such is the waste of the last four years; the waste caused by the failure of the economic machine to function properly, a failure to produce and distribute, which makes inadequate the income of nearly every group in the community. So long as the economic machine fails to operate at its potential capacity the income of each group will continue to be insufficient. So long as our economy provides vastly less to each group in the community than our resources in men and materials make possible, the incomes of everyone will be inadequate.

Consider the reaction of the country to the first three years of depression. Down and down went the curves of business activity. Longer and longer grew the lines of idle workers and the rows of idle machines. The whole constituted a challenge to the American people to act *as a body*, to remedy a ridiculous situation which had developed out of their *acting separately.*

Why was this challenge to American intelligence and action not met in the first three years of depression? We have grown up in a tradition which says that if economic forces are let alone all will come out right in the end. In the past we have regarded social interference in the interest of economic continuity as highly improper. This supremely crucial function we abandoned to private initiative, operating through the price system and controlled by competition. Such a system had worked in the past—haltingly and after a fashion. In the first year of the depression there may have been justification for waiting for recovery in the interest of protecting this principle. In the second year, was there justification? In the third year, with more than a quarter of our working population out of work and agricultural income reduced to a third its former size, had not the time come for positive action by the community as a body instead of by individuals alone?

A year ago the people of this country voted on precisely this question. And with an overwhelming majority they chose a President with a mandate for positive action; and he assumed his delegated duty with a gallantry which the whole nation unmistakably approved. The change involved in this was of major importance in the development of this country. It meant a shift from *laissez faire* to positive effort. It implied an effort by the community through its government to restore exchangeability by positive action. It placed directly on the shoulders of the new administration the responsibility for bringing about recovery from one of the deepest depressions this country has ever known.

The immediate reasons for this popular demand for positive action are clear. The terrific waste of depression, the hardships suffered by individuals through no fault of their own, the failure of business leadership to cope with the forces of depression, these all led to the insistent demand for change, a demand which would respect no allegiance to theory or preconceptions. How this demand was to be carried out, what action was to be undertaken, was not clear; but a policy of *laissez faire* was no longer to be countenanced.

What positive measures could be undertaken? Preliminary to their understanding is an assessment of the underlying developments which led to this general demand for governmental activity. This takes us directly into economic analysis. Those people who have so extravagantly praised the beauties of *laissez faire* have always done so on the assumption of highly flexible prices and a degree of freedom in competition. Actually the breakdown came at a time when our economy was a spotted reality of competition and control—with the control entrusted to irresponsible trustees. In 1929 we did not have a system of free competition and flexible prices. True, in some areas, like farming, we have had highly flexible prices and a considerable number of individuals actively competing in both production and price. If prices throughout our economy had been as flexible as those in the farm area were, it is quite possible that the 1929 depression would have been of minor consequence. The truth was, however, that an important part of our economy had prices which were not responsive—as theoretically they should have been—to changes in supply or demand. At the furthest extreme are railroad and public-utility rates, steel rails and many other goods and services whose prices were fixed over very considerable periods of time. In such occupations and areas, the whole impact of changes in demand are taken in the form of changes in production without any changes in price.

Intermediate between the extremes of flexible price and fixed price, lies most of industry. In this area prices are fixed for shorter periods of time but are periodically revised over longer periods of time. Thus, in varying degrees, changes in demand are met by changes in production, and more slowly and over a longer time only, by changes in price.

This matter of temporary or more permanently fixed prices is vitally important. This fixity is a major disturbing influence in a system which is theoretically competitive. Consider a concrete case—the production of automobiles. The manufacturer of cars will set a wholesale price on his cars at the beginning of the season. Presumably he will set a price which he expects will sell as many cars in the year as will make his total profits at that price as large as possible. Once the price is set, any drop in demand for cars will result, not in a drop in price, but in a drop in production. Men will be discharged and machines will become idle. Because of lessening employment and lessening incomes, there is likely to be a further drop in demand for cars. If this condition were typical of all industry the resulting condition would be one which we describe as depression. It is, of course, true that once or twice a year the prices of cars will be revised. But in the intermediate periods, prices are fixed, and changing demand is reflected only in changing production, with a direct effect on the income of consumers. It is this fact which is of major significance. It is this price inflexibility which causes an initial drop in demand to induce unemployment. In this manner, the rigidity of some prices and the flexibility of others tends to make production in our system unstable, deranging the balance between prices and production in different fields. We have a choice, if the situation is to be remedied, of really restoring competition or of extending the areas of rigidity until they include all prices of real social consequence.

Notice how differently the depression has affected different parts of our economy. In the agricultural area, in which prices are highly flexible, the drop in effective demand during the depression has caused a great drop in prices, while production has declined little. The farmers are working as hard as ever, but they get less for their product. Throughout most of industry, the effect of the depression has been essentially different. Prices have dropped relatively little compared to the drop in agricultural prices. The fall in demand has been met for the most part by reduced production. The income of the workers as a body has dropped as rapidly as that of the farm group, not primarily because wages were lower (though that has been important), but because of being out of employment. Thus, while the cash incomes of farmers as a body and of wage workers as a body have fallen off to an almost equal degree, one has fallen because of a fall in prices and the other because of a fall in production.

This difference in the effect of the depression in agriculture and in industry is of great importance because it suggests that quite different methods for restoring balance must be applied in the different fields. Restoration of balance would require a lowering of production and a lifting of prices in agriculture, but a lifting of production and in some cases even a lowering of prices in industry.

This difference in the effect of the depression on prices and on production is of vital importance. It is the key to many of the apparent conflicts between the agricultural and the industrial programs. Even for different industries the relative effect on prices and on production has been different; some with fatally flexible prices and maintained production, others with rigid prices and flexible production. Perhaps the picture of the depression is best portrayed by thinking of all the different economic activities distributed along a scale according to the amenability of prices to change. As has been suggested, most agricultural activities and certain industries are at one end of the scale and at the other extreme are certain more or less monopolized trades. Between these extremes are ranged the bulk of industry. If we think of the prices and production of different commodities as having been roughly in balance in 1926, the effect of the depression was to reduce prices at the flexible end of the scale and to maintain production there, while at the other end prices were being maintained and production was dropping.

To restore exchangeability in such a situation we can do one of two things: we can lift the flexible prices to the level of the rigid ones, and simultaneously increase production in the fixed-price areas; or we can reduce the rigid prices to the level of the flexible ones, and reduce production in the flexible-price areas.

The advantages of the first path toward the restoration of exchangeability are clear; and it is this path which has been taken by the administration. The major advantage of lifting prices—of lifting most those which have fallen most and lifting not at all those which have not fallen—grows out of the burden of debt created at the old price level. To lower all prices to the level of those which had fallen most would be to overburden the debtors in the country and to endanger the solvency of our many great debtor institutions. Elementary justice thus required a lifting of the flexible prices to parity with the prices which had not dropped, rather than the more difficult course of revising downward those which had remained fixed.

Here, then, is the more immediate objective of recovery: to raise prices in the area of flexibility, to raise production in the area of rigidity, and raise both prices and production in the intermediate areas of industry until all groups attain the ready exchangeability which they once had. How is this immediate objective to be reached? From here on we must take up each element of the recovery program separately, remembering that each element is essential and that each depends for its success on the development of the other parts of the program.

The agricultural program may be considered first. Here the immediate problem is to increase the farmers' incomes by asking the industrial population to pay a fair exchange price for food. The exposition of the way in which the industrial population is to be enabled not only to pay more for food but also to consume more of its own products is deferred here. For the present, notice that the intention is to perfect a synchronized program which will increase the farmers' incomes by approximately the amount which the industrial population's purchasing power is reduced. I say "approximately" because it is hoped that some of the farmers' increased incomes will come from a reduction in spreads and margins. Such a shift in power to buy might seem to involve no net advance toward recovery; yet two benefits should be noticed. First, no recovery can occur until the farmers are able to buy industrial products on an ample scale; therefore, the raising of farm income even at the immediate expense of the urban population would be a definite step forward if it secured for farmers a more adequate income. Second, there would be a direct expansion of purchasing. Since the increased purchasing of the farm population would be exactly counterbalanced in the initial stage by decreased power to purchase on the part of the industrial population, a net gain in total purchases would arise only as the increased prices for farm products induced a more rapid expenditure of the forty billions of dollars involved.

It is believed that a greater expenditure would be induced by giving farmers more income than by saving it for consumers. If this is true a definite increase in business, in total expenditure, and in total income, would result. So the farm program, by raising prices, on the one hand restores price balance, and on the other hand induces increased total expenditure.

The methods being employed in raising farm prices are foretold. It is well recognized by economists that in the area in which prices are highly flexible, as in agriculture, it is possible to raise prices only by reducing supply or by increasing demand. The total recovery program involves both, though the A.A.A. program, taken alone, involves mostly a reduction in production. The need for this reduction is greater because of long accumulated surpluses traceable to the shift of this country from debtor to creditor status during the War. This shift involved such a reduction in our agricultural exports as to unsettle all the relationships which had been established during our long history as an exporter of raw products. Nor can we count on any immediate change. Combined with a positive program for reducing farm production, and as an aid in bringing about reduction, the processing tax has been employed as a means for raising the price paid by the consumer so that it constitutes more nearly an adequate remuneration for the farmer. The proceeds of the processing tax have been distributed in a manner to insure the reduction of crop acreage. So supply is limited to demand.

The third part of the program involves an effort to increase farm exports, a difficult program and a program on which little reliance can be placed for dealing with the existing crop surplus. However, no opportunity is being overlooked, such as furtherance of world commodity controls. Not much can be done of a permanent nature, however, unless we are willing to admit on far easier terms than are at present in force upwards of half a billion dollars in foreign commodities in exchange for our agricultural goods.

Still another element in the recovery program is of a long-run nature; the effort to remove some 40,000,000 acres of land from cultivation, an effort which has beneficial incidental results, such as the arrest of erosion and the conservation of the soil. The relation sought in this way between farm and industrial activity is of a permanent sort and belongs not in the category of emergency action but of long-time planning of land and population.

All this agricultural effort ought to increase farmers' incomes; and if the industrial program is carried on adequately the whole community must benefit. At the same time success in raising prices to the farmer necessarily rests on the corresponding success of the industrial plan. Through the action just described the supply of farm products is being reduced. Complete success, however, demands that we also increase the demand. If the unemployed population can be returned to work they will be in a position to buy more farm products. This is the farmers' interest in the spread of employment and increased wages. The two are inextricably related.

When we come to the industrial sector of the recovery program, the immediate objectives are almost exactly the reverse of those in the agricultural sector. The main problem is, in some industries, to raise volume of production and volume of pay rolls without increasing price; in other industries, to raise volume of production and volume of wages with an increase in price but not an increase at all commensurate with the increase in the price of agricultural products.

At first thought you will ask how the wage bill can be increased by an industry without increasing the prices charged. This is the very crux of the recovery program. It was by reducing production and wages in some industries, without a corresponding drop in prices, that we destroyed exchangeability. To restore it the process must be reversed. In many industries the declining volume of production in the last three years has increased overhead costs per unit of product.

In order to meet this increasing cost, the industrialists have, on the one hand, maintained prices at nearly their former level, and, on the other hand, have reduced wage rates and employment. In this way they shifted the burden of reduction to the workers, brought on unemployment and destroyed purchasing power.

To regain exchangeability, it is necessary that the increased direct costs of operation attributable to paying higher wages should be absorbed by profit takers without any increase in prices. This involves spreading overhead and increasing wages so that the increased volume of production can be purchased by workers, or in part by workers and in part by farmers who receive more from the workers for the commodities they supply.

It must be recognized, of course, that there are many industries which fall between the two extremes of price flexibility and price rigidity. In such industries, the regaining of exchangeability requires that only part of the increased costs due to increased wages be absorbed by the industry through a wider spreading of overhead costs, while the remainder of the increased costs is passed on to the consumer. In still other industries in which prices have fallen very greatly over their earlier level, a return to an economic balance would undoubtedly require that the whole of the increased costs be passed on to the consumer. In such cases, the worker would be directly benefited at the expense of the consumer, a condition properly parallel to that in respect to agricultural products.

Many important industries should have regarded themselves as belonging in the first two classes, in which the whole, or an important part, of the increased labor costs would be absorbed in the expectation of an increased volume of activity. Unfortunately for the rapid progress of the recovery program, most industries have acted as if they belonged in the third class, and have passed the whole of the increased labor costs to the consumer. Indeed, in many cases, it looks as if more than the increased costs had been passed on, at least in the primary areas of production. For this reason, the recovery program may be slowed up; in fact if the raising of prices beyond the increased costs is widely pursued, the recovery program will be seriously impaired.

It will be seen that the most important consideration in all this is that increased payments should be made to workers without a corresponding increase in charges made to the consumer. The reverse of this has taken place during the depression. Less and less money has been paid out in pay rolls, while the prices of industrial products have shown no corresponding decline. The reversal of this process is necessary to recovery.

Because of the importance of this, it would seem that insufficient attention has been given to classifying industries according to the extent to which the increased costs could be properly passed on to the consumer and the extent to which they ought to be absorbed by the industry. To the extent that industry effectively supports the present program, the increased wages paid out will represent new purchasing power, a net gain in the demand for the products of industry and agriculture, and a real step forward toward recovery. To the extent that a lifting of prices out of proportion to increased costs occurs, we will have retarded progress. The balance of gain or loss from the industrial sector is the responsibility now of industry itself. The opportunity has been provided. If there is failure it will be yet another example of the inability of industry to coöperate; and this time there will not even be the excuse of antitrust restrictions. If further and more drastic controls become necessary it will be because industry has demonstrated its inability to conceive and carry out, even under the best auspices, that program of enlightened self-interest from which *laissez-faire* economists have professed to expect so much.

There are certain considerations which should be held to firmly. Even if all the increased costs from higher wages should be passed on to consumers, so long as no increases in prices beyond this were imposed, there would still be some net gain. The raising of prices would undoubtedly increase total expenditures. It would do this by inducing some of those who now hold part of our forty billion dollars to expend not only their current receipts but part of their savings, thereby increasing the flow of money and causing a net increase in the demand for goods. This would be a step in the right direction, though it might not carry very far or very rapidly. In essence, the industrial effort will have been a failure if the wages paid out by industry do not on the whole increase more rapidly than the prices charged by industry as a whole. In the hurly-burly of code-making [of the NRA], this fact has too often been lost sight of.

So far we have covered the agricultural and industrial programs.

A third major factor consists of public and civil works. Through these programs, it is intended that a large volume of new purchasing power shall be created. By these expenditures, workers are given increased power to buy. This power to buy means that the money paid out for these purposes will go directly for the purchase of goods. The public-works program is getting under way. There have been difficult problems of organization. Like any effort of this sort results are slow to appear in the early stages. But a formidable momentum is now apparent. An increasing volume of funds is going out each week and will soon come to significant result. I often think, in this connection, of the slump which preceded the War. It takes about as long to build up a program of peace construction as it does to organize for war. The efforts are similar; and the time required cannot be greatly shortened.

These, then, are the main features of the program. The complete success of each depends upon the success of the others, carried on as parallel drives in the grand strategy. They constitute a reasoned whole which should bear us to success. The failure of any one of these three attacks to attain its objective means the partial failure of the others, and the necessity of beginning anew. There are other things being done which play into and strengthen these major elements: attempts to expand credit; the bolstering up of existing credit so that it will not be a depressing influence or cause hardship while the machine is set in motion; encouragement for the expansion of private construction, a process which will put purchasing power into circulation without adding to the goods which come immediately to market; the protection of consumers so that their choices can be carried out on a basis of reflection instead of in a welter of conflicting and exaggerated claims; the protection of the debtor against the worst consequences of threatened dispossession; relief for the unemployed, which amounts by now to a characteristically American form of unemployment insurance.

The success or failure of these will not jeopardize the whole. The success or failure of the three great branches of the program—reducing production and raising prices to the farmer, increasing production and raising wages to the industrial worker faster than industrial prices are raised, and the putting into circulation of a new flow of buying power— these are the central core of the recovery drive conceived to be undertaken by the community as a whole. It is, I believe, adequate. It is in many ways unorthodox. It runs counter to the accepted notions of the doctrinaire—convinced believers in *laissez-faire* like it no better than communists. It is tentative, but still carefully hammered out of the iron of reality. We believe it to be the instrument of our present salvation; but we believe in no part of it so fanatically that we are unwilling to change. And this, of course, is the reason for proceeding through permissive powers with a calculated avoidance of any commitment whatever to doctrine.

The sheer hard economics of the situation in which we find ourselves makes certain demands on human nature from which recoil is natural. Sacrifice is demanded. Promise is also offered, of course, but the sacrifice seems much easier to concentrate on than the promise; and those who are squeezed give themselves whole-heartedly to opposition. All the old shibboleths, behind which vested interests have always hidden, are trotted out to do their stuff. The noise is tremendous and all the faint-hearted are quickly intimidated. To pursue a considered program in the midst of this welter of recrimination and special pleading is the task to which we have now to give ourselves.

There is no reason to suppose that our measures are unsound or that any of the experimental procedures have yet failed. They have not achieved utopia; but no one who was intimately concerned with their fashioning supposed that they would. Only the hangers-on, and those whose hopes outran their intelligence, believed that results would be seen before the causes of those results had become operative. There is complaint from many sources; and no administrator can be deaf to it. But what it was hoped to do in two, four or six years, none of us expected to see in eight months. Yet we have, I think, in all modesty, some reasonable ground for pride. The organization necessary to our eventual aims has been, if not perfected, yet set up in measurably competent fashion. And the long-time effort is being pursued by it with singular energy and determination. Besides this, however, it is only just to say that the immediate demands of a population hungry, cold and in despair have been met. We have not turned aside from any responsibility; we have not asked anyone else to do what it seemed possible for us to do.

The most captious critic, I believe, after careful assessment of the efforts of this administration, would be forced to admit that such an outpouring of loyal and devoted effort has seldom before been seen. I wish it were possible for me to describe for you, in any adequate words, the phenomena of sacrifice, of self-imposed discipline, of giving everything which was possessed by heart and hand and brain, which I have seen so intimately among my colleagues in these past months. I have no lack whatever of confidence in the results to come when the time is ripe for them to come; I have, however, a miserable feeling of the inadequacy, in this case, of the test of results. I wish my fellow citizens could have seen the ordeal, got something of its feel and color, so that adequate honor might be paid where it is due. I do not speak of any of those whose names you may have seen in the press or of whom you may have heard reports. It is truly the unknown servants of the Republic who have deserved well of their country in this crisis.

I have called some of them to Washington myself. Others have called more. They have come with fresh minds, clean motives, and unselfish aspirations. Numbers have come from this university [Columbia] at sacrifices known only to themselves. And their only reward will be unspectacular: the personal sense of having served in a crisis to re-create the gigantic strength of America. Those who have come from this and from other universities have come quietly and gone to work in prosaic ways. They have found that what they had to do was really only an extension and an intensification of what they were used to doing. But under the lash of need they have been driven almost unbearably.

I have had a chance to see the truth of the saying that ours is a government of men. The fiction that it is a government of laws would, I think, never have attained its great prestige if the right men had been called to govern. Much has been said lately of the new institutions which have been invented, of the changes which have overtaken hitherto accepted arrangements. It is possible to overemphasize this idea. In fact, a careful examination of the new legislation will disclose that its novel characteristic is its provision of freedom for action by those who have to do the acting. The powers granted are mostly permissive; the rules written are mandates for performance. Everything depends on men.

The center of the present storm is in the economic field. It is natural that economists should be our greatest dependence for guidance as well as for skillful administration. This university and others have not finished their task by thinning the existing ranks and making temporary loans to government. The end of the demand is not in sight; perhaps it never will be. Perhaps it must be assumed as a regular burden from now on. This requires, of course, a return from economics to political economy as the needed discipline. Economics belonged to *laissez-faire;* the world has turned its back on that. The danger is that universities may not find it out, but may continue to turn over and over the sterile dust of free-competitive principles. Men trained in this kind of thinking are handicapped now; it is the greatest single difficulty with economists in government that they can think only of ways to emasculate the government in its dealings with economic phenomena, because they carry in their heads a formula of noninterference. Political economists are what is needed, men not ridden by preconceptions, careful analysts who recognize logical needs and dare to follow them across their concepts to conclusions in simple operating arrangements, even if this requires the government to do novel things. I say this because for a long time I have been saying it and the event has proved the necessity. Some important part of the effort of our universities has gone to stuffing students with preconceptions which are shattered the moment they meet the economic realities of everyday life. The departments of political economy in our universities are not yet conceiving their problem in the terms to which they must ultimately come—or else go the way of the academic classics with which they really belong.

The most grudging consent to our recovery program comes from these departments of economics; they appear to have forgotten how little they liked the logical alternative when they were living with it a year ago. Seemingly they would rather have us fail than to succeed in unorthodox ways. People who find themselves in such a frame of mind belong with the Bourbons, the Malthusians and other historical diehards after whom deluges have come.

It is quite impossible to predict the shape our newly invented economic institutions may take in the future. That seems to me, in any case, unimportant. What is important is that we have undertaken a venture which is theoretically new in the sense that it calls for control rather than drift. In the years to come much ingenuity will be needed in the effort to isolate and strengthen the nerve centers of industrial civilization. We have yet to discover in determinate fashion what efforts are naturally those of common service, and so require a high degree of socialization, and what ones can safely be left to relatively free individual or group contrivance. We are turning away from the entrusting of crucial decisions, and the operation of institutions whose social consequences are their most characteristic feature, to individuals who are motivated by private interests. It will take a long time to learn how this may be done effectively. But the longest step toward its accomplishment was taken when the new and untrod path was entered on. It is my earnest hope that the university which has been my home during so many active years, and from whose encouragement I and others have drawn strength, may enter on these tasks with courage and determination. The link between this institution and that one which I am at the moment serving in Washington is a natural one. The university is a place for learning and for renewal. It is the source on which government must depend for inspiration, for criticism, for expert service; the source, also, of that political economy out of which the new industrial state must be forged.

XXIII. INTRODUCTION

The single best source of the "realism" of the depression is *The Folklore of Capitalism*, 1937, written by Thurman W. Arnold (born in 1891). With wit and learning, he dissected the sacred cows of traditional America. His rejection of rationalism and faith in organized power led him to dismiss the ideological warfare of the depression as hugely irrelevant to the brute facts. Americans, in Arnold's view, had been concerned with the future and not with the present, with the ideal and not with the actual, and with the symbol, not with the concrete. Holding tenaciously to a fact wherever he could uncover one, Arnold demonstrated on virtually every page of his work how deeply he was committed to the unphilosophical dimensions of pragmatism. Rejecting assumptions and ideals at every turn, Arnold's work was more than gay iconoclasm. *The Folklore of Capitalism* is a perfectly characteristic example of depression realism.

XXIII.

Thurman W. Arnold
THE FOLKLORE OF CAPITALISM
1937

The folklore of 1937 was expressed principally by the literature of law and economics. Here were found elaborately framed the little pictures which men had of society as it ought to be. Of course, this literature

SOURCE. Thurman W. Arnold, *The Folklore of Capitalism,* New Haven: Yale University Press, 1937, pp. 46–47, 58–71, and 77–82. Reprinted with the permission of Yale University Press.

was not called folklore. No one thought of sound principles of law or economics as a religion. They were considered as inescapable truths, as natural laws, as principles of justice, and as the only method of an ordered society. This is a characteristic of all vital folklore or religion. The moment that folklore is recognized to be only folklore it ceases to have the effect of folklore. It descends to the place of poetry or fairy tales which affect us only in our romantic moments. For example, years ago Mr. Justice Cardozo pointed out that law was really literature. This is true. Yet if it were generally recognized to be true, the particular kind of literature known as law would not have the kind of influence it has today.

The effect of the peculiar folklore of 1937 was to encourage the type of organization known as industry or business and discourage the type known as government. Under the protection of this folklore the achievements of American business were remarkable. There was no questioning of myths which supported independent empires by those engaged in those enterprises. So-called private institutions like General Motors never lost their direction through philosophical debate. The pioneer efforts at industrial organization in this country had been wasteful beyond belief, but bold and confident.

With respect to political government, however, our superstitions had the opposite effect. They were not a cohesive force, but a destructive and disintegrating one. The pioneer efforts of the Government were timid, indecisive, and ineffective. When it became necessary for the Government to fill gaps in the national structure in which private business enterprise was an obvious failure, the myths and folklore of the time hampered practical organization at every turn. Men became more interested in planning the culture of the future—in saving posterity from the evils of dictatorship or bureaucracy, in preventing the American people from adopting Russian culture on the one hand, or German culture on the other—than in the day-to-day distribution of food, housing, and clothing to those who needed them. Mystical attacks on practical measures achieved an astonishing degree of success. Debaters and orators rose to the top in such an atmosphere and technicians twiddled their thumbs, unable to use their skills. . . .

MEDIEVAL ATTITUDES IN LAW AND ECONOMICS

The years before and during the great depression in America, which were feudal in their economic organization, present a spectacle of a continuous search for a set of rational formulas designed to enable men to govern with a minimum of exercise of judgment, and with a minimum of personal power. The historian of the future will be amazed at a great people's simple belief that sound legal and economic principles, discovered by close students of these mysteries, were the only means to national salvation. He will be equally amazed at the naive fears that opportunistic action or judgment based not upon learning but on political expediency, whatever its temporary benefits, would necessarily lead to disaster if it did not fit into some preconceived theory. The history of the time is the story of men who struggled gallantly and unsuccessfully to make government correspond to this theory about it. It is intelligible only if we start out with a bird's-eye view of what men thought were the principles which made the social structure survive.

. . . The "thinking man" . . . was essential to all political debate. Without him, public discussion of rational principles and systems of government would have been impossible. He was the great spirit which hovered over all governmental institutions.

This particular type of folklore had ceased to affect medicine in 1937. Medical principles were not supposed to be a matter which was to be thought out, in the way governmental principles were thought out. The difference between the attitudes of medical science and physical science was very subtle, particularly since the political scientist of 1937 always *claimed* to be doing the same thing as the physical scientist. That difference therefore cannot be defined; it can only be illustrated.

Thirty years ago medical men were still fighting for principle, just as political men are fighting for it today. There were the homeopathic and the allopathic schools of medicine. The thinking man was supposed to choose between these two schools in hiring his physician. There was much public debate on their merits. Disciples of each school were supposed to stand together as a matter of party loyalty. They were the missionaries of a medical creed.

Today the public is no longer asked to choose between conflicting medical principles (at least not to the same extent). Medicine has been taken over by men of skill rather than men of principle. The medical sects, such as chiropractic, which still argues fundamental principle in the way the political scientist argues it, are unimportant. There is little left in medicine for thinking men to debate. Physicians are chosen on a guess as to their expertness. Hospitals no longer take sides. Therefore the concept of the "thinking man" is no longer essential.

In advertising the "thinking man" has gone so completely that a modern advertising agency would be amazed at the suggestion that the best way to sell goods is by making a rational appeal.

In government the concept still reigns supreme. Men are still asked to diagnose the ills of social organization through the darkened lenses of "schools" of legal or economic theory. They still worry about choosing a "system" of government. Fact-minded persons who do not believe in the "thinking man" and who do not expect to gain political objectives by making rational appeals to him are not considered respectable. They are called "politicians" and not "political scientists." The political scientists are the high priests of our governmental mythology. The politician is still in the position of the Jewish money lender of the Middle Ages.

In examining that curious folklore, still a powerful influence in 1937, the future historian will observe that during the first half of the twentieth century the principles of government were divided into two great branches, law and economics. Each had its specialists, who were supposed to work hand in hand in the joint enterprise of discovering the true principles of government. The law, on the one hand, preserved those great moral values of freedom and individualism by pointing out that the opportunistic action, which seemed best for the moment, often concealed dangerous moral traits. It was supposed to guard us against well-meaning individuals who, in their desire to alleviate human suffering and promote efficiency for the present, were leading us into future bureaucracy, regimentation, and dictatorship. Economics, on the other hand, supplied the principles which, if properly studied, would make incoherent legislative bodies act with unity and coherence, and which, if properly propagandized among the solid citizenry, would insure the selection of legislators who could distinguish between sound and unsound principles. Between the two sets of principles it was thought possible to avoid the personal element in government.

The future historian will also mark the paradox that there was little agreement on what were the sound theories in 1937, and at the same time almost unanimous agreement that good government followed only upon the selection of sound theories. No program for the alleviation of any pressing problem could win any sort of acceptance without having behind it some theory logically consistent with the more general superstitions concerning the function of government. Men believed that there were several defined systems of government—Capitalism, Communism, Fascism—which bright men had thought up and lesser men accepted, all of them in operation in various parts of the world. It was the duty of the American people to make a free-will choice between them. The great ideological battle in 1937 was whether Capitalism was worth preserving. Most people thought it should be preserved. There were many intelligent humanitarian people, however, who thought that it should be abandoned and a new system inaugurated, usually called Socialism. This new system on paper seemed preferable to Capitalism. Yet it was constantly pointed out by its opponents that if one tried to obtain Socialism, one got either Fascism or Communism, with their attendant evils of regimentation, bureaucracy, dictatorship, and so on, and that individualism disappeared.

It was a complicated business, this preservation of the capitalistic system in 1937 against the other "isms" and alien ideals. There was first the task of defining what Capitalism really was. This was a constant process. It had to be done every day and each new restatement led only to the necessity of further definition. The preservation of Capitalism also required that practical plans be tested by expert economic theorists who looked at each practical measure through the spectacles of economic abstractions, in order not to be confused by immediate objectives. Thus child labor had to be debated, not on the basis of whether it was desirable for children to work, but in the light of its effect on the American home in ten years, if it were followed to its logical conclusion. Measures for the conservation of oil, or regulation of agriculture, had to be considered without relation to immediate benefits either to oil or agriculture. Tendencies were regarded as far more important than immediate effects, and the danger to posterity actually seemed more real than the danger to existing persons.

The capitalistic system in America had two sets of rules, one economic and the other legal, determining what the limits of governmental control should be. Economic theory had no separate institution to speak ex cathedra, other than the two political parties, each of which hired experts to study it and advise them. Whatever was produced by any political platform had to have its background of scholarly research. It was the duty of each party to consult only sound economists. Legal theory, on the other hand, was manufactured by the Supreme Court of the United States. There were two parties in the Supreme Court of the United States, each with its own legal theory. However, it was generally agreed that what the majority of judges thought was the real essence of the Constitution. It was not left to the people to decide between sound and unsound legal theory, and therefore the opinions of dissenting judges, unlike the opinions of dissenting economists, were not available in political debate, at least prior to Roosevelt's attack on the Court. This was because law concerned the spiritual welfare of the people and preserved their form of government, whereas economics concerned only their material welfare. In spiritual things it is essential that men do right according to some final authority. There was thought to be no such compelling reason to prevent them from ruining themselves economically.

The general idea of the Supreme Court's function is represented by the [idea that] . . . the economic and social legislation of the day is thrown out of the august portals of the Supreme Court, stripped of the plausible humanitarian disguises which had deceived both the President and Congress. This gives a very accurate picture of what the great mass of conservative people thought the Court was doing for them. They did not trust themselves to decide whether a humanitarian or practical scheme was really government by edict, or would lead to government by edict. They knew that such things seldom appeared on the surface, and that they required great learning to analyze. However, more intelligent people required a more complicated explanation, because they preferred long words to pictures. Hence the years of the depression produced thousands of learned dissertations, which came to every possible sort of conclusion as to the constitutionality of various measures. These articles did not make the law clear. They did, however, make it clear that there was such a thing as law, which experts could discover through reason.

It was this faith in a higher law which made the Supreme Court the greatest unifying symbol in American government. Here was the one body which could still the constant debate, and represent to the country the ideal of a government of fundamental principles. On this Court the whole ideal of a government of laws and not of the competing opinions of men appeared to depend. Here only was there a breathing spell from the continual din of arguments about governmental philosophy which were never settled.

The legislative branches of the Government were under constant suspicion, and their acts were presumed to be malevolent. The incompetency of Congress was an assumed fact everywhere. The great trouble with the legislative branches was that they were influenced by an unlearned, untheoretical, illogical, and often corrupt force called "politics." Politics was continually putting unworthy persons in power, as opposed to business, where, because of economic law, only worthy persons rose to the top. A body influenced by political considerations could not give any disinterested judgments as to the soundness of any economic theory. Hence Congress was constantly picking unsound theories, listening to unsound economists, and letting the practical convenience of the moment overweigh the needs of posterity. Politicians were the kind of people who would not care if a thing called bureaucracy was established as long as it gave them jobs.

The only trustworthy check against unsound economic theory was not the politician, but that great body of thinking men and women who composed the better class of the public. Yet even such people were easily confused in those days when the noise of competing theories was loudest. The only way of straightening them out was by constant preaching, which had the weakness of all preaching throughout the centuries, in that sin and heresy were always rising against it. Hence the age-old cry of the disappointed preacher to his erring flock was constantly heard in the land. . . .

It might seem strange . . . to the reader, examining this most interesting folklore from a detached point of view, that the sound economists did not demand a Supreme Court of Economics. Why should they entrust to popular judgment this scholarly task, when they refused to entrust to popular judgment the somewhat easier task of legal reasoning?

The answer to this question takes us into some of the unexamined religious assumptions which the folklore of 1937 had in common with the Christian religion which was its heritage. It went back to the paradox of the relationship of sin and virtue, and the mystical nature of free will. God, according to an earlier theology, had his choice of making men keep to the straight and narrow path by discipline, or by persuasion. Weighing the advantages of these two different methods, he preferred to make him free to sin in order to make a more noble fellow out of him. Neither God nor the economists of 1937 desired a nation of slaves. Therefore the economists would have rejected as unthinkable the organization of a Supreme Court of Economics, on the ground that even a benevolent dictatorship is bad because it abolishes freedom. It had been evident for a long time that the only possible method of making *laissez faire* economics, or indeed any other planned system of economic principles work, would be to force people to accept them. But it was far better to trust to the feeble judgment of the common herd, and to guide them through love of virtue and fear of hell, of Inflation, or Bureaucracy, or Regimentation, or whatever name hell happened to have in the particular field of learning, at the particular time. Of course, the results were discouraging to the economists. They regretted man's tendency to follow false economic reasoning, just as the preachers regretted man's tendency to sin. Nevertheless, they felt that the only refuge was in a deeper search for the Word and in more fervent preaching.

This was the way that most intelligent, socially minded, "thinking men" thought. Of course, those who actually ran the Government were compelled to act on an entirely different set of assumptions. Politicians were interested in getting votes, and such high-sounding theory had nothing whatever to do with the process. Everybody knew this, but it was regarded as a shameful thing that it should be so. Therefore, the efforts of reformers were directed toward abolishing this distressing phenomenon. They argued that if men who did not stoop to use political tricks would only go into politics, and if people only would elect them, then political tricks would disappear from government. The efforts along this line achieved about the same success as the age-old effort to abolish sensuality from love. Everyone realized this, but considered it no excuse for abandoning the effort.

LAW AND OBEDIENCE TO AUTHORITY

There was only one area where the prevailing theory limited the operation of group free will. Men could choose between sound and unsound economic theories, but they must not be permitted to choose between sound and unsound constitutional theories. To prevent them from erring on this point, a scholargarchy was set up, with complete autocratic power. To a superficial observer, this might seem a denial of the beauty of group free will, but closer examination showed that it was not. For the function of the Supreme Court was not to prevent people from choosing what kind of constitution they desired, but to prevent them from changing their form of government *without knowing it.* Congress in its ignorance was constantly passing laws with purely practical objectives, which really changed the constitution without giving people a chance to exercise their free will on that important subject. Therefore some autocratic power had to be set up to apply the complicated scholarly techniques to such measures, not to prevent the people from exercising their free will on the Constitution, but to prevent them from doing it inadvertently.

Immersed in such theories, no student of government, economics, or law could look at the conduct of the institutions about which he was thinking without the same sort of nausea that an idealistic lover of bees and butterflies feels when she overturns a stone and sees some big black bugs crawling about in a loathsome manner. A similar attitude produced the same results in the study of government as it would have produced in biology. Facts about social organization of which men did not approve were not treated as facts, but as sins.

From this point of view it became the duty of everyone to denounce organized political factions as low things unworthy of the attention of courageous statesmen. Party platforms were the only reality—not the social and political pressures which force such platforms into a series of inconsistent compromises. The remedy was to ignore the pressures and make the platforms courageous and consistent. We were supposed to elect to office only those persons who did not care whether they were reelected or not.

Of course, no political party could carry out these principles without political suicide, but this only meant that political parties were shot through with politics. Hence everyone demanded the kind of political party which thought more of posterity than getting votes for its leaders. Everyone realized, of course, that this was impossible, and the conflict created spiritual trouble, indecision, and a greater variety of literary and oratorical nonsense than the world has ever known heretofore.

To find peace, men denounced government by men, and sought relief by reciting principles. The fundamental assumption of the folklore about government during the great depression was that principles could be more trusted than organizations. Organizations were dangerous because of their tendency to err and stray. Principles, provided that they were sound, endured forever, and could alone make up for the constant tendency of social groups to backslide.

THE DAWN OF A DIFFERENT ATTITUDE
TOWARD INDIVIDUAL MALADJUSTMENTS

All this folklore persisted in a time when the theory of free will, sin, and repentance was disappearing from the thinking about individuals' troubles. Psychiatrists and psychologists no longer explained individual conduct on the basis of a free-will choice between good and evil. Such a way of thinking had led in the past to curing the insane by preaching away the devil which had entered the patient. By 1937 people had lost interest in theoretical ethical principles for maladjusted individuals. The term "sinner" had gone from all sophisticated psychology. The concept of the devil had disappeared from the anatomy of the individual mind. Indeed, the idea that any man was a single integrated individual had disappeared, and it was recognized that each individual was a whole cast of characters, each appearing on the stage under the influence of different stimuli. In diagnosing an individual's maladies, the psychiatrist found out what his fantasies were and, without bothering whether they were true or false, attempted to cure him by recognizing these fantasies as part of the problem.

The psychiatrists, like physicians, were not concerned with the theoretical definition of the good mind, or the perfect human body. Even where they read of such definitions by their more theoretical brethren, they did not attempt to fit their particular patients into these molds. Ignoring the speculation of what the man would be in twenty years, or the effect of their treatment on posterity, they proceeded to make the insane person as comfortable and as little of a nuisance to himself and his fellow man as possible, from day to day. They did not spend their time deploring insanity, or the existence of psychopathic personalities. Their attitude toward their patients was rather one of intense interest. And in this atmosphere curative techniques developed, and men actually learned.

THE FAITH IN PRINCIPLES
RATHER THAN ORGANIZATIONS

In 1937 there was little of this point of view in legal or economic thinking. The point of view of the psychiatrist had long been part of the stock in trade of that low class called politicians. However, the attitude seldom was in evidence when respectable people talked or thought about government. There were exceptions here and there in colleges, but that influence had failed to reach the minds of respectable editorial writers, forward-looking reformers, or molders of public opinion. The conception of social institutions as having free will, and winning their salvation by a free-will selection of the right principles; the idea that politics, pressure groups, lobbying, powerful political machines existed because people had sinful yearnings in that direction; the economic idea that depressions were the result of tinkering with economic laws and preventing the automatic working of an abstract law which would have functioned properly had it not been for bad men who threw this law out of gear—these were held as articles of faith by conservatives and radicals alike.

This faith, held so implicitly, was sorely tried during the years of the great depression. As in every time of great travail, from the great plagues on to today, prayers went up in all directions. These prayers, from businessmen, labor leaders, and socialists, had one element in common. They all showed distrust of any form of organized control. No one would admit that man should govern man. No one would observe the obvious fact that lay everywhere under their noses, that human organizations rise to power, not by following announced creeds, but by the development of loyalties and institutional habits. All these devoted people thought that the world could only attain that state of static perfection which alone was worth aiming at, by studying and developing the proper theories, and then following them, not by force, but by their own free will. Thus far the ideals of the Socialist party, the Liberty League, Dr. Townsend, and the budget balancers were all identical. The only difference between them was the proper application of the general principles on which all right-thinking men agreed. . . .

Of course, the God to lead us out of our economic bewilderment was not always the God of the Church. Lawyers found one in the Constitution. Huge organizations like the Liberty League and the Crusaders sought the truth from this document and the learned decisions elaborating it. They produced briefs, law-review articles, and sermons in publications devoted to the elucidation of the law. Like all great bodies of literature, the Constitution was marched in all conceivable directions. An inflation of legal learning took place, the like of which the world has never seen. In the Middle Ages, men sought the "Word" just as diligently, but the available material resources did not permit so many thousands to seek it at the same time, and the printing presses were not so efficient then as now.

The Constitution, however, was only one symbol. Men feverishly attempted to make all written law march toward safety, security, and peace, through logical certainty. Millions were spent on restating all the law at once, and hundreds of learned men were employed by an organization called the "American Law Institute." Prominent lawyers gathered from all parts of the nation to hear the law, as it ought logically to be, read to them for their agreement and approbation.

The purely religious character of these exercises was shown in the complete lack of selfish interest in nearly all of those who participated in them. They sought nothing for themselves in this quest for simplified principle. No discouragement halted that search. Indeed, the obstacles were what made the search entrancing. The American Law Institute was ceremony of the very purest sort, dedicated to the ideal that this was a government of law and not of men. Some of the members of the Liberty League may have had a few selfish interests to further, but it is very doubtful if even these people thought about those interests directly, so absorbed were they in the search for ultimate truth, so preoccupied in contemplation of the future to the exclusion of the present. And in so far as the great membership of this institution was concerned, most of them were acting directly against the common sense interests which they would instantly have recognized if the phobias which motivated them had been brushed aside.

A poll of the Institute of Public Opinion showed that at least 30 per cent of even the unemployed men preferred the conservative to the liberal label. Persons on relief who had seen better days and were imbued with middle-class culture felt it only proper that they should be pauperized before aid was extended them. It was common to find persons who had gone bankrupt devoting the rest of their lives to working for their creditors. Some of these persons demanded new philosophies of government and became Socialists, or Communists, or whatnot. Few of them demanded with any articulate political force actual bread instead of religious principles. Only a few groups like the ex-soldiers, a few of the industrial leaders, and the politicians seemed to catch the beauty of the old proverb that "a bird in the hand is worth two in the bush." They achieved cash bonuses out of the tangled political situation, while most of their fellows were seeking symbols.

The deep hold which this highly religious folklore had upon the small business or professional man, a majority of our industrial leaders, and our press is evidenced by the fact that in 1936 the Constitution became for them a sort of abracadabra which would cure all disease. Copies of the Constitution, bound together with the Declaration of Independence and Lincoln's Gettysburg Address, were distributed in cigar stores; essays on the Constitution were written by high school students; incomprehensible speeches on the Constitution were made from every public platform to reverent audiences which knew approximately as much about the history and dialectic of that document as the masses in the Middle Ages knew about the Bible—in those days when people were not permitted to read the Bible. The American Liberty

League was dedicated to Constitution worship. Like the Bible, the Constitution became the altar whenever our best people met together for tearful solemn purposes, regardless of the kind of organization. Teachers in many states were compelled to swear to support the Constitution. No attempt was made to attach a particular meaning to this phrase, yet people thought it had deep and mystical significance, and that the saying of the oath constituted a charm against evil spirits. The opponents of such oaths became equally excited, and equally theological about the great harm the ceremony might do. Nor was Constitution worship limited to upper strata. The Ku Klux Klan and similar disorderly organizations took the Constitution as their motto for the persecution of Jews and Catholics. In May, 1936, Michigan discovered a state-wide organization of misguided psychopathic personalities which had conducted a series of floggings simply because it was caught up by the solemnity of a ritual. No one could belong who did not take a solemn oath that he was a supporter of the Constitution. The most interesting fact about this order was that it was recruited largely from the underprivileged and the unemployed.

Only radical parties refused to worship the Constitution, but the spirit of the age was such that they, too, put their faith in the written doctrines which they themselves had framed. Thus, the Socialist party, a group which could have no other conceivable purpose than to organize a protest vote, split wide apart in the crucial year of 1936 on purely theological doctrine.

When in 1937 the President proposed to put more liberal judges on the Court, liberals like Oswald Garrison Villard and John T. Flynn joined with the *New York Herald Tribune* to denounce this sacrilege. A group of men with completely irreconcilable views joined together in reciting the book of common prayer.

The essential characteristics of this type of thinking may be described as follows:

1. Everyone was so completely preoccupied with government as it ought to be that no action which was politically possible could escape condemnation in the terms of that ideal. Expediency was not a good public excuse for necessary imperfections.

2. Everyone was so much more concerned with the future life of social institutions than with the present that it seemed immaterial what happened to the legislation of the day directed only at temporary needs. Nothing could be considered really important unless it fitted into what

was conceived to be the moral future of the nation. No one could quite explain what the moral future of the nation was, and therefore on such a question they were always willing to accept the word of any duly constituted authority whose remarks fitted their particular prejudices.

3. Everyone was more interested in the spiritual government than in the temporal. Temporal government consisted of business and politics. The theory was that these things ran themselves, the one being impelled by beneficent economic laws, which operated because of the inherent balance of human nature, and the other being an invention of the devil which ran automatically because of the weakness of human nature.

4. No one ever read the economic theory or the constitutional theory which kept the spiritual government in bounds. Nor was there any faith in any particular type of expert. The faith was in the pontifical nature of the utterances ex cathedra, and the belief in the centuries of learning supposed to lie back of them. Not everyone liked the particular set of such principles which happened to be uppermost. But they were convinced that further study and the elimination of politics from government would give them a set which they would like.

The attitude which we have just been describing colored all thinking and all public utterance wherever the activities of government were concerned. It completely confused the activities of government by subjecting them to unreal standards under which no human organization could operate. The election of 1936 brought out the fact that a very large number of people, roughly representing the more illiterate and inarticulate masses of people, had lost their faith in the more prominent and respected economic preachers and writers of the time, who for the most part were aligned against the New Deal. They repudiated the advice of the newspapers which they bought and read because they were more immediately affected by the economic pressures of the time which were depriving them of security. Nevertheless, after the election, people continued to talk in the old phrases as before. The political leadership which was demanded was also required to be cast in old formulas and these old formulas continued to confuse its direction. Although there were signs of a change in attitude everywhere, organized learning had not yet caught up.

B. The Tenant

XXIV. INTRODUCTION

In the summer of 1936, James Agee (1909-1955) was commissioned to write an article about the tenant farmer in the United States. In collaboration with Walker Evans, who took the remarkable photographs for the volume that eventually resulted, Agee wrote of the lives of three tenant families who raised cotton in Alabama. The article grew to book length, and was published as *Let Us Now Praise Famous Men,* a book which was, according to Evans, ". . . the reflection of one resolute, private rebellion. Agee's rebellion was . . . self-damaging, deeply principled, infinitely costly, and ultimately priceless."

Selections cannot do justice to Agee's accomplishment. In his often torrential prose, Agee showed what is hard to imagine. He wrote of the desperately poor and oppressed in America, not merely with compassion but with genuine, and occasionally overwhelming, affection. He saw and wrote of individuals, not of an abstract social question. Usually controlling but almost never obscuring his own rage, Agee's book is a quiet scream about the fragile lives of his subjects. No other writer of the period equaled Agee's creative combination of realism and humanism.

The selections that follow are Agee's description of picking cotton, as well as of the food tenants ate. His simultaneous attraction and repulsion can be found in these selections, along with a small part of the portrait he drew of the southern tenant farmer. His poetry of privation is represented somewhat in these excerpts, but the reader would do well to experience the longer work for himself.

XXIV.

James Agee

LET US NOW PRAISE FAMOUS MEN

1936

WORK 2: COTTON

Cotton is only one among several crops and among many labors: and all these other crops and labors mean life itself. Cotton means nothing of the sort. It demands more work of a tenant family and yields less reward than all the rest. It is the reason the tenant has the means to do the rest, and to have the rest, and to live, as a tenant, at all. Aside from a few negligibilities of minor sale and barter and out-of-season work, it is his one possible source of money, and through this fact, though his living depends far less on money than on the manipulations of immediate nature, it has a certain royalty. It is also that by which he has all else besides money. But it is also his chief contracted obligation, for which he must neglect all else as need be; and is the central leverage and symbol of his privation and of his wasted life. It is the one crop and labor which is in no possible way useful as it stands to the tenant's living; it is among all these the one which must and can be turned into money; it is among all these the one in which the landowner is most interested; and it is among all these the one of which the tenant can hope for least, and can be surest that he is being cheated, and is always to be cheated. All other tasks are incidental to it; it is constantly on everyone's mind; yet of all of them it is the work in which the tenant has least hope and least interest, and to which he must devote the most energy. Any less involved and self-contradictory attempt to understand what cotton and cotton work 'means' to a tenant would, it seems to me, be false to it. It has the doubleness that all jobs have by which one stays alive and in which one's life is made a cheated ruin, and the same sprained and twilight effect on those who must work at it: but because it is only one among the many jobs by which a tenant family must stay alive, and deflects all these others, and receives still other light from

SOURCE. James Agee and Walker Evans, *Let Us Now Praise Famous Men,* Boston: Houghton Mifflin, 1960, pp. 326–329, 336–342, and 415–417. Copyright 1960 by Walker Evans. Reprinted with the permission of the publisher, Houghton Mifflin Company.

their more personal need, reward, and value, its meanings are much more complex than those of most jobs: it is a strong stale magnet among many others more weak and more yielding of life and hope. In the mind of one in whom all these magnetisms are daily and habituated from his birth, these meanings are one somber mull: yet all their several forces are pulling at once, and by them the brain is quietly drawn and quartered. It seems to me it is only through such a complex of meanings that a tenant can feel, toward that crop, toward each plant in it, toward all that work, what he and all grown women too appear to feel, a particular automatism, a quiet, apathetic, and inarticulate yet deeply vindictive hatred, and at the same time utter hopelessness, and the deepest of their anxieties and of their hopes: as if the plant stood enormous in the unsteady sky fastened above them in all they do like the eyes of an overseer. To do all of the hardest work of your life in service of these drawings-apart of ambiguities; and to have all other tasks and all one's consciousness stained and drawn apart in it: I can conceive of little else which could be so inevitably destructive of the appetite for living, of the spirit, of the being, or by whatever name the centers of individuals are to be called: and this very literally: for just as there are deep chemical or electric changes in all the body under anger, or love, or fear, so there must certainly be at the center of these meanings and their directed emotions; perhaps most essentially, an incalculably somber and heavy weight and dark knotted iron of subnausea at the peak of the diaphragm, darkening and weakening the whole body and being, the literal feeling by which the words a broken heart are no longer poetic, but are merely the most accurate possible description.

Yet these things as themselves are withdrawn almost beyond visibility, and the true focus and right telling of it would be in the exact textures of each immediate task.

Of cotton farming I know almost nothing with my own eyes; the rest I have of Bud Woods. I asked enough of other people to realize that every tenant differs a little in his methods, so nothing of this can be set down as 'standard' or 'correct'; but the disonances are of small detail rather than of the frame and series in the year. . . . I have decided, too, to try to use my imagination a little, as carefully as I can. I must warn you that the result is sure to be somewhat inaccurate: but it is accurate anyhow to my ignorance, which I would not wish to disguise.

From the end of the season and on through the winter the cotton and the corn stand stripped and destroyed, the cotton black and brown, the corn gray and brown and rotted gold, much more shattered, the banks of woodland bare, drenched and black, the clay dirt sombered wet or hard with a shine of iron, peaceful and exhausted; the look of trees in a once full-blown country where such a burning of war has gone there is no food left even for birds and insects, all now brought utterly quiet, and the bare homes dark with dampness, under the soft and mourning midwinter suns of autumnal days, when all glows gold yet lifeless, and under constrictions of those bitter freezings when the clay is shafted and sprilled with ice, and the aching thinly drifted snows which give the land its shape, and, above all, the long, cold, silent, inexhaustible, and dark winter rains:

In the late fall or middle February this tenant, which of the three or of the millions I do not care—a man, dressed against the wet coldness, may be seen small and dark in his prostrated fields, taking down these sometimes brittle, sometimes rotted forests of last year's crops with a club or with a cutter, putting death to bed, cleaning the land: and late in February, in fulfillment of an obligation to his landlord, he borrows a second mule and, with a two-horse plow, runs up the levees, that is, the terraces, which shall preserve his land; this in a softening mild brightness and odoriferousness of presaging spring, and a rustling shearing apart of the heavy land, his mules moving in slow scarce-wakened method as of work before dawn, knowing the real year's work to be not started yet, only made ready for. It is when this is done, at about the first of March, that the actual work begins, with what is planted where, and with what grade and amount of fertilizer, determined by the landlord, who will also, if he wishes, criticize, advise, and govern at all stages of planting and cultivation. But the physical work, and for that matter the knowledge by which he works, is the tenant's, and this is his tenth or his fortieth year's beginning of it, and it is of the tenant I want to tell. . . .

Picking season. Late in August the fields begin to whiten more rarely with late bloom and more frequently with cotton and then still thicker with cotton, a sparkling ground starlight of it, steadily bursting into more and more millions of points, all the leaves seeming shrunken smaller; quite as at night the whole frontage of the universe is more and more thoroughly printed in the increasing darkness; and the wide cloudless and tremendous light holds the earth clamped and trained as beneath a vacuum bell and burningglass; in such a brilliance that half and two thirds of the sky is painful to look into; and in this white maturing oven the enlarged bolls are streaked a rusty green, then bronze, and are split and splayed open each in a loose vomit of cotton. These split bolls are now *burrs,* hard and edged as chiseled wood, pointed nearly as thorns, spread open in three and four and five gores or cells. It is slow at first, just a few dozen scattered here and there and then a few tens of dozens, and then there is a space of two or three days in which a whole field seems to be crackling open at once, and at this time it seems natural that it must be gone into and picked, but all the more temperate and experienced tenants wait a few days longer until it will be fully worth the effort: and during this bursting of bolls and this waiting, there is a kind of quickening, as if deep under the ground, of all existence, toward a climax which cannot be delayed much longer, but which is held in the tensions of this reluctance, tightening, and delay: and this can be seen equally in long, sweeping drivings of a car between these spangling fields, and in any one of the small towns or the county seats, and in the changed eyes of any one family, a kind of tightening as of an undertow, the whole world and year lifted nearly upon its crest, and soon beginning the long chute down to winter: children, and once in a while a very young or a very old woman or man, whose work is scarcely entered upon or whose last task and climax this may be, are deeply taken with an excitement and a restlessness to begin picking, and in the towns, where it is going to mean money, the towns whose existence is for it and depends on it, and which in most times of year are sunken in sleep as at the bottom of a sea: these towns are sharpening awake; even the white hot streets of a large city are subtly changed in this season: but Gudger and his wife and Ricketts and Woods, and most of the heads of the million and a quarter families who have made this and are to do the working of taking it for their own harm and another's use, they are only a little more quiet than usual, as they might be if they were waiting for a train to come in, and keep looking at the fields, and judging them; and at length one morning (the Ricketts women are already three days advanced in ragged work), Gudger says, Well:

Well; I reckin tomorrow we'd better start to picking:

And the next morning very early, with their broad hats and great sacks and the hickory baskets, they are out, silent, their bodies all slanted, on the hill: and in every field in hundreds of miles, black and white, it is the same: and such as it is, it is a joy which scarcely touches any tenant; and is worn thin and through in half a morning, and is gone for a year.

It is simple and terrible work. Skill will help you; all the endurance you can draw up against it from the roots of your existence will be thoroughly used as fuel to it: but neither skill nor endurance can make it any easier.

Over the right shoulder you have slung a long white sack whose half length trails the ground behind. You work with both hands as fast and steadily as you can. The trick is to get the cotton between your fingertips at its very roots in the burr in all three or four or five gores at once so that it is brought out clean in one pluck. It is easy enough with one burr in perhaps ten, where the cotton is ready to fall; with the rest, the fibers are more tight and tricky. So another trick is, to learn these several different shapes of burr and resistance as nearly as possible by instinct, so there will be no second trying and delay, and none left wasted in the burr; and, too, as quickly to judge what may be too rotted and dirtied to use, and what is not yet quite ready to take: there are a lot suspended between these small uncertainties, and there should be no delay, no need to use the mind's judgement, and few mistakes. Still another trick is, between these strong pulls of efficiency, proper judgement, and maximum speed, not to hurt your fingers on the burrs any worse than you can help. You would have to try hard, to break your flesh on any one burr, whether on its sharp points or its edges; and a single raindrop is only scarcely instrumental in ironing a mountain flat; but in each plucking of the hand the fingers are searched deep in along these several sharp, hard edges. In two hours' picking the hands are just well limbered up. At the end of a week you are favoring your fingers, still in the obligation of speed. The later of the three to five times over the field, the last long weeks of the season, you might be happy if it were possible to exchange them for boils. With each of these hundreds of thousands of insertions of the hands, moreover, the fingers are brought to a small point, in an action upon every joint and tendon in the hand. I suggest that if you will try, three hundred times in succession, the following exercise: touch all five fingertips as closely as possible into one point, trying meanwhile to hold loose cotton in the palm of the hand: you will see that this can very quickly tire, cramp and deteriorate the whole instrument, and will understand how easily rheumatism can take up its strictures in just this place.

Meanwhile, too, you are working in a land of sunlight and heat which are special to just such country at just that time of year: sunlight that stands and stacks itself upon you with the serene weight of deep sea water, and heat that makes the jointed and muscled and fine-structured body glow like one indiscriminate oil; and this brilliant weight of heat is piled upon you more and more heavily in hour after hour so that it can seem you are a diving bell whose strained seams must at any moment burst, and the eyes are marked in stinging sweat, and the head, if your health is a little unstable, is gently roaring, like a private blowtorch, and less gently beating with aching blood: also the bag, which can hold a hundred pounds, is filling as it is dragged from plant to plant, four to nine burrs to a plant to be rifled swiftly, and the load shrugged along another foot or two and the white row stretched ahead to a blur and innumerably man-ifolded in other white rows which have not yet been touched, and younger bolls in the cleaned row behind already breaking like slow popcorn in the heat, and the sack still heavier and heavier, so that it pulls you back as a beast might rather than a mere dead weight: but it is not only this: cotton plants are low, so that in this heat and burden of the immanent sun and of the heavying sack you are dragging, you are continuously somewhat stooped over even if you are a child, and are bent very deep if you are a man or a woman. A strong back is a godsend, but not even the strongest back was built for that treatment, and there combine at the kidneys, and rill down the thighs and up the spine and athwart the shoulders the ticklish weakness of gruel or water, and an aching that is increased in geometric progressions, and at length, in the small of the spine, a literal and persistent sensation of yielding, buckling, splintering, and breakage: and all of this, even though the mercy of nature has hardened your flesh and has anesthetized your nerves and your powers of reflection and of imagination, yet reaches in time the brain and the more mirror-like nerves, and thereby is redoubled upon itself much more powerfully than before: and this is all compounded upon you during each successive hour of the day and during each successive day in a force which rest and food and sleep only partly and superficially refresh: and though, later in the season, you are relieved of the worst of the heat, it is in exchange at the last for a coolness which many pickers like even less well, since it so slows and chills the lubricant garment of sweat they work in, and seriously slows and stiffens the fingers which by then at best afford an excruciation in every touch.

The tenants' idiom has been used ad nauseam by the more un-speakable of the northern journalists but it happens to be accurate: that picking goes on each day from can to can't: sometimes, if there is a feeling of rush, the Ricketts continue it by moonlight. In the blasting heat of the first of the season, unless there is a rush to beat a rain or to make up an almost completed wagonload, it is customary to quit work an hour and a half or even two hours in the worst part of the day and to sit or lie in the shade and possible draft of the hallway or porch asleep or dozing after dinner. This time narrows off as the weeks go by and a sense of rush and of the wish to be done with it grows on the pickers and is tightened through from the landlord. I have heard of tenants and pickers who have no rest-period and no midday meal, but those I am acquainted with have it. It is of course no parallel in heartiness and variety to the proud and enormous meals which farm wives of the wheat country prepare for harvest hands, and which are so very zestfully regarded by some belated virgilians as common to what they like to call the American Scene. It is in fact the ordinary every day food, with perhaps a little less variety than in the earlier summer, hastily thrown together and heated by a woman who has hurried in exhausted from the field as few jumps as possible ahead of her family, and served in the dishes she hurriedly rinsed before she hurried out on the early morning as few jumps as possible behind them. When they are all done, she hurries through the dish washing and puts on her straw hat or her sun-bonnet and goes on back into the field, and they are all at it in a strung-out little bunch, the sun a bitter white on their deeply bent backs, and the sacks trailing, a slow breeze idling in the tops of the pines and hickories along the far side but the leaves of the low cotton scarcely touched in it, and the whole land, under hours of heat still to go, yet listed subtly forward toward the late end of the day. They seem very small in the field and very lonely, and the motions of their industry are so small, in range, their bodies so slowly moving, that it seems less that they are so hard at work than that they are bowed over so deeply into some fascination or grief. . . .

The biscuits are large and shapeless, not cut round, and are pale, not tanned, and are dusty with flour. They taste of flour and soda and damp salt and fill the mouth stickily. They are better with butter, and still better with butter and jam. The butter is pallid, soft, and unsalted, about the texture of coldcream; it seems to taste delicately of wood and wet cloth; and it tastes 'weak.' The jam is loose, of little berries, full of light raspings of the tongue; it tastes a deep sweet purple tepidly watered, with a very faint sheen of a sourness as of iron. Field peas are olive-brown, the shape of lentils, about twice the size. Their taste is a cross between lentils and boiled beans; their broth is bright with seasoning of pork, and of this also they taste. The broth is soaked up in bread. The meat is a bacon, granular with salt, soaked in the grease of its frying: there is very little lean meat in it. What there is is nearly as tough as rind; the rest is pure salted stringy fat. The eggs taste of pork too. They are fried in it on both sides until none of the broken yolk runs, are heavily salted and peppered while they fry, so that they come to table nearly black, very heavy, rinded with crispness, nearly as dense as steaks. Of milk I hardly know how to say; it is skimmed, blue-lighted; to a city palate its warmth and odor are somehow dirty and at the same time vital, a little as if one were drinking blood. There is even in so clean a household as this an odor of pork, of sweat, so subtle it seems to get into the very metal of the cooking-pans beyond any removal of scrubbing, and to sweat itself out of newly washed cups; it is all over the house and all through your skin and clothing at all times, yet as you bring each piece of food to your mouth it is so much more noticeable, if you are not used to it, that a quiet little fight takes place on your palate and in the pit of your stomach; and it seems to be this odor, and a sort of wateriness and discouraged tepidity, which combine to make the food seem unclean, sticky, and sallow with some invisible sort of disease, yet this is the odor and consistency and temper and these are true tastes of home; I know this even of myself; and much as my reflexes are twitching in refusal of each mouthful a true homesick and simple fondness for it has so strong hold of me that in fact there is no fight to speak of and no faking of enjoyment at all. And even later, knowing well enough of such food what an insult it is to those who must spend their lives eating it, and who like it well enough, and when I am sick with it, I have also fondness for it, and when this fails, a funny kind of self-scorning determination that I shall eat for a few weeks what a million people spend their lives eating, and feel that whatever discomfort it brings me is little enough and willingly taken on, in the scale of all it could take to even us up.

XXV. INTRODUCTION

The most influential social novel of the depression was *The Grapes of Wrath*, 1939, by John Steinbeck (born in 1902). Steeped in the culture and mythology of the Salinas Valley of California, Steinbeck sketched the lives of the deposed Okies with a blend of compassion and simplicity. It is true, as many literary critics have pointed out, that Steinbeck's characters are essentially stereotypic and monodimensional. As Agee was virtually obsessed with the individual and human implications of the social situation, so Steinbeck was, by and large, concerned with the social consequences of human tragedy. The social realism of the period, of which *The Grapes of Wrath* is the prime example, often meant that the social background became the foreground. In that sense, *The Grapes of Wrath* is an attempt to tell the dramatic story of the function and practice of American society as it impinged on the lives of tenant farmers. The impersonality of the social system was often, perhaps too often, at the center of Steinbeck's literary imagination. Alfred Kazin, a literary historian, put it well:

"Though the book *The Grapes of Wrath* was as urgent and as obvious a social tract for its time as *Uncle Tom's Cabin* had been for another, it was also the first novel of its kind to dramatize the inflictions of the crisis without mechanical violence. The bitterness was there, as it should have been, the sense of unspeakable human waste and privation and pain. But in the light of Steinbeck's strong sense of fellowship, his simple indignation at so much suffering, the Joads, while essentially symbolic marionettes, did illuminate something more than the desperation of the time: they became a living and challenging part of the forgotten American procession. Though the characters were essentially stage creations, the book brought the crisis that had severed Americans from their history back into it by recalling what they had lost through it. It gave them a design, a sense of control, where out of other depression novels they could get only the aimless bombardment of rage."

Steinbeck's sense of community as well as his understanding of the nature of the Great Depression inform the following selections.

XXV.

John Steinbeck

THE GRAPES OF WRATH

1939

The owners of the land came onto the land, or more often a spokesman for the owners came. They came in closed cars, and they felt the dry earth with their fingers, and sometimes they drove big earth augers into the ground for soil tests. The tenants, from their sun-beaten dooryards, watched uneasily when the closed cars drove along the fields. And at last the owner men drove into the dooryards and sat in their cars to

SOURCE. John Steinbeck, *The Grapes of Wrath*, New York: Viking Press, 1939, pp. 42–53 and 315–326. Copyright 1939 by John Steinbeck. Reprinted with the permission of The Viking Press, Inc.

talk out of the windows. The tenant men stood beside the cars for a while, and then squatted on their hams and found sticks with which to mark the dust.

In the open doors the women stood looking out, and behind them the children—corn-headed children, with wide eyes, one bare foot on top of the other bare foot, and the toes working. The women and the children watched their men talking to the owner men. They were silent.

Some of the owner men were kind because they hated what they had to do, and some of them were angry because they hated to be cruel, and some of them were cold because they had long ago found that one could not be an owner unless one were cold. And all of them were caught in something larger than themselves. Some of them hated the mathematics that drove them, and some were afraid, and some worshiped the mathematics because it provided a refuge from thought and from feeling. If a bank or a finance company owned the land, the owner man said, The Bank—or the Company—needs—wants—insists—must have—as though the Bank or the Company were a monster, with thought and feeling, which had ensnared them. These last would take no responsibility for the banks or the companies because they were men and slaves, while the banks were machines and masters all at the same time. Some of the owner men were a little proud to be slaves to such cold and powerful masters. The owner men sat in the cars and explained. You know the land is poor. You've scrabbled at it long enough, God knows.

The squatting tenant men nodded and wondered and drew figures in the dust, and yes, they knew, God knows. If the dust only wouldn't fly. If the top would only stay on the soil, it might not be so bad.

The owner men went on leading to their point: You know the land's getting poorer. You know what cotton does to the land; robs it, sucks all the blood out of it.

The squatters nodded—they knew, God knew. If they could only rotate crops they might pump blood back into the land.

Well, it's too late. And the owner men explained the workings and the thinkings of the monster that was stronger than they were. A man can hold land if he can just eat and pay taxes; he can do that.

Yes, he can do that until his crops fail one day and he has to borrow money from the bank.

But—you see, a bank or a company can't do that, because those creatures don't breathe air, don't eat side-meat. They breathe profits; they eat the interest on money. If they don't get it, they die the way you die without air, without side-meat. It is a sad thing, but it is so. It is just so.

The squatting men raised their eyes to understand. Can't we just hang on? Maybe the next year will be a good year. God knows how much cotton next year. And with all the wars—God knows what price cotton will bring. Don't they make explosives out of cotton? And uniforms? Get enough wars and cotton'll hit the ceiling. Next year, maybe. They looked up questioningly.

We can't depend on it. The bank—the monster has to have profits all the time. It can't wait. It'll die. No, taxes go on. When the monster stops growing, it dies. It can't stay one size.

Soft fingers began to tap the sill of the car window, and hard fingers tightened on the restless drawing sticks. In the doorways of the sun-beaten tenant houses, women sighed and then shifted feet so that the one that had been down was now on top, and the toes working. Dogs came sniffing near the owner cars and wetted on all four tires one after another. And chickens lay in the sunny dust and fluffed their feathers to get the cleansing dust down to the skin. In the little sties the pigs grunted inquiringly over the muddy remnants of the slops.

The squatting men looked down again. What do you want us to do? We can't take less share of the crop—we're half starved now. The kids are hungry all the time. We got no clothes, torn an' ragged. If all the neighbors weren't the same, we'd be ashamed to go to meeting.

And at last the owner men came to the point. The tenant system won't work any more. One man on a tractor can take the place of twelve or fourteen families. Pay him a wage and take all the crop. We have to do it. We don't like to do it. But the monster's sick. Something's happened to the monster.

But you'll kill the land with cotton.

We know. We've got to take cotton quick before the land dies. Then we'll sell the land. Lots of families in the East would like to own a piece of land.

The tenant men looked up alarmed. But what'll happen to us? How'll we eat?

You'll have to get off the land. The plows'll go through the dooryard.

And now the squatting men stood up angrily. Grampa took up the land, and he had to kill the Indians and drive them away. And Pa was born here, and he killed weeds and snakes. Then a bad year came and he had to borrow a little money. An' we was born here. There in the door—our children born here. And Pa had to borrow money. The bank owned the land then, but we stayed and we got a little bit of what we raised.

We know that—all that. It's not us, it's the bank. A bank isn't like a man. Or an owner with fifty thousand acres, he isn't like a man either. That's the monster.

Sure, cried the tenant men, but it's our land. We measured it and broke it up. We were born on it, and we got killed on it, died on it. Even if it's no good, it's still ours. That's what makes it ours—being born on it, working it, dying on it. That makes ownership, not a paper with numbers on it.

We're sorry. It's not us. It's the monster. The bank isn't like a man.

Yes, but the bank is only made of men.

No, you're wrong there—quite wrong there. The bank is something else than men. It happens that every man in a bank hates what the bank does, and yet the bank does it. The bank is something more than men, I tell you. It's the monster. Men made it, but they can't control it.

The tenants cried, Grampa killed Indians, Pa killed snakes for the land. Maybe we can kill banks—they're worse than Indians and snakes. Maybe we got to fight to keep our land, like Pa and Grampa did.

And now the owner men grew angry. You'll have to go.

But it's ours, the tenant men cried. We—

No. The bank, the monster owns it. You'll have to go.

We'll get our guns, like Grampa when the Indians came. What then?

Well—first the sheriff, and then the troops. You'll be stealing if you try to stay, you'll be murderers if you kill to stay. The monster isn't men, but it can make men do what it wants.

But if we go, where'll we go? How'll we go? We got no money.

We're sorry, said the owner men. The bank, the fifty-thousand-acre owner can't be responsible. You're on land that isn't yours. Once over the line maybe you can pick cotton in the fall. Maybe you can go on relief. Why don't you go on west to California? There's work there, and it never gets cold. Why, you can reach out anywhere and pick an orange. Why, there's always some kind of crop to work in. Why don't you go there? And the owner men started their cars and rolled away.

The tenant men squatted down on their hams again to mark the dust with a stick, to figure, to wonder. Their sunburned faces were dark, and their sun-whipped eyes were light. The women moved cautiously out of the doorways toward their men, and the children crept behind the women, cautiously, ready to run. The bigger boys squatted beside their fathers, because that made them men. After a time the women asked, What did he want?

And the men looked up for a second, and the smolder of pain was in their eyes. We got to get off. A tractor and a superintendent. Like factories.

Where'll we go? the women asked.

We don't know. We don't know.

And the women went quickly, quietly back into the houses and herded the children ahead of them. They knew that a man so hurt and so perplexed may turn in anger, even on people he loves. They left the men alone to figure and to wonder in the dust.

After a time perhaps the tenant man looked about—at the pump put in ten years ago, with a goose-neck handle and iron flowers on the spout, at the chopping block where a thousand chickens had been killed, at the hand plow lying in the shed, and the patent crib hanging in the rafters over it.

The children crowded about the women in the houses. What we going to do, Ma? Where we going to go?

The women said, We don't know, yet. Go out and play. But don't go near your father. He might whale you if you go near him. And the women went on with the work, but all the time they watched the men squatting in the dust—perplexed and figuring.

The tractors came over the roads and into the fields, great crawlers moving like insects, having the incredible strength of insects. They crawled over the ground, laying the track and rolling on it and picking it up. Diesel tractors, puttering while they stood idle; they thundered when they moved, and then settled down to a droning roar. Snub-nosed monsters, raising the dust and sticking their snouts into it, straight down the country, across the country, through fences, through dooryards, in and out of gullies in straight lines. They did not run on the ground, but on their own roadbeds. They ignored hills and gulches, water courses, fences, houses.

The man sitting in the iron seat did not look like a man; gloved, goggled, rubber dust mask over nose and mouth, he was a part of the monster, a robot in the seat. The thunder of the cylinders sounded through the country, became one with the air and the earth, so that earth and air muttered in sympathetic vibration. The driver could not control it— straight across country it went, cutting through a dozen farms and straight back. A twitch at the controls could swerve the cat', but the driver's hands could not twitch because the monster that built the tractor, the monster that sent the tractor out, had somehow got into the driver's hands, into his brain and muscle, had goggled him and muzzled him—goggled his mind, muzzled his speech, goggled his perception, muzzled his protest. He could not see the land as it was, he could not smell the land as it smelled; his feet did not stamp the clods or feel the warmth and power of the earth. He sat in an iron seat and stepped on iron pedals. He could not cheer or beat or curse or encourage the extension of his power, and because of this he could not cheer or whip or curse or encourage himself. He did not know or own or trust or beseech the land. If a seed dropped did not germinate, it was nothing. If the young thrusting plant withered in drought or drowned in a flood of rain, it was no more to the driver than to the tractor.

He loved the land no more than the bank loved the land. He could admire the tractor—its machined surfaces, its surge of power, the roar of its detonating cylinders; but it was not his tractor. Behind the tractor rolled the shining disks, cutting the earth with blades—not plowing but surgery, pushing the cut earth to the right where the second rows of disks cut it and pushed it to the left; slicing blades shining, polished by the cut earth. And pulled behind the disks, the harrows combing with iron teeth so that the little clods broke up and the earth lay smooth. Behind the harrows, the long seeders—twelve curved iron penes erected in the foundry, orgasms set by gears, raping methodically, raping without passion. The driver sat in his iron seat and he was proud of the straight lines he did not will, proud of the tractor he did not own or love, proud of the power he could not control. And when that crop grew, and was harvested, no man had crumbled a hot clod in his fingers and let the earth sift past his fingertips. No man had touched the seed, or lusted for the growth. Men ate what they had not raised, had no connection with the bread. The land bore under iron, and under iron gradually died; for it was not loved or hated, it had no prayers or curses.

At noon the tractor driver stopped sometimes near a tenant house and opened his lunch: sandwiches wrapped in waxed paper, white bread, pickle, cheese, Spam, a piece of pie branded like an engine part. He ate without relish. And tenants not yet moved away came out to see him, looked curiously while the goggles were taken off, and the rubber dust mask, leaving white circles around the eyes and a large white circle around nose and mouth. The exhaust of the tractor puttered on, for fuel is so cheap it is more efficient to leave the engine running than to heat the Diesel nose for a new start. Curious children crowded close, ragged children who ate their fried dough as they watched. They watched hungrily the unwrapping of the sandwiches, and their hunger-sharpened noses smelled the pickle, cheese, and Spam. They didn't speak to the driver. They watched his hand as it carried food to his mouth. They did not watch him chewing; their eyes followed the hand that held the sandwich. After a while the tenant who could not leave the place came out and squatted in the shade beside the tractor.

"Why, you're Joe Davis's boy!"

"Sure," the driver said.

"Well, what you doing this kind of work for—against your own people?"

"Three dollars a day. I got damn sick of creeping for my dinner—and not getting it. I got a wife and kids. We got to eat. Three dollars a day, and it comes every day."

"That's right," the tenant said. "But for your three dollars a day fifteen or twenty families can't eat at all. Nearly a hundred people have to go out and wander on the roads for your three dollars a day. Is that right?"

And the driver said, "Can't think of that. Got to think of my own kids. Three dollars a day, and it comes every day. Times are changing, mister, don't you know? Can't make a living on the land unless you've got two, five, ten thousand acres and a tractor. Crop land isn't for little guys like us any more. You don't kick up a howl because you can't make Fords, or because you're not the telephone company. Well, crops are like that now. Nothing to do about it. You try to get three dollars a day someplace. That's the only way."

The tenant pondered. "Funny thing how it is. If a man owns a little property, that property is him, it's part of him, and it's like him. If he owns property only so he can walk on it and handle it and be sad when it isn't doing well, and feel fine when the rain falls on it, that property is him, and some way he's bigger because he owns it. Even if he isn't successful he's big with his property. That is so."

And the tenant pondered more. "But let a man get property he doesn't see, or can't take time to get his fingers in, or can't be there to walk on it —why, then the property is the man. He can't do what he wants, he can't think what he wants. The property is the man, stronger than he is. And he is small, not big. Only his possessions are big—and he's the servant of his property. That is so, too."

The driver munched the branded pie and threw the crust away. "Times are changed, don't you know? Thinking about stuff like that don't feed the kids. Get your three dollars a day, feed your kids. You got no call to worry about anybody's kids but your own. You get a reputation for talking like that, and you'll never get three dollars a day. Big shots won't give you three dollars a day if you worry about anything but your three dollars a day."

"Nearly a hundred people on the road for your three dollars. Where will we go?"

"And that reminds me," the driver said, "you better get out soon. I'm going through the dooryard after dinner."

"You filled in the well this morning."

"I know. Had to keep the line straight. But I'm going through the dooryard after dinner. Got to keep the lines straight. And—well, you know Joe Davis, my old man, so I'll tell you this. I got my orders wherever there's a family not moved out—if I have an accident—you know, get too close and cave the house in a little—well, I might get a couple of dollars. And my youngest kid never had no shoes yet."

"I built it with my hands. Straightened old nails to put the sheathing on. Rafters are wired to the stringers with baling wire. It's mine. I built it. You bump it down—I'll be in the window with a rifle. You even come too close and I'll pot you like a rabbit."

"It's not me. There's nothing I can do. I'll lose my job if I don't do it. And look—suppose you kill me? They'll just hang you, but long before you're hung there'll be another guy on the tractor, and he'll bump the house down. You're not killing the right guy."

"That's so," the tenant said. "Who gave you orders? I'll go after him. He's the one to kill."

"You're wrong. He got his orders from the bank. The bank told him, 'Clear those people out or it's your job.' "

"Well, there's a president of the bank. There's a board of directors. I'll fill up the magazine of the rifle and go into the bank."

The driver said, "Fellow was telling me the bank gets orders from the East. The orders were, 'Make the land show profit or we'll close you up.' "

"But where does it stop? Who can we shoot? I don't aim to starve to death before I kill the man that's starving me."

"I don't know. Maybe there's nobody to shoot. Maybe the thing isn't men at all. Maybe, like you said, the property's doing it. Anyway I told you my orders."

"I got to figure," the tenant said. "We all got to figure. There's some way to stop this. It's not like lightning or earthquakes. We've got a bad thing made by men, and by God that's something we can change." The tenant sat in his doorway, and the driver thundered his engine and started off, tracks falling and curving, harrows combing, and the phalli of the seeder slipping into the ground. Across the dooryard the tractor cut, and the hard, foot-beaten ground was seeded field, and the tractor cut through again; the uncut space was ten feet wide. And back he came. The iron guard bit into the house-corner, crumbled the wall, and wrenched the little house from its foundation so that it fell sideways, crushed like a bug. And the driver was goggled and a rubber mask covered his nose and mouth. The tractor cut a straight line on, and the air and the ground vibrated with its thunder. The tenant man stared after it, his rifle in his hand. His wife was beside him, and the quiet children behind. And all of them stared after the tractor. . . .

Once California belonged to Mexico and its land to Mexicans; and a horde of tattered feverish Americans poured in. And such was their hunger for land that they took the land—stole Sutter's land, Guerrero's land, took the grants and broke them up and growled and quarreled over them, those frantic hungry men; and they guarded with guns the land they had stolen. They put up houses and barns, they turned the earth and planted crops. And these things were possession, and possession was ownership.

The Mexicans were weak and fled. They could not resist, because they wanted nothing in the world as frantically as the Americans wanted land.

Then, with time, the squatters were no longer squatters, but owners; and their children grew up and had children on the land. And the hunger was gone from them, the feral hunger, the gnawing, tearing hunger for land, for water and earth and the good sky over it, for the green thrusting grass, for the swelling roots. They had these things so completely that they did not know about them any more. They had no more the stomach-tearing lust for a rich acre and a shining blade to plow it, for seed and a windmill beating its wings in the air. They arose in the dark no more to hear the sleepy birds' first chittering, and the morning wind around the house while they waited for the first light to go out to the dear acres. These things were lost, and crops were reckoned in dollars, and land was valued by principal plus interest, and crops were bought and sold before they were planted. Then crop failure, drought, and flood were no longer little deaths within life, but simple losses of money. And all their love was thinned with money, and all their fierceness dribbled away in interest until they were no longer farmers at all, but little shopkeepers of crops, little manufacturers who must sell before they can make. Then those farmers who were not good shopkeepers lost their land to good shopkeepers. No matter how clever, how loving a man might be with earth and growing things, he could not survive if he were not also a good shopkeeper. And as time went on, the business men had the farms, and the farms grew larger, but there were fewer of them.

Now farming became industry, and the owners followed Rome, although they did not know it. They imported slaves, although they did not call them slaves: Chinese, Japanese, Mexicans, Filipinos. They live on rice and beans, the business men said. They don't need much. They wouldn't know what to do with good wages. Why, look how they live. Why, look what they eat. And if they get funny—deport them.

And all the time the farms grew larger and the owners fewer. And there were pitifully few farmers on the land any more. And the imported serfs were beaten and frightened and starved until some went home again, and some grew fierce and were killed or driven from the country. And the farms grew larger and the owners fewer.

And the crops changed. Fruit trees took the place of grain fields, and vegetables to feed the world spread out on the bottoms: lettuce, cauliflower, artichokes, potatoes—stoop crops. A man may stand to use a scythe, a plow, a pitchfork; but he must crawl like a bug between the rows of lettuce, he must bend his back and pull his long bag between the cotton rows, he must go on his knees like a penitent across a cauliflower patch.

And it came about that owners no longer worked on their farms. They farmed on paper; and they forgot the land, the smell, the feel of it, and remembered only that they owned it, remembered only what they gained and lost by it. And some of the farms grew so large that one man could not even conceive of them any more, so large that it took batteries of bookkeepers to keep track of interest and gain and loss; chemists to test the soil, to replenish; straw bosses to see that the stooping men were moving along the rows as swiftly as the material of their bodies could stand. Then such a farmer really became a storekeeper, and kept a store. He paid the men, and sold them food, and took the money back. And after a while he did not pay the men at all, and saved bookkeeping. These farms gave food on credit. A man might work and feed himself; and when the work was done, he might find that he owed money to the company. And the owners not only did not work the farms any more, many of them had never seen the farms they owned.

And then the dispossessed were drawn west—from Kansas, Oklahoma, Texas, New Mexico; from Nevada and Arkansas families, tribes, dusted out, tractored out. Carloads, caravans, homeless and hungry; twenty thousand and fifty thousand and a hundred thousand and two hundred thousand. They streamed over the mountains, hungry and restless—restless as ants, scurrying to find work to do—to lift, to push, to pull, to pick, to cut—anything, any burden to bear, for food. The kids are hungry. We got no place to live. Like ants scurrying for work, for food, and most of all for land.

We ain't foreign. Seven generations back Americans, and beyond that Irish, Scotch, English, German. One of our folks in the Revolution, an' they was lots of our folks in the Civil War—both sides. Americans.

They were hungry, and they were fierce. And they had hoped to find a home, and they found only hatred. Okies—the owners hated them because the owners knew they were soft and the Okies strong, that they were fed and the Okies hungry; and perhaps the owners had heard from their grandfathers how easy it is to steal land from a soft man if you are fierce and hungry and armed. The owners hated them. And in the towns, the storekeepers hated them because they had no money to spend. There is no shorter path to a storekeeper's contempt, and all his admirations are exactly opposite. The town men, little bankers, hated Okies because there was nothing to gain from them. They had nothing. And the laboring people hated Okies because a hungry man must work, and if he must work, if he has to work, the wage payer automatically gives him less for his work; and then no one can get more.

And the dispossessed, the migrants, flowed into California, two hundred and fifty thousand, and three hundred thousand. Behind them new tractors were going on the land and the tenants were being forced off. And new waves were on the way, new waves of the dispossessed and the homeless, hardened, intent, and dangerous.

And while the Californians wanted many things, accumulation, social success, amusement, luxury, and a curious banking security, the new barbarians wanted only two things—land and food; and to them the two were one. And whereas the wants of the Californians were nebulous and undefined, the wants of the Okies were beside the roads, lying there to be seen and coveted: the good fields with water to be dug for, the good green fields, earth to crumble experimentally in the hand, grass to smell, oaten stalks to chew until the sharp sweetness was in the throat. A man might look at a fallow field and know, and see in his mind that his own bending back and his own straining arms would bring cabbages into the light, and the golden eating corn, the turnips and carrots.

And a homeless hungry man, driving the roads with his wife beside him and his thin children in the back seat, could look at the fallow fields which might produce food but not profit, and that man could know how a fallow field is a sin and the unused land a crime against the thin children. And such a man drove along the roads and knew temptation at every field, and knew the lust to take these fields and make them grow strength for his children and a little comfort for his wife. The temptation was before him always. The fields goaded him, and the company ditches with good water flowing were a goad to him.

And in the south he saw the golden oranges hanging on the trees, the little golden oranges on the dark green trees; and guards with shotguns patrolling the lines so a man might not pick an orange for a thin child, oranges to be dumped if the price was low.

He drove his old car into a town. He scoured the farms for work. Where can we sleep the night?

Well, there's Hooverville on the edge of the river. There's a whole raft of Okies there.

He drove his old car to Hooverville. He never asked again, for there was a Hooverville on the edge of every town.

The rag town lay close to water; and the houses were tents, and weed-thatched enclosures, paper houses, a great junk pile. The man drove his family in and became a citizen of Hooverville—always they were called Hooverville. The man put up his own tent as near to water as he could get; or if he had no tent, he went to the city dump and brought back cartons and built a house of corrugated paper. And when the rains came the house melted and washed away. He settled in Hooverville and he scoured the countryside for work, and the little money he had went for gasoline to look for work. In the evening the men gathered and talked together. Squatting on their hams they talked of the land they had seen.

There's thirty thousan' acres, out west of here. Layin' there. Jesus, what I could do with that, with five acres of that! Why, hell, I'd have ever'thing to eat.

Notice one thing? They ain't no vegetables nor chickens nor pigs at the farms. They raise one thing—cotton, say, or peaches, or lettuce. 'Nother place'll be all chickens. They buy the stuff they could raise in the dooryard.

Jesus, what I could do with a couple pigs!

Well, it ain't yourn, an' it ain't gonna be yourn.

What we gonna do? The kids can't grow up this way.

In the camps the word would come whispering, There's work at Shafter. And the cars would be loaded in the night, the highways crowded —a gold rush for work. At Shafter the people would pile up, five times too many to do the work. A gold rush for work. They stole away in the night, frantic for work. And along the roads lay the temptations, the fields that could bear food.

That's owned. That ain't our'n.

Well, maybe we could get a little piece of her. Maybe—a little piece. Right down there—a patch. Jimson weed now. Christ, I could git enough potatoes off'n that little patch to feed my whole family!

It ain't our'n. It got to have Jimson weeds.

Now and then a man tried; crept on the land and cleared a piece, trying like a thief to steal a little richness from the earth. Secret gardens hidden in the weeds. A package of carrot seeds and a few turnips. Planted potato skins, crept out in the evening secretly to hoe in the stolen earth.

Leave the weeds around the edge—then nobody can see what we're a-doin'. Leave some weeds, big tall ones, in the middle.

Secret gardening in the evening, and water carried in a rusty can.

And then one day a deputy sheriff: Well, what you think you're doin'?

I ain't doin' no harm.

I had my eye on you. This ain't your land. You're trespassing.

The land ain't plowed, an' I ain't hurtin' it none.

You goddamned squatters. Pretty soon you'd think you owned it. You'd be sore as hell. Think you owned it. Get off now.

And the little green carrot tops were kicked off and the turnip greens trampled. And then the Jimson weed moved back in. But the cop was right. A crop raised—why, that makes ownership. Land hoed and the carrots eaten—a man might fight for land he's taken food from. Get him off quick! He'll think he owns it. He might even die fighting for the little plot among the Jimson weeds.

Did ya see his face when we kicked them turnips out? Why, he'd kill a fella soon's he'd look at him. We got to keep these here people down or they'll take the country. They'll take the country.

Outlanders, foreigners.

Sure, they talk the same language, but they ain't the same. Look how they live. Think any of us folks'd live like that? Hell, no!

In the evenings, squatting and talking. And an excited man: Whyn't twenty of us take a piece of lan'? We got guns. Take it an' say, "Put us off if you can." Whyn't we do that?

They'd jus' shoot us like rats.

Well, which'd you ruther be, dead or here? Under groun' or in a house all made of gunny sacks? Which'd you ruther for your kids, dead now or dead in two years with what they call malnutrition? Know what we et all week? Biled nettles an' fried dough! Know where we got the flour for the dough? Swep' the floor of a boxcar.

Talking in the camps, and the deputies, fat-assed men with guns slung on fat hips, swaggering through the camps: Give 'em somepin to think about. Got to keep 'em in line or Christ only knows what they'll do! Why, Jesus, they're as dangerous as niggers in the South! If they ever get together there ain't nothin' that'll stop 'em.

QUOTE: In Lawrenceville a deputy sheriff evicted a squatter, and the squatter resisted, making it necessary for the officer to use force. The eleven-year-old son of the squatter shot and killed the deputy with a .22 rifle.

Rattlesnakes! Don't take chances with 'em, an' if they argue, shoot first. If a kid'll kill a cop, what'll the men do. Thing is, get tougher'n they are. Treat 'em rough. Scare 'em.

What if they won't scare? What if they stand up and take it and shoot back? These men were armed when they were children. A gun is an extension of themselves. What if they won't scare? What if some time an army of them marches on the land as the Lombards did in Italy, as the Germans did on Gaul and the Turks did on Byzantium? They were land-hungry, ill-armed hordes too, and the legions could not stop them. Slaughter and terror did not stop them. How can you frighten a man whose hunger is not only in his own cramped stomach but in the wretched bellies of his children? You can't scare him—he has known a fear beyond every other.

In Hooverville the men talking: Grampa took his lan' from the Injuns.

Now, this ain't right. We're a-talkin' here. This here you're talkin' about is stealin'. I ain't no thief.

No? You stole a bottle of milk from a porch night before last. An' you stole some copper wire and sold it for a piece of meat.

Yeah, but the kids was hungry.

It's stealin', though.

Know how the Fairfiel' ranch was got? I'll tell ya. It was all gov'ment lan', and could be took up. Ol' Fairfiel', he went into San Francisco to the bars, an' he got him three hunderd stew bums. Them bums took up the lan'. Fairfiel' kep' 'em in food an' whiskey, an' then when they'd proved the lan', ol' Fairfiel' took it from 'em. He used to say the lan' cost him a pint of rotgut an acre. Would you say that was stealin'?

Well, it wasn't right, but he never went to jail for it.

No, he never went to jail for it. An' the fella that put a boat in a wagon an' made his report like it was all under water 'cause he went in a boat—he never went to jail neither. An' the fellas that bribed congressmen and the legislatures never went to jail neither.

All over the State, jabbering in the Hoovervilles.

And then the raids—the swoop of armed deputies on the squatters' camps. Get out. Department of Health orders. This camp is a menace to health.

Where we gonna go?

That's none of our business. We got orders to get you out of here. In half an hour we set fire to the camp.

They's typhoid down the line. You want ta spread it all over?

We got orders to get you out of here. Now get! In half an hour we burn the camp.

In half an hour the smoke of paper houses, of weedthatched huts, rising to the sky, and the people in their cars rolling over the highways, looking for another Hooverville.

And in Kansas and Arkansas, in Oklahoma and Texas and New Mexico, the tractors moved in and pushed the tenants out.

Three hundred thousand in California and more coming. And in California the roads full of frantic people running like ants to pull, to push, to lift, to work. For every manload to lift, five pairs of arms extended to lift it; for every stomachful of food available, five mouths open.

And the great owners, who must lose their land in an upheaval, the great owners with access to history, with eyes to read history and to know the great fact: when property accumulates in too few hands it is taken away. And that companion fact: when a majority of the people are hungry and cold they will take by force what they need. And the little screaming fact that sounds through all history: repression works only to strengthen and knit the repressed. The great owners ignored the three cries of history. The land fell into fewer hands, the number of the dispossessed increased, and every effort of the great owners was directed at repression. The money was spent for arms, for gas to protect the great holdings, and spies were sent to catch the murmuring of revolt so that it might be stamped out.

The changing economy was ignored, plans for the change ignored; and only means to destroy revolt were considered, while the causes of revolt went on.

The tractors which throw men out of work, the belt lines which carry loads, the machines which produce, all were ignored; and more and more families scampered on the highways, looking for crumbs from the great holdings, lusting after the land beside the roads. The great owners formed associations for protection and they met to discuss ways to intimidate, to kill, to gas. And always they were in fear of a principal—three hundred thousand—if they ever move under a leader—the end. Three hundred thousand, hungry and miserable; if they ever know themselves, the land will be theirs and all the gas, all the rifles in the world won't stop them. And the great owners, who had become through their holdings both more and less than men, ran to their destruction, and used every means that in the long run would destroy them. Every little means, every violence, every raid on a Hooverville, every deputy swaggering through a ragged camp put off the day a little and cemented the inevitability of the day.

The men squatted on their hams, sharp-faced men, lean from hunger and hard from resisting it, sullen eyes and hard jaws. And the rich land was around them.

D'ja hear about the kid in that fourth tent down?

No, I jus' come in.

Well, that kid's been a-cryin' in his sleep an' a-rollin' in his sleep. Them folks thought he got worms. So they give him a blaster, an' he died. It was what they call black-tongue the kid had. Comes from not gettin' good things to eat.

Poor little fella.

Yeah, but them folks can't bury him. Got to go to the county stone orchard.

Well, hell.

And hands went into pockets and little coins came out. In front of the tent a little heap of silver grew. And the family found it there.

Our people are good people; our people are kind people. Pray God some day kind people won't all be poor. Pray God some day a kid can eat.

And the associations of owners knew that some day the praying would stop.

And there's the end.

C. Neo-orthodoxy

XXVI. INTRODUCTION

At the end of the depression decade, the editors of *The Christian Century* asked a number of people to describe how the experiences of the 1930's had changed their minds. Reinhold Niebuhr (born in 1892) contributed an essay, reprinted here, which was his own confession of disillusionment with the pieties and illusions of liberalism, especially in its cultural and theological manifestations.

He reported that the traditional Christian homilies had no effect when he delivered them from his pulpit in Detroit, that the experiences of a preacher in the depression proved, at least to him, that a mere continuation of liberal Christianity—whether the social Gospel or not —with its emphasis on the inherent goodness of man as well as its smiling faith in the inevitability of progress, was simply futile. As the depression destroyed one after another of his previously held alternatives to social action and intellectual commitment, Niebuhr was virtually compelled to embrace a new theological position which was, as he knew, not fundamentally new except in its application. This position, reminiscent of Augustine and Calvin, with its political and economic implications, became part of the vanguard of what came to be called "neo-orthodoxy." Correctly suggesting a return to an earlier theology, neo-orthodoxy became an integral part of the depression's search for a realism that would not only permit but help men to deal with brute facts that could no longer be mishandled or ignored with impunity.

The basis on which Niebuhr built his entire system was a new acceptance of an older theological attitude: as he grew increasingly fascinated with the existence of evil, he necessarily grew increasingly dissatisfied with the optimism inherent in liberalism. Men, he argued, must necessarily fail, must necessarily plan badly and execute blindly. Rediscovering original sin, the concept of a fatally flawed human nature, he was led to reject classical economics, as well as political democracy that was not based on economic democracy. He was persuaded that Marxists understood the nature of the political process, although he accused them of sharing liberal pieties in their common celebration of man's supposed limitless potentialities.

The intellectual softness of liberalism, its boundless faith in man, its guilt over the peace of Versailles, led to Munich, led to capitulation to the frank barbarism of fascism. He implied that the illusions of liberal democracy made it unable to manage, or indeed, even to comprehend power. Already decadent liberalism, as a result of willful blindness, refused or was unable to see that economic democracy was essential if political democracy was to be saved. It could see neither the need to socialize property nor the difficulties of achieving some measure of economic justice. Crippled in foreign affairs, this kind of culture would find itself unable to deal with its own most determined enemies; crippled in domestic policy, it seemed bent on continuing the same responses to problems that had produced the crisis of depression in the first place.

The orthodoxy Niebuhr proposed was intended to be deeply involved in this world, and yet it was supposed never to lose sight of the ultimate and other-worldly destination of mankind. It must inform political and economic decisions, and look to the final judgment before the throne of Christ. Above all, neo-orthodoxy could flourish, as he suggested, only in the ruins of those old illusions and assumptions that had created a liberal world, a world which, at the close of the 1930's, seemed unable to heal itself within or protect itself from without. Annihilation seemed to be the alternative to his theological "realism."

XXVI.

Reinhold Niebuhr

TEN YEARS THAT SHOOK MY WORLD

1939

. . . About midway in my ministry which extends roughly from the peace of Versailles to the peace of Munich, measured in terms of Western history, I underwent a fairly complete conversion of thought which involved rejection of almost all the liberal theological ideals and ideas with which I ventured forth in 1915. I wrote a book, my first, in 1927 which when now consulted is proved to contain almost all the theological windmills against which today I tilt my sword. These windmills must have tumbled shortly thereafter for every succeeding volume expresses a more and more explicit revolt against what is usually known as liberal culture.

SOURCE. Reinhold Niebuhr, "Ten Years That Shook My World," *The Christian Century,* Vol. LVI, No. 17 (April 26, 1939), pp. 542–546. Copyright 1939 Christian Century Foundation. Reprinted with the permission of *The Christian Century.*

While my critics accuse me of inconstancy my own biased judgment is that there is no inconstancy in the development of my thought since that day, though there is a gradual theological elaboration of what was at first merely socio-ethical criticism. Since the war was the revelation of the internal anarchy of Western civilization, the existence of which bourgeois culture was inclined to deny, and since the peace of Versailles was the revelation of vindictive passions which liberalism imagined were banished from the world, and since the peace of Munich proves that one cannot simply correct the injustices of conquest by the injustice which results from capitulation to tyranny, I conclude that the whole of contemporary history proves that liberal culture has not seen the problem of mankind in sufficient depth to understand its own history. Its too simple moralism has confused issues at almost every turn.

The contemporary problem is brought into theological focus if it is recognized that liberal Christianity is essentially an appropriation of the genuine achievements, and an accommodation to the characteristic prejudices, of this bourgeois culture which first came to flower in the Renaissance, which gained some triumphs and suffered some checks in the Reformation, which reached its zenith in the early part of this century, which revealed its internal anarchy in the World War and its inability to defend itself against lower forms of civilization in the present hour. In terms of politics and economics the bourgeois world is the world of the business man, of expanding commerce and industry, of economic imperialism, transmuted in a period of decay into economic nationalism.

In terms of culture, the bourgeois civilization produced what is generally known as liberalism. This liberalism, I must hasten to add, is something more than either the spirit of tolerance on the one hand or liberal economic theory on the other hand. The liberalism of classical economics, upon which capitalism is built (though it must disavow its own presuppositions in its period of decay) is only one characteristic fruit of the liberal culture. The faith of classical economic theory, that economic activity left to itself, without political interference, would gradually achieve a perfect harmony and justice, was merely one, though a very fateful, error derived from the general liberal assumption that man is essentially a very harmless animal, if only he can be held within the harmonies of nature and of reason from which the fanaticism of religion had beguiled him.

The spirit of tolerance in the liberal culture is of course a real gain. It belongs by right to any profound Christianity which understands the ambiguity of all human actions, the imperfection of all human ideals and the peril of self-righteous fanaticism in all human conflict. It must be admitted, however, that traditional Christianity, both Catholic and Protestant, had so frequently allowed the loyalty and worship, which belongs to God alone, to be appropriated for relative, social, political, economic and theological positions, that it had given rationalists good reason to believe that fanatic cruelty was the chief by-product, or possibly even the chief product, of religion.

It may be observed, however, that those who move away from a liberal culture have both the obligation and the possibility of proving that they have a securer foundation for the spirit of tolerance than traditional liberalism afforded. In secular liberalism the spirit of tolerance is either rooted in a deep skepticism and pessimism which must finally culminate in the intolerable sneer of Pilate, "What is truth?" or it is based on an untenable optimism which believes, with Professor [John] Dewey, that men of good will must, if they meditate upon the issues of life long and profoundly enough, arrive at a "common faith." Professor Dewey's notion that divisions in the human family are chiefly derived from anachronistic religious dogmas ought, incidentally, to be fairly well refuted now by the force of the tragic events of contemporary history.

In any profound Christianity the spirit of tolerance must be derived from the knowledge that, however necessary it may be to judge one another and even to fight one another on the moral and political level, we are all sinners who stand under God's ultimate judgment. It is this consciousness of a divine judgment which must persuade us to recognize the validity of Christ's admonition, "Judge not that ye be not judged," or of St. Paul's exhortation: "Therefore thou art inexcusable, O man, whosoever thou art that judgest; for wherein thou judgest another, thou condemnest thyself; for thou that judgest doest the same thing."

If liberalism as a creed is more than the liberal spirit of toleration on the one hand and more than laissez faire economics on the other, what is it? I should say primarily faith in man; faith in his capacity to subdue nature, and faith that the subjection of nature achieves life's final good; faith in man's essential goodness, to be realized either when man ceases to be spiritual and returns to nature (romanticism), or when he ceases to be natural and becomes rational; and finally, faith in human history which is conceived as a movement upward by a force immanent within it. Whether this faith rests upon Darwin or upon Hegel, that is, whether nature is believed to guarantee progress or whether progress is conceived of as man's "gradual spiritualization" and his emancipation from natural impulses, prejudices and parochial attachments, the optimistic conclusion is the same.

It is instructive to note that liberal culture was always divided against itself on the question whether it should regard human nature and human history primarily from the standpoint of man's relation to nature or from the standpoint of his rational transcendence over nature. In this conflict between the naturalists and idealists, the idealists had something of the Christian doctrine of the dignity of man as made in the image of God, and the naturalists had something of the Christian doctrine of man as a creature who must not pretend to be more than he is. But between them they lost the uneasy conscience of the Christian and expressed themselves in terms of an easy conscience. Whatever was wrong with man, the cause was some defect in his social organization or some imperfection in his education which further social history and cultural development would correct.

I may say that though I express my opposition to liberal civilization politically in terms of Marxian politics, I regard Marxian culture as participating essentially in all the liberal illusions. It also believes in the goodness of man, once capitalism has been destroyed. It also believes in an inevitable progress on the other side of the revolution. It has a catastrophic view of history, but only provisionally so. The destruction of capitalism is, for it, the final destruction of evil. This error must not be taken lightly, even by those of us who believe that the Marxian analysis of the relation of economics to politics is essentially correct.

The Marxian misunderstanding of man has contributed to the development of a tyranny in Russia which almost, though not quite, rivals fascist tyranny. Objectively it cannot be as bad, because it is impossible to destroy all the universal hopes in communism, which distinguish it from the franker tribal mania of fascism. Subjectively, this decay in Russia may be worse, because it extinguishes a new hope in a world in which all the old lights are going out. I feel genuinely sorry for my friends who seem to be under a spiritual necessity to deny obvious facts about Russian tyranny.

In a sense, the really tragic end of a liberal culture is to be found in the peace of Munich. What was best in that culture was outraged by the peace of Versailles and what was shallowest in it came to the conclusion that the horrors of a peace of conquest could be expiated by a peace of capitulation. Thus it lost its last chance to save what is genuine and universal in its life against the threat of a new barbarism. It fondly imagines that the decay of the modern world may still be healed by belatedly yielding "justice" to Germany, when it is obvious that Germany, and the fascist world in general, is no longer interested in justice, but bent upon the display of its power and the exercise of a dominion which asks no questions about justice in either the Christian or the liberal sense.

Liberal moralism is, in short, unable to cope either with man's immediate political or with his ultimate religious problems. It does not know how to check evil and historical injustice in politics, because it would like to operate against injustice in terms of perfect moral purity. The ultimate religious problem of evil in man does not arise for it, because it is always waiting for the perfect education or perfect social order which will make man moral. It does not understand man in the full dimension of his spirit, and does not see that precisely because he is a child of God and made in God's image, he cannot be contained in, or easily checked by, either the harmony of nature or the prudence of reason.

It would, of course, be grossly unfair not to recognize that liberal Chrstianity made a genuine contribution to true Christianity by appropriating some of the achievements of this culture. Through some of these appropriations liberal Christianity purified Christian theology of some of its grievous historical errors. One of these was the insistence of Christian orthodoxy that a religious explanation of natural events was also a scientific explanation and obviated the necessity of tracing the natural sequence of events and their secondary causation.

But religion is constitutionally indifferent to the problem of secondary causation. This indifference becomes a sin when theology is made into a bad science and the sense of ultimate meaning and creation is allowed to obscure the problem of natural causation. In accommodating itself to the "scientific spirit," liberal Christianity therefore rightly clarified an ancient confusion, though it must be admitted that it was frequently betrayed thereby into a world view in which its essential theism was transmuted into a vague pantheism.

A second great gain of liberal Christianity, derived from the achievements of modern culture, was the application of the scientific historical method to its own records. Ethically, this emancipated Christianity from the necessity of regarding any moral attitude, fortuitously enshrined in its own canon, as final and authoritative. It permitted the Christian law of love to stand out in Christian ethics as the only final norm. Theologically, this scientific spirit saved Christianity from the corruption of the profound principle, *credo ut intelligam*, into a tyranny of theological authority over human reason. These gains of liberal Christianity must not be imperiled. It would be truer to say that they must not be sacrificed, though they will be imperiled. Frantic and hysterical retreats to orthodoxy are bound to imperil them. This advance must be protected against those who think it a gain to return to theological obscurantism from the shallows of a too simple rationalism.

But liberal Christianity quite obviously accepted the prejudices as well as the achievements of modern culture. It was pathetically eager to justify itself before the "modern mind" and failed to realize that this modern mind was involved in a very ancient human sin. It imagined itself the final mind. It thought of itself as God, the final arbiter of truth and destiny.

In seeking to persuade the modern mind that Christianity is respectable and intelligent, the liberals sacrificed most of the essential Christian positions. Christ was transmuted into the good man Jesus, who could charm all men to become as good as he was. The classic Christology of the God-man was repudiated, though innumerable reservations sought to hide the repudiation. It was not recognized that this absurd doctrine of the God-man Christ contains the whole essence of the Christian faith—its belief that God transcends history and yet makes himself known in history; that history measured by Christ is tragic and ends tragically for it crucifies Christ; that only God is able to resolve the conflict between what man is and what he ought to be, a conflict in which all men stand; that God cannot do this by simply wiping out history and transmuting it into eternity, but by redeeming history, but that the redemption of history involves more than persuading man to follow the law of God. It involves God's taking upon himself the inevitable violation of that law.

Liberal Christianity, in short, tended to follow modern culture in estimating both the stature and the virtue of man. It did not recognize that man is a spirit who can find a home neither in nature nor in reason, but only in God. The power of human self-transcendence (the true image of God) is such that man can and does break every restraint set by nature or reason. His very capacities are occasions for sin in him. It is because he is made in the image of God that man can be tempted to make himself God, to seek to overcome his natural insecurity by pretensions of power which involve him in more insecurity; to seek to hide the finiteness of his intelligence by pretensions of absolute truth, which involve him in cruel fanaticisms; to seek to transcend his insignificance by claims of importance which are both ridiculous and dangerous.

All these things man does, not because his pure mind is impeded by the inertia of his animal nature, but because he is the only animal who is involved in history and yet stands outside of it, the only creature who has a glimpse of the eternal beyond the finite and is incited to pretend an eternal significance for all his finite interests, values and ideals.

For this reason, the simple reinterpretation of the Kingdom of God into the law of progress, in the thought of liberal Christianity, is an equally serious betrayal of essential insights of the Christian faith to the prejudices of modern culture. Obviously there is progress of all kinds in human history, including progress in aerial bombing and the effective use of the radio for the dissemination of political lies. There is progress from immaturity to maturity in every field of endeavor. But there is not a single bit of evidence to prove that good triumphs over evil in this constant development of history. History points to a goal beyond itself, and not merely to an eternity which negates history.

This is what all biblical religion tries to say in words and symbols which outrage reason, as they must. For reason cannot contain this idea, though, if it is astute enough, it can uncover the absurdity of alternative propositions. Liberal Christianity sought to efface these irrationalities of biblical apocalypticism by discovering that Jesus had, indeed, some difficulty in freeing his thought about the Kingdom of God from outworn forms of Jewish thought, but that he is to be commended for almost achieving this desirable emancipation in the end and thus approximating what an enlightened modern man believes about history.

Yet from the standpoint of mere history the final story about this Jesus is that he was crucified. That he was raised from the dead and will come again in glory—*that* faith belongs to another dimension which is beyond history, and yet without which history would be either meaningless or filled with tragic meaning only.

Christianity, in short, faces the tremendous task of extricating itself from the prejudices and illusions of a culture which is rapidly sinking with the disruption of the civilization which gave it birth. This is not yet fully realized in America, because the prospects and hopes of our civilization are sufficiently brighter than in Europe to give liberal illusions a tougher vitality and a slower death here. This task of emancipation is a tremendous one, partly because liberalism as a culture is still superior to many of the cultures which threaten to displace it politically. It is certainly superior to the primitive and Nietzschian romanticism which expresses itself in fascist politics. It may even prove superior to socialism, if socialism sacrifices the achievements of democracy as it has done in Russia.

One of the real tragedies of our era is that the very democracy which is the great achievement of liberalism cannot be maintained if liberalism is not transcended as a culture. The problem of achieving economic justice is obviously more difficult than liberalism had imagined. The prerequisite of economic justice is a tolerable equilibrium of economic power, which in a technical age means the socialization of property. The excessive moralism of liberalism makes it impossible to see either the necessity of this end or the rigorous means which will be required to achieve it. Liberalism seems unable to move toward the economic democracy which is required to maintain its political democracy. Nor does it seem able to protect what is still left of its political democracy against the threat of a new barbarism; which is what makes the peace of Munich so significant.

If I believe that the Christian understanding of man could help solve some of these crucial issues and could conserve the best achievements of liberalism better than traditional liberalism can conserve them, I do not for that reason wish merely to hitch Christian faith to this or to that political task. Christianity faces ultimate issues of life which transcend all political vicissitudes and achievements. But the answer which Christian faith gives to man's ultimate perplexities and the hope which it makes possible in the very abyss of his despair, also throw light upon the immediate historical issues which he faces. Christianity is not a flight into eternity from the tasks and decisions of history. It is rather the power and the wisdom of God which makes decisions in history possible and which points to proximate goals in history which are usually obscured either by optimistic illusions or by the despair which followed upon the dissipation of these illusions. Christianity must therefore wage constant war, on the one hand against political religions which imagine some proximate goal and some conditioned good as man's final good, and on the other hand against an otherworldliness which by contrast gives these political religions a seeming validity.

For this reason, any new orthodoxy which seeks to persuade men that because all men must finally be made manifest before the judgment seat of Christ, they are not to regard the momentary judgments, the proximate goals and the relative values of history seriously, must be regarded as a heresy as dangerous as any simple optimism. In every experience of life, Christ appears in many guises to the believer. He is the judge in comparison with whom I am found to fall short and to be an unprofitable servant. He is the redeemer who gives my life a new center of loyalty and a new source of power. He is, however, also the law, the logos, the essential structure of life, which I must seek to obey, even though I fall short in my obedience. He is what I am essentially, and therefore what I ought to be.

Liberal Christianity emphasized that fact rather too simply. The new orthodoxy rightly insists that he is also what I can never be. He is therefore the source of my despair. Only in that despair and in repentance can he become the source of a new hope. This second emphasis is true enough. Only it will tempt us "to continue to sin that grace may abound" if we do not preserve what is genuinely Christian in liberal Christian moralism: the insistence that Christ is our law, our ideal, our norm, and the revelation of our essential being.

All this is not very autobiographical, after all. The only autobiographical note which I can add, in conclusion, is that such theological convictions which I hold today began to dawn upon me during the end of a pastorate in a great industrial city. They dawned upon me because the simple little moral homilies which were preached in that as in other cities, by myself and others, seemed completely irrelevant to the brutal facts of life in a great industrial center. Whether irrelevant or not, they were certainly futile. They did not change human actions or attitudes in any problem of collective behavior by a hair's breadth, though they may well have helped to preserve private amenities and to assuage individual frustrations.

These convictions which dawned in my pastorate have been further elaborated in a teaching position in a theological seminary. Greater leisure has given me opportunity to discover the main currents and emphases of the classical ages of Christian thought, and to find insights there which have been long neglected and which are yet absolutely essential to modern man, or indeed to man of any age.

However, since I am not so much scholar as preacher, I must confess that the gradual unfolding of my theological ideas has come not so much through study as through the pressure of world events. Whatever measure of Christian faith I hold today is due to the gradual exclusion of alternative beliefs through world history. As did Peter, I would preface my confession, "Thou hast words of eternal life," with the question, "Lord, to whom shall we go?" Even while imagining myself to be preaching the gospel, I had really experimented with many modern alternatives to Christian faith, until one by one they proved unavailing.

CHAPTER 5

Social Responsibilities

A. War

XXVII. INTRODUCTION

The devastation and brutality of World War II created a new world for Americans as well as for others. Many of the old questions seemed still relevant, while the old answers increasingly came to seem inappropriate and to miss the point of Auschwitz, the atomic bomb and international conflict, continuing industrialism and democratic aspirations. As the possibility of universal death became real for the first time in human history, questions of responsibility, engagement, and alienation became more and more pressing.

Early in World War II, before America's entrance into the conflict, an American poet accused his fellow writers and scholars in America of betraying their responsibilities to western civilization. Archibald Macleish (born in 1892) accused American intellectuals of having isolated themselves in a collective ivory tower. Such being the case, he asserted, contemporary American intellectuals had failed to understand the nature of the world in which they lived. Nazism was a war against mind and civilization as well as a war against the bodies of men. The fragmentation of intellectual life in America, he wrote, had destroyed intellectual responsibility. The older conception of the republic of letters—a concept that was applicable to many of the writers in the first decades of the twentieth century—was at least partly built on the assumption that the productive intellectuals had a responsibility to their society not merely as citizens, but also as intellectuals. American intellectuals had become less than whole men as a result of the bifurcation of intellectual life. The failure of America's scholars and writers to live up to the social responsibilities, coupled perhaps with a failure of nerve, would necessarily contribute to the destruction of those very things intellectuals in America, as elsewhere, believed to be most precious. "How could we sit back as spectators of a war against ourselves?" Macleish demanded to know.

XXVII.

Archibald Macleish

THE IRRESPONSIBLES

1940

History—if honest history continues to be written—will have one question to ask of our generation, people like ourselves. It will be asked of the books we have written, the carbon copies of our correspondence, the photographs of our faces, the minutes of our meetings in the famous rooms before the portraits of our spiritual begetters. The question will be this: Why did the scholars and writers of our generation in this country, witnesses as they were to the destruction of writing and of scholarship in great areas of Europe and to the exile and the imprisonment and murder of men whose crime was scholarship and writing—witnesses also to the rise in their own country of the same destructive forces with the same impulses, the same motives, the same means—why did the scholars and the writers of our generation in America fail to oppose those forces while they could —while there was still time and still place to oppose them with the arms of scholarship and writing?

It is a question the historians will ask with interest—the gentle, detached, not altogether loving interest with which historians have always questioned the impotent spirits of the dead. Young men working in the paper rubbish of our lives, the old journals, the marginal notations, the printed works, will discover (or so they will think) that the scholars and the writers of our generation in this country had been warned of danger as men were rarely warned before. They will discover (or so they will think) that the common inherited culture of the West, by which alone our scholars and our writers lived, had been attacked in other countries with a stated and explicit purpose to destroy. They will discover that that purpose had been realized. They will discover that a similar purpose backed by similar forces, created by similar conditions, was forming here. And it will seem to them strange—ironical and strange—that the great

SOURCE. Archibald Macleish, *The Irresponsibles,* New York: Duell, Sloan and Pearce, 1940, pp. 3–34. Reprinted with the permission of the Houghton Mifflin Company. Copyright 1940 by Archibald Macleish.

mass of American scholars and American writers made no effort to defend either themselves or the world by which they lived.

They will make of course the necessary reservations. They will note that societies of scholars and associations of writers adopted resolutions declaring their devotion to civilization. They will note that certain young novelists and poets, the most generous and gallant of their time, unable to endure the outrage and injustice, gave up their lives as writers and enlisted in the hopeless armies to fight brutality with force. But of those who truly faced this danger not with their bodies but their minds, of those who fought the enemies of the intellect with the weapons of the intellect, devoting to that warfare all the strength, all the imagination, all the resources of courage and inventiveness, all the watchfulness by day and night, all the last reserves of hope and skill and pain which men must use whose lives and more than lives are put in danger—of those who fought this danger with the weapons by which this danger could be overcome, they will record the names of very few. And they will ask their question. Why did we, scholars and writers in America in this time, we who had been warned of our danger not only by explicit threats but by explicit action, why did we not fight this danger while the weapons we used best —the weapons of ideas and words—could still be used against it?

It is not a question for which we are altogether unprepared. We have been writing out our answer for many years now in action and inaction, in words and in silence—in learned articles in the scientific journals and in controversial articles in the general magazines, in blank faces after the passionate words, in bored eyes refusing to believe. The answer we have prepared, the answer we have written out for history to find, is the answer Leonardo is said to have given Michelangelo when Michelangelo blamed him for his indifference to the misfortunes of the Florentines. It is the answer of our kind at many other times and places. "Indeed," said Leonardo, "indeed the study of beauty has occupied my whole heart." The study of beauty, the study of history, the study of science, has occupied our whole hearts and the misfortunes of our generation are none of our concern. They are the practical and political concern of practical and political men but the concern of the scholar, the concern of the artist, is with other, purer, more enduring things.

This is the answer we have written down for history to find. I doubt whether it will satisfy the ironic men who come to plague us on that waterfront where Teresias was made to drink the blood and answer.

I think indeed it will not satisfy them. For it has not satisfied ourselves. We say with great firmness and authority, speaking by our words and by our silence, that the misfortunes of our generation are economic and political misfortunes from which the scholar can safely hold himself apart. We say this with all the authority of the political scientists of the past to whom the misfortunes of the people were always political and economic and of no concern to the poet, the pure scholar, the artist intent upon his art. We say it also with the authority of the political scientists of the present to whom all phenomena of whatever kind are, by hypothesis, economic and political. But though we say it we do not believe it. For we have observed these misfortunes. They have been acted out for us to see. And what we have seen is this: that the misfortunes of our time are not the misfortunes the philosophers, the theorists, the political scientists have described to us. They are not the practical concern of the practical man and therefore matters of indifference to the scholar. On the contrary, it is the practical man and the practical man alone—the man whose only care is for his belly and his roof—who can safely be indifferent to these troubles. The things he lives by are not menaced. And it is precisely the scholar, the poet—the man whose care is for the structures of the intellect, the houses of the mind—whose heart is caught. For it is the scholar's goods which are in danger.

It is perhaps because we have seen this and yet refuse to see it—because we know one thing and yet continue to declare another—that our minds are so confused and our counsels so bewildering. Nothing is more characteristic of the intellectuals of our generation than their failure to understand what it is that is happening to their world. And nothing explains that failure as precisely as their unwillingness to see what they have seen and to know what they do truly know. They have seen the crisis of their time—they have seen it spelled out, played out, fought out as few observers ever before in history saw the tragedy exposed. They know its ending. And yet they continue to pretend they do not know. They continue to speak of the crisis of their time as though the war in Europe were that crisis—and the war, they say, is no concern of theirs. They continue to speak of the crisis as though the imperialistic maneuvers, the struggles for markets, the propaganda in the news- papers and the radio, were the crisis—and the maneuvers of imperialism, the propaganda of the press and the struggles for trade they say are no concern of theirs. And yet they know—they know very well because they have seen—that these things are not the crisis but merely its reflections in the mirrors of action. They know that behind the war, behind the diplomatic gestures, behind the black print on the page and the hysterical voices on the air there is something deeper and more dangerous—more dangerous to *them*. They know that it is a condition of men's minds which has produced these things—a condition which existed and exists not only in Europe but in other parts of the world as well and not least in our own country. And they know that this condition of men's minds is not a practical, a political, phenomenon of no concern to the scholar and the man of thought but something very different.

It is not, for example, a matter of purely practical and political interest that great numbers of men in various parts of the world wish passionately and even violently to give up the long labor of liberty and to surrender their wills and their bodies and even their minds to the will of a leader, so that they may achieve at least the dignity of order, at least the dignity of obedience. It is not a matter of purely practical and political significance that whole nations of men have gladly and willingly released themselves not only from their rights as individuals but from their responsibilities as individuals so that they are no longer compelled to feel or to respect the individual humanity of others—or to feel or to respect the things that individual humanity has, over many centuries, created. It is not a matter of purely practical and political importance that governments which once, whatever they may have practiced, protested a respect for learning and the arts, should now permit themselves to show not only the power but worse, far worse, the *willingness,* the *purpose,* to enslave both learning and the arts. It is not a matter of purely practical and political importance that societies which once made part of the community of Western culture should now attempt by murder and outrage and exile to root out that culture and to replace it with private and parochial sciences and private and parochial arts so that frontiers are armed, for the first time in the history of the West, not only along the rivers and the mountains and the boundaries of nations, but across the common earth of culture, the free land that was never fenced before.

I think no honest man will say that these are matters of practical and political significance alone. I think any man who considers with coolness, and without the preconceptions of the dogmas, the character of the crisis of his time will admit, because he will have no choice but to admit, that this crisis is in essence a cultural crisis—a revolt of certain classes, certain conditions of men against the inherited culture of the West and against all common culture—a revolt by no means limited to those nations alone where it has been successful. Wars we have had before—many wars; murder also; inquisition of scholars; torture of askers; suppression and mutilation of truth. But in the past these things have been done, however hypocritically, in the name of truth, in the name of humanity—even in the name of God. The forms of culture were preserved—and in the preservation of a civilization as in the preservation of an art the forms are everything. What is new and unexampled in the times we live in is *the repudiation of the forms.* What is new is a cynical brutality which considers moral self-justification unnecessary and therefore—and this is perhaps its worst indecency— dispenses even with the filthy garment of the hypocrite. To use brutality and force, not in the name of Right nor in the name of God, but in the name of force alone, is to destroy the self-respect and therefore the dignity of the individual life without which the existence of art or learning is inconceivable. To lie, not in the name of truth, but in the name of lies, is to destroy the common basis of communication without which a common culture cannot exist and a work of learning or of art becomes unintelligible.

The truth is—the plain and simple truth of which we have so many painful evidences—that the disorder of our time, whatever else it may now be or may become, is in its essentials a revolt against the common culture of the West. For against what but the common culture did this disorder continue to struggle in Germany long after it had overthrown the former state? There was no domestic danger for it to fear. Against what but the Western respect for the dignity of the individual was aimed the long series of outrages against the Jews? The Jews were impotent when they were subjected to the worst abuses. Against what but the Western respect for the common, the nationless, creation of the artist was aimed the destruction of the work of men like Thomas Mann? Thomas Mann had already been repudiated by his people when they accepted the government of his enemies. Against what but the Western belief in the wholeness of Western civilization was aimed the assault upon a church which was no longer a danger to any ruler and the fabrication of a paganism which needed only the blond sopranos on the ends of wires to be Wagner at his worst?

Intellectuals in America and elsewhere—writers, scientists, the men of learning—have attempted to ignore these questions. They have pretended to themselves that the burning of books, the exiling of artists, the invention of mythologies were merely incidents—afterthoughts— decorations: that the true crisis was the crisis of food, the crisis of arms, the crisis created by political forces, by economic collapse,—that they had, and needed have, no truck with it. They have been wrong. These things are not incidents. They are not afterthoughts. They are the essential nature of the revolution of our age. For without this attack upon the habits of the mind, the reliances of the spirit, that revolution could not, by any possibility, have succeeded.

The revolution of our age—the revolution which has finally emerged and declared itself in action—is not the great revolution of the masses of which generous men once dreamed: and which other and less generous men have now so meanly and so bloodily betrayed. The revolution of the masses was a revolution which proposed to set up one faith against another faith, one culture against another culture: a faith in man, a faith in the power of the patterns of men's lives, against a faith in institutions and in money; a culture of the people against a culture of the exploiters of the people. The revolution which has finally and successfully emerged in action has no such faith and no such culture.

It is a revolution of negatives, a revolution of the defeated, a revolution of the dispossessed, a revolution of despair. It is a revolution created out of misery by dread of yet more misery, a revolution created out of disorder by terror of disorder. It is a revolution of gangs, a revolution *against*. And the enemy it is against, the enemy it must destroy, is the enemy which, in all times and in all civilizations, has stood against the revolutions of the gangs—the rule of moral law, the rule of spiritual authority, the rule of intellectual truth. To establish the negative revolutions, the revolutions of which the only aim is power, the revolutions which have no means but force, it is necessary first to destroy the authority of the unseen sayings of the mind. It is necessary to destroy the things the mind has made. Caliban in the miserable and besotted swamp is the symbol of this revolution. As long as the unseen beauty in the air retains its voices and its seductive music and its stinging whips the revolutions of the gangs are clumsy, blundering, grotesque and foolish. They can bellow and threaten and boast and gesture with their arms but in the end the invisible voices of the air, the invisible power of the ideal will master them. They have one hope of success and only one—the destruction of the whole system of ideas, the whole respect for truth, the whole authority of excellence which places law above force, beauty above cruelty, singleness above numbers.

It is the distinction of our time—perhaps unhappily its most memorable distinction—that it and it alone has provided the formula by which this overthrow could be achieved. Only in our time has the revolution of the gangs discovered a strategy and a leadership brutal enough, cynical enough, cunning enough to destroy the entire authority of the inherited culture and thereafter to seal the doors against the searching and the asking of the scholar's mind, the artist's mind, so that the revolution of force, the revolution of despair could flower and fulfill its possibilities. Only in our time has the revolution of the gangs shown itself openly and admittedly as the thing it is—a revolution of cruelty, cunning and despair against the authority and the discipline of the mind.

It is to this disorder and not to some political and partisan dissension, not to some accidental economic breakdown—practical and political matters for the men of politics and practice—it is to this direct, explicit and intentional attack upon the scholar's world and the scholar's life and the scholar's work that American scholarship has been indifferent. Or if not indifferent, then inactive, merely watchful—fearful, watchful and inactive. And it is there that history will place its questions.

How could we sit back as spectators of a war against ourselves?

Did we suppose the newly discovered techniques of deception, of falsehood as a military force, of strategic fraud, were incapable of reaching us—incapable of crossing sea water? We had seen their methods drive their conquests through the countries of the world more rapidly than Alexander or Napoleon or Tamerlane or any other conqueror or killer.

Or was it something else we thought? Did we believe others would defend us? Did we think the issue was an issue of strategy, an issue of battles? Did we think the British and the French would win their war and so defend us? But we knew very well, because we had seen, that this war was not a war fought in the open on the military front, but a war fought in the back street and the dark stair—a war fought within the city, within the house, within the mind—a war of treason: a war of corruption: a war of lies. And against treason and corruption and lies, battle fleets and grand armies are impotent.

The questions answer themselves and yet provide no answer. For if we did not believe we were safe by sea water, or if we did not believe others would save us, then our failure to act in our own defense becomes a curious thing. What has prevented us from acting? Lack of courage? It is difficult to indict a generation for lack of courage. Lack of wisdom? There is wisdom enough in other matters.

I think, speaking only of what I have seen myself and heard—I think it is neither lack of courage nor lack of wisdom, but a different reason which has prevented our generation of intellectuals in this country from acting in their own defense. I think it is the organization of the intellectual life of our time. Specifically, I think it is the division and therefore the destruction of intellectual responsibility. The men of intellectual duty, those who should have been responsible for action, have divided themselves into two castes, two cults—the scholars and the writers. Neither accepts responsibility for the common culture or for its defense.

There was a time a century ago, two centuries ago, when men who practiced our professions would have accepted this responsibility without an instant's hesitation. A century ago the professions of the writer and the scholar were united in the single profession of the man of letters and the man of letters was responsible in everything that touched the mind. He was a man of wholeness of purpose, of singleness of intention—a single intellectual champion, admittedly responsible for the defense of the inherited tradition, avowedly partisan of its practice. Where those who practice our several professions divide the learned world and the creative world between them in irresponsible and neutral states, the man of letters inhabited both learning and the world of letters like an empire.

He was a man of learning whose learning was employed not for its own sake in a kind of academic narcissism but for the sake of decent living in his time. He was a writer whose writing was used not to mirror an abstract and unrelated present but to illuminate that present by placing it in just relation to its past. He was therefore and necessarily a man who admitted a responsibility for the survival and vitality of the common and accumulated experience of the mind, for this experience was to him the air he breathed, the perspective of his thinking. Learning to him was no plump pigeon carcass to be picked at for his private pleasure and his private fame but a profession practiced for the common good. Writing was not an ornament, a jewel, but a means to ends, a weapon, the most powerful of weapons, a weapon to be used. Whatever threatened learning or the ends of learning challenged the man of letters. Whatever struck at truth or closed off question or defiled an art or violated decency of thinking struck at him. And he struck back with every weapon masters of the word could find to strike with. Milton defending freedom of the mind in sentences which outlive every name of those who struck at freedom, Voltaire displaying naked to the grin of history the tyrants who were great until he made them small, Bartolomé de las Casas gentling cruel priests and brutal captains with the dreadful strokes of truth—Las Casas, Milton and Voltaire were men of letters—men who confessed an obligation to defend the disciplines of thought not in their own but in the general interest.

Had men like these been living in our time—had the intellectuals of our time been whole and loyal—it would, I think, have been impossible for the revolution of the gangs to have succeeded where success has been most dangerous—in the perversion of the judgments of the mind. Murder is not absolved of immorality by committing murder. Murder is absolved of immorality by bringing men to think that murder is not evil. This only the perversion of the mind can bring about. And the perversion of the mind is only possible when those who should be heard in its defense are silent.

They are silent in our time because there are no voices which accept responsibility for speaking. Even the unimaginable indecencies of propaganda—even the corruption of the word itself in Germany and Russia and in Spain and elsewhere—even the open triumph of the lie, produced no answer such as Voltaire in his generation would have given. And for this reason—that the man who could have been Voltaire, who could have been Las Casas, does not live: the man of intellectual *office,* the man of intellectual *calling,* the man who *professes* letters— professes an obligation as a servant of the mind to defend the mind's integrity against every physical power—professes an obligation to defend the labors of the mind and the structures it has created and the means by which it lives, not only privately and safely in his study, not only strictly and securely in the controversies of the learned press, but publicly and at the public risk and danger of his life. He does not exist because the man of letters no longer exists. And the man of letters no longer exists because he has been driven from our world and from our time by the division of his kingdom. The single responsibility, the wholeness of function of the man of letters, has been replaced by the divided function, the mutual antagonism, the isolated irresponsibility of two figures, each free of obligation, each separated from a portion of his duty—the scholar and the writer.

Why this substitution has come about—whether because the methods of scientific inquiry, carried over into the humanities, destroyed the loyalties and habits of the mind or for some other reason, I leave to wiser men to say. The point is that there has been a substitution. The country of the man of letters has been divided between his heirs. The country that was once the past and present—the past made useful to the reasons of the present, the present understood against the knowledge of the past—the country that was once the past and present brought together in the mind, is now divided into past on one side, present on the other.

Past is the scholar's country; present is the writer's. The writer sees the present on the faces of the world and leaves the past to rot in its own rubbish. The scholar digs his ivory cellar in the ruins of the past and lets the present sicken as it will. A few exceptions noted here and there—men like Thomas Mann—the gulf between these countries is complete. And the historical novels fashionable at the moment, the vulgarizations of science, the digests of philosophy only define its depth as a plank across a chasm makes the chasm deeper. That it should be necessary to throw such flimsy flights from one side to the other of the learned world shows how deeply and disastrously the split was made.

That scholarship suffers or that writing suffers by the change is not asserted. Scholarship may be more scientific; writing may be purer. Indeed there are many who believe, and I among them, that the time we live in has produced more first-rate writers than any but the very greatest ages, and there are scholars of a scholarship as hard, as honest, as devoted as any we have known. But excellence of scholarship and writing are not now in question. What matters now is the defense of culture—the defense truly, and in the most literal terms, of civilization as men have known it for the last two thousand years. And there the substitution for the man of letters of the scholar and the writer, however pure the scholarship, however excellent the writing, is a tragic and immeasurable loss. For neither the modern scholar nor the modern writer admits responsibility for the defense. They assert on the contrary, each in his particular way, an irresponsibility as complete as it is singular.

The irresponsibility of the scholar is the irresponsibility of the scientist upon whose laboratory insulation he has patterned all his work. The scholar has made himself as indifferent to values, as careless of significance, as bored with meanings as the chemist. He is a refugee from consequences, an exile from the responsibilities of moral choice. He has taught himself to say with the physicist—and with some others whom history remembers—"What is truth?" He has taught himself with the biologist to refrain from judgments of better or worse. His words of praise are the laboratory words—objectivity—detachment—dispassion. His pride is to be scientific, neuter, skeptical, detached—superior to final judgment or absolute belief. In his capacity as scholar the modern scholar does not occupy the present. In his capacity as scholar he loves the word—but only the word which entails no judgments, involves no decisions, accomplishes no actions. Where the man of letters of other centuries domesticated the past within the rustling of the present, making it stand among us like the meaning of a statue among trees, the modern scholar in his capacity as scholar leaves the present and returns across the past where all the men are marble. Where the man of letters of other centuries quarried his learning from the past to build the present the modern scholar quarries his learning from the past to dig the quarries.

It is not for nothing that the modern scholar invented the Ph.D. thesis as his principal contribution to literary form. The Ph.D. thesis is the perfect image of his world. It is work done for the sake of doing work—perfectly conscientious, perfectly laborious, perfectly irresponsible. The modern scholar at his best and worst is both these things—perfectly conscientious, laborious and competent: perfectly irresponsible for the saving of his world. He remembers how in the Civil Wars in England the scholars, devoted only to their proper tasks, founded the Royal Society. He remembers how through other wars and other dangers the scholars kept the lamp of learning lighted. He does not consider that the scholars then did other things as well as trim the lamp wicks. He does not consider either that the dangers change and can be greater. He has his work to do. He has his book to finish. He hopes the war will not destroy the manuscripts he works with. He is the pure, the perfect type of irresponsibility—the man who acts as though the fire could not burn him because he has no business with the fire. He knows because he cannot help but know, reading his papers, talking to his friends—he knows this fire has consumed the books, the spirit, everything he lives by, flesh itself—in other countries. He knows this but he will not know. It's not his business. Whose business is it then? He will not answer even that. He has his work to do. He has his book to finish . . .[sic]

The writer's irresponsibility is of a different kind. Where the modern scholar escapes from the adult judgments of the mind by taking the disinterested man of science as his model, the modern writer escapes by imitation of the artist. He practices his writing as a painter does his painting. He thinks as artist—which is to say he thinks without responsibility to anything but truth of feeling. He observes as artist—which is to say that he observes with honesty and truthfulness and without comment. His devotion, as with every honest painter, is devotion to the thing observed, the actual thing, the thing without its consequences or its antecedents, naked of judgment, stripped of causes and effects, The invisible world, the intellectual world, the world of the relation of ideas, the world of judgments, of values, the world in which truth is good and lies are evil—this world has no existence to the honest artist or to the honest writer who takes the artist for his model. His duty is to strip all this away—to strip away the moral preference, the intellectual association.

He sees the world as a god sees it—without morality, without care, without judgment. People look like this. People act like that. He shows them looking, acting. It is not his business why they look so, why they act so. It is enough that he should "make them happen." This is the whole test, the whole criterion, of the work of the writer-artist—to show things as they "really happen"; to write with such skill, such penetration of the physical presence of the world, that the action seen, the action described, will "really happen" on his page. If he concerns himself with motive at all he concerns himself with the "real" motive, meaning the discreditable motive which the actor conceals from himself. His most searching purpose is to find, not the truth of human action, but the low-down, the discreditable explanation which excuses him from care. The suggestion that there are things in the world—ideas, conceptions, ways of thinking—which the writer-artist should defend from attack: the suggestion above all that he was under obligation to defend the inherited culture, would strike him as ridiculous.

Artists do not save the world. They practice art. They practice it as Goya practiced it among the cannon in Madrid. And if this war is not Napoleon in Spain but something even worse than that? They practice art. Or they put the art aside and take a rifle and go out and fight. But not *as artists*. The artist does not fight. The artist's obligations are obligations to his art. His responsibiliy—his one responsibility—is to his art. He has no other. Not even when his art itself, his chance to practice it, his need to live where it is practiced, may be in danger. The writer-artist will write a bloody story about the expense of blood. He will present the face of agony as it has rarely been presented. But not even then will he take the weapon of his words and carry it to the barricades of intellectual warfare, to the storming of belief, the fortifying of conviction where alone this fighting can be won.

There are examples in history of civilizations made impotent by excess of culture. No one, I think, will say of us that we lost our intellectual liberties on this account. But it may well be said, and said with equally ironic emphasis, that the men of thought, the men of learning in this country were deceived and rendered impotent by the best they knew. To the scholar impartiality, objectivity, detachment were ideal qualities he taught himself laboriously and painfully to acquire. To the writer objectivity and detachment were his writer's pride. Both subjected themselves to inconceivable restraints, endless disciplines to reach these ends. And both succeeded. Both writers and scholars freed themselves of the subjective passions, the emotional preconceptions which color conviction and judgment. Both writers and scholars freed themselves of the personal responsibility associated with personal choice. They emerged free, pure and single into the antiseptic air of objectivity. And by that sublimation of the mind they prepared the mind's disaster.

If it is a consolation to the philosophers of earlier civilizations to know that they lost the things they loved because of the purity of their devotion, then perhaps this consolation will be ours as well. I doubt if we will profit by it or receive much praise.

B. Cold War

XXVIII. INTRODUCTION

The threat of Communism, as understood by literate and thoughtful Americans, required a continuing search for principles of foreign relations that would achieve at least some degree of verisimilitude. The growth of Soviet power made it plain that the old American assumption of virtual omnipotence was disabling and dangerous. The painful search for the possible in America's foreign affairs was conducted with particular clarity by George Kennan (born in 1904) in a series of articles in *Foreign Affairs*. The article reprinted here is Kennan's sermon to America about the need to reconstruct an important part of the national mythology so that our actions would be guided by predictable and desirable consequences, not by a continued search for ways by which America could reorganize the world. Kennan asked that Americans consider what kind of Russia would be possible and desirable, as those terms would be defined by Americans. He found it imperative to say that there was no necessary danger or evil in Russians being Russians. Although he hoped that America would abandon its traditional posture of moral superiority in foreign affairs, Kennan made it clear that he was himself deeply enmeshed in the American tradition.

His own faith assumed that evil could not endure, and that the evil aspects of the Soviet Union would therefore inevitably collapse because of their own moral deficiencies. Returning almost full circle in American intellectual history, Kennan's essential position was that America should become a model to the rest of the world, the same position that John Winthrop had taken in 1630. The policy of containment, as elaborated by Kennan, rested on the assumption that the Kremlin walls would crack in the foreseeable future. It was America's responsibility both to herself and to the world, therefore, to frustrate the spread of Communism long enough for what Kennan believed to be "the internal contradictions" of the regime to begin their corrosive work. The faith supporting Kennan's position made it more, rather than less, intimately bound to the traditional American conception of foreign affairs. It may perhaps be that the intense Americanism of Kennan's position contributed to the influence he had on the formulation of American policy.

XXVIII.

George F. Kennan
AMERICA AND THE RUSSIAN FUTURE
1951

The very virulence with which Americans reject the outlook and practice of those who now hold power in the Kremlin implies in the strongest possible way the belief in, and desire for, an alternative—for some other Russian outlook and some other set of practices in Russia to take the place of those we know today. Yet we may be permitted to ask whether there is any clear image in our minds of what that outlook

SOURCE. George F. Kennan, "America and the Russian Future," *Foreign Affairs*, Vol. XXIX, No. 3 (April, 1951), pp. 351–370. Copyright 1951 by the Council on Foreign Relations, Inc., New York. Reprinted with the permission of *Foreign Affairs*.

and those practices might be, and of the ways by which Americans might promote progress toward them. At the present time, in particular, when the coexistence of the two systems on the same planet has led to such immense strains and anxieties everywhere, and to so much despair of its successful continuation, there is a tendency on the part of many people to permit the image of a different and more acceptable Russia to become eclipsed by, or even identified with, the question of victory or defeat in a future war. Some Americans are already reverting, merely in contemplation of a possible war, to the American bad habit of assuming that there is something final and positive about a military decision—that it is the ending of something, and the happy ending, rather than a beginning.

There could, of course, be no greater error than this, quite apart from any consideration of the blood and sacrifice which war involved. A war against Soviet power which could be said to be relatively successful militarily . . . would in itself assure little or nothing in the way of progress toward the achievement of the sort of alternative we might wish; at the most it would only make more immediate various aspects of a problem which already exists and which every American who objects to Soviet behavior must, in consistency, have in mind anyway, war or no war. That is the problem of the kind of Russia which we would prefer to see; the kind with which we ourselves could, let us say, live easily; the kind which would permit the existence of a much more stable world order; the kind to which it would be both realistic and suitable for us to aspire.

This problem of the possibility of a different and preferable Russia is not really a question of war or peace. War in itself will not bring about such a Russia. Indeed it would be most unlikely to lead in that direction unless accompanied by many wise and strenuous efforts besides the military one. And a continued absence of major war will not preclude the coming of a different Russia. All of that depends upon a great many other things which would have to be done by a great many people, either in war or in peace. Not all of these things can be done by Americans. So far as direct action is concerned, the bulk of them cannot be. But our possibilities for influencing the outcome are significant; and we must remember that there may be times when our efforts may be capable of swinging the balance one way or the other. For that reason our own relationship to the Russian future is something worth our most strenuous thought and attention. And in our efforts to determine it, two things are of major importance: (1) that we should know what we want; and (2) that we should know how to conduct ourselves in order to facilitate, rather than to impede, the coming into being of what we want. The word "facilitate" is used advisedly; for we are dealing here with a foreign country, and our role can be at best a marginal one, supplementary to a far more important role which others must play.

What sort of Russia would we like to see before us, as our partner in the world community?

Perhaps the first thing to get straight here is the sort of Russia there is no use looking for. And such a Russia—the kind we may *not* look for—is easy to describe and envisage, for it would be a capitalistic and liberal-democratic one, with institutions closely resembling those of our own republic.

If we look first at the question of the economic system, we see at once that Russia has scarcely known private enterprise as we are familiar with it in this country. Even in pre-Revolutionary times the Russian Government always had a close hold on a number of economic activities, notably transportation and the armament industry, which in our country have traditionally, or at least normally, been private. . . . Whatever private enterprise may have been in Tsarist Russia, it had not yet come to hold anything resembling the respect and significance in the eyes of the people that it had acquired in the older mercantile countries by the beginning of this century. Perhaps with time it would have. The prospects were steadily improving. Examples of efficient and progressive industrial management existed in Russia before the Revolution, and were increasing.

But all this, it must be remembered, was a long time ago. Thirty-three years have elapsed since the Revolution. Those years, in the strenuous conditions of Soviet life, have witnessed the passing of a full generation. Of the people capable of influencing the course of events in Russia today only an insignificant minority recall the pre-Revolutionary days at all. The younger generation has no comprehension or concept of anything but the state capitalism that the Soviet regime has enforced. And what we are talking about here is something not even in the present but in the indefinite future.

Bearing all this in mind, we see that there is no Russian national understanding which would permit the early establishment in Russia of anything resembling the private enterprise system as we know it.

This is not to say that some such understanding will not some day develop. It may, if circumstances are favorable. But it will never be a system identical to our own. And no one will usefully be able to force the pace, particularly no one from the outside.

It is true that the term "Socialism" has been used for so many years in close intimacy with the term "Soviet" that it is now hateful to many people, both within and without the borders of the Soviet Union. But it is easy to draw wrong conclusions from this phenomenon. It is conceivable that retail trade and the performance of the small individual services which have so much to do with the pleasantness of daily life may some day return in large measure to private hands in Russia. In agriculture, as we shall see presently, there will certainly be an extensive return to private ownership and initiative. There is a further possibility that the system of mutual production-cooperation by groups of artisans (*artels*)—a system peculiarly rooted in Russian tradition and under-standing—may some day point the way to economic institutions which could represent a highly important and promising innovation in the approach to modern problems of labor and capital. But large sections of economic life known to us as the normal provinces of private enterprise will almost certainly remain in national hands for a long time to come in Russia, regardless of the identity of the political authority. This should surprise no American, nor should it offend any. There is no reason why the form of Russian economic life, beyond certain major exceptions that will be mentioned below, should be considered a matter of vital concern to the outside world.

Agriculture deserves a special place in our thinking on this subject. Agricultural enterprise is the Achilles heel of the Soviet system. Left in private hands, it constitutes a concession to human freedom and individual initiative—a concession which the true Bolshevik finds abhorrent. Forcibly collectivized, it requires an elaborate apparatus of restraint if the farmer is to be made to stay on his land and to produce. The forced collectivization of the farming population is probably today the greatest single cause of discontent in the Soviet Union, except possibly the excessive cruelty of the police, with which it is intimately connected. It may be taken for granted that one of the first acts of any future progressive authority in Russia would be to abolish this hated system of agricultural serfdom and to restore to the farmers the pride and incentives of private land ownership and free disposal of agricultural commodities. Collective farms may continue to exist; and they probably will, for the most abhorrent feature of the present system is not the concept of producer-cooperation itself but the element of restraint that underlies its application. The collectives of the future will be voluntary cooperatives, however, not shotgun marriages.

Turning to the political side, it was said above that we could not expect to see the emergence of a liberal-democratic Russia along American patterns. This cannot be too strongly emphasized. It does not mean that future Russian regimes will necessarily be unliberal. There is no liberal tradition finer than the strain which has existed in the Russia of the past. Many Russian individuals and groups of this day are deeply imbued with that tradition, and will do all in their power to make it the dominant element in the Russian future. In that effort, we may wish them well without reservation. But we will be doing them no favor if we permit ourselves to expect too much to happen too fast, or look to them to produce anything resembling our own institutions. These Russian liberals will have no easy road to walk. They will find in their country a young generation that has known nothing but Soviet power and has been trained to think subconsciously in the terms of that power even when it has resented and hated it. Many features of the Soviet system will stick, if only for the reason that everything has been destroyed which might seem to have constituted an alternative to them. And some features will deserve to stick, for no system that lasts over decades is entirely without merits. Any program of government for a future Russia will have to adjust itself to the fact that there has been this Soviet interlude, and that it has left its positive marks as well as its negative ones. And no members of future Russian governments will be aided by doctrinaire and impatient well-wishers in the West who look to them, just because they are seeking a decent alternative to what we know today as Bolshevism, to produce in short order a replica of the Western democratic dream.

Above all, it behooves us Americans, in this connection, to repress, and if possible to extinguish once and for all, our inveterate tendency to judge others by the extent to which they contrive to be like ourselves. In our relations with the people of Russia it is important, as it has never been important before, for us to recognize that our institutions may not have relevance for people living in other climes and conditions and that there can be social structures and forms of government in no way resembling our own and yet not deserving of censure. . . .

Forms of government are forged mainly in the fire of practice, not in the vacuum of theory. They respond to national character and to national realities. There is a great good in the Russian national character, and the realities of that country scream out today for a form of administration more considerate of that good. Let us hope that it will come. But when Soviet power has run its course, or when its personalities and spirit begin to change (for the ultimate outcome could be of one or the other), let us not hover nervously over the people who come after, applying litmus papers daily to their political complexions to find out whether they answer to our concept of "democratic." Give them time; let them be Russians; let them work out their internal problems in their own manner. The ways by which peoples advance toward dignity and enlightenment in government are things that constitute the deepest and most intimate processes of national life. There is nothing less understandable to foreigners, nothing in which foreign interference can do less good. There are, as we shall see presently, certain features of the future Russian state that *are* of genuine concern to the outside world. But these do not include the form of government itself, provided only that it keep within certain well-defined limits, beyond which lies totalitarianism.

What, then, do they include? To what kind of a Russia may we reasonably and justly look forward? What attributes are we, as responsible members of the world community, entitled to look for in the personality of a foreign state, and of Russia in particular?

We may look, in the first place, for a Russian government which, in contrast to the one we know today, would be tolerant, communicative and forthright in its relations with other states and peoples. It would not take the ideological position that its own purposes cannot finally prosper unless all systems of government not under its control are subverted and eventually destroyed. It would dispense with this paranoiac suspiciousness we know so well, and consent to view the outside world, ourselves included, as it really is and always has been: neither entirely good nor entirely bad, neither entirely to be trusted nor entirely to be mistrusted. . . . It would consent to recognize that this outside world is not really preoccupied with diabolical plots to invade Russia and inflict injuries on the Russian people. Viewing the outside world in this way, the statesmen of a future Russia could approach it with tolerance and forbearance and practical good humor, defending their national interests as statesmen must, but not assuming that these can be furthered only at the expense of the interests of others, and vice versa.

No one asks for a naive and childlike confidence; no one asks for a fatuous enthusiasm for all that is foreign; no one asks that the genuine and legitimate differences of interest which have always marked, and will always continue to mark, the relations beweeen peoples be ignored. We must expect Russian national interests not only to continue to exist but to be vigorously and confidently asserted. But in a regime that we could recognize as an improvement over what we know today we would expect that this would be done in an atmosphere of emotional sanity and moderation: that the foreign representative would not continue to be viewed and treated as one possessed of the devil; that it would be conceded that there might be such a thing as innocent and legitimate curiosity about a foreign country, which could be permitted to be gratified without fatal detriment to that country's national life; that it would be recognized that there might be individual foreign business aspirations which did not aim at the destruction of the Russian state; that it would be admitted, finally, that persons desirous of travelling across international borders might have, and are even apt to have, motives other than "espionage, sabotage and diversion"—such trivial motives, in fact, as the enjoyment of travel or the peculiar impulses that move people to wish to visit relatives from time to time. In short, we may ask that the grotesque system of anachronisms known as the Iron Curtain be lifted from the world, and that the Russian people, who have so much to give and so much to receive as mature members of the world community, cease to be insulted by a policy that treats them as children, too immature to have normal contact with the adult world, too undependable to be let out alone.

Secondly, while recognizing that the internal system of government is in all essential respects Russia's own business and may well depart drastically from our own, we are entitled to expect that the exercise of governmental authority will stop short of that fairly plain line beyond which lies totalitarianism. Specifically, we may expect that any regime which claims to contrast favorably with that which we have before us today will refrain from enslaving its own labor—industrial and agricultural. There is a reason for this: a reason even more solid than the shock we experience at witnessing the sickening details of this type of oppression. When a regime sets out to enslave its own working population in this way, it requires for the maintenance of the arrangement so vast an apparatus of coercion that the imposition of the Iron Curtain follows almost automatically. No ruling group likes to admit that it can govern its people only by regarding and treating them as criminals. For this reason there is always a tendency to justify internal oppression by pointing to the menacing iniquity of the outside world. And the outside world must be portrayed, in these circumstances, as very iniquitous indeed—iniquitous to the point of caricature. Nothing short of this will do. Carefully hiding the realities behind the Iron Curtain, the regime depicts "abroad" to its own people in every lurid hue of hideousness, as anxious mothers attempt to intimidate their children and fortify their own authority by embroidering the image of that sinister "something" which "will get you if you don't watch out."

In this way, excess of internal authority leads inevitably to unsocial and aggressive conduct as a government among governments, and is a matter of concern to the international community. The world is not only heartily sick of this comedy by reason of the endless and wearisome falsehoods it involves, but it has learned to recognize it as something so irresponsible and dangerous that, maintained for any length of time, it easily becomes a major hazard for world peace and stability. It is for this reason that we, while recognizing that all distinctions as between freedom and authority are relative and admitting that 90 per cent of them are no business of ours when they affect a foreign country, still insist that there is an area here in which no government of a great country can move without creating the most grievous and weighty problems for its neighbors. That is precisely the area in which the regime of Hitler found itself at home, and in which the Soviet Government has moved for at least these past fifteen years. We may state bluntly that we can recognize no future Russian regime as one with which we could have a satisfactory relationship unless it keeps out of this danger area.

The third thing we may hope from a new Russia is that it will refrain from pinning an oppressive yoke on other peoples who have the instinct and the capacity for national self-assertion. In mentioning this matter, we are entering upon a delicate subject. There is no more difficult and treacherous one in the entire lexicon of political issues. In the relationships between the Great-Russian people and nearby peoples outside the confines of the old Tsarist Empire, as well as non-Russian national groups that were included within that empire, there is no conceivable pattern of borders or institutional arrangements which, measured against the concepts prevailing to date, would not arouse violent resentments and involve genuine injustices in many quarters. If people in that part of the world are going to go on thinking of national borders and minority problems in the way that they have thought of them in the past and continue to think of them today, Americans would do well to avoid incurring any responsibility for views or positions on these subjects; for any specific solutions they may advocate will some day become a source of great bitterness against them, and they will find themselves drawn into controversies that have little or nothing to do with the issue of human freedom. . . .

These, then, are the things for which an American well-wisher may hope from the Russia of the future: that she lift forever the Iron Curtain, that she recognize certain limitations to the internal authority of government, and that she abandon, as ruinous and unworthy, the ancient game of imperialist expansion and oppression. If she is not prepared to do these things, she will hardly be distinguishable from what we have before us today, and to hasten the arrival of such a Russia would not be worth the care or thought of a single American. If she is prepared to do these things, then Americans will not need to concern themselves more deeply with her nature and purposes; the basic demands of a more stable world order will then have been met, and the area in which a foreign people can usefully have thoughts and suggestions will have been filled.

So much, then, for the kind of Russia we would like to see. How should we, as Americans, conduct ourselves in order to promote the realization of, or at least an advance toward, such a Russia?

In our thinking on this subject we must be careful to distinguish between direct action, i.e., action on our part directly affecting persons and events behind what is now the Iron Curtain, and indirect action, by which we mean action taken in respect to other things—with respect, let us say, to ourselves or to our relations with other people—and affecting the Soviet world only obliquely and incidentally.

Most regrettably, as the world is today, the possibility for direct action by Americans toward the ends discussed above must be examined both in terms of a possible war and in terms of the continuation of the present state of "no major war." The first of these contingencies must unfortunately be discussed first, for it has become the dominant prospect in the minds of many people.

If war comes, what can we do directly to promote the emergence of a more desirable Russia? We can hold steadily and clearly in mind the image of the kind of Russia we would like to see and assure that military operations are shaped in such a way as to permit it to come into existence.

The first part of this task is a negative one: not to let ourselves be diverted by irrelevant or confusing concepts of war aims. We can avoid, this time, the tyranny of slogans. We can avoid confusing ourselves with grandiose and unrealistic, or even meaningless, phrases designed simply to make us feel better about the bloody and terrible business in which we are engaged. We can remember that war—a matter of destruction, brutalization and sacrifice, of separations, domestic disintegration, and the weakening of the deeper fabrics of society—is a process which of itself can achieve no positive aims: that even military victory is only the prerequisite for some further and more positive achievement which it makes possible but by no means assures. We can have the moral courage, this time, to remind ourselves that major international violence is, in terms of the values of our civilization, a form of bankruptcy for us all—even for those who are confident that they are right; that all of us, victors and vanquished alike, must emerge from it poorer than we began it and farther from the goals we had in mind; and that, since victory or defeat can signify only relative degrees of misfortune, even the most glorious military victory would give us no right to face the future in any spirit other than one of sorrow and humbleness for what has happened and of realization that the road ahead, toward a better world, is long and hard—longer and harder, in fact, than it would have been had it been possible to avoid a military cataclysm altogether.

Remembering these things, we will be less inclined to view military operations as ends in themselves, and should find it easier to conduct them in a manner harmonious with our political purposes. If it should fall to us to take up arms against those who today dispose over the Russian people, we can try not to give that people the impression that we are their enemies, or consider them ours. We can try to make them understand the necessity of such hardships as we cannot avoid inflicting on them. We can endeavor to hold constantly before them the evidences of a sympathetic understanding for their past and interest in their future. We can give them the feeling that we are on their side, and that our victory, if it comes, will be used to provide them with a chance to shape their own destiny in the future to a pattern happier than that which they have known in the past. For all of this it is important that we bear in mind what Russia has been, and can be, and not permit political differences to becloud that picture.

National greatness is a difficult thing to define. Every nation is made up of individuals; and among individuals, as is known, there is no uniformity. Some are charming, others irritating; some are honest, others not exactly so; some are strong, others weak; some command admiration, others, by general agreement, are anything but admirable. This is true in our own country; it is true in Russia. Just what, in these circumstances, national greatness consists of, is hard to say. Certainly it rarely consists of those qualities in which a people thinks itself great; for in nations, as in individuals, the outstanding virtues are generally not the ones for which we fancy ourselves distinguished.

Yet that there *is* such a thing as national greatness is clear; and that the Russian people possess it in high degree is beyond question. They are a people whose progress out of darkness and squalor has been a painful one, marked by enormous sufferings and punctuated by heart-rending setbacks. Nowhere on the face of the globe has the tiny flame of faith in the dignity and charity of man flickered more precariously under the winds that tore at it. Yet it has never gone out; it is not extinguished today even in the heart of the Russian land and whoever studies the struggle of the Russian spirit through the ages can only bare his head in admiration, before those Russian people who kept it alight through their sacrifices and sufferings.

The record of Russian culture to date has proven that this struggle has a significance far wider than the confines of the traditional Russian territory; it is a part, and an extremely important part, of the general cultural progress of mankind. We have only to look at the people of Russian birth or origin living and working in our midst—the engineers, the scientists, the writers, the artists—to know that this is true. It would be tragic if our indignation over Soviet outlooks and policies led us to make ourselves the accomplices of Russian despotism by forgetting the greatness of the Russian people, losing our confidence in their genius and their potential for good, and placing ourselves in opposition to their national feelings. The vital importance of this becomes even clearer when we reflect that we in the outside world who believe in the cause of free-dom will never prevail in any struggle against the destructive workings of Soviet power unless the Russian people are our willing allies. That goes for peace, and it goes for war. The Germans, though not fighting at that time in the cause of freedom, learned to their sorrow the impossibility of combatting simultaneously both the Russian people and the Soviet Government.

The greatest difficulty here, of course, lies in the mute and helpless position in which the Russian people find themselves as subjects of a totalitarian regime. Our experiences with Germany have demonstrated that we have not succeeded very well, as a nation, in understanding the position of the man who lives under the yoke of modern despotism. Totalitarianism is not a national phenomenon; it is a disease to which all humanity is in some degree vulnerable. To live under such a regime is a misfortune that can befall a nation by virtue of reasons purely historic and not really traceable to any particular guilt on the part of the nation as a whole. Where circumstances weaken the powers of resistance, to a certain crucial degree, the virus triumphs. If individual life is to go on at all within the totalitarian framework it must go on by arrangement with the regime, and to some extent in connivance with its purposes. Furthermore, there will always be areas in which the totalitarian government will succeed in identifying itself with popular feelings and aspirations. The relationship between citizen and political authority under totalitarianism is therefore inevitably complicated: it is never pat and simple. Who does not understand these things cannot understand what is at stake in our relations with the peoples of such countries. These realities leave no room for our favored conviction that the people of a totalitarian state can be neatly divided into collaborators and martyrs and that there will be none left over. People do not emerge from this relationship unscathed: when they do emerge they need help, guidance and understanding, not scoldings and sermons.

We will get nowhere with an attitude of emotional indignation directed toward an entire people. Let us rise above these easy and childish reactions and consent to view the tragedy of Russia as partly our own tragedy, and the people of Russia as our comrades in the long hard battle for a happier system of man's coexistence with himself and with nature on this troubled planet.

So much for what we do if, contrary to our hopes and our wishes, a war so much talked about should prove impossible to avoid. But supposing we are faced with a continuation of the present state of absence of major warfare? What should our course of action be then?

First of all, have we any grounds to hope, in these circumstances, that there might be changes in Russia of the kind that we are here envisaging? There are no objective criteria for the answer to this question. There is no "proof" one way or another. The answer rests on something which is partly a matter of opinion and judgment, but partly, admittedly, an act of faith. The writer believes the answer to be a positive one: that we are indeed justified in hoping, and holding it possible, that there may be such changes. But in substantiation of this view it is possible to say only the following.

There can be no genuine stability in any system which is based on the evil and weakness in man's nature—which attempts to live by man's degradation, feeding like a vulture on his anxieties, his capacity for hatred, his susceptibility to error, and his vulnerability to psychological manipulation. Such a system can represent no more than the particular frustrations and bitterness of the generation of men who created it, and the cold terror of those who have been weak or unwise enough to become its agents.

I am not speaking here of the Russian Revolution as such. That was a more complicated phenomenon, with deeper roots in the logic of history. I am speaking of the process by which something claiming to be a hopeful turn in human events, claiming to lead toward a decrease rather than an increase in the sum total of human injustice and oppression, evolved into the shabby purgatory of the police state. Only men with a profound sense of personal failure could find satisfaction in doing to others those things which are always involved in such a system; and whoever has had occasion to look deeply into the eyes of a Communist police officer will have found there, in that dark well of disciplined hatred and suspicion, the tiny gleam of despairing fright which is the proof of this statement. Those who begin by clothing a personal lust for power and revenge with the staggering deceits and oversimplifications of totalitarianism end up by fighting themselves—in a dreary, hopeless encounter which projects itself onto the subject peoples and makes of their happiness and their faith its battlefield.

Men of this sort can bequeath something of the passion of the struggle to those of their close associates who inherit their power. But the process of inheritance cannot be carried much further. People can move along, themselves, as by some force of habit, on the strength of an emotional drive acquired at second hand; but it is no longer theirs to transmit to others. The impulses that thrust men of one generation into so despairing an attitude toward themselves and toward the popular masses in whom they like to see themselves reflected become progressively uninteresting to succeeding generations. The cruelties, the untruths, the

354   SOCIAL RESPONSIBILITIES

endless deriding of man's nature practised in the concentration camps: all these institutions of the police state, though they may first have something of the lurid fascination that manifestations of danger and anarchy always exert in a well-regulated and composed society, sooner or later end up— like some stale and repetitious pornography—by boring everybody, including those who practise them.

Many of the servants of totalitarian power, it is true, having debased themselves more than their victims and knowing that they have barred themselves from any better future, may cling despairingly to their unhappy offices. But despotism can never live just by the fears of the jailers and hangmen alone; it must have behind it a driving political will. In the days when despotic power could be closely associated with a dynasty or an inherited oligarchy, such a political will could be more enduring. But then, by the same token, it had to take a more benevolent and constructive interest in the people over whom it ruled and from whose labors it fed. It could not afford to live by their total intimidation and degradation. Dynastic continuity compelled it to recognize an obligation to the future, as well as to the present and the past.

The modern police state does not have these qualities. It represents only a fearful convulsion of society, springing from the stimulus of a given historical moment. Society may be grievously, agonizingly ill from it. But society—being something organic, marked by change and renewal and adjustment—will not remain this way indefinitely. The violent maladjustments which caused the convulsion will eventually begin to lose their actuality, and the instinct for a healthier, less morbid, more interesting life will begin to assert itself.

These, then, are the reflections which give the writer, for one, faith that if the necessary alternatives are kept before the Russian people, in the form of the existence elsewhere on this planet of a civilization which is decent, hopeful and purposeful, the day must come—soon or late, and whether by gradual process or otherwise—when that terrible system of power which has set a great people's progress back for decades and has lain like a shadow over the aspirations of all civilization will be distinguishable no longer as a living reality, but only as something surviving partly in recorded history and partly in the sediment of constructive, organic change which every great human upheaval, however unhappy its other manifestations, manages to deposit on the shelf of time.

But how these changes are to come about is something which cannot be foreseen. If there are, indeed, such things as laws of political development, they will surely play a part here; but then they would be the laws of development peculiar to the phenomenon of modern totalitarianism, and these have not yet been adequately studied and understood. Whether such laws exist or not, developments will be modified both by national character and by the tremendous part which the fortuitous unquestionably plays in the shaping of human events.

These things being so, we must admit with respect to the future of government in Russia, we see "as through a glass, darkly." Superficial evidences would not seem to leave much room for hope that the changes we would wish to see in the attitudes and practises of government in Moscow could come about without violent breaks in the continuity of power, that is, without the overthrow of the system. But we cannot be sure of this. Stranger things have happened—though not much stranger. And, in any case, it is not our business to prejudge the question. It is not necessary for us, merely in order to shape our own conduct in a way conducive to our own interests, to decide what we admittedly cannot really know. We should allow, here, for all possibilities, and should exclude none. The main thing is that we keep clearly in mind the image of what we would like to see in the personality of Russia as an actor on the world stage, and let that be our guide in all our dealings with Russian political factions, including both that which is in power and those which are in opposition to it. And if it should turn out to be the will of fate that freedom should come to Russia by erosion from despotism rather than by the violent upthrust of liberty, let us be able to say that our policy was such as to favor it, and that we did not hamper it by preconception or impatience or despair.

Of one thing we may be sure: no great and enduring change in the spirit and practice of government in Russia will ever come about primarily through foreign inspiration or advice. To be genuine, to be enduring and to be worth the hopeful welcome of other peoples such a change would have to flow from the initiatives and efforts of the Russians themselves. It is a shallow view of the workings of history which looks to such things as foreign propaganda and agitation to bring about fundamental changes in the lives of a great nation. Those who talk of overthrowing the Soviet system by propaganda point, by way of justification of their thesis, to the intensive workings of the Soviet propaganda machine and to the various facets of subversive activity conducted, inspired or encouraged by the Kremlin throughout the world. They forget that the outstanding fact about such activities, on the record of the thirty-three years over which they have been assiduously conducted, has been their general failure. In the end, military intimidation or invasion has been generally necessary for the actual spread of the Soviet system. . . .

For these reasons, the most important influence that the United States can bring to bear upon internal developments in Russia will continue to be the influence of example: the influence of what it is, and not only what it is to others but what it is to itself. This is not to say that many of those things which are now preoccupying the public mind are not of unquestioned importance: such things as physical strength, armaments, determination and solidarity with other free nations. It is not to deny the urgent and overriding necessity for a wise and adroit foreign policy, designed to release and make effective all those forces in the world which, together with our own, can serve to convince the masters of the Kremlin that their grand design is a futile and unachievable one, persistence in which promises no solution of their own predicaments and dilemmas. In fact, there can be no question but that these must remain major preoccupations if war is to be avoided and time is to be gained for the working of more hopeful forces. But they can only remain sterile and negative if they are not given meaning and substance by something which goes deeper and looks further ahead than the mere prevention of war or the frustration of imperialistic expansion. To this, there is general agreement; but what is this "something"? Many people think it only a question of what we urge upon others, in other words, a question of external propaganda. I would submit that it is primarily a question of what we urge upon ourselves. It is a question of the spirit and purpose of American national life itself. Any message we may try to bring to others will be effective only if it is in accord with what we are to ourselves, and if this is something sufficiently impressive to compel the respect and confidence of a world which, despite all its material difficulties, is still more ready to recognize and respect spiritual distinction than material opulence.

Our first and main concern must still be to achieve this state of national character. We need worry less about convincing others that we have done so. In the lives of nations the really worthwhile things cannot and will not be hidden. Thoreau wrote: "There is no ill which may not be dissipated, like the dark, if you let in a stronger light upon it. . . . If the light we use is but a paltry and narrow taper, most objects will cast a shadow wider than themselves." Conversely, if our taper is a strong one we may be sure that its rays will penetrate to the Russian room and eventually play their part in dissipating the gloom which prevails there. No iron curtain could suppress, even in the innermost depths of Siberia, the news that America had shed the shackles of disunity, confusion and doubt, had taken a new lease of hope and determination, and was setting about her tasks with enthusiasm and clarity of purpose.

C. Resource Allocation

XXIX. INTRODUCTION

The growing wealth of the United States in the post-war period carried with it a number of important and sobering questions. The problem of seemingly chronic unemployment resisted solution, as did the question of the proper allocation of national resources in the interest of the public sector of the American economy. That second area was addressed most persuasively by John Kenneth Galbraith (born in 1908) in *The Affluent Society*, 1958. The chapter reprinted here is "The Theory of Social Balance," in which the central idea of the book is made clear. Galbraith's argument that private affluence creates public squalor had been suggested earlier by other economists, but the firmness and lucidity of his work earned him a wide audience.

XXIX.
John Kenneth Galbraith
THE AFFLUENT SOCIETY
1958

The final problem of the productive society is what it produces. This manifests itself in an implacable tendency to provide an opulent supply of some things and a niggardly yield of others. This disparity carries to the point where it is a cause of social discomfort and social unhealth. The line which divides our area of wealth from our area of poverty is roughly that which divides privately produced and marketed goods and services from publicly rendered services. Our wealth in the first is not

SOURCE. John Kenneth Galbraith, *The Affluent Society*, Boston: Houghton Mifflin, 1958, pp. 251–269. Copyright 1958 by John Kenneth Galbraith. Reprinted with the permission of the publisher, Houghton Mifflin Company.

only in startling contrast with the meagerness of the latter, but our wealth in privately produced goods is, to a marked degree, the cause of crisis in the supply of public services. For we have failed to see the importance, indeed the urgent need, of maintaining a balance between the two.

This disparity between our flow of private and public goods and services is no matter of subjective judgment. On the contrary, it is the source of the most extensive comment which only stops short of the direct contrast being made here. In the years following World War II, the papers of any major city—those of New York were an excellent example—told daily of the shortages and shortcomings in the elementary municipal and metropolitan services. The schools were old and overcrowded. The police force was under strength and underpaid. The parks and playgrounds were insufficient. Streets and empty lots were filthy, and the sanitation staff was underequipped and in need of men. Access to the city by those who work there was uncertain and painful and becoming more so. Internal transportation was overcrowded, unhealthful, and dirty. So was the air. Parking on the streets had to be prohibited, and there was no space elsewhere. These deficiencies were not in new and novel services but in old and established ones. Cities have long swept their streets, helped their people move around, educated them, kept order, and provided horse rails for vehicles which sought to pause. That their residents should have a nontoxic supply of air suggests no revolutionary dalliance with socialism.

The discussion of this public poverty competed, on the whole successfully, with the stories of ever-increasing opulence in privately produced goods. The Gross National Product was rising. So were retail sales. So was personal income. Labor productivity had also advanced. The automobiles that could not be parked were being produced at an expanded rate. The children, though without schools, subject in the playgrounds to the affectionate interest of adults with odd tastes, and disposed to increasingly imaginative forms of delinquency, were admirably equipped with television sets. We had difficulty finding storage space for the great surpluses of food despite a national disposition to obesity. Food was grown and packaged under private auspices. The care and refreshment of the mind, in contrast with the stomach, was principally in the public domain. Our colleges and universities were severely overcrowded and underprovided, and the same was true of the mental hospitals.

The contrast was and remains evident not alone to those who read.

The family which takes its mauve and cerise, air-conditioned, power-steered, and power-braked automobile out for a tour passes through cities that are badly paved, made hideous by litter, blighted buildings, billboards, and posts for wires that should long since been put underground. They pass on into a countryside that has been rendered largely invisible by commercial art. (The goods which the latter advertise have an absolute priority in our value system. Such aesthetic considerations as a view of the countryside accordingly come second. On such matters we are consistent.) They picnic on exquisitely packaged food from a portable icebox by a polluted stream and go on to spend the night at a park which is a menace to public health and morals. Just before dozing off on an air mattress, beneath a nylon tent, amid the stench of decaying refuse, they may reflect vaguely on the curious unevenness of their blessings. Is this, indeed, the American genius?

In the production of goods within the private economy it has long been recognized that a tolerably close relationship must be maintained between the production of various kinds of products. The output of steel and oil and machine tools is related to the production of automobiles. Investment in transportation must keep abreast of the output of goods to be transported. The supply of power must be abreast of the growth of industries requiring it. The existence of these relationships—coefficients to the economist—has made possible the construction of the input-output table which shows how changes in the production in one industry will increase or diminish the demands on other industries. To this table, and more especially to its ingenious author, Professor Wassily Leontief, the world is indebted for one of its most important of modern insights into economic relationships. If expansion in one part of the economy were not matched by the requisite expansion in other parts—were the need for balance not respected—then bottlenecks and shortages, speculative hoarding of scarce supplies, and sharply increasing costs would ensue. Fortunately in peacetime the market system operates easily and effectively to maintain this balance, and this together with the existence of stocks and some flexibility in the coefficients as a result of substitution, insures that no serious difficulties will arise. We are reminded of the existence of the problem only by noticing how serious it is for those countries—Poland or, in a somewhat different form, India—which seek to solve the problem by planned measures and with a much smaller supply of resources.

Just as there must be balance in what a community produces, so there must also be balance in what the community consumes. An increase in the use of one product creates, ineluctably, a requirement for others. If we are to consume more automobiles, we must have more gasoline. There must be more insurance as well as more space on which to operate them. Beyond a certain point more and better food appears to mean increased need for medical services. This is the certain result of the increased consumption of tobacco and alcohol. More vacations require more hotels and more fishing rods. And so forth. With rare exceptions—shortages of doctors are an exception which suggests the rule—this balance is also maintained quite effortlessly so far as goods for private sale and consumption are concerned. The price system plus a rounded condition of opulence is again the agency.

However, the relationships we are here discussing are not confined to the private economy. They operate comprehensively over the whole span of private and public services. As surely as an increase in the output of automobiles puts new demands on the steel industry so, also, it places new demands on public services. Similarly, every increase in the consumption of private goods will normally mean some facilitating or protective step by the state. In all cases if these services are not forthcoming, the consequences will be in some degree ill. It will be convenient to have a term which suggests a satisfactory relationship between the supply of privately produced goods and services and those of the state, and we may call it social balance.

The problem of social balance is ubiquitous, and frequently it is obtrusive. As noted, an increase in the consumption of automobiles requires a facilitating supply of streets, highways, traffic control, and parking space. The protective services of the police and the highway patrols must also be available, as must those of the hospitals. Although the need for balance here is extraordinarily clear, our use of privately produced vehicles has, on occasion, got far out of line with the supply of the related public services. The result has been hideous road congestion, an annual massacre of impressive proportions, and chronic colitis in the cities. As on the ground, so also in the air. Planes collide with disquieting consequences for those within when the public provision for air traffic control fails to keep pace with private use of the airways.

But the auto and the airplane, versus the space to use them, are merely an exceptionally visible example of a requirement that is pervasive. The more goods people procure, the more packages they discard and the more trash that must be carried away. If the appropriate sanitation services are not provided, the counterpart of increasing opulence will be deepening filth. The greater the wealth the thicker will be the dirt. This indubitably describes a tendency of our time. As more goods are produced and owned, the greater are the opportunities for fraud and the more property that must be protected. If the provision of public law enforcement services do not keep pace, the counterpart of increased well-being will, we may be certain, be increased crime.

The city of Los Angeles, in modern times, is a near-classic study in the problem of social balance. Magnificently efficient factories and oil refineries, a lavish supply of automobiles, a vast consumption of hand-somely packaged products, coupled with the absence of a municipal trash collection service which forced the use of home incinerators, made the air nearly unbreathable for an appreciable part of each year. Air pollution could be controlled only by a complex and highly developed set of public services—by better knowledge stemming from more research, better policing, a municipal trash collection service, and possibly the assertion of the priority of clean air over the production of goods. These were long in coming. The agony of a city without usable air was the result.

The issue of social balance can be identified in many other current problems. Thus an aspect of increasing private production is the appear-ance of an extraordinary number of things which lay claim to the inter-est of the young. Motion pictures, television, automobiles, and the vast opportunities which go with the mobility, together with such less en-chanting merchandise as narcotics, comic books, and pornographia, are all included in an advancing gross national product. The child of a less opulent as well as a technologically more primitive age had far fewer such diversions. The red schoolhouse is remembered mainly because it had a paramount position in the lives of those who attended it that no modern school can hope to attain.

In a well-run and well-regulated community, with a sound school system, good recreational opportunities, and a good police force—in short a community where public services have kept pace with private production—the diversionary forces operating on the modern juvenile may do no great damage. Television and the violent mores of Hollywood and Madison Avenue must contend with the intellectual discipline of the school. The social, athletic, dramatic, and like attractions of the school also claim the attention of the child. These, together with the other recreational opportunities of the community, minimize the tendency to delinquency. Experiments with violence and immorality are checked by an effective law enforcement system before they become epidemic.

In a community where public services have failed to keep abreast of private consumption things are very different. Here, in an atmosphere of private opulence and public squalor, the private goods have full sway. Schools do not compete with television and the movies. The dubious heroes of the latter, not Miss Jones, become the idols of the young. The hot rod and the wild ride take the place of the more sedentary sports for which there are inadequate facilities or provision. Comic books, alcohol, narcotics, and switchblade knives are, as noted, part of the increased flow of goods, and there is nothing to dispute their enjoyment. There is an ample supply of private wealth to be appropriated and not much to be feared from the police. An austere community is free from temptation. It can be austere in its public services. Not so a rich one.

Moreover, in a society which sets large store by production, and which has highly effective machinery for synthesizing private wants, there are strong pressures to have as many wage earners in the family as possible. As always all social behavior is part of a piece. If both parents are engaged in private production, the burden on the public services is further increased. Children, in effect, become the charge of the community for an appreciable part of the time. If the services of the community do not keep pace, this will be another source of disorder.

Residential housing also illustrates the problem of the social balance, although in a somewhat complex form. Few would wish to contend that, in the lower or even the middle income brackets, Americans are munificently supplied with housing. A great many families would like better located or merely more houseroom, and no advertising is necessary to persuade them of their wish. And the provision of housing is in the private domain. At first glance at least, the line we draw between private and public seems not to be preventing a satisfactory allocation of resources to housing.

On closer examination, however, the problem turns out to be not greatly different from that of education. It is improbable that the housing industry is greatly more incompetent or inefficient in the United States than in those countries—Scandinavia, Holland, or (for the most part) England—where slums have been largely eliminated and where *minimum* standards of cleanliness and comfort are well above our own. As the experience of these countries shows, and as we have also been learning, the housing industry functions well only in combination with a large, complex, and costly array of public services. These include land purchase and clearance for redevelopment; good neighborhood and city planning, and effective and well-enforced zoning; a variety of financing and other aids to the housebuilder and owner; publicly supported reasearch and architectural services for an industry which, by its nature, is equipped to do little on its own; and a considerable amount of direct or assisted public construction for families in the lowest income brackets. The quality of the housing depends not on the industry, which is given, but on what is invested in these supplements and supports.

The case for social balance has, so far, been put negatively. Failure to keep public services in minimal relation to private production and use of goods is a cause of social disorder or impairs economic performance. The matter may now be put affirmatively. By failing to exploit the opportunity to expand public production we are missing opportunities for enjoyment which otherwise we might have had. Presumably a community can be as well rewarded by buying better schools or better parks as by buying bigger automobiles. By concentrating on the latter rather than the former it is failing to maximize its satisfactions. As with schools in the community, so with public services over the country at large. It is scarcely sensible that we should satisfy our wants in private goods with reckless abundance, while in the case of public goods, on the evidence of the eye, we practice extreme self-denial. So, far from systematically exploiting the opportunities to derive use and pleasure from these services, we do not supply what would keep us out of trouble.

The conventional wisdom holds that the community, large or small, makes a decision as to how much it will devote to its public services. This decision is arrived at by democratic process. Subject to the imperfections and uncertainties of democracy, people decide how much of their private income and goods they will surrender in order to have public services of which they are in greater need. Thus there is a balance, however rough, in the enjoyments to be had from private goods and services and those rendered by public authority.

It will be obvious, however, that this view depends on the notion of independently determined consumer wants. In such a world one could with some reason defend the doctrine that the consumer, as a voter, makes an independent choice between public and private goods. But given the dependence effect—given that consumer wants are created by the process by which they are satisfied—the consumer makes no such choice. He is subject to the forces of advertising and emulation by which production creates its own demand. Advertising operates exclusively, and emulation mainly, on behalf of privately produced goods and services. Since management and emulative effects operate on behalf of private production, public services will have an inherent tendency to lag behind. Automobile demand which is expensively synthesized will inevitably have a much larger claim on income than parks or public health or even roads where no such influence operates. The engines of mass communication, in their highest state of development, assail the eyes and ears of the community on behalf of more beer but not of more schools. Even in the conventional wisdom it will scarcely be contended that this leads to an equal choice between the two.

The competition is especially unequal for new products and services. Every corner of the public psyche is canvassed by some of the nation's most talented citizens to see if the desire for some merchantable product can be cultivated. No similar process operates on behalf of the nonmerchantable services of the state. Indeed, while we take the cultivation of new private wants for granted we would be measurably shocked to see it applied to public services. The scientist or engineer or advertising man who devotes himself to developing a new carburetor, cleanser, or depilatory for which the public recognizes no need and will feel none until an advertising campaign arouses it, is one of the valued members of our society. A politician or a public servant who dreams up a new public service is a wastrel. Few public offenses are more reprehensible.

So much for the influences which operate on the decision between public and private production. The calm decision between public and private consumption pictured by the conventional wisdom is, in fact, a remarkable example of the error which arises from viewing social behavior out of context. The inherent tendency will always be for public services to fall behind private production. We have here the first of the causes of social imbalance.

Social balance is also the victim of two further features of our society —the truce on inequality and the tendency to inflation. Since these are now part of our context, their effect comes quickly into view.

With rare exceptions such as the post office, public services do not carry a price ticket to be paid for by the individual user. By their nature they must, ordinarily, be available to all. As a result, when they are improved or new services are initiated, there is the ancient and troublesome question of who is to pay. This, in turn, provokes to life the collateral but irrelevant debate over inequality. As with the use of taxation as an instrument of fiscal policy, the truce on inequality is broken. Liberals are obliged to argue that the services be paid for by progressive taxation which will reduce inequality. Committed as they are to the urgency of goods . . . they must oppose sales and excise taxes. Conservatives rally to the defense of inequality—although without ever quite committing themselves in such uncouth terms—and oppose the use of income taxes. They, in effect, oppose the expenditure not on the merits of the service but on the demerits of the tax system. Since the debate over inequality cannot be resolved, the money is frequently not appropriated and the service not performed. It is a casualty of the economic goals of both liberals and conservatives for both of whom the questions of social balance are subordinate to those of production and, when it is evoked, of inequality.

In practice matters are better as well as worse than this statement of the basic forces suggests. Given the tax structure, the revenues of all levels of government grow with the growth of the economy. Services can be maintained and sometimes even improved out of this automatic accretion.

However, this effect is highly unequal. The revenues of the federal government, because of its heavy reliance on income taxes, increase more than proportionately with private economic growth. In addition, although the conventional wisdom greatly deplores the fact, federal appropriations have only an indirect bearing on taxation. Public services are considered and voted on in accordance with their seeming urgency. Initiation or improvement of a particular service is rarely, except for purposes of oratory, set against the specific effect on taxes. Tax policy, in turn, is decided on the basis of the level of economic activity, the resulting revenues, expediency, and other considerations. Among these the total of the thousands of individually considered appropriations is but one factor. In this process the ultimate tax consequence of any individual appropriation is *de minimus,* and the tendency to ignore it reflects the simple mathematics of the situation. Thus it is possible for the Congress to make decisions affecting the social balance without invoking the question of inequality.

Things are made worse, however, by the fact that a large proportion of the federal revenues are pre-empted by defense. The increase in defense costs has also tended to absorb a large share of the normal increase in tax revenues. The position of the federal government for improving the social balance has also been weakened since World War II by the strong, although receding, conviction that its taxes were at artificial wartime levels and that a tacit commitment exists to reduce taxes at the earliest opportunity.

In the states and localities the problem of social balance is much more severe. Here tax revenues—this is especially true of the General Property Tax—increase less than proportionately with increased private production. Budgeting too is far more closely circumscribed than in the case of the federal government—only the monetary authority enjoys the pleasant privilege of underwriting its own loans. Because of this, increased services for states and localities regularly pose the question of more revenues and more taxes. And here, with great regularity, the question of social balance is lost in the debate over equality and social equity.

Thus we currently find by far the most serious social imbalance in the services performed by local governments. The F.B.I. comes much more easily by funds than the city police force. The Department of Agriculture can more easily keep its pest control abreast of expanding agricultural output than the average city health service can keep up with the needs of an expanding industrial population. One consequence is that the federal government remains under constant pressure to use its superior revenue position to help redress the balance at the lower levels of government.

Finally, social imbalance is the natural offspring of persistent inflation. Inflation by its nature strikes different individuals and groups with highly discriminatory effect. The most nearly unrelieved victims, apart from those living on pensions or other fixed provision for personal security, are those who work for the state. In the private economy the firm which sells goods has, in general, an immediate accommodation to the inflationary movement. Its price increases are the inflation. The incomes of its owners and proprietors are automatically accommodated to the upward movement. To the extent that wage increases are part of the inflationary process, this is also true of organized industrial workers. Even unorganized white collar workers are in a milieu where prices and incomes are moving up. The adaption of their incomes, if less rapid than that of the industrial workers, is still reasonably prompt.

The position of the public employee is at the other extreme. His pay scales are highly formalized, and traditionally they have been subject to revision only at lengthy intervals. In states and localities inflation does not automatically bring added revenues to pay higher salaries and incomes. Pay revision for all public workers is subject to the temptation to wait and see if the inflation isn't coming to an end. There will be some fear—this seems to have been more of a factor in England than in the United States —that advances in public wages will set a bad example for private employers and unions.

Inflation means that employment is pressing on the labor supply and that private wage and salary incomes are rising. Thus the opportunities for moving from public to private employment are especially favorable. Public employment, moreover, once had as a principal attraction a high measure of social security. Industrial workers were subject to the formidable threat of unemployment during depression. Public employees were comparatively secure, and this security was worth an adverse salary differential. But with improving economic security in general this advantage has diminished. Private employment thus has come to provide better protection against inflation and little worse protection against other hazards. Though the dedicated may stay in public posts, the alert go.

The deterioration of the public services in the years of inflation has not gone unremarked. However, there has been a strong tendency to regard it as an adventitious misfortune—something which, like a nasty shower at a picnic, happened to blight a generally good time. Salaries were allowed to lag, which was a pity. This is a very inadequate view. Discrimination against the public services is an organic feature of inflation. Nothing so weakens government as persistent inflation. The public administration of France for many years, of Italy until recent times, and of other European and numerous South American countries have been deeply sapped and eroded by the effects of long-continued inflation. Social imbalance reflects itself in inability to enforce laws, including significantly those which protect and advance basic social justice, and in failure to maintain and improve essential services. One outgrowth of the resulting imbalance has been frustration and pervasive discontent. Over much of the world there is a rough and not entirely accidental correlation between the strength of indigenous communist parties or the frequency of revolutions and the persistence of inflation.

A feature of the years immediately following World War II was a remarkable attack on the notion of expanding and improving public services. During the depression years such services had been elaborated and improved partly in order to fill some small part of the vacuum left by the shrinkage of private production. During the war years the role of government was vastly expanded. After that came the reaction. Much of it, unquestionably, was motivated by a desire to rehabilitate the prestige of private production and therewith of producers. No doubt some who joined the attack hoped, at least tacitly, that it might be possible to sidestep the truce on taxation vis-à-vis equality by having less taxation of all kinds. For a time the notion that our public services had somehow become inflated and excessive was all but axiomatic. Even liberal politicians did not seriously protest. They found it necessary to aver that they were in favor of public economy too.

In this discussion a certain mystique was attributed to the satisfaction of privately supplied wants. A community decision to have a new school means that the individual surrenders the necessary amount, willy-nilly, in his taxes. But if he is left with that income, he is a free man. He can decide between a better car or a television set. This was advanced with some solemnity as an argument for the TV set. The difficulty is that this argument leaves the community with no way of preferring the school. All private wants, where the individual can choose, are inherently superior to all public desires which must be paid for by taxation and with an inevitable component of compulsion.

The cost of public services was also held to be a desolating burden on private production, although this was at a time when the private production was burgeoning. Urgent warnings were issued of the unfavorable effects of taxation on investment. . . . This was at a time when the inflationary effect of a very high level of investment was causing concern. The same individuals who were warning about the inimical effects of taxes were strongly advocating a monetary policy designed to reduce investment. However, an understanding of our economic discourse requires an appreciation of one of its basic rules: men of high position are allowed, by a special act of grace, to accommodate their reasoning to the answer they need. Logic is only required in those of lesser rank.

Finally it was argued, with no little vigor, that expanding government posed a grave threat to individual liberties. . . .

With time this attack on public services has somewhat subsided. The disorder associated with social imbalance has become visible even if the need for balance between private and public services is still imperfectly appreciated.

Freedom also seemed to be surviving. Perhaps it was realized that all organized activity requires concessions by the individual to the group. This is true of the policeman who joins the police force, the teacher who gets a job at the high school, and the executive who makes his way up the hierarchy of Du Pont. If there are differences between public and private organization, they are of kind rather than of degree. As this is written the pendulum has in fact swung back. Our liberties are now menaced by the conformity exacted by the large corporation and its impulse to create, for its own purposes, the organization man. This danger we may also survive.

Nonetheless, the postwar onslaught on the public services left a lasting imprint. To suggest that we canvass our public wants to see where happiness can be improved by more and better services has a sharply radical tone. Even public services to avoid disorder must be defended. By contrast the man who devises a nostrum for a nonexistent need and then successfully promotes both remains one of nature's noblemen.

D. The American Negro

XXX. INTRODUCTION

The single most important question of social responsibility in post-war America was occasioned by the civil rights movement. The question of the nation's responsibility to and for the American Negro produced a large body of writing that sought to understand the Negro as a psychological and social fact. Ralph Ellison (born in 1914) in *The Invisible Man*, 1947, made a relatively early, influential, and sensitive contribution to an understanding of such issues.

It is the prologue to his novel that is reprinted here. In a brief space, with great intensity, Ellison suggested that the "Negro problem" was created by others, that the Negro was now a symbol produced by the imagination, hopes, and fears of white men. It was necessary for the Negro to accept at least the possibility of life as a hibernation, "a covert preparation for a more overt action," as he put it. Whether freedom for the Negro would come from his hate or from his love was one question, and another was the meaning of the concept of freedom itself. He was strong enough to assert that the ostensible irresponsibility of the Negro was a function of the white man's inability to face the problem. Ellison was willing to accept the principle of irresponsibility because, as he asked, to whom or to what could an invisible man be responsible? Responsibility for the actions of the American Negro therefore belonged to those who had created the problem in the first place, the white American.

There are more explicit statements of the Negroes' fight for some kind of liberation, but Ellison's early book remains one of the most moving and courageous, as the following passage shows.

XXX.

Ralph Ellison

INVISIBLE MAN

1947

I am an invisible man. No, I am not a spook like those who haunted Edgar Allan Poe; nor am I one of your Hollywood-movie ectoplasms. I am a man of substance, of flesh and bone, fiber and liquids—and I might even be said to possess a mind. I am invisible, understand, simply because people refuse to see me. Like the bodiless heads you see sometimes in circus sideshows, it is as though I have been surrounded by mirrors of hard, distorting glass. When they approach me they see only my surroundings, themselves, or figments of their imagination—indeed, everything and anything except me.

Nor is my invisibility exactly a matter of a bio-chemical accident to my epidermis. That invisibility to which I refer occurs because of a peculiar disposition of the eyes of those with whom I come in contact. A matter of the construction of their *inner* eyes, those with which they look through their physical eyes upon reality. I am not complaining, nor am I protesting either. It is sometimes advantageous to be unseen, although it is most often rather wearing on the nerves. Then too, you're constantly being bumped against by those of poor vision. Or again, you often doubt if you really exist. You wonder whether you aren't simply a phantom in other people's minds. Say, a figure in a nightmare which the sleeper tries with all his strength to destroy. It's when you feel like that, out of resentment, you begin to bump people back. And, let me confess, you feel that way most of the time. You ache with the need to convince yourself that you do exist in the real world, that you're a part of all the sound and anguish, and you strike out with your fists, you curse and you swear to make them recognize you. And, alas, it's seldom successful.

One night I accidentally bumped into a man, and perhaps because of the near darkness he saw me and called me an insulting name. I sprang at him, seized his coat lapels and demanded that he apologize. He was a

SOURCE. Ralph Ellison, *Invisible Man,* New York: Random House, 1947, pp. 3–12. Copyright 1947 by Ralph Ellison. Reprinted by permission of Random House, Inc.

tall blond man, and as my face came close to his he looked insolently out of his blue eyes and cursed me, his breath hot in my face as he struggled. I pulled his chin down sharp upon the crown of my head, butting him as I had seen the West Indians do, and I felt his flesh tear and the blood gush out, and I yelled, "Apologize! Apologize!" But he continued to curse and struggle, and I butted him again and again until he went down heavily, on his knees, profusely bleeding. I kicked him repeatedly, in a frenzy because he still uttered insults though his lips were frothy with blood. Oh yes, I kicked him! And in my outrage I got out my knife and prepared to slit his throat, right there beneath the lamplight in the deserted street, holding him in the collar with one hand, and opening the knife with my teeth —when it occurred to me that the man had not *seen* me, actually; that he, as far as he knew, was in the midst of a walking nightmare! And I stopped the blade, slicing the air as I pushed him away, letting him fall back to the street. I stared at him hard as the lights of a car stabbed through the darkness. He lay there, moaning on the asphalt; a man almost killed by a phantom. It unnerved me. I was both disgusted and ashamed. I was like a drunken man myself, wavering about on weakened legs. Then I was amused: Something in this man's thick head had sprung out and beaten him within an inch of his life. I began to laugh at this crazy discovery. Would he have awakened at the point of death? Would Death himself have freed him for wakeful living? But I didn't linger. I ran away into the dark, laughing so hard I feared I might rupture myself. The next day I saw his picture in the *Daily News,* beneath a caption stating that he had been "mugged." Poor fool, poor blind fool, I thought with sincere compassion, mugged by an invisible man!

Most of the time (although I do not choose as I once did to deny the violence of my days by ignoring it) I am not so overtly violent. I remember that I am invisible and walk softly so as not to awaken the sleeping ones. Sometimes it is best not to awaken them; there are few things in the world as dangerous as sleepwalkers. I learned in time though that it is possible to carry on a fight against them without their realizing it. For instance, I have been carrying on a fight with Monopolated Light & Power for some time now. I use their service and pay them nothing at all, and they don't know it. Oh, they suspect that power is being drained off, but they don't know where. All they know is that according to the master meter back there in their power station a hell of a lot of free current is disappearing somewhere into the jungle of Harlem. The joke, of course, is that I don't live in Harlem but in a border area. Several years ago (before

I discovered the advantages of being invisible) I went through the routine process of buying service and paying their outrageous rates. But no more. I gave up all that, along with my apartment, and my old way of life: That way based upon the fallacious assumption that I, like other men, was visible. Now, aware of my invisibility, I live rent-free in a building rented strictly to whites, in a section of the basement that was shut off and forgotten during the nineteenth century, which I discovered when I was trying to escape in the night from Ras the Destroyer. But that's getting too far ahead of the story, almost to the end, although the end is in the beginning and lies far ahead.

The point now is that I found a home—or a hole in the ground, as you will. Now don't jump to the conclusion that because I call my home a "hole" it is damp and cold like a grave; there are cold holes and warm holes. Mine is a warm hole. And remember, a bear retires to his hole for the winter and lives until spring; then he comes strolling out like the Easter chick breaking from its shell. I say all this to assure you that it is incorrect to assume that, because I'm invisible and live in a hole, I am dead. I am neither dead nor in a state of suspended animation. Call me Jack-the-Bear, for I am in a state of hibernation.

My hole is warm and full of light. Yes, *full* of light. I doubt if there is a brighter spot in all New York than this hole of mine, and I do not exclude Broadway. Or the Empire State Building on a photographer's dream night. But that is taking advantage of you. Those two spots are among the darkest of our whole civilization—pardon me, our whole *culture* (an important distinction, I've heard)—which might sound like a hoax, or a contradiction, but that (by contradiction, I mean) is how the world moves: Not like an arrow, but a boomerang. (Beware of those who speak of the *spiral* of history; they are preparing a boomerang. Keep a steel helmet handy.) I know; I have been boomeranged across my head so much that I now can see the darkness of lightness. And I love light. Perhaps you'll think it strange that an invisible man should need light, desire light, love light. But maybe it is exactly because I *am* invisible. Light confirms my reality, gives birth to my form. A beautiful girl once told me of a recurring nightmare in which she lay in the center of a large dark room and felt her face expand until it filled the whole room, becoming a formless mass while her eyes ran in bilious jelly up the chimney. And so it is with me. Without light I am not only invisible, but formless as well; and to be unaware of one's form is to live a death. I myself, after existing some twenty years, did not become alive until I discovered my invisibility.

That is why I fight my battle with Monopolated Light & Power. The deeper reason, I mean: It allows me to feel my vital aliveness. I also fight them for taking so much of my money before I learned to protect myself. In my hole in the basement there are exactly 1,369 lights. I've wired the entire ceiling, every inch of it. And not with fluorescent bulbs, but with the older, more-expensive-to-operate kind, the filament type. An act of sabotage, you know. I've already begun to wire the wall. A junk man I know, a man of vision, has supplied me with wire and sockets. Nothing, storm or flood, must get in the way of our need for light and ever more and brighter light. The truth is the light and light is the truth. When I finish all four walls, then I'll start on the floor. Just how that will go, I don't know. Yet when you have lived invisible as long as I have you develop a certain ingenuity. I'll solve the problem. And maybe I'll invent a gadget to place my coffee pot on the fire while I lie in bed, and even invent a gadget to warm my bed—like the fellow I saw in one of the picture magazines who made himself a gadget to warm his shoes! Though invisible, I am in the great American tradition of tinkers. That makes me kin to Ford, Edison and Franklin. Call me, since I have a theory and a concept, a "thinker-tinker." Yes, I'll warm my shoes; they need it, they're usually full of holes. I'll do that and more.

Now I have one radio-phonograph; I plan to have five. There is a certain acoustical deadness in my hole, and when I have music I want to *feel* its vibration, not only with my ear but with my whole body. I'd like to hear five recordings of Louis Armstrong playing and singing "What Did I Do to Be so Black and Blue"—all at the same time. Sometimes now I listen to Louis while I have my favorite dessert of vanilla ice cream and sloe gin. I pour the red liquid over the white mound, watching it glisten and the vapor rising as Louis bends that military instrument into a beam of lyrical sound. Perhaps I like Louis Armstrong because he's made poetry out of being invisible. I think it must be because he's unaware that he *is* invisible. And my own grasp of invisibility aids me to understand his music. Once when I asked for a cigarette, some jokers gave me a reefer, which I lighted when I got home and sat listening to my phonograph. It was a strange evening. Invisibility, let me explain, gives one a slightly different sense of time, you're never quite on the beat. Sometimes you're ahead and sometimes behind. Instead of the swift and imperceptible flowing of time, you are aware of its nodes, those points where time stands still or from which it leaps ahead. And you slip into the breaks and look around. That's what you hear vaguely in Louis' music.

Once I saw a prizefighter boxing a yokel. The fighter was swift and amazingly scientific. His body was one violent flow of rapid rhythmic action. He hit the yokel a hundred times while the yokel held up his arms in stunned surprise. But suddenly the yokel, rolling about in the gale of boxing gloves, struck one blow and knocked science, speed and footwork as cold as a well-digger's posterior. The smart money hit the canvas. The long shot got the nod. The yokel had simply stepped inside of his opponent's sense of time. So under the spell of the reefer I discovered a new analytical way of listening to music. The unheard sounds came through, and each melodic line existed of itself, stood out clearly from all the rest, said its piece, and waited patiently for the other voices to speak. That night I found myself hearing not only in time, but in space as well. I not only entered the music but descended, like Dante, into its depths. And *beneath the swiftness of the hot tempo there was a slower tempo and a cave and I entered it and looked around and heard an old woman singing a spiritual as full of Weltschmerz as flamenco, and beneath that lay a still lower level on which I saw a beautiful girl the color of ivory pleading in a voice like my mother's as she stood before a group of slaveowners who bid for her naked body, and below that I found a lower level and a more rapid tempo and I heard someone shout:*

"Brothers and sisters, my text this morning is the 'Blackness of Blackness.'"

And a congregation of voices answered: "That blackness is most black, brother, most black ..."

"In the beginning ..."

"At the very start," they cried.

"... there was blackness ..."

"Preach it ..."

"... and the sun ..."

"The sun, Lawd ..."

"... was bloody red ..."

"Red ..."

"Now black is ..." the preacher shouted.

"Bloody ..."

"I said black is ..."

"Preach it, brother ..."

"... an' black ain't ..."

"Red, Lawd, red: He said it's red!"

"Amen, brother ..."

"Black will git you ..."

"Yes, it will ..."

"... an' black won't ..."

"Naw, it won't!"

"It do ..."

"It do, Lawd ..."

"... an' it don't."

"Halleluiah ..."

"... It'll put you, glory, glory, Oh my Lawd, in the WHALE'S BELLY."

"Preach it, dear brother ..."

"... an' make you tempt ..."

"Good God a-mighty!"

"Old Aunt Nelly!"

"Black will make you ..."

"Black ..."

"... or black will un-make you."

"Ain't it the truth, Lawd?"

And at that point a voice of trombone timbre screamed at me, "Git out of here, you fool! Is you ready to commit treason?"

And I tore myself away, hearing the old singer of spirituals moaning, "Go curse your God, boy, and die."

I stopped and questioned her, asked her what was wrong.

"I dearly loved my master, son," she said.

"You should have hated him," I said.

"He gave me several sons," she said, "and because I loved my sons I learned to love their father though I hated him too."

"I too have become acquainted with ambivalence," I said. "That's why I'm here."

"What's that?"

"Nothing, a word that doesn't explain it. Why do you moan?"

"I moan this way 'cause he's dead," she said.

"Then tell me, who is that laughing upstairs?"

"Them's my sons. They glad."

"Yes, I can understand that too," I said.

"I laughs too, but I moans too. He promised to set us free but he never could bring hisself to do it. Still I loved him ..."

"Loved him? You mean . . . ?"

"Oh yes, but I loved something else even more."

"What more?"

"Freedom."

"Freedom," I said. "Maybe freedom lies in hating."

"Naw, son, it's in loving. I loved him and give him the poison and he withered away like a frost-bit apple. Them boys woulda tore him to pieces with they homemade knives."

"A mistake was made somewhere," I said, "I'm confused." And I wished to say other things, but the laughter upstairs became too loud and moan-like for me and I tried to break out of it, but I couldn't. Just as I was leaving I felt an urgent desire to ask her what freedom was and went back. She sat with her head in her hands, moaning softly; her leather-brown face was filled with sadness.

"Old woman, what is this freedom you love so well?" I asked around a corner of my mind.

She looked surprised, then thoughtful, then baffled. "I done forgot, son. It's all mixed up. First I think it's one thing, then I think it's another. It gits my head to spinning. I guess now it ain't nothing but knowing how to say what I got up in my head. But it's a hard job, son. Too much is done happen to me in too short a time. Hit's like I have a fever. Ever' time I starts to walk my head gits to swirling and I falls down. Or if it ain't that, it's the boys; they gits to laughing and wants to kill up the white folks. They's bitter, that's what they is . . ."

"But what about freedom?"

"Leave me 'lone, boy; my head aches!"

I left her, feeling dizzy myself. I didn't get far.

Suddenly one of the sons, a big fellow six feet tall, appeared out of nowhere and struck me with his fist.

"What's the matter, man?" I cried.

"You made Ma cry!"

"But how?" I said, dodging a blow.

"Askin' her them questions, that's how. Git outa here and stay, and next time you got questions like that, ask yourself!"

He held me in a grip like cold stone, his fingers fastening upon my windpipe until I thought I would suffocate before he finally allowed me to go. I stumbled about dazed, the music beating hysterically in my ears. It was dark. My head cleared and I wandered down a dark narrow passage, thinking I heard his footsteps hurrying behind me. I was sore, and into my being had come a profound craving for tranquillity, for peace and quiet, a state I felt I could never achieve. For one thing, the trumpet was blaring and the rhythm was too hectic. A tom-tom beating like heart-thuds began drowning out the trumpet, filling my ears. I longed for water and I heard it rushing through the cold mains my fingers touched as I felt my way, but I couldn't stop to search because of the footsteps behind me.

"Hey, Ras," I called. "Is it you, Destroyer? Rinehart?"

No answer, only the rhythmic footsteps behind me. Once I tried crossing the road, but a speeding machine struck me, scraping the skin from my leg as it roared past.

Then somehow I came out of it, ascending hastily from this underworld of sound to hear Louis Armstrong innocently asking,

> *What did I do*
> *To be so black*
> *And blue?*

At first I was afraid; this familiar music had demanded action, the kind of which I was incapable, and yet had I lingered there beneath the surface I might have attempted to act. Nevertheless, I know now that few really listen to this music. I sat on the chair's edge in a soaking sweat, as though each of my 1,369 bulbs had everyone become a klieg light in an individual setting for a third degree with Ras and Rinehart in charge. It was exhausting—as though I had held my breath continuously for an hour under the terrifying serenity that comes from days of intense hunger. And yet, it was a strangely satisfying experience for an invisible man to hear the silence of sound. I had discovered unrecognized compulsions of my being—even though I could not answer "yes" to their promptings. I haven't smoked a reefer since, however; not because they're illegal, but because to *see* around corners is enough (that is not unusual when you are invisible). But to hear around them is too much; it inhibits action. And despite Brother Jack and all that sad, lost period of the Brotherhood, I believe in nothing if not in action.

Please, a definition: A hibernation is a covert preparation for a more overt action.

Besides, the drug destroys one's sense of time completely. If that happened, I might forget to dodge some bright morning and some cluck would run me down with an orange and yellow street car, or a bilious bus! Or I might forget to leave my hole when the moment for action presents itself.

Meanwhile I enjoy my life with the compliments of Monopolated Light & Power. Since you never recognize me even when in closest contact with me, and since, no doubt, you'll hardly believe that I exist, it won't matter if you know that I tapped a power line leading into the building and ran it into my hole in the ground. Before that I lived in the darkness into which I was chased, but now I see. I've illuminated the blackness of my invisibility—and vice versa. And so I play the invisible music of my isolation. The last statement doesn't seem just right, does it? But it is; you hear this music simply because music is heard and seldom seen, except by musicians. Could this compulsion to put invisibility down in black and white be thus an urge to make music of invisibility? But I am an orator, a rabble rouser—Am? I *was,* and perhaps shall be again. Who knows? All sickness is not unto death, neither is invisibility.

I can hear you say, "What a horrible, irresponsible bastard!" And you're right. I leap to agree with you. I am one of the most irresponsible beings that ever lived. Irresponsibility is part of my invisibility; any way you face it, it is a denial. But to whom can I be responsible, and why should I be, when you refuse to see me? And wait until I reveal how truly irresponsible I am. Responsibility rests upon recognition, and recognition is a form of agreement. Take the man whom I almost killed: Who was responsible for that near murder—I? I don't think so, and I refuse it. I won't buy it. You can't give it to me. *He* bumped *me, he* insulted *me.* Shouldn't he, for his own personal safety, have recognized my hysteria, my "danger potential"? He, let us say, was lost in a dream world. But didn't *he* control that dream world—which, alas, is only too real!—and didn't *he* rule me out of it? And if he had yelled for a policeman, wouldn't *I* have been taken for the offending one? Yes, yes, yes! Let me agree with you, I was the irresponsible one; for I should have used my knife to protect the higher interests of society. Some day that kind of foolishness will cause us tragic trouble. All dreamers and sleepwalkers must pay the price, and even the invisible victim is responsible for the fate of all. But I shirked that responsibility; I became too snarled in the incompatible notions that buzzed within my brain. I was a coward . . . [*sic*]

But what did *I* do to be so blue? Bear with me.

CHAPTER 6

Apocalypse

XXXI. INTRODUCTION

Norman O. Brown (born in 1913) delivered the Phi Beta Kappa address at Columbia University in 1960. A professor of comparative literature at the University of Rochester, Brown was trained as a classicist, became a Freudian, and continued to move out to the verges of knowledge. He wrote *Life Against Death: The Psychoanalytical Meaning of History* in 1959; its influence has increased steadily. Committed to a metahistory, Brown's address to the students at Columbia inevitably invites a comparison with Emerson's earlier Phi Beta Kappa address, which Brown's resembles. Rejecting rationalism and science, Brown called for a liberation of the demonic yet Christian spirits who lived in some men. Leaning away from a superannuated scholarship and reliance on reason, Brown turned toward poetry, magic, and miracle. Standing firmly on the same tradition on which the New England Transcendentalists stood, Brown, in the manner and the style of Emerson, called for a renewal of the American Dream, a renewal that was predicated on a rejection of the past, another old American idea. Standing in the mists of the landscape he occupies, Brown's address at Columbia constitutes a radical rejection of civilization— American and other. The political and social dimensions are missing altogether, while regeneration of the individual through the release of what D. H. Lawrence once called the private and internal holy ghosts in each man was not the necessary precondition to social reconstruction, but was an end in itself.

The entire address is reprinted here.

XXXI.

Norman O. Brown

APOCALYPSE: THE PLACE OF MYSTERY IN THE LIFE OF THE MIND
1961

I didn't know whether I should appear before you—there is a time to show and a time to hide; there is a time to speak, and also a time to be silent. What time is it? It is fifteen years since H. G. Wells said Mind was at the End of its Tether—with a frightful queerness come into life: there is no way out or around or through, he said; it is the end. It is because I think mind is at the end of its tether that I would be silent. It is because I think there is a way out—a way down and out—the title of Mr. John Senior's new book on the occult tradition in literature—that I will speak.

Mind at the end of its tether: I can guess what some of you are thinking—*his* mind is at the end of its tether—and this could be; it scares me but it deters me not. The alternative to mind is certainly madness. Our greatest blessings, says Socrates in the *Phaedrus,* come to us by way of madness—provided, he adds, that the madness comes from the god. Our real choice is between holy and unholy madness: open your eyes and look around you—madness is in the saddle anyhow. Freud is the measure of our unholy madness, as Nietzsche is the prophet of the holy madness, of Dionysus, the mad truth. Dionysus has returned to his native Thebes; mind—at the end of its tether—is another Pentheus, up a tree. Resisting madness can be the maddest way of being mad.

And there is a way out—the blessed madness of the maenad and the bacchant: "Blessed is he who has the good fortune to know the mysteries of the gods, who sanctifies his life and initiates his soul, a bacchant on the mountains, in holy purifications." It is possible to be mad and to be unblest; but it is not possible to get the blessing without the madness; it is not possible to get the illuminations without the derangement. Derange-

SOURCE. Norman O. Brown, "Apocalypse," *Harper's Magazine,* Vol. 222, No. 1332 (May, 1961), pp. 47–49. Copyright 1961 by Harper's Magazine, Inc. Reprinted with the permission of Norman O. Brown.

ment is disorder: the Dionysian faith is that order as we have known it is crippling, and for cripples; that what is past is prologue; that we can throw away our crutches and discover the supernatural power of walking; that human history goes from man to superman.

No superman I; I come to you not as one who has supernatural powers, but as one who seeks for them, and who has some notions which way to go to find them.

Sometimes—most times—I think that the way down and out leads out of the university, out of the academy. But perhaps it is rather that we should recover the academy of earlier days—the Academy of Plato in Athens, the Academy of Ficino in Florence, Ficino who says, "The spirit of the god Dionysus was believed by the ancient theologians, and Platonists to be the ecstasy and abandon of disencumbered minds, when partly by innate love, partly at the instigation of the god, they transgress the natural limits of intelligence and are miraculously transformed into the beloved god himself: where, inebriated by a certain new draft of nectar and by an immeasurable joy, they rage, as it were, in a bacchic frenzy. In the drunkenness of this Dionysian wine, our Dionysius (the Areopagite) expresses his exultation. He pours forth enigmas, he sings in dithyrambs. To penetrate the profundity of his meanings, to imitate his quasi-Orphic manner of speech, we too require the divine fury."

At any rate the point is first of all to find again the mysteries. By which I do not mean simply the sense of wonder—that sense of wonder which is indeed the source of all true philosophy—by mystery I mean secret and occult; therefore unpublishable; therefore outside the university as we know it; but not outside Plato's Academy, or Ficino's.

Why are mysteries unpublishable? First because they cannot be put into words, at least not the kind of words which earned you your Phi Beta Kappa keys. Mysteries display themselves in words only if they can remain concealed; this is poetry, isn't it? We must return to the old doctrine of the Platonists and Neo-Platonists, that poetry is veiled truth; as Dionysus is the god who is both manifest and hidden; and as John Donne declared, with the Pillar of Fire goes the Pillar of Cloud. This is also the new doctrine of Ezra Pound, who says: "Prose is not education but the outer courts of the same. Beyond its doors are the mysteries. Eleusis. Things not to be spoken of save in secret. The mysteries self-defended, the mysteries that cannot be revealed. Fools can only profane them. The dull can neither penetrate the secretum nor divulge it to others." The mystic academies, whether Plato's or Ficino's, knew the limitations of words and drove us on beyond them, to go over, to go under, to the learned ignorance, in which God is better honored and loved by silence than by words, and better seen by closing the eyes to images than by opening them.

And second, mysteries are unpublishable because only some can see them, not all. Mysteries are intrinsically esoteric, and as such an offense to democracy: is not publicity a democratic principle? Publication makes it republican—a thing of the people. The pristine academies were esoteric and aristocratic, self-consciously separate from the profane vulgar. Democratic resentment denies that there can be anything that can't be seen by everybody; in the democratic academy truth is subject to public verification; truth is what any fool can see. This is what is meant by the so-called scientific method: so-called science is the attempt to democratize knowledge—the attempt to substitute method for insight, mediocrity for genius, by getting a standard operating procedure. The great equalizers dispensed by the scientific method are the tools, those analytical tools. The miracle of genius is replaced by the standardized mechanism. But fools with tools are still fools, and don't let your Phi Beta Kappa key fool you. Tibetan prayer wheels are another way of arriving at the same result: the degeneration of mysticism into mechanism—so that any fool can do it. Perhaps the advantage is with Tibet: for there the mechanism is external while the mind is left vacant; and vacancy is not the worst condition of the mind. And the resultant prayers make no futile claim to originality or immortality; being nonexistent, they do not have to be catalogued or stored.

The sociologist Simmel sees showing and hiding, secrecy and publicity, as two poles, like Yin and Yang, between which societies oscillate in their historical development. I sometimes think I see that civilizations originate in the disclosure of some mystery, some secret; and expand with the progressive publication of their secret; and end in exhaustion when there is no longer any secret, when the mystery has been divulged, that is to say profaned. The whole story is illustrated in the difference between ideogram and alphabet. The alphabet is indeed a democratic triumph; and the enigmatic ideogram, as Ezra Pound has taught us, is a piece of mystery, a piece of poetry, not yet profaned. And so there comes a time—I believe we are in such a time—when civilization has to be renewed by the discovery of new mysteries, by the undemocratic but sovereign power of the imagination, by the undemocratic power which makes poets the unacknowledged legislators of mankind, the power which makes all things new.

The power which makes all things new is magic. What our time needs is mystery: what our time needs is magic. Who would not say that only a miracle can save us? In Tibet the degree-granting institution is, or used to be, the College of Magic Ritual. It offers courses in such fields as clairvoyance and telepathy; also (attention physics majors) internal heat: internal heat is a yoga bestowing supernatural control over body temperature. Let me succumb for a moment to the fascination of the mysterious East and tell you of the examination procedure for the course in internal heat. Candidates assemble naked, in midwinter, at night, on a frozen Himalayan lake. Beside each one is placed a pile of wet frozen undershirts; the assignment is to wear, until they are dry, as many as possible of these undershirts before dawn. Where the power is real, the test is real, and the grading system dumfoundingly objective. I say no more. I say no more; Eastern Yoga does indeed demonstrate the existence of supernatural powers, but it does not have the particular power our Western society needs; or rather I think that each society has access only to its own proper powers; or rather each society will only get the kind of power it knows how to ask for.

The Western consciousness has always asked for freedom: the human mind was born free, or at any rate born to be free, but everywhere it is in chains; and now at the end of its tether. It will take a miracle to free the human mind: because the chains are magical in the first place. We are in bondage to authority outside ourselves: most obviously—here in a great university it must be said—in bondage to the authority of books. There is a Transcendentalist anticipation of what I want to say in Emerson's Phi Beta Kappa address on the American Scholar:

"The books of an older period will not fit this. Yet hence arises a grave mischief. The sacredness which attaches to the act of creation, the act of thought, is transferred to the record. Instantly the book becomes noxious: the guide is a tyrant. The sluggish and perverted mind of the multitude having once received this book, stands upon it, and makes an outcry if it is destroyed. Colleges are built on it. Meek young men grow up in libraries. Hence, instead of Man Thinking, we have the bookworm. I had better never see a book than to be warped by its attraction clean out of my own orbit, and make a satellite instead of a system. The one thing in the world, of value, is the active soul."

How far this university is from that ideal is the measure of the defeat of our American dream.

This bondage to books compels us not to see with our own eyes; compels us to see with the eyes of the dead, with dead eyes. Whitman, likewise in a Transcendentalist sermon, says, "You shall no longer take things at second or third hand, nor look through the eyes of the dead, nor feed on the specters in books." There is a hex on us, the specters in books, the authority of the past; and to exorcise these ghosts is the great work of magical self-liberation. Then the eyes of the spirit would become one with the eyes of the body, and god would be in us, not outside. God in us: *entheos:* enthusiasm; this is the essence of the holy madness. In the fire of the holy madness even books lose their gravity, and let themselves go up into the flame: "Properly," says Ezra Pound, "we should read for power. Man reading should be man intensely alive. The book should be a ball of light in one's hand."

I began with the name of Dionysus; let me be permitted to end with the name of Christ: for the power I seek is also Christian. Nietzsche indeed said the whole question was Dionysus versus Christ; but only the fool will take these as mutually exclusive opposites. There is a Dionysian Christianity, an apocalyptic Christianity, a Christianity of miracles and revelations. And there always have been some Christians for whom the age of miracle and revelation is not over; Christians who claim the spirit; enthusiasts. The power I look for is the power of enthusiasm; as condemned by John Locke; as possessed by George Fox, the Quaker; through whom the houses were shaken; who saw the channel of blood running down the streets of the city of Litchfield; to whom, as a matter of fact, was even given the magic internal heat—"The fire of the Lord was so in my feet, and all around me, that I did not matter to put on my shoes any more."

Read again the controversies of the seventeenth century and discover our choice: we are either in an age of miracles, says Hobbes, miracles which authenticate fresh revelations; or else we are in an age of reasoning from already received Scripture. Either miracle or Scripture. George Fox, who came up in spirit through the flaming sword into the paradise of God, so that all things were new, he being renewed to the state of Adam which he was in before he fell, sees that none can read Moses aright without Moses' spirit; none can read John's words aright, and with a true understanding of them, but in and with the same divine spirit by which

John spake them, and by his burning shining light which is sent from God. Thus the authority of the past is swallowed up in new creation; the word is made flesh. We see with our own eyes and to see with our own eyes is second sight. To see with our own eyes is second sight.

Twofold Always. May God us keep
From single vision and Newton's sleep.